THE KOROWAI OF IRIAN JAYA

OXFORD STUDIES IN ANTHROPOLOGICAL LINGUISTICS
William Bright, *General Editor*

The Korowai of Irian Jaya

Their Language in Its Cultural Context

GERRIT J. VAN ENK
and
LOURENS DE VRIES

New York   Oxford
OXFORD UNIVERSITY PRESS
1997

Oxford University Press

Oxford   New York

Athens   Auckland   Bangkok   Bogota   Bombay   Buenos Aires
Calcutta   Cape Town   Dar es Salaam   Delhi   Florence   Hong Kong
Istanbul   Karachi   Kuala Lumpur   Madras   Madrid   Melbourne
Mexico City   Nairobi   Paris   Singapore   Taipei   Tokyo   Toronto   Warsaw

and associated companies in

Berlin   Ibadan

Copyright © 1997 by Gerrit J. van Enk and Lourens de Vries

Published by Oxford University Press, Inc.
198 Madison Avenue, New York, New York 10016

Oxford is a registered trademark of Oxford University Press

Library of Congress Cataloging-in-Publication Data
Enk, Gerrit J. van.
    The Korowai of Irian Jaya : their language in its cultural context / Gerrit J. van Enk and
Lourens de Vries.
        p.   cm. — (Oxford studies in anthropological linguistics ; 9)
    ISBN 0-19-510551-6
    1. Korowai language—Social aspects.   I. Vries, Lourens de.   II. Title.   III. Series.
PL6621.K68E55   1997
499'.12—dc21   96-47024

9 8 7 6 5 4 3 2 1

Printed in the United States of America
on acid-free paper

PREFACE

This book is a first step in the study of the fascinating language and culture of the Korowai, a Papuan community of treehouse dwellers in the magnificent rainforest of southern Irian Jaya, Indonesia, in the area between the upper Becking and Eilanden rivers (see map 2, Korowai area). The Korowai came into contact with outsiders only recently, in the beginning of the 1980s. Yaniruma, a village with a mixed Kombai and Korowai population, was opened in 1980 by the first missionary in this area, Johannes Veldhuizen, who built an airstrip there. Other Korowai villages are Manggél (1986), Yafufla (1987), and Mabül (1989).

Gert van Enk lived in Yaniruma as a missionary of the ZGK (Mission of the Reformed Churches in the Netherlands) and was involved in the ministry of GGRI (the Reformed Churches of Indonesia) between February 1987 and September 1990. Lourens de Vries worked as a linguist with ZGK in the Wambon, Kombai, and Korowai area from 1982 to 1991. He lived in Yaniruma from February 1984 to July 1985 and from June 1990 to March 1991. Furthermore, he paid numerous short visits to the Korowai area as a linguistic consultant for the ZGK missionaries Veldhuizen, Venema, and van Enk. Since all these missionaries studied the Korowai language for shorter or longer periods and shared their data, this book is built on the work of all of them.

It should be pointed out that the (oral) texts collected by Gert van Enk played a central role in writing the sections on morphosyntax, discourse coherence, and cultural patterns.

Since these texts were collected in the framework of van Enk's personal language learning and culture study, most of them were written in the practical Korowai orthography, with graphemes selected from the Indonesian alphabet and without marking stress. Because of this, stress is marked only in chapter 2 and in the Korowai vocabularies at the end of the book. Of course, affixation affects stress placement, and for the lexical category most involved in affixation—verbs—stress placement is extensively discussed in chapter 3.

We thank the Consistory of the Gereformeerde Kerk van Groningen-Noord (the Netherlands), the Netherlands Organisation for Scientific Research (the Irian Jaya Studies Programme), the Projects Division of the Department of Languages and Cultures of South-East Asia and Oceania of Leiden University, and the Faculty of the Arts of the University of Amsterdam for granting the time and the funds needed to complete this book.

We thank William Bright, Bernard Comrie, William Foley, Ger Reesink, Paul Taylor, and Bert Voorhoeve for comments and discussion. We are indebted to the Summer Institute of Linguistics for the Shoebox program, a data management program for the field linguist, which proved very useful for interlinearising, glossary making, and building up databases (Wimbish 1990).

We thank Marianne van Enk-Bos, George Steinmetz, Michel Top, Johannes Veldhuizen, and Rijke de Wolf for permission to use their photographs in this book.

The book has the following organisation. Chapter 1 sketches the physical, cultural, historical, and linguistic background of the Korowai community. Chapter 2 presents Korowai phonology and morphophonemics. Chapter 3 discusses Korowai morphology. Chapter 4 presents some major morphosyntactic patterns of coherence in discourse. Chapter 5 discusses Korowai kinship terminology. Chapter 6 has texts selected to illustrate patterns of grammar, discourse, and culture.

We have decided to present the annotated texts as a chapter of this book and not as an appendix since the annotated texts are more than just illustrations for patterns described in earlier chapters. The texts are important documents in their own right, windows to the world of the Korowai, and, it is hoped, also inspiring sources for future researchers.

Appendix 1 presents a comparative word list with Korowai and Kombai basic lexical items. Appendix 2 has Korowai–English and English–Korowai vocabularies, and appendix 3 lists Korowai loanwords from Indonesian. Appendix 4 lists the Korowai inhabitants registered in the administrative units Yaniruma and Manggél in 1992. Appendix 5 presents a list of references to the Korowai in the mission magazine *Tot aan de einden der aarde*.

With this book, we want to make our data on Korowai easily accessible to the scholarly community. We have tried to bring our readers as close as possible to the fascinating reality of the Korowai language and oral literature. The book is theoretically eclectic, and we have tried to use general terminology as much as possible and to keep references to the linguistic literature to a minimum. Where we used a specific theoretical model (e.g., in the chapter on kinship terms), we did so because we were convinced it served the clear presentation of complex facts.

Little has been written on the area between the Upper Digul and the Eilanden rivers of southeast Irian Jaya (and hardly anything was published; cf. the bibliography on Irian Jaya by van Baal, Galis, and Koentjaraningrat 1984). Most sources are rare and hard to find and are often in Dutch or in Indonesian, many of them reports and articles in mission books and periodicals by Dutch missionaries of the Reformed churches (ZGK) who have been allowed to work in the area since 1956. We have decided to use those few sources and refer to them, since they often contain valuable information, for future research also.

In their overview of the anthropological research of Irian Jaya, van Baal, Galis, and Koentjaraningrat (1984: 80) observe that 'the lowlands are being neglected in spite of overwhelming evidence that the cultural variation of the lowland tribes exceeds that of the highland peoples by far.' Much of this cultural variation will disappear in the near future. In this context, they view the Awyu-speaking tribes to the right of the Digul River as 'the white gaps which are really appalling'.

This book is meant not only as a first step in the study of the Korowai but also as an urgent appeal for anthropologists, linguists, and others to continue with the study of the Korowai and to start with the study of the Ulakhin, the Kopka, the Tsawkwambo, and other isolated and totally unknown groups living just south of the central ranges in southeastern Irian Jaya.

Enumatil   G. J. v E.
Leiden   L. de V.
October 1996

CONTENTS

ABBREVIATIONS AND SYMBOLS

Phonetics

Phonetic symbols in this book are taken from the International Phonetic Alphabet.

Kinship

Kinship notational conventions follow Lounsbury (1964: 358–359):

> F = father; M = mother; B = brother; S = sister; H = husband; W = wife; s = son;
> d = daughter; P = parent
>
> ♂ = male (ego, kinsman, or linking kinsman); ♀ = female (ego, kinswoman, or
> linking kinswoman)

Notice also the following usages of dots in the extension rules. Compare the following examples:

> . . . ♂Ss = male linking relative's son (where the dots imply that the male sign
> cannot represent ego, that is, that it cannot be the initial terminus of the
> genealogical chain);
>
> ♂Ss = any male person's sister's son (where the male in question may be either
> ego or a linking relative standing in the chain between ego and the designated
> kin type);
>
> MB . . . = mother's brother's . . . (i.e., mother's brother as a link in the genealogical chain beween ego and a kinsman to be designated);

MB = mother's brother or mother's brother's (i.e, mother's brother either as the designated relative or as a link to some other designated relative traced through him).

Other Abbreviations

*	unacceptable form	INTNS	intensifier
1	first person	INTROG	interrogative
2	second person	IRR	irrealis mood
3	third person	ITER	iterative aspect
NON-1	second and third person	LOC	locative relation
		lit.	literally
ADDR	addressee	MOD	modifier
ADH	adhortative mood	N	noun
ADJ	adjective	NCLAN	clan name
ADV	adverb	NEAR	near past or future
ADVERS	adversative	NEG	negation
AFFIRM	affirmative	NFAM	family name
ATTENT	attention	NGEOGR	geographic name
CAUS	causative	NKIN	kinship noun
CIRCUM	circumstantial	NORN	ornithological name
COMIT	comitative	NPROP	proper name
CONN	connective	NREL	relational noun
DEICT	deictic	NTRIBE	tribe name
DESID	desiderative	NUM	numeral
DIMIN	diminutive	OBJ	object
DISJ	disjunctive	ONOMAT	onomatopoeia
DS	different subject (switch reference)	PART	particle
		PAUSE	pause
EFF	effort	PERF	perfect
EMPH	emphasis	PERS	personal (pronoun)
et al.	*et alii*, and others	PKIN	plural kinship nouns
EXCLM	exclamation	PL	plural
EXP	expectation	plos.	plosive
FOC	focus	POS	positive
HAB	habitual	POS.EXP	positive expectation question
h.l.	hoc loco, in this context	POSS	possessive (pronoun)
HOD	hodiernum	POSTP	postposition
IMM	immediate future or past	POTENT	potential mood
IMP	imperative mood	prenas.	prenasalised
IMPOS	impossibility mood	PROGR	progressive aspect
INDEF	indefinite	Q	question-marker
INF	infinitive	Q-clitic	question clitic
INGRES	ingressive	Q-word	question words
INTENT	intentional mood	QUOTE	quote-marking element

REAL	realis	V	vowel
SG	singular	VB	verb
SR	switch reference	vd.	voiced
SS	same subject	vl.	voiceless
	(switch reference)	VOC	vocative
SUB	subordinator	ZGK	Mission of the Reformed
SUPP	support verb		Churches
TOP	topic	*TADEDA*	*Tot aan de einden der*
TR	transitional sound		*aarde* (ZGK mission
TREL	temporal relation		periodical)

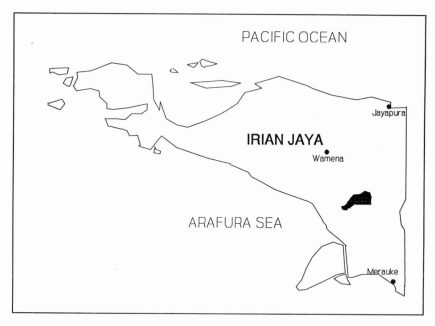

Map 1 Irian Jaya with inset of the Korowai Area

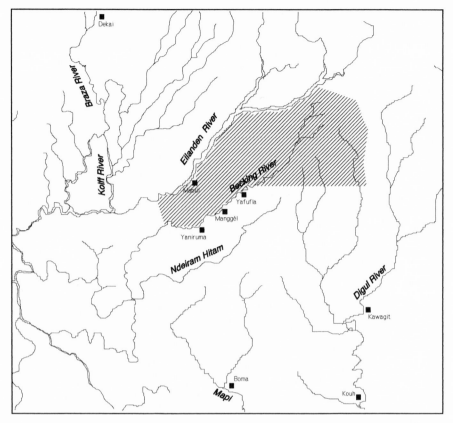

Map 2   Korowai Area

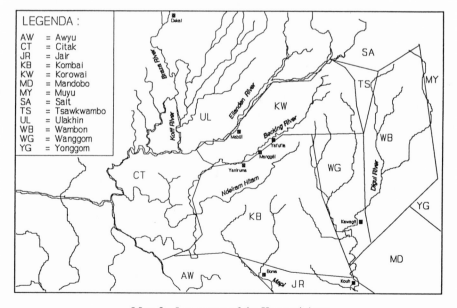

Map 3   Languages of the Korowai Area

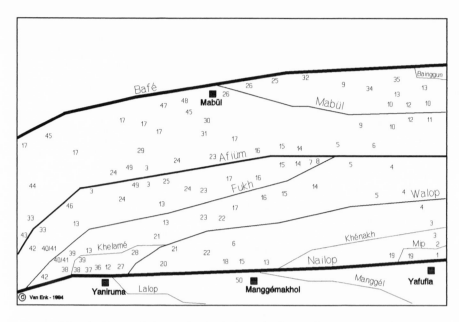

Map 4   Korowai clan territories (schematized map, downstream area)

LEGEND:

Bafé = Eilanden River
Lalop = Sokom River
Nailop = Becking River

The numbers on the map refer to the names of the Korowai clans; clan territories listed
below (cf. chapter 1 for an alphabetical list).

1. Maliap	18. Bolüop	35. Lebolanop
2. Marüo	19. Mifanop	36. Milofakhanop*
3. Molonggatun	20. Faülanop	37. Bilambanén
4. Yanikhatun	21. Nambul	38. Molonggai
5. Makhél	22. Manianggatun	39. Wahüop
6. Dajo	23. Khelékhatun	40. Nailop
7. Khaul	24. Laménggatun	41. Kimbekhom
8. Nandup	25. Lefilkhei	42. Gifanop
9. Lemakha	26. Khawékh Baféyanop	43. Bisom
10. Bumkhei	27. Daifuf Khawékh	44. Khendi
11. Khalikhatun	28. Walifuf Khawékh	45. Layol
12. Sendékh	29. Sinanggatun	46. Yenggél
13. Khenei	30. Mendé	47. Walofekhatun
14. Khomei Khajakhatun	31. Bafiga	48. Walüalüp
15. Khomei Walüfekhatun	32. Awop	49. Khandunanop
16. Khomei Walofekhatun	33. Gagoanop	50. Aimbon*
17. Nggokhoni	34. Ngguali	

The names marked with an asterisk refer to clans of Kombai origin.

THE KOROWAI OF IRIAN JAYA

The Korowai People

The Korowai are a Papuan people living in the Kecamatan (subdistrict) Kouh of the district Merauke of the Indonesian province Irian Jaya, in the area between the upper Becking and Eilanden rivers (see figure 1–1) and east of the headwaters of the Becking River.

The Korowai people call their language *koluf-aup* 'Korowai language'. The noun *aup* means 'voice; word; story; language'. The origin of the name *kolufo* and its Indonesian version, *Korowai*, is not known. There are around 4,000 speakers of the Korowai language.

The term *kolufo-yanop* 'Korowai person; Korowai people' denotes people who share the same language, *koluf-aup*, rather than a unit like a tribe. The clan, not the tribe, is the all-important unit. Since we lived in Yaniruma, a village on the border between the Kombai and Korowai, we had the most intensive contacts with the Korowai clans who live on the western banks of the Becking River in the proximity of Yaniruma, and the dialect of those clans is described.

The aim of this chapter is to provide a background for the patterns of language and discourse and for the corpus of annotated texts presented in this book.

First, we give some historical background, followed by the physical-geographical context and the cultural-geographical context (relations with neighbouring languages and neighbouring societies, settlement patterns, and clan territories). The means of subsistence are discussed, as are some aspects of the way in which the Korowai construct the notions of universe and of humankind. Furthermore, some concepts are mentioned that play a central role in major ideological structures. Finally, we discuss Korowai oral tradition and its genres.

Figure 1–1   The Eilanden River with tributary. George Steinmetz, 1995.

Recent history of contact

We shall now summarise the first period of contacts between the Korowai and out-siders, from 1978 to the early 1990s, paying attention also to the first stage of *kampong* formation.[1] Here we sketch the history of contact from the perspective of the outsid-ers. The *Khenil-khenil* text in chapter 6 presents a fascinating account of the same period of (first) contacts from the Korowai point of view.[2]

Kampong formation (Indonesian: *pembukaan kampong*) refers to the building of Indonesian-style villages (*kampong*) where people from different clans (and often of different tribes) live together, integrated in the Indonesian administrative system.

For ethnic groups like the Korowai, this change means that they descended from their high treehouses (see figure 1–2; the average height is between 8 and 12 metres) on their own clan territories to live in *kampong* houses on stilts, of a maximum of 2 metres, in neat rows. Since the Korowai are not used to living together with people of different clans (and tribes) and on the soil of other clans, the initial stage of a *kampong* is usually conflict-ridden, and a sharp increase of *khakhua* accusations and *khakhua* trials is connected with *kampong* formation [see below, some central ideo-logical notions, under *khakhua* '(male) witch'].

Connected with *kampong* formation and with living in the *kampong* are the use of iron axes instead of stone axes; the use of Indonesian-style clothing instead of penis gourds and skirts; the institutions of local government, church, clinic, and school; and the money economy. No wonder the Korowai initially experienced the *kampong* as the world turned upside down (see *Khenil-khenil* in chapter 6).

The first systematic efforts to contact the Korowai started in 1978. After eighteen months of survey trips by helicopter and boat and on several occasions accompanied by the Reverend Jaap Groen, Johannes Veldhuizen, a Dutch missionary of the Mission of the Reformed Churches (ZGK), decided to enter the Korowai territories via the southwestern route from the Citak area in March 1978. After several trips in dugout canoes, the first meeting with the Korowai people took place on October 4, 1978.

In the first stage, it was the Citak-Kombai man Nggop who played a key role in establishing relationships with people of the Korowai clans Molonggai and Sendékh.[3] On March 30, 1979, Veldhuizen obtained permission from the Kombai man Yanggio Ambüakharun to open a mission station at the mouth of the small stream Yaniruma, along the bank of the Sokom River (Korowai: Lalop), not far from where the Sokom River flows into the Becking River (Korowai: Nailop). On October 18 of that same

Figure 1–2 Exceptionally high treehouse on the Gifanop territory, upriver from Manggél village. George Steinmetz, 1995.

year, two Papuan evangelists settled in Yaniruma—Kepsan Kurufe, a Kombai man, and Kristian Wandenggei, a Wanggom man, both from the Upper Digul area. In the early 1980s, an elementary school that taught in Indonesian and a clinic were opened.

In these first years of the mission station, contacts were initiated and maintained with Korowai from the north bank of the Becking River and Kombai people from the area north of the Ndeiram Hitam River.[4] Soon the Kombai outnumbered the Korowai in Yaniruma, and this domination was strengthened when in 1983 the local government moved the inhabitants of the Kombai–Nombéakha village Firu (Korowai: Filup) to Yaniruma (van Enk 1993: 25, n. 63).[5] Some Korowai people built houses in the Korowai section of Yaniruma, but they used them only from time to time, for example, when they worked for the mission to build the airstrip or to make roads. The goods of the small shop in Yaniruma (iron axes, salt, fishhooks) attracted Korowai people from clans in the vicinity of Yaniruma. In the southwestern border area, some Korowai families of three Gifanop subclans moved to the Citak village Mbasman and others to the small Citak village Mu.

Since 1983, accompanied by fellow missionary Henk Venema, Veldhuizen made trips up the Becking River. In 1985, the first Korowai village was opened: Funbaum, on the Manianggatun clan territory, between the Walop River and the Becking. This village, or *kampong*, was opened by the then old Mukhalé Manianggatun.[6] Later this *kampong* was moved to the Nakhilop location, only one hour's walk from Yaniruma, upriver on the north bank of the Becking River.[7]

Not far from Nakhilop, an Indonesian film crew led by Dea Sudarman did most of the shooting for the anthropological documentary *Korowai* in 1986–1987, focussing on the construction of a treehouse and on a sago grub feast that was held at that time (Sudarman 1987). This film was made for the Indonesian Foundation of Social Sciences, chaired by the Indonesian anthropologist Selo Soemardjan, who also visited the Korowai area in 1986. At the same time the Indonesian Department of Social Affairs set up a community development project in Yaniruma.

In 1986, a new Korowai village was opened, as a result of the initiative of the Kombai man Füneya Aimbon, where the Manggél River flows into the Becking. The new village, named Manggél, or Manggémakhol,[8] three hours' walk upriver from Yaniruma on the south bank of the Becking River, also absorbed some of the inhabitants of Nakhilop, which was abandoned in 1987 after witchcraft-related conflicts. The Kombai evangelist Wandeyop Weremba of Nakhilop also moved to Manggél.[9]

The Reverend van Enk took over the missionary task of Venema in 1987 and started systematically exploring the Korowai territories northeast of Yaniruma, further away from the Becking. Contacts were established with people living on the banks of the Fukh and Afiüm rivers and later also with those living between the Afiüm and the Eilanden River (Korowai: Bafé).

In 1988, the Kombai man Bofo Khomei gave permission to build a *kampong* on his territory.[10] The new village took its name from the river Yafufla, which flows into the Becking close to the village. The evangelist Kepsan Kurufe coordinated the building of Yafufla and moved to the village in 1990.

In the course of 1989, the local government of the Kouh subdistrict organised an expedition, led by the secretary of the subdistrict Dominikus Amutai, to where the Mabül River flows into the Eilanden River. This trip, held in connection with the upcoming National Census of 1990, led to the formation of the *kampong* Mabül.[11]

Tourists and petty traders regularly visited Mabül, coming upriver from Senggo, the head village of the Citak-Mitak subdistrict. The mission placed an evangelist in Mabül in 1992, the Awyu man Albertus Fiokho.

Following a raid in 1990 by Kombai groups on Korowai territories east of Yafufla, in which several people were killed, the police of the Sektor Kouh sent a patrol to Yafufla. This patrol led to contacts with Korowai groups from unpacified areas.[12]

A film crew of the Japanese television production corporation Nexus, cooperating with Dea Sudarman, filmed in September 1990 in the clan territories of the Faülanop and Manianggatun, the (upstream) Dajo, and very far up the Becking River.

The area along the Becking River between Yaniruma and Yafufla having been pacified, tour operators started to organise some trips to real and fake treehouses in that Kombai–Korowai border area where the *kampongs* had become rather stable settlements.

In the 1980s, an oil company (Conoco) and a mineral company (Allied International) searched for oil and alluvial gold in the Korowai area, but their survey explorations did not lead to further activities.

Using his own observations during short visits and interviews with the missionaries Veldhuizen and Venema, Rijke de Wolf wrote a short novel in Dutch, published in 1992 under the title *Sapuru*; this is a work of fiction that portrays the daily life of the Korowai in and around Yaniruma as de Wolf (1992) perceived it.[13]

Also in 1992, van Enk organised a major expedition, together with the evangelist of Manggél, Wandeyop Weremba, that started from Yafufla in a northerly direction to the area close to the mouth of the Bainggun River in the Eilanden Rivier, where Bumkhei people were contacted.[14]

In 1993, an American film crew led by Judy D. Hallett, in cooperation with Paul M. Taylor of the Smithsonian Institution, made an anthropological documentary, mainly in the area of the downstream Dajo clan. One of the issues in that film is the *khakhua*-related eating of human flesh in traditional Korowai culture (see Some central ideological notions below).

In July and August 1995, Johannes Veldhuizen and Gert van Enk, accompanied by the reporter Alexander Smoltczyk and the photographer George Steinmetz, went to the uncontacted Sayakh and Lén-Bainggatum clan territories. This expedition resulted in a number of unique photographs that were published in the German magazine *Geo* and the American magazine *National Geographic* (see Smoltczyk and Steinmetz 1996, Steinmetz 1996).

Summarising the history of contact, we can say that apart from incidental trips by ZGK mission personnel deeper into Korowai land, direct and regular contacts between outsiders and Korowai people have been limited to the pacified parts of the border river areas (Mabül on the Eilanden River and the *kampongs* along the Becking River). Most of the Korowai clans still live in isolation and have not been contacted; in fact, it is not clear today where the northern border runs.

Physical geography

The Korowai are scattered in an area mostly covered with swampy, mixed tropical rainforests (cf. Beversluis 1954: 277, 288ff., and van Steenis 1954: 239f.) between two big rivers, the Eilanden and the Becking, which flow from northeast to west.

The Korowai land is very sparsely populated since interclan conflicts, the *khakhua* complex (see below, Some central ideological notions), and diseases like tropical malaria, tuberculosis, elephantiasis, and severe anemia constantly engender victims. Sometimes vast territories are empty because all the people living there have died.

The area is divided into many dozens of clan territories. The inhabited parts of the territories usually are low but mostly dry soils (*bayom*) or somewhat higher sandy soils (*nenim*) between wide swamps (*waliop*), which contain large acreages of sago trees. High banks of rivers and streams are also often inhabited. The most important rivers, which have concentrations of treehouses on their banks, are the Afiüm, Walop, Mabül, Nèlaf, and Fukh. The Korowai themselves make a distinction between the high grounds in the middle of the two border rivers, the Eilanden (Bafé) and Becking (Nailop), and the low grounds close to the big border rivers.[15] Both the Korowai living on the banks lower on the big rivers and the so-called Stone Korowai (Indonesian: Korowai Batu; Korowai: ilolkolufo),[16] that is, upriver Korowai, know the Ndeiram Hitam (Lemé), a major river in the neighbouring Kombai area.[17]

Although Korowai land is still lowland (the elevation is around 100 metres above sea level), ranges of hills form the transition to the foothills of the central New Guinea mountain range; from these higher points (*fium* 'hill') and from the banks of the very wide Eilanden River the mountains are visible in the north when the weather is clear.[18] Rocky spurs of the central mountains dominate the landscape along the banks of the uppermost parts of the Eilanden and the Becking rivers. The Korowai know the bigger rivers of the trans-Eilanden area.[19]

Along the banks of the Becking, there are areas with sediments of fine-grained clay, whereas in the vicinity of Yaniruma a light loam is found in some places. Between the Afiüm and Fukh rivers the soil is mostly sandy, partly covered with *nibung* palm trees (*Oncosperma filamentosum*; Korowai *betél*), instead of the usual mixed and very diverse rainforest.

The Korowai do not know lakes or other wide surfaces of water, except for the very wide Eilanden River. The Korowai area is too far from the sea to experience the effect of the tides, even in extremely dry periods, and the water of the Becking and the Eilanden is always drinkable (and full of fish).

The climate is a transition between that of the Lower Digul area and that of the trans-Eilanden area. There is no clear transition between east monsoon and west monsoon because the rainfall after the end of the latter often increases toward the end of May (see Braak 1954: 47; cf. map in Petocz 1987: 18–19). The last three months of the year are usually very hot; at the same time, these months contribute much to the annual rainfall of over 5 metres.[20]

Cultural geography

In this section, Korowai language and culture are tentatively placed in the context of surrounding languages and (Irian Jaya south coast) cultures. The local configuration of clan territories and new settlement patterns of recent years are also indicated.

Linguistic relationships

Approximately 1,000 languages are spoken on New Guinea; about 250 of these belong to the Austronesian family. The remainder, about 750 languages, called non-Austronesian or Papuan languages, cannot be said to derive from one ancestral language and are organised in more than sixty language families (Foley 1986; Wurm 1982). One of these Papuan language families is the Awyu-Ndumut family, to which Korowai belongs.[21] The Awyu-Ndumut family of southeast Irian Jaya is spoken between the Eilanden and Digul rivers; it is surrounded by the Asmat, Ok, Marind, and Mek families (Voorhoeve 1975: 27; Silzer and Heikkinen 1991: 23). Other languages of the Awyu family are Wambon (Drabbe 1959; de Vries and Wiersma 1992); Mandobo (Drabbe 1959); Awyu, Aghu, and Jair (Drabbe 1957); Kombai (de Vries 1993b); Tsawkwambo, Sawi, and Pisa (Drabbe 1950); and Sjiagha-Yenimu (Drabbe 1950).

The Korowai language has the following characteristics. Korowai has a seven-vowel system, including a front rounded close vowel /ü/. There are nineteen consonants, including prenasalised stops. Voiced stop consonants have implosive allophones.

Korowai's verb morphology is complex, featuring sentence-medial forms, although these medial forms are not very elaborate. Independent verb forms are extensively used medially in clause chaining, with switch-reference conjunctions linking them to the next clause in the chain. Especially in narratives, the clause chains are connected by tail-head linkage. See Healy (1966) and Longacre (1972) for clause chaining and tail-head linkage in Papuan languages. Korowai employs suffixes in the verb morphology. The category conflation of second and third person in Korowai verb paradigms (both in singular and plural) occurs commonly in Papuan languages, especially in the nonsingular (Haiman 1980: xxxix; Wurm 1982: 83). The clause has a strict S O V pattern.

The nominal morphology is simple. Nouns have no nonsingular forms, with the exception of kinship nouns and a few other nouns. The numerals are based on body parts used as tallies, as in many Papuan languages (Laycock 1975; de Vries 1995a).

With these characteristics, Korowai can be regarded as a fairly typical Papuan language from a typological point of view, although the term 'typical Papuan language' is a dangerous one given the bewildering diversity of Papuan languages.

Korowai has the Awyu language Kombai as its southern neighbour. Korowai and Kombai share a long border, and the Korowai and Kombai people in the border area have marriage alliances. Our Korowai informants have their clan territories not far from the border with the Kombai language. Yet the lexical correspondence between Kombai and Korowai, as reflected in the cognation percentage of basic lexical items, is only 22% (see appendix 1).

To the east, Tsawkwambo is spoken, an Awyu language. The missionary Versteeg (1983: 21) estimated the number of speakers of Tsawkwambo to be around 500, living in and around the village Waliburu. According to the initial survey by Versteeg (22), Korowai and Tsawkwambo have a lexical correspondence between 15% and 19%.

The northern boundary of the Korowai language is not clear. It could be that it borders with the Kopka language, which according to the survey of Kroneman and Peckham (1988) could very well be a Lowland Ok family language. But there could also be unknown groups living between the Korowai and the Kopka people. At the time of our research, it was not yet possible to enter the area of the northern Korowai clans. Korowai has a cognation percentage of 9% with Kopka in 200 items of the initial survey list of Kroneman and Peckham. The Kopka language is spoken in the foothills of the central ranges in and around the village of Seradela (which has an airstrip), located south of the Una language, a Mek language spoken in the mountain villages Sumtamon, Bomela, and Langda. East of Kopka, the Samboka language is spoken, a member of the Somahai family. The initial survey by Kroneman and Peckham indicates that a small corridor of Lowland Ok languages extends from the border with Papua New Guinea into Irian Jaya, separating the Awyu languages from the Mek and Mountain Ok languages spoken in the southern slopes of the ranges. This Lowland Ok corridor ends where the Somahai family begins.

To the southwest, Citak, of the Asmat-Kamoro family (Voorhoeve 1980), is spoken (see map 3, Languages). We counted only three (possible) cognates in a list of 85 Citak basic vocabulary items given in Kroneman and Peckham (1988), a list of Citak items of the Tiau dialect of Citak collected by the Reverend Kruidhof in 1979. To the northwest, Ulakhin is spoken, a totally unkown language.

The lexical correspondence percentages given above are from initial survey work and should be taken only as very rough indications of the relations of the Korowai language with the languages in its surroundings.

The Korowai people are in the initial stage of a process of integration into the wider Indonesian community. The great majority of the Korowai are monolingual, with only people living in the border river villages having some knowledge of local (pidginised) varieties of Indonesian (Bahasa Indonesia, the national language of Indonesia). Via this relatively young group of speakers Indonesian loan words are rapidly entering the Korowai lexicon. The loans are adapted in various degrees, both phonologically and semantically, to Korowai patterns. For example the Korowai word *anggaman* 'church service; catechism class' is based on the Indonesian word *agama* 'religion'. Appendix 3 is a list of Indonesian loans. Indonesian verbs are integrated into the Korowai language by a productive morphological derivation with the support-verb *mo* (see Derivation of verbs in chapter 3). This strategy, to integrate Indonesian verbs with *mV-* verbs, is found in all Awyu languages. See, for example, table 1–1.

Cultural relationships

When considering the place of Korowai culture in the context of the surrounding cultures and societies, the scarcity of information the latter is the first thing to observe. For example, hardly anything is known about the ethnic and linguistic groups

Table 1–1   Verb forms

Indonesian		Korowai	
beristirahat	'to pause'	isila-mo-	'to pause'
berdoa	'to pray'	berdoa-mo-	'to pray'
kembali	'to return'	kembali-mo-	'to return'
kasih kerja	'to give work'	kasikelaja-mo-	'to set under penal servitude'

in the trans-Eilanden area, although some Korowai clans maintain relationships with those groups in the form of marriage alliances.[22] It is also assumed (cf. Pétrequin and Pétrequin 1993: 50–53, 260ff.) that stone axes from the Langda area, on the south slopes of main ranges in the eastern highlands, where the Una language is spoken, reached the Korowai via exchange relationships with people in the trans-Eilanden area. The treehouses of the Ulakhin, one of the groups in the trans-Eilanden (see map 3), resemble those of the Korowai. Somewhat more is known of the ethnic groups south (Kombai, Wambon, Wanggom), west (Citak, an Asmat group), and east (Tsawkwambo) of the Korowai, although hardly anything is published.

In terms of material culture and technology, the Korowai do not differ significantly from their eastern and southern neighbours. Treehouse and bivouac construction, production of weaponry (shields, bows, arrows, knives, spears), fishing and hunting technology, methods of raising pigs, techniques of sago production, and horticultural techniques are basically the same as in the Kombai (which the Korowai call Aim) and Tsawkwambo areas.

The material culture of the Korowai differs significantly from that of the Citak, their southwestern neigbours, because of differences in ecological and cultural conditions. The Citak (which the Korowai call Banam) live in an area with vast treeless swamps and lakes filled with water plants. They used to be headhunters, raiding surrounding tribes like the Korowai. Accordingly, the Citak have a sophisticated canoe-building culture, with long war canoes in which they stand. Being water people, they have a wide range of fishing techniques and instruments. The Korowai are land people, and their big rivers are shallow, with vast stonebanks, making canoes useless for most of the time.

We shall now survey some more nonmaterial aspects of Korowai culture in the light of what is known from some other southcoast cultures of Irian Jaya.

Decorative motifs

In decorative motifs (*woliol* 'decorative motif; drawing; symbol; picture') carved in wood and bamboo (*woliol aombo* 'he plants *woliol*'), the Korowai themselves point out differences with the Kombai, especially in the variety of decorative motifs for *déponagél* (smoking pipes) and *wakhél* (arrow shafts) (see also figure 1–3). However, the motifs on the *wolumon* (shields) painted in white, red, and black correspond to the Kombai shield motifs.

A type of body decoration by burn scars (*nggawalalun*) seems to be specific for the Korowai. It is not found in immediately surrounding tribes. The scars form regular rows of buds on arms, breast, and belly of males and females (see figure 1–4).

The Korowai know a game in which figures are formed in the air with the help of a string and two or four hands. The motifs created in this game (animals and other natural phenomena) resemble those of the Kaowerawédj of the mid-Mamberamo River area (cf. van Eechoud 1962: plate 26).

Musical tradition

As far as musical culture is concerned, there is a striking contrast between Korowai and Kombai. The Korowai do not have the strong and complex tradition of song,

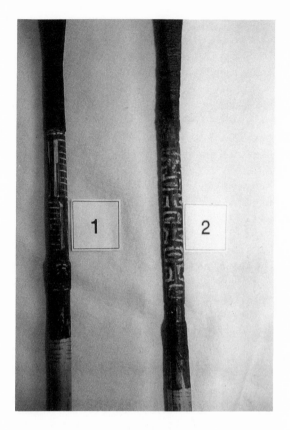

Figure 1–3 *Woliol* arrow
shafts: (1) *yenalfayan* type;
(2) *yumfayan* type.
Marianne van Enk-Bos, 1994.

dance, and instrumental music of the Kombai. The Korowai say that their fellow tribesmen northeast of Yafufla have imitated (= borrowed) the songs and dances of the Kombai. We see the same borrowing tendency in the western Korowai area, where the Korowai have borrowed melodies and themes from the Citak, an Asmat tribe with an exceptionally rich song tradition.[23] The Citak melodies and themes appear in Korowai 'worksongs' (*èponaup*),[24] that is, songs that accompany daily activities like sago pounding, in the melodies produced with the Jew's harp (*kombéof-aup* 'voice/ sound of the *kombéop* or Jew's harp'), and in the dances performed during feasts (see also Sago, below).

The bamboo Jew's harp of the Korowai is of the type described by Kunst (1967: ill. 6e and d) and by Bakx (1992: photo 11). It is played by men, and there are melody traditions from fathers to sons. Surrounding groups also know the instrument, generally called *kombéop* in Awyu languages. The drums of the Citak and the bamboo flutes of the Kombai are not used by the Korowai.

Oral tradition

Just like the neighbouring cultures, the Korowai have a rich oral tradition (cf. below, Oral tradition, and chapter 6). When these neighbouring cultures came in contact with outsiders, the new experiences were flexibly and quickly incorporated into the oral tradition. For example, in Kombai myths one finds references to wristwatches, rice, heaven and hell, the devil, and so on. Since the contacts between outsiders and the Korowai are very recent and involve only a few clans in border areas, the texts of the Korowai oral tradition that we recorded do not show clear signs of such adaptive incorporation and seem to reflect to a great extent the oral tradition of an Awyu community in precontact days.

There are traditional differences among the various ethnic groups concerning openness for contacts with others, and these differences no doubt have their impact on the oral traditions. The Muyu and the Mandobo, for example, have a reputation of being traders (cf. Boelaars 1970; Schoorl 1957) who far more easily cross the boundaries of their clan territories than the Korowai, for whom the clan territory is

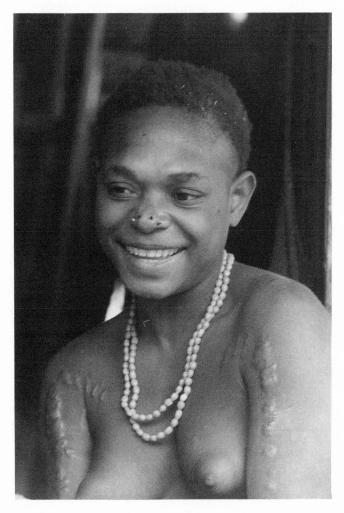

Figure 1–4   *Nggawalun* burn scar decoration of Nggènggè Dajo. Johannes Veldhuizen, 1987.

their world. The ancestral lands give them all they need, and they do not like foreigners to cross these lands. The Korowai were traditional victims of the neighbouring Citak, a headhunting Asmat tribe. This has contributed also to the tendency to withdraw to their own territory and to the view of the world outside as threatening and hostile rather than inviting.

Ideological structures and rituals

In key concepts and central rituals, there is a rather sharp dividing line between Asmat groups like the Citak and Awyu groups like the Korowai, Kombai, Wambon, and Mandobo.

The Korowai share with the other Awyu groups the *khakhua* concept, or rather the whole complex of *khakhua*-related concepts (see below, Some central ideological notions). *Khakhua* is the name for the persons (always males) with an inner urge or disposition to perform lethal cannibalistic witchcraft, that is, eating the vital organs of their victims. The Korowai have an obsessive fear of *khakhua* and have a very harsh punishment of men with that criminal disposition: the 'witch' is executed and eaten, after a trial that often involves torture. Perhaps even stronger than the fear of 'witches' is the fear of being accused of lethal witchcraft (cf. Groen 1991: 28, 34 for the corresponding Kombai concept of *kakua*). The consumption of human flesh occurs only in this *khakhua* context in Awyu cultures and is not connected with the punishment of other crimes like theft or with headhunting.

The Korowai do not practise headhunting, which was widespread in southern Irian Jaya before pacification, for example, by the Citak (Baas 1990: 3ff., 8), Yéi-Nan (van Baal 1982: 57), Marind (van Baal 1966: 710ff., 745ff.) and Jaqay (Boelaars 1981: 157–169).

According to Baas, the Citak headhunting raids on the Korowai and the Kombai stopped in 1966, but the fear of them is still very strong among the Kombai along the Ndeiram Hitam River and among the Korowai along the Becking River. Coordinated offensive actions of allied clans against other clans or tribes, as occur in the Kombai area, have not been observed in the Korowai (van Enk 1990a: 16f.).

The Korowai not only share the key concept of *khakhua* with Awyu groups like Kombai and Wambon, a concept central to the way in which the Korowai interpret death, but also the sago grub feast, the central ritual of the continuity of life (see Sago below). The sago grub feasts of the Tsawkwambo (Griffioen and Veldhuizen 1978; Stam 1978: 164–165) and of the Kombai (Venema 1989, in press) are very much the same as that of the Korowai, with a long, ceremonial festival bivouac in the vicinity of a sacred location (*wotop*).

Pig sacrifices are performed by both Korowai (see *The Pig Sacrifice* in chapter 6) and Kombai, but pig festivals as known in the upper Digul area (Mandobo: Boelaars 1970: 173–186, 227; Muyu: Schoorl 1957: 88–92, 98ff.), in the Mappi area (Jaqay: Boelaars 1981: 173–183), and further south (Marind: van Baal 1966: 839–847) are not known to Korowai and Kombai.

Forms of ritualised homosexuality, in the context of headhunting or of initiation, that occur in Marind Anim, Yèi-Nan, and Yaqay societies (van Baal 1966, 1982: 57; Boelaars 1981), do not seem to occur in Korowai society.

The Korowai are familiar with the theme of the destruction by the creator-spirit with fire and water of a primordial, rejected creation. This theme occurs, for example, in the origin myth *Ginol Silamtena* (see chapter 6) and is found in several other tribes in southern Irian Jaya, for example, Kombai and Jair (Griffioen 1983: 11; Kamma 1978: 2).

The idea of reincarnation of the 'soul' is found in Kombai, Wanggom, and Wambon thinking but is most articulate in Korowai thinking about the afterlife (see Mankind below). In other aspects, Korowai views on the afterlife are significantly different from the 'two-roads' views of Kombai and Mandobo. The Korowai dead travel one road to the one land of the dead (*bolüplefupé*) 'at the edge of the clan territories', but the Kombai and Mandobo dead face the option of two roads that lead to two different places, one good and one bad. These views are embedded in the Romalü tradition of the Kombai (de Vries 1993b: 112) and the Tomalüp tradition of the Mandobo (Boelaars 1970: 203).[25]

The change of humans into animals (and back) by applying magic (*khomi-/khomé* 'to transform') is a theme in Korowai folktales and totem stories (see, e.g., *A Folktale about the Fofumonalin Brothers* in chapter 6); however, the Korowai say that they no longer know how to perform this magic, adding that the tribes along the Digul River do know this magic, which was confirmed by informants from that area.[26]

Social and political organisation; kinship

In social and political organisation, the Korowai can be compared with Kombai, Wambon, Mandobo, and other Awyu groups. The patriclan is the central unit of social, economic, and political organisation. The emotional ties to the clan territory, the inalienable soil of the clan, are very strong. Marriage is exogamous and polygynous and forms an essential cohesion device among Korowai clans and also between Korowai clans and neighbouring Citak and Kombai clans.

Physically, mentally, and verbally strong males called *letél-abül* (lit. strongman) or *khén-mengg(a)-abül* ('man with aggression/fierceness') dominate the clan, but their leadership is never institutionalised and is not hereditary.[27] In the absence of organised raids against other groups, found in societies that practise headhunting, like the neighbouring Citak, institutionalised forms of war leadership did not emerge. Strong patriclans dominate weaker clans in their environment, but again, this does not lead to institutionalised forms of authority of one clan over another. The *Mukhalé* text in chapter 6 reflects this tendency in the political organization: there is a total absence of central authority, and aggressive leaders in some clans (like Mukhalé) may temporarily acquire regional political power that is tied to their person.

The kinship terminology of the Korowai follows the same Omaha pattern found in Kombai (de Vries 1987) and Mandobo (Boelaars 1970). The central opposition between cross and parallel relationships is morphologically expressed in the morpheme *sa-* (e.g., *lal* 'parallel female child' versus *sa-lal* 'cross female child').

There are also clear parallels with neighbouring Awyu groups in kinship behaviour. Perhaps the strongest parallel is kinship behaviour related to the avunculate, an institution found in many New Guinea societies. Van Baal (1981: 83) describes the avunculate as follows:

The marriage of a girl into another group establishes an alliance between the groups concerned. The factuality of this alliance is reflected in the widely spread custom known as the avunculate, the institutionalized relationship between a mother's brother and his sister's children which obliges the uncle to act as the children's protector, helper or mentor, all as the case may be.

In Korowai society, the avunculate certainly is relevant. When one of his sister's children is in danger, '*mom* (MB) and his *sabül* (Ss) or *salal* (Sd) sleep in one place until the danger is over', to quote one of the informants. When *mom* (MB) dies, his *sabül* demands compensation payment from *mom's* people, usually a pig. *Mom* (MB) often coarranges the marriage of his sister's children. These patterns of avuncular behaviour have also been found in the Kombai society (de Vries 1987).

The Omaha I skewing rule (see chapter 5) by which *mom* 'uncle' is extended from MB to MBs, MBss, and so on functions in this institutional context of the avunculate to define the class of potential legal and social successors of the mother's brother.

The avunculate has been found to be reflected in marriage arrangements in Korowai, Kombai, and Mandobo. In the fierce competition to get a wife, a young man invokes the help of his protector, the MB, who gives him one of his (classificatory) daughters. This preferred MBd cross-cousin marriage of the Mandobo (Boelaars 1970: 76–79) and Wambon (Drabbe 1959) has an interesting variant in the Korowai and Kombai societies. There the preference is to marry MMBd, called *makh* 'grandmother' in Korowai (see Grandparents' generation in chapter 5), who address their wife with the word 'grandmother' if she is a MMBd. The Kombai once explained the preference for MMBd, in contrast with the MBd, as follows: 'The MBd is too close, we like to jump one'.

Another recurrent pattern of kinship behaviour is connected with the institution of the levirate. When the bridal payments (see figure 1–5) for a woman have been completed, the brothers of her husband have rights over her and her children when her husband dies; they either marry her to another or one of them marries her. The Korowai terms *khaimon* (HB) and *khamokh* (♂BW) (see chapter 5) function in this context to express the fact that a man is the legal successor of his brother as husband of his BW.

A third pattern of kinship behaviour that is also found with other (Awyu) groups in the area is affinal avoidance, especially between a man and his wife's mother. They cannot eat from one fireplace or use the same utensils. They should not see each other. A man is not allowed to use the name of his WM, not even in reference. If a man does not respect these restrictions, he does not respect his bride-givers. Violations of the WM taboos cause sickness in the children of the man who violates them. In the affinal kinship terminology, there is a general term for WP (*ban*) with a very broad range of reference, in contrast to a specific term that singles out WM(S) (*bandakhol*).

Counting system

The number systems of the languages of the Awyu family can be subdivided into two groups (cf. de Vries 1995a): body-part tally systems (fingers-arm-head systems) and counting on hands and feet.

Figure 1–5   Part of bridal payment. Johannes Veldhuizen, 1984.

Kombai, Korowai, Wambon, and Mandobo have body-part tally systems. In these systems, counting starts on the little finger of the left hand until the thumb is reached and then goes up the arm to the highest point on the head, the turning point, after which counting goes down again via the other arm until the little finger of the right hand is reached, the end point. Crucial for these systems is that the nouns denoting the body parts are also used as numerals. For example, the noun meaning 'wrist' also means 'six' because the wrist is the first counting point on the arm after the first five points on the hand (the fingers).

This method of counting by the Wambon, Kombai, Korowai, and Mandobo contrasts with the counting on hands and feet practised by the Citak, described by Kruidhof (n.d.), the western Asmat family neighbour of Kombai and Korowai. Notwithstanding the contacts between the Citak and the Kombai and Korowai clans, the northern Awyu languages spoken in the foothills of the central mountain range seem to link up with the mountain tribes in the counting system (up and down the arms), whereas the Awyu groups in the south (Sjiagha-Yenimu and Aghu) and southwest (Pisa) seem to link up with the Asmat family in which counting on hands and feet is the norm. Korowai counting (*lamo* 'to count') is described in Numerals, in chapter 3 (cf. de Vries 1995a for numeral systems of Awyu languages).

Territories and treehouses of Korowai clans

In this section, we present an outline of the traditional housing and settlement patterns of Korowai clans. The Korowai live in treehouses (*khaim*) on ancestral territories (*bolüp*) that belong to patriclans (*gun; yanogun*).

Territories

Not much is known about how the boundaries of the territories are established and maintained and about land rights. There are indications that there is a distinction between land-using and landholding rights. The Korowai say that the territorial divisions are based on decrees of the ancestors (*mbolombolop*). Some etiological fragments in the folktale traditions (*wakhatum*) and in totem stories (*laibolekha mahüon*) that we recorded (see below, Oral tradition, for genres) serve as a foundation for the geographical position of certain groups.

Throughout the Korowai area, there are stretches of land not specifically claimed by clans. Sometimes these are called *laléo-bolüp* 'territories of the spirits' (see below, Some central ideological notions, for the *laléo* concept). There are sacred parts or sacred places (*wotop*) on most territories, connected with the spirits of the ancestors (*mbolombolop*).[28] Sago grub festivals and pig sacrifices take place close to the sacral area of the territory.

The territory or ancestral land is the *Lebensraum*, the living space of the clan in the full sense of the word. This idea of living space comes to the fore when uninvited or unwanted outsiders enter the territory. This is felt to be a threat to and a violation of the living space, a threat to life itself, and the reaction can be to kill the intruder(s). The arrival of outsiders with clothing (called *laléo* 'spirit') on Korowai clan territories was experienced as the end of the world (*lamotelokhai* 'the world is coming to its end'). Notice that the Korowai noun *lamol* means 'clan territory' but also 'world, universe'(see *laléo en lamol/wola* concept in Some central ideological notions, below).

Some clans have subclans, like the Khomei,[29] who are subdivided into three groups, the Khomei Khayakhatun, the Khomei Walofekhatun, and the Khomei Walüfekhatun.[30] These subclans have their own territories, which (partly) border on one another. Other clans with such subdivisions are the Gifanop and the Khawékh.

Some clans have the same name and a distant kinship relation, but the distance between them, both in geographical position and kinship relatedness, is greater than in the case of the subclans. The geographical position may then be used to distinguish them, often in terms of (position on) rivers and streams; for example, see table 1–2. We have observed that people of these geographically separate clans of the same name

Table 1–2   Terms of geographical position

Afiüm Lemakha	'Afiüm River Lemakha'
Bafé Lemakha	'Eilanden River Lemakha'
Nèlaf Lefilkhei	'Nèlaf River Lefilkhei'
Walüpta Lefilkhei	'Halfway-Lefilkhei'
Khosübolekha Dajo	'Downstream Dajo'
Khülolekha Dajo	'Upstream Dajo'
Khabülop Nggokhoni	'Offspring Nggokhoni'
Khosübol Nggokhoni	'Downstream Nggokhoni'
Khülolkha Nggokhoni	'Upstream Nggokhoni'
Makhol Nggokhoni	'(River) Mouth Nggokhoni'
Sendékh Baféyanop	'Sendékh Eilanden River people'
Sendékh Nailofanop	'Sendékh Becking River people'

address one another with (classificatorily applied) sibling terms. The same phenomenon occurs between people of clans with names that have some sound correspondences, like the Wafüop and the Wahüop people.

It is possible that two clans with different names share one territory. When this is the case, the names of the clans can be combined:

Aremél-Dondon

Dajo-Lemakha

Khenei-Sakhén

Khaul-Nandup

Yawol-Sayakh

We have not enough data to interpret such combinations, for example, in terms of moietylike structures. There are indications that some clans traditionally exchange women, such as the Khomei Khajakhatun and the Lefilkhei Nélafanop.

In the course of the years 1987 through 1992, a beginning was made in the registration of Korowai clans and their geographical distribution. An alphabetical list with fifty clans and their location is presented in table 1–3.

Table 1–3   Location of clans

Clan name	Clan territory no.	Clan name	Clan territory no.
Aimbon	(50)*	Laménggatun	(24)
Awop	(32)	Layol	(45)
Bafiga	(31)	Lebolanop	(35)
Bilambanén	(37)	Lefilkhei	(25)
Bisom	(43)	Lemakha	(9)
Bolüop	(18)	Makhél	(5)
Bumkhei	(10)	Maliap	(1)
Daifuf Khawékh	(27)	Manianggatun	(22)
Dajo	(6)	Marüo	(2)
Faülanop	(20)	Mendé	(30)
Gagoanop	(33)	Mifanop	(19)
Gifanop	(42)	Milofakhanop	(36)*
Nggokhoni	(17)	Molonggai	(38)
Ngguali	(34)	Molonggatun	(3)
Khalikhatun	(11)	Nailop	(40)
Khandunanop	(49)	Nambul	(21)
Khaul	(7)	Nandup	(8)
Khawékh Baféyanop	(26)	Sendékh	(12)
Khelékhatun	(23)	Sinanggatun	(29)
Khendi	(44)	Wahüop	(39)
Khenei	(13)	Walifuf Khawékh	(28)
Khomei Khajakhatun	(14)	Walofekhatun	(47)
Khomei Walofekhatun	(16)	Walüalüp	(48)
Khomei Walüfekhatun	(15)	Yanikhatun	(4)
Kimbekhom	(41)	Yenggél	(46)

The numbers following the clan names refer to the numbers on the schematic map of Korowai clan territories (see map 4). The asterisk-marked names indicate Kombai clans living on enclave Kombai territories.

The clans in table 1–4 have been registered, but their precise location is not yet sufficiently clear.

The treehouse

The treehouse, *khaim* [see figures 1–6 (exterior) and 1–7 (interior)], is the usual housing of the clan. Two or, rarely, three treehouses stand on one clearing in the jungle. The treehouses can be up to 35 metres above the ground, but most are between 8 and 12 metres high.

The treehouse has great significance for the Korowai; in some sense it can be seen as a microcosmos in which the clan lives and moves, an idea that occurs in the film documentaries of both Sudarman (1987) and Taylor and Hallett (1994), which contain valuable information on Korowai treehouses and their construction.

The bigger treehouses have, just like the festival bivouacs, separate sections for men and women. Some treehouses also have separate stairs and entrances leading to these sections (*yafin bol* 'stair hole' or 'entrance'). The stairs (*yafin*) are made from thin poles with notches in which to place the feet. This *yafin* pole is tied with its upper end to the floor platform (*bülan, ülekhal*) of the treehouse and to the veranda (*lambiakh*) with rattan. The lower end of the *yafin* pole hangs loose. Since the upper end of the pole rises about 1 metre above the floor platform, visible through the opening in the treehouse, the movements of the pole always signal to the people inside that someone is ascending [cf. lines (14) and (15) of *The Resurrection Story* lines (10)–(11) of *Mukhalé* in chapter 6].

Table 1–4   Unlocated clans

Clan name	Clan name
Abüm	Khülolekha Yawol
Aifu	Lakhayukh
Aremél	Lénayon
Bainggatun	Maelanop
Balümanop	Malinggatun
Bambüokh	Mesokhatun
Bandéop	Munanop
Basén	Naliop
Baul	Nambén
Dambol	Nanduop
Dendükhatun	Sakhatun
Dondon	Sakhén
Eniakhatun	Sakhüp
Gelianop	Sayakh
Kanil	Sian
Khakheyu	Silokhanop
Khalafekha Molonggai	Wafüop
Khaufanop	Wakhonom
Khosübolekha Yawol	

Figure 1–6   Treehouse on Bilambanén territory. Johannes Veldhuizen, 1986.

Both the stairs and the threshold beam in the entrance to a new treehouse (*abüokh-dil* 'door beam') are smeared with animal fat (*yabén*) to guarantee continuous welfare. A similar thing is done when a pig trap (*al*) is used for the first time. Smearing (*béalmo* 'to smear') with animal fat occurs also in two contexts in the myth of origin *Ginol Silamtena* (see chapter 6).[31]

The higher treehouses make use of in-between platforms, connected with *gawil* stairs, which are fastened at *both* ends, whereas the *yafin* stairs are fastened only at the upper end. The stairs that lead to the highest floor, where the people live, are always of the *yafin* type in treehouses with in-between platforms.

The fire (*melil, menil, alun*) in one or more fireplaces (*meli-bol* 'fire-hole'; see figure 1–8) occupies a central position in the treehouse. Food is prepared and shared around the fireplace, which gives warmth in cold weather. The verb *alü* means both 'to warm' and 'to cook'. The people sleep around the fire, which is kept smouldering during the night.

Figure 1–7   Interior of treehouse on Khomei-Kajakhatun territory, with the wife of Khemayop-Khomei. Gerrit van Enk, 1988.

The fireplace is constructed of small spars, filled with a layer of leaves and clay, and suspended in a hole in the floor with rattan (*nan*). The biggest threat to the treehouse is fire. When people have lost control of the fire in the fireplace, the rattan of the fireplace is cut, causing the whole fireplace to drop out of the house.

When the fire is lighted for the first time in the new treehouse, a very small piece of sago is put into the smouldering fire until it burns. This burnt piece of sago is put into the roofing. Again, the aim is to ensure that much game will be brought into the house.

In building a treehouse, first a big banian tree (*baül*) or a big *wambon* tree (*Ponnetia pinniata*; Indonesian: *matoa*) is selected to function as the central pole (*khokhül*). Working from temporary building platforms, the Korowai remove those branches of the selected tree that stand in the way of the treehouse to be erected. Then, from the same working platforms, they build the floor, supported by four to ten supporting poles (*khaim-fénop* 'treehouse poles'). Before the supporting poles are planted, *wanum* leaves or *khakhlakh* grass stalks are used to cover the holes in which the supporting poles will be planted. This is to prevent demons (*laléo*) and male witches (*khakhua*) to enter the treehouse along the supporting poles (see below, Some central ideological notions).

The floor (*bülan*) of the treehouse is constructed by using spars. The downmost cross beams [*dil* '(cross) beam'],[32] together with the bottom beams (*lal*), form the basis for the floor. The floor is covered with bark of the *nibung* palm tree (*betél*) or of the *dal* tree (*dal-khal* 'skin/bark of the *dal* tree').[33]

After the floor, the walls (*damon*) of the treehouse are made from wooden shafts of leaves of the sago tree, fastened in frameworks of small spars that form the front and back walls of the house (*bon-damon* 'front/back wall' versus *léam-damon* 'side wall').[34] Finally, the roof (*lél*) is made from sago leaves. The roof consists of two wings (*lél-baul*) that form an angle of about 70 degrees.

When the building of the treehouse is completed, small holes (*bol* 'opening') are formed in the roof, at the front and back, to guarantee plenty of game. The idea is that game animals have access to the treehouse through these holes or doors, which

Figure 1–8 Fireplace; sago consumption. Name of woman unknown. Johannes Veldhuizen, 1986.

are named after the game wanted, such as *küal-bol* 'cassowary holes/doors', *gol-bol* 'pig holes/doors'.

A well-built treehouse is strong and can be used for about five years. During that period, the only part that needs major maintenance efforts is the roof. Treehouses that are about to be abandoned because of their bad state may, in exceptional cases, be used as a place in which to leave behind the dead body of an inhabitant. But normally the dead are buried close to or under the treehouse. The shallow graves (*mébol* 'earth-hole; grave') are respected and maintained by the surviving inhabitants of the treehouse.

Korowai villages: settlement and housing patterns

Under the influence of the mission and later also the local government, some Korowai people, mostly those of the border areas along the Becking and Eilanden rivers, settled in villages. This *kampong* formation took place in the period 1979 to 1992 and implied a drastic modernisation of social life. Being located in border areas, most of these villages have a mixed population of Korowai and Kombai people (Yaniruma and Yafufla) or of Korowai and Citak (Mbasman). The villages Manggél (on the Becking) and Mabül (on the Eilanden) until now have only Korowai inhabitants.

The villages are divided into *rukun tetangga* (Indonesian for 'neighbourhoods' or 'village sections'), which are also administrative units.[35] Korowai terms for *village* are *khambom* (from Indonesian: *kampung, kampong*) and *kelaja* (from Indonesian: *kerja* 'work, labour'). The village is associated with work because it is in villages that one can earn money by working. In villages with mixed populations, the division into *rukun tetangga* follows tribal divisions. The village sections have a simple structure: one rather wide street, with two rows of houses on either side.

The village houses, called *khaü* (treehouses are called *khaim*), usually consist of a rectangular space divided into two or three rooms.[36] The structure is built on poles (*fénop*) about 150 centimetres high. The frame of the house is made of roughly cut wood (*donggop* 'spar'). The floor (*bülan*) is covered with bark of the *nibung* palm (*betél*) or with split aerial roots (*makhil*). The walls consist of ribs of sago leaves (*bunggul*; Indonesian: *gaba-gaba*). The roof (*lél*) is made of sago leaves. Often, a small, separate structure behind the house but connected to it by a kind of veranda functions as a kitchen.

We shall now discuss the settlement pattern and population of the individual villages. For their precise locations, see maps 2 and 3.

Yaniruma

The village Yaniruma (Korowai: Yaniluma) was opened in October 1979; the village soon had two sections, a Korowai *rukun tetangga* (RT 1) and a Kombai *rukun tetangga* (RT 2) (see above for the Indonesian administrative term *RT*). In the Korowai section live people from the following clans: Bilambanén, Gifanop, Khawékh, Molonggai, Sendékh, and Wahüop (See map 4). Kombai relatives from these Korowai people also found a place in this section. The Kombai clans involved are Aimbak-harun, Ambüakharun, Milofakhanop, and Khombonggai. In the Kombai section live people from the following clans: Alera, Bolaru, Buakewo, Eluaru, Kambuaru, Kinggo, Kumanopohu, Liparu, Rakhuno, Rerefano, and Seharuba. These clans have their territories mainly along the Ndeiram Hitam River (called Lemé in Korowai and Semé in Kombai) and around the Kombai village Ugo. The Kombai village section is called Amboruma, after a small stream close to that section.

A third village section (RT 3) came into existence when the government decided that the Nombéakha people, a group of Kombai clans with their own dialect and customs and living in the village Firu (a few hours downriver from Yaniruma on the Becking), had to move to Yaniruma. In the early 1990s the majority of these Nombéakha clans lived more or less permanently in Yaniruma: Alera, Ambraru, Barikul, Givaru, Faulano, Kembom, Khwaino, Tomakio, and Tünakhakü.

During the 1991–1992 census, 320 persons were registered as inhabitants of Yaniruma: eighty-five persons in twenty-two households in the Korowai section (RT 1), seventy-nine persons in twenty-two households in the Kombai section (RT 2), and 155 persons in twenty-four households in the Nombéakha section (RT 3).[37]

Mu, Jaim, and Mbasman

Korowai people from the border area with the Citak moved into the two smaller vil-lages Mu and Jaim and the bigger village Mbasman in the beginning of the 1980s. These three villages have mixed Korowai and Citak populations. We have no quan-titative data on the population of these villages, which belong administratively to the Citak-Mitak district (Senggo), whereas the other Korowai villages belong to the dis-trict Kouh.

Manggél

The development of the village Manggél on the bank of the Manggél River, opened in 1986, was connected with the abandonment of the village Nakhilop.[38] Gert van Enk periodically lived in Manggél, and the Indonesian Christian development foun-dation YAPPER organised village community activities in this village. In 1992, the following Korowai clans were registered as inhabitants of Manggél: Aimbon (mixed Kombai and Korowai), Bolüop, Khenei, Khomei-Khayakhatun, Khomei-Walofekhatun and Khomei-Walüfekhatun, Khosübolekha Dajo, Khülolekha Dajo, Mifanop, Molonggatun, and Nandup. The 1992 census counted sixty-five to seventy Korowai inhabitants in twenty-six households.

Yafufla

The opening of the Kombai-Korowai village Yafufla was the result of the decision in 1987 of the Kombai man Bofo Khomei, who had affinal ties with the Korowai clans Mariap and Malüo (cf. map 4). These clans live more than six hours upriver by foot from Yaniruma on the north bank of the Becking River. The village was built on the south bank, in the Kombai territory of Bofo Khomei. In 1992, there were thirty Kombai persons in nine households in Yafufla, of the Kombai clans Bandifaru, Khomei, Kinggo, Kubalopohu, and Liparu, and forty-five Korowai persons in thirteen households, from the clans Aifü, Bainggatun, Lénggatun, Makhé, Malinggatun, Malüo, Mariap, and Wafüop.

Mabül

Mabül, on the Eilanden River (coordinates 139, 35° 5, 40°), had in 1992 fifty-seven inhabitants in sixteen households, of the following clans: Alemél, Awop, Bafiga, Bisom, Guali, Khalikhatun, Lefilkhei, Lemakha, Maüp, and Khawékh (Baféyanop).[39]

Férman

This village has been abandoned.[40] Férman was a small village, unique because of its central location in the Korowai area, in the territory of the Khomei Khayakhatun, on the bank of the Fukh River. The village was opened in April 1990 by people from Khomei, Nggokhoni, and Khelékhatun groups (van Enk 1993: 25, n. 62). Other clans represented in the list of the 1992 local census are (Khülolekha) Dajo, Khalikhatun, Lefilkhei, Molonggatun, Nanokhatun, and Walofekhatun, a total of thirty-two persons in fifteen households.

IN THE COURSE OF 1992, an administrative reorganisation took place in southern Irian Jaya. This meant for Yaniruma and Manggél the elevation to the status of *desa*, the lowest unit of Indonesian civil administration. Yafufla became a *kampung* of the Desa Manggél, and Mabül became a *kampung* of Yaniruma.

Notwithstanding this integration of Korowai villages in the Indonesian administrative system, there is much absenteeism in the villages, caused by a number of cultural and economic factors: (1) the participation in the preparation of a series of sago grub festivals, which take months (building long bivouacs; felling sago trees; collecting grubs, firewood, stones, etc.). Just as the Muyu attributed the organisation of pig festivals for their village absenteeism (Schoorl 1957: 170ff.), the Korowai cited sago grub festivals as their reason to stay in the jungle for long periods; (2) the often very long distances between the villages and the clan territories, where the sago acreages and fishing and hunting grounds are located; (3) the fear of lethal witchcraft and of accusations of witchcraft, especially during epidemics (cf. Schoorl 1957: 176); (4) the respect of older clan members, who often reject the modernisation of social life implied by living in villages.[41] The older people view the villages also as places where there is no morality, because young people live there without older people to enforce social and moral norms.

Means of subsistence

This section is an outline of the major means of subsistence of the Korowai, except for the production of sago, which is important enough to be discussed separately.

Horticulture

The Korowai can be described as primitive horticulturalists who apply shifting cultivation. Sago (at least ten species are cultivated; general terms: *kho, khosül, ndaü*) and bananas (more than ten species; general terms: *dup, dendü, sakhu*) are the basic food items. The gardens (*yasim*) in the clearings (*umbontafekho*) around the treehouses are used primarily for planting bananas (*dup aobotop*). Sweet potatoes (*khaw 'Ipomoea batatas'*) and *Colocasia* tubers (*simbelu*) are cultivated also, in the gardens around the treehouse or in gardens further away. The leaves of sweet potatoes are also eaten. In the immediate vicinity of treehouses and houses in the villages, tobacco (*dépon, saukh, sü*) is grown.

Gathering

In the jungle surrounding the treehouse and especially along riverbanks, various green-leaf vegetables, grass species, and cane species are collected. Sugar canes (*Saccharum officinarum*; Korowai: *baliam*) are popular as sweets and as a source of energy during journeys. A full-flavoured grass species, called *gelén* by the Korowai, is collected to be eaten together with sago. The young, rich inflorescence of the *Saccharum edule* (Korowai: *bu, godunalé*) is also combined with sago. Various cucumber species (Cucurbitaceae spp., Korowai: *ukh, lamül*) are collected. Wild fruits (*duop*) are collected during the various seasons, like the sweet fruits of the *Ponnetia pinniata* (*béan, wambon*) and wild apples (*labulop*), both sources of vitamin C. Also bound to seasons is the gathering of the fruits of the *Pandanus* (*mahüankho*; Indonesian *buah merah*) and the breadfruits, or *Artocarpus* (*yawol*).

Domestication

Domesticated pigs (*belüfekha*)[42] are raised (*khendé*) by the women. Piglets live, just like dogs (*méan, muman, khendép* 'dog'), with the family in the treehouse.[43] When fully grown, the domesticated pigs get their place in the vicinity of the treehouse, sometimes within fences. The domestication of pigs does not primarily serve the production of meat for the family but rather institutionalised exchange relations that require pigs, for example, in marriage transactions or to recompensate for deaths or offences (cf. the *kholofudamo* concept in Some central ideological notions, below). In this same framework of exchange and recompensation, pigs are sacrificed to ancestral spirits.

Dogs are kept to assist in hunting and for their teeth (*banggil* 'dog teeth'), which in the form of long strings have a high exchange value.

Hunting

Hunting is a male occupation; big game is exclusively hunted by adult males.[44] Wild pigs are tracked (*bétop abokhai/abolai*) and shot (*ülmekho*) with bows and arrows (*ati-khayo*) or caught in pitfalls (*bu*) or in pig traps (*al*) with a special fence construction. Once caught, the pigs are pierced with spears (*mal*) or shot with arrows.

The meat of wild pigs is for direct consumption. Their teeth are used for decoration of the nose (*yagua* 'nose decoration of pig teeth') and the neck (*bésam* 'pigteeth necklace').

Cassowaries (*küal, sandum, sanip*) are hunted with bows and arrows or with rattan ropes (*nan*) strung at a height across likely cassowary paths to break (*bamolmo*) their necks. The meat is eaten, the very hard thigh bones are used for the production of arrowtips (*khekhin* 'cassowary-bone arrow') and daggers (*yal*), and the cap (*debap*) and the feathers are used for body decoration.

After the slaughter [*(m)bumo*], the meat of wild pigs and cassowaries is stewed and packed in parcels of leaves [*lakhilmo* 'to wrap in small package' or *lakhup duo* 'stew (in big package) with hot stones'] or it is smoked on a smoking rack (*sim*) over the fireplace in the treehouse. The blood (*büngga*) of pigs, mixed with their fat (*yabén*), is used to make a kind of blood sausage.

Small game may also be hunted by the young. Small game comprises snakes (*anol, émol*); lizard and salamander species (*mafüm yegun kholfunè*);[45] all kinds of rodents (*duo gun kholfunè*); marsupials (e.g., the *amékhesimdop, füon,* or *khayal* species); varans and iguanas (*buél-bajom*); and flying foxes (*yemül*) and smaller bats (like the *makhayal, lokhetikh,* and *sahüo* species), some of which are classified as birds (*dél*). Birds (collective noun *délamol*) that are hunted, are the wild chicken (*wakhum*); *Goura cristata* (*aülém*); and Blith's hornbill (*khawil*), the beak of which is used as a penis gourd (*khawisip*) for special, festive occasions.

Small children hunt very small game—such as frogs (*khugol*), lizards, and various big insects like the locust species *bakhuom* and *danggup*—using *kailon* arrows, little arrows made of (sago) leaf ribs (see figure 1–9).[46]

Fishing

Fishing, done by both men and women, is an important supplement to the generally protein-poor diet of the Korowai. Fish (*khelé*) may be caught by using poison, with which the water is 'hit' (*maun ümbaté*). Fish is also shot (*ülmekho*) with arrows over a bait, usually an ants' nest. Also, fish is caught in basketlike constructions (*khanél*; see figure 1–10) placed in a dam made of mud, branches, and leaves (*maun makhol yefoleté*).[47] Finally, fish is caught by scooping (*ali*), which occurs when the water is low and parts of the river can be isolated by dams. Then the water is scooped out.

Korowai who visit the villages buy nylon thread (*nèlon*) and metal hooks (*kuasél*, lit. 'pointed shell') to fish with living bait, especially green locusts (*bakhuom*). Also modern is to fish from a dugout canoe (*alèp*). Originally, the Korowai were not very much canoe oriented, in contrast to their Citak neighbours.

Some frequently caught fish species are *dül* (Indonesian: *ikan duri*, i.e., *Arius maculatus* v. sagor) and various other sheatfish species (*gum, lüma,* or *khalom*). Also caught are *lefül* or *mandun* (Indonesian: '*ikan kakap batu*', i.e., *Lobotes surinamensis*) and the palua fish (Indonesian: *ikan sembilang*, i.e., *Plotosus canius* v. angguilaris). Just like the meat of big game, the meat of big fish can be stewed in parcels of leaves or smoked. Smaller fish are grilled (*alü*) in a smouldering fire.

In addition to fish, some other kinds of food (*maun langga* 'water food') are obtained from the river, namely, shrimp species like *abém, betül,* and *khakhu*, as well

Figure 1–9   *Kailon* arrows shot into roof of festival bivouac. Michel Top, 1993.

as mudcrabs like *kulekham* and *khomulo*. River tortoise species like the *abéap*, *bif*, and *wayo* are caught and cooked in their shells.

Crocodiles (*semail*), living in the upper parts of the Becking River, were not hunted in the precontact period. Now they are hunted because of the high prices paid for their skins.[48] The bones of crocodiles (*semail-kholol*) play a role in magic aimed at manipulating the water levels in the river. When the river dries up during a long dry spell, the bone of a crocodile and a fresh fruit of the *Pandanus* (*mahüan-khosol*) are suspended in shallow water. The result is rain in the evening.[49]

Fishing and hunting are governed by taboos and restrictions (*ayulekha*), some of which have their basis in totem traditions (*laibolekha mahüon*). There are various kinds of fishing and hunting magic.[50]

Sago

Sago (*Metroxylon* spp.; cf. Petocz 1987: 31,43; van Steenis 1954: 267) plays a very prominent role in the life of the Korowai, both in everyday life and in the sacred ritu-

Figure 1–10   Fisherman from Sayakh clan holding a *khanél* fishing basket. George Steinmetz, 1995.

als of the sago grub feast. In this section, attention is given to some aspects of the production and consumption of sago and to the sago grub festival.

Production

The noun *kho* refers to both the sago palm tree and to sago flour as the staple food of the Korowai.[51] The Korowai distinguish at least ten subspecies of sago palm trees.[52] Depending on the subspecies, sago trees take ten to twelve years to mature. Regularly making new acreages of sago trees and planting young sago sprouts within existing acreages is seen as a sign of virtuous responsibility.[53]

For the production of sago flour, just before flowering (when the amount of starch in the tree is maximal) the men cut (*ülmaté*) the sago palm, after which they cut the trunk in a few big pieces, which they split (*domaté*), with a kind of crowbar (*dulekhil*). With a special stick (*yafikh*), women chisel and pound (*lamü*) the inside of the trunk to loosen the fibres. Then they put the pounded fibres in bags and transport them from where the sago palm was felled to a nearby spot where there is a stream or well. At that place the washing out of the sago flour takes place. The women set up a structure consisting of (at least) two connected woody shafts (*inggenun, khejo*) of sago leaves (see figure 1–11). The women place filters of bark at the connection points. In the first shaft, the mixture of water and fibres is pressed and kneaded (*geli*). The fibres remain in the first, higher shaft while the suspension of sago flour flows through the filter of bark into the second, lower shaft, at the end of which sago fibres (that have been washed out already) are placed in such a way that the water slowly runs away and the sago flour settles. The flour is packed into heavy balls wrapped in sago leaves. These balls, or big lumps, of sago are called *ndaülakh*. During the pounding and the washing, the women usually sing in the rhythm of the work (*èponaup* 'worksong').

Sago flour is only one of the uses of the sago tree, albeit a crucial one. Some of the other functions are the following. From rotting sago trunks, sago grubs (*non* or *gèkh*; see figure 1–12) are collected (see the sago grub festival below). Fresh marrow from the top of mature sago trees (which just have been felled) or from very young sago palms (*aun, sél*) is eaten raw and considered a special treat. The frayed fibres (*sékh*) of the upper end of the stem are used to make skirts (also called *sékh*) for the women and filters (*fiop*) for the bamboo pipes (*déponagél*). The hard leaf stems (*khejo*) of the mature sago palm are used to close the walls of the treehouse (*damon*, clearly visible in figure 1–7) and horizontally as hanging places to store food (*banibol*). The leaves of the sago palm tree also have various uses. They are woven to hold big lumps of sago for transport or folded to package food that is stewed in the fire (*lakhilmo*). They are also folded to form the roof (*lél*) of the treehouse.

Consumption

Sago is prepared for consumption in various ways. The most simple and most frequent way is to grill (*alü*) the sago in the fire (see figure 1–8). A small lump of sago is placed in the fire until the outer layer is done (*dobongga*). That layer (*abéakh*) is

Figure 1–11   *Inggenun* sago washing structure. Marianne van Enk-Bos, 1992.

Figure 1–12   Sago grubs and sago beetles. Johannes Veldhuizen, 1987.

peeled off with the fingers and eaten, while the remaining lump is placed back in the fire; the procedure is repeated with the next layers (*gaul*) until the last layer or piece (*mup*) is ready to be eaten. Packed in leaves, sago may also be stewed (*lakhilmo*), sometimes mixed with vegetables, mushrooms, meat, fish, or sago grubs. Bigger meat stew packets are always mixed with pulverized sago.

It is striking that sago, even the smallest amount, is *always* shared (*mbalamo; banté*) with those who are around the fireplace; not sharing or skipping (*malomekho*) someone is a deed of enmity.

Sago grub festivals

The precise meanings[54] and procedures of the Korowai sago grub festival (*gil*; see figure 1–13) are not known.[55] The expression for organising and celebrating a sago grub festival is *non ü-alü-lekhelimo*, lit. 'sago grub cut-bake-finish'. Our observations of various Korowai sago grub festivals, which were held in the pacified border zone along the Becking, gave sufficient indications that they follow the same general pattern of action and have the same meaning (ritualising the continuity of life) as the sago grub festivals of the Kombai (cf. Venema 1989) and the Tsawkwambo (cf. Griffioen and Veldhuizen 1978).[56] During these feasts, there is an intensive exchange of goods in the context of establishing and maintaining social relationships (see *kholofudamo* in Some central ideological notions, below).

Because of the system of chain invitations (A invites B, B invites C, C invites D, etc.), also known from Kombai feasts, sago grub festivals have an important function in interclan and even intertribe contacts. Together with the invitation, a *saündal* may be given to the invited guest. The *saündal* (see figure 1–14) is a rib of the leaf of a sago palm tree in which splinters or small sticks have been stuck. The invited person takes one little stick out of the *saündal* every day, and when he or she has reached the last stick, which is twice as long as the others, the day of the feast has arrived. The *saündal* in figure 1–14 is a 'modern' one since it represents the time span of two weeks of seven days each. The opposition between workdays and Sundays is reflected in this *saündal* by the distinction between the long sticks (Sundays) and the short sticks (workdays).

We refer to Venema (1989) for this general pattern of sago grub festivals and limit our discussion to some aspects that play a role in the texts of chapter 6.

The preparations for the sago grub festival and the celebration itself take almost three months. The phases of the moon (*alümekhon*) play an important role in the planning and execution of various stages of the festival (see table 1–5).

The first step in the preparatory phase is the construction of a (very) long festival bivouac (see figure 1–15), big enough to house the several hundred people who attend the festival. In the centre of the bivouac, a sacred pole is erected (*khandin fénop*), which, being much higher than the bivouac, pierces the roof. The sacred pole is surrounded by a sacred fence (*khandin damon*). Within the fence, there is, from the very beginning of the preparations, a continuous, sacred fire (*khandin menil*) that is guarded all the time by the fire guard (*milon* or *milon-abül* '*milon*-man'), who during his office is subject to all kinds of taboos. For example, he is not allowed to have sex, and for his short walks during the fire watch, he has always to place his feet in

Figure 1–13 Festival bivouac for sago grub feast in vicinity of Yaniruma. Johannes Veldhuizen, 1985.

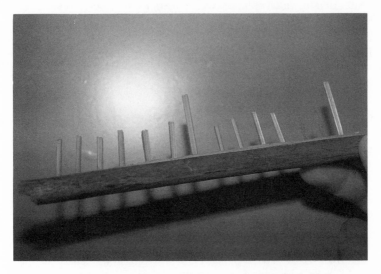

Figure 1–14   *Saündal.* Marianne van Enk-Bos, 1990.

his own footprints (*bétom*). *Milon* is the name not only of the guard of the sacred fire but also of a sago subspecies, which is mentioned in the context of sexual fertility and procreation in the Ginol Silamtena myth, when the original couple has sex for the first time. Sago grubs who have matured in rotting trunks of the *milon* sago are very fat and greasy, and in the Silamtena myth satisfactory and fertile heterosexual intercourse is linked to the anointment of sexual organs with *milon* grub fat [see line (36) in *Ginol Silamtena* in chapter 6].

Table 1–5   Moon phases

Term[a]	Translation	Code
wakhol lulo	'new moon (invisible)'	NM
sol alümekhon	'toward first quarter'	1Q–
wakhol khonggételombo	'first quarter'	1Q
wakhotalélelo	'waxing moon'	1Q+
wakhol üwaimbo	'about full moon'	FM–
wakhol khonggétalé	'full moon'	FM
wakhol lutenalelo	'after full moon'	FM+
wakhol khakhelimbo	'waning moon'	3Q–
wakhol khakhelilmo	'third quarter'	3Q
wakhol lulondemo	'toward new moon'	3Q+

[a]Alternative moon-phase expressions are 'toward first quarter': *khenil alümekhon = alümekhon sol falé* 'the moon is just visible'; 'full moon': *wakhol khonggételo* 'the moon is big'; 'after full moon': *wakhol hièntenalelo* 'the moon becomes small'. The expression *wakhol khakhelilmo* means lit. 'the moon has split'.

Just before the start of the construction of the festival bivouac, the production of sago grubs (*non, gèkh*) begins. This is done as follows. After felling the sagopalm (*gèkh ülmo* lit. 'to fell the grubs'), the trunk is cut into pieces, split open, tied up, covered with sago leaves, and left to rot. The sago beetle (*khip*, i.e., Scarabaeidae spp.; see figure 1–12; cf. Gressitt and Hornabrook 1985: 30ff.) then comes and places its eggs in the trunk. The grubs feed on the rotting tree. After one month, the tight packaging of the rotting tree in the leaves is renewed, both to help the rotting process and to prevent pigs from eating the trunk. After two months, the packaged parts of the trunk are opened and the full-grown, very fat sago grubs, a source of joy to the Korowai, are collected.

While the grubs are maturing in the felled sago trees, the members of the feast-giving clan, assisted by members of related clans, complete the festival location: racks (*balin*) are built in the long bivouac for storing the sago and the grubs; firewood and cooking stones are collected; several smaller bivouacs are built for guests, who spend several nights at the festival location; and large amounts of leaves of the sago are cut to package sago grubs, sago, and stew parcels. During the last week before the festival proper, sago is produced in large amounts. This sago is meant for the guests (*balin ndaü* 'festival sago', lit. storage-rack sago) during the feast but also for the people involved in the preparations (*bani-khau ndaü* 'leafstem-inside sago'), that is, sago for direct consumption, which is stored in wooden leaf stems of the sago leaves.

When the grubs are mature, one group collects them and another group fetches bananas, sugar canes, sweet potatoes, and *gelén* and *bu* vegetables (see above, Means of subsistence) and places these on racks in front of the long bivouac, in the shadow (*khüfolun-ta*).

Figure 1–15   Aerial view of sago grub festival bivouac. George Steinmetz, 1995.

The celebration starts after the arrival of the closest relatives of the feast-givers with the first distribution of sago, grubs, and other food. The next day big groups of other guests arrive. They enter dancing (*lamé/tamé*) and singing (*bonanam*), and immediately after the entrance dance they are assigned a place in the bivouac and are given food.

Two fashions of dancing occur in the context of sago grub feasts. The *khasam* dance is a special form of running dance performed when guests arrive and enter the feast house (see figure 1–16). While dancing they shout a staccato '*wo-wè-wo-wo-wo-wo-wo-wo-wo-wo-wo-wo-wè-wo-wo*', which is followed by a long-stretched, vibrating '*yo-o-o-o-o-o-o-o-o-o-o-o-o-o*' and finally by a sudden interrupted '*hüüüüüüüüüüüü*', simultaneously accompanied by the clattering of bows and arrows. The *külomo* dance moves forward with froglike and vigorous jumps, from left to right, changing the position of the body in angles of 45 degrees with every jump. This dance has been observed on the way to sago grub festivals.

Sometimes the dancing is used to clear a path to the festival location. While dancing, the dancers tred on scrubs and bushes and cut them down. The verb *oldintai* (or *olaibo*) is used to denote this combination of clearing a path and dancing [see, e.g., the text of *Aibum*, lines (10)–(11) in chapter 6].

During the evening and night, grubs mixed with sago are constantly stewed between heated stones in big leaf packets, and groups of guests dance from one end of the bivouac to the other. Very early in the morning, the first groups of guests depart. The next day, closing rituals take place in the presence of just the members of the clan; they focus on fertility and prosperous growth, such as the breaking down of

Figure 1–16 *Khasam* entrance dance of arriving guests at sago grub feast. Johannes Veldhuizen, 1985.

the sacred fence (*khandin fénop/du*) and the singing of the *Gom* song (see chapter 6). In *The Gom Song*, the boys of the clan are called on to grow and procreate, and the sago trees are called on to grow and multiply. The remains of the fence are transported to and thrown away at the 'downstream end' (*sübap*) of the festival place. Afterward the boys who are present shoot a hail of *kailon* arrows into the inside of the roof (*lébaul*) of the bivouac (see figure 1–9). The *kailon* shooting has the motive expressed in the *Gom* song: to further the growth of new sago (*menèl melukhai* 'it will grow fast'). In the *Ginol Silamtena* myth (see chapter 6), the *kailon* shooting also occurs but not in the context of the sago grub festival. Rather, the creator-spirit Ginol shoots the backbone part of the mythical pig Faül into its high position to form the sky on a hail of *kailon* arrows [see line (20)].

The Korowai relate the diverse stages in the preparation and celebration of the grub feast with specific times, in which the phases of the moon play an important role (see table 1–5), as do parts of the day (see table 1–6). The timetable for the Korowai grub feast is shown in table 1–7, which gives the 'script' of the preparation and celebration. The table is based on detailed information given by Fénélun Molonggai on July 5, 1990, in Yaniruma and verified by various other informants.

Korowai views of the universe and mankind

The Universe

In this section, we briefly mention some concepts that we think play a role in Korowai cosmology, the way in which the Korowai construct the notion of the universe. We do not know enough to give a more comprehensive sketch of their cosmology. The following concepts are discussed: *bolübolüp* 'the places', *bolüplefupé* 'world of the dead', *méanmaél* 'the great water', and *dalibün/khulbün* 'the sky'.

Very tentatively, we can say that the Korowai conceptualise the universe in terms of concentric circles. The innermost circle is the world of the living (*bolübolüp* "the places"). The *bolübolüp* are the places where the daily life of people, animals, and spirits (*laléo*) takes place, which can be perceived by ordinary human beings. This domain is divided into the worlds, or territories, of the different clans or tribes (*bolüp*). There does not seem to be a special realm for the spirits.[57]

The second circle is called *bolüplefupé* '(at) the end or margin of the *bolübolüp*', which is considered the realm of the dead. The souls of the deceased people who go

Table 1–6 Division of the day

Term	Translation	Code
sol walemémodo	'just becoming light'	early
walédo/walelé	'at daybreak'	daybreak
debünenul	'early in the morning'	morning
lefüta/lefütalé	'at noon'	noon
folétop	'in the afternoon'	afternoon
gülédo	'becoming dark'	dark
gülnanggaup	'at night'	night

Table 1–7 The Korowai sago grub festival timetable

Time	Activity	Translation
	A. First Preparations	
Month 1		
1Q–	1. khandin-melil	'lighting of the sacred fire'
	2. milon—mütebolekha abül alo	'sacred fire guard—the one who is ahead'
	3. gèkh ülmo	'cutting sago trees for breeding grubs'
3Q+	4. kho mukhto dainta di fu laméleté	'packaging sago trunk sections in leaves'
	B. Preparing the Festival Location	
Month 2		
1Q–	5. gil bolüp fahüomaté	'clearing of festival location (by cutting trees
day 1		and removing bushes)
day 2	6. donggop lai dueté	'planting poles for the festival bivouac'
day 3	7. makhil bandolenè difeté	'transporting building materials'
1Q	8. lél alifeté	'building the roof with sago leaves'
	9. ün taileté	'constructing the ridge at the roof'
FM	10. ilol bando laté	'collecting stones for food preparation'
	11. melil bameté/deté	'cleaving firewood'
3Q–	12. khaülenalenalena aleté	'building small bivouacs for the guests'
	C. Harvest	
3Q	13. khosül (balindaü) üeté	'cutting sago (for consumption during the
Month 3		celebrations)'
1Q–	14. balindaü üeté	'cutting festival sago'
day 1	15. banikhaup ndaü üeté	'cutting sago for consumption during further
		preparations'
day 2	16. lul deté	'cutting leaves (for wrapping grubs)'
	17. khokhüneni bando laté[a]	'collecting garden products'
day 3	18. gèkh khelèlmaté/domaté	'opening of rotting sago trunks to collect
		mature grubs'
	D. Storage	
1Q	19. gèkh lakhup dueté[b]	'stewing grubs'
day 1	20. gèkh lefu balinta fenè feté	'storing of (fresh) grubs on the rack'
	21. lefu alü fetédakhu balinta fenè feté	'storing of stewed grubs on the rack'
day 2 (morning)	22. gil giolmanofè gil lokhteté	'the feast-givers take position at the festival place (while others continue to collect the mature grubs)'
afternoon	23. yebunmengga lulmengga wélmengga bando lenè	'collecting rattan (ropes), leaves (for wrapping food), and materials for torches

[a]Fénélun Molonggai gave the following enumeration: *Dufekho baliampeko gelémpekho bufekho khawfekho* 'bananas, sugarcanes, *gelén* grass, tebui kan (*Saccharum edule*), and sweet potatoes'.

[b]Concerning the first amounts of grubs, the informant said, *lefufé yanop khopésambatélekha fédofédomaté* 'the one part they use to give to the special persons invited' and a *lefufé fenè feté* 'the other part they just store' (for common consumption during the festival).

Table 1–7 (*continued*)

Time	Activity	Translation
	E. Last Preparations	
(dark)	24. yanoptekhé khatédo lelip laté	'(feast-givers) go out and accompany the people who continued to work at the grubs and bring them to the festival bivouac'
	25. gèkh lamo fu lefulmekho ilol menil aleté	'packaging grubs and heating stones'
	26. gèkhtamonfekho aleté dainta khandun fofeté	'stewing packaged grubs under hot stones'
day 3	27. lamontenalena melibol yanifekho aleté	'stewing small packages at different fireplace(s)'
	F. Celebrations Start (Presence of Relatives)	
(early)	28. yekhené kho alü langgamaté	'they bake and eat their (own) sago'
	29. gèkh fo sambilefè bantetédo lé külmekheté[c]	'they distribute a part of the grubs among their closest kinsmen who eat them)'
	G. Celebrations Continue (Presence of Guests)	
noon	30. khopésambatélekha yanop lamébomaté	'entrance of the guests invited'
	31. ndaü alü banteté	'distribution of baked sago among guests'
FM	32. gèkhfekho khokhünenifekho	'they eat grubs and garden products until
day 1	lè külmekhete	satisfied'
	33. lefugop wai gilfodo lefugop yeté	'some groups of guests depart; others stay overnight'
day 2	34. debünenul yekhenép wai gilfo sendifkhayan	'early in the morning all of them depart'
	H. Sacral Part of the Celebrations—Finale I	
day 3	35. gil giolmanofè yekhenép gèkh domaté	'the feast-givers collect grubs again'
(night)	36. gèkh alü batédo	'they continue to stew grubs all night'
3Q	37. nikhül wafil lefu günè balutédo walelé	'groups of women and men keep dancing until daybreak'
(morning)	38. khandindamon demé	'breaking down the sacred fence'
	39. gèkhfekho ndaüfekho bantenè lefulmekho	'final distribution of grubs and sago'
	40. lé lefulmekhetédakhu wai yekhenép gilfaté	'final meal and departure (of all people)'
	I. End of the Feast—Finale II	
(dark)	41. gil giolmanofè wofakhüp éfeluté	'feast-givers stay overnight at the spot'
3Q+ (daybreak)	42. yekhené khaikhaim wai gilfaté	'they finally go to their treehouses'

[c]According to Fénélun Molonggai, the *lambil* consists of the *nabul* 'wife's sibling', *mom* 'mother's brother', *aw* 'elder sister', *modol* 'younger sister', *afé* 'elder brother', and *mofekha* 'younger brother' (see chapter 5 for these kinship terms).

this realm of the dead 'at the end of the places' again have a bodily existence. The realm of the dead is structured just like the world of the living in terms of clans and tribes and their territories. The first and second circles (the worlds of the living and the dead) are connected by the big road (*debülop-talé* 'road-big'), which runs through a twilight jungle. The souls of the deceased (*yanopkhayan*) travel this road to the realm of the dead, but the road is also used by those souls who through reincarnation manifest themselves again in the land of the living (see *yanopkhayan* in Mankind, below).

Surrounding the realms of the living and the dead, the third concentric circle is the endless great water, called *méan-maél* or *méan-maun* 'the dog-water' by the Korowai. Another term for the great water is *atiafunakh* 'the surrounding water'. We do not know whether the Korowai relate these 'dog' terms for the mythical world sea, or 'great water', to the mythical dog who appears in the *Ginol Silamtena* myth of origin [line (18); see chapter 6]. In the context of ideas about the final destruction of the universe, a threathening role is assigned to the big fish (*ndewé*) that populate the great water (*lamol/wola*).

Finally, above all of this, there is the firmament (*dalibün; khulbün* 'the sky'), where the planets and the stars have their place. In the Ginol Silamtena myth of origin, sun, moon, and stars are produced together with humankind in one deed of creation (see line 27). Neither in the myths of origin nor in the folktales (*wakhatum*) do the heavenly bodies receive any special significance. The position of the stars (*belil*) does not seem to be assigned any special meaning.[58] The moon (*wakhol*) functions especially as the marker of time and as a source of light.[59] The word *mamün* 'sun' also means 'warmth', and the warmth of the sun is ascribed healing power.[60] Solar eclipses are associated with the end of the world (see *lamol/wola* below, Some central ideological notions), just as are thunderstorms (*fup-aun nenilfo*, lit. 'wind-rain very much'). The (normal) word for rainbow is *anol*, which also means snake. We do not know what the relationship between the two meanings of *anol* is (or if there is any).

As for the relationship between the earth (*wola, lamol*) and the firmament (*dalibün, khulbün*), in the myth of origin *Ginol Silamtena* (chapter 6) it is told how the firmament above was formed out of the backbone (*müfekholol*) of the slaughtered mythical pig and the world down here out of the chestbone of the mythical pig Faül.[61]

Mankind

In this section, we mention some concepts that we think have an important place in how the Korowai construct the concept of man, the human personality. Again, we do not pretend to come up with an analysis of the Korowai view of mankind. Some key terms marking aspects of the person are the following, the glosses often being only imperfect indications of the meanings of the terms: *yanop* 'man, person', *yanopkhayan* 'soul', *maf* 'shadow/ghost', and *lokhül* 'body'.

The term *yanop* 'man' refers to humans, in opposition to animals and spirits. It primarily denotes persons of the same clan or of the same family,[62] but the term may also be used for persons of nonrelated groups and even of other tribes. There is a special term for 'individual'—*imban*.[63] Individual persons are always thought of as members of a group (cf. the term *yanogun* in Cultural geography, above).

The term *yanopkhayan* 'soul' comprises *yanop* 'person' and the intensifier *khayan* 'very', thus 'the very person, the true person, the essence of a person, the personality'. The *yanopkhayan* is located behind the breastbone (*banggolol*) of a human being. When the *yanopkhayan* leaves the body, it leaves either through the crown of the head or the intestines. The souls of people who died or have lost consciousness walk along the big road (*debüloptalé*). When the soul meets a blockage on the big road (*lül aületé*),[64] made by those relatives who preceded him or her, this means that the soul must return (*wokhelimekho lailo lai*) to the land of the living, so he or she regains consciousness (*mesip khaféntelo* 'again he is alive'). When there is no roadblock, the soul proceeds to the light at the end of the road, where he or she is received by relatives in his or her own clan territory in the realm of the dead. The newly arrived *yanopkhayan* is given dried meat to eat. The *yanopkhayan* can marry in the realm of the dead (*bolüplefupé*), but they do not have children.

The *yanopkhayan* of the most despised and feared category of persons in the land of the living, the *khakhua* '(male) witches', also go to the realm of the dead. There is no separate place where deceased bad people go, as in some neighbouring cultures (e.g., Mandobo) that are possibly under Christian influence (see above, Cultural relationships).

After a certain length of time the *yanopkhayan* can be summoned to return to the land of the living by entering the body of a baby just before birth. The decision concerning the return (*khomungga mahüon*)[65] is taken by the council of the clan in the realm of the dead. When a *yanopkhayan* returns to the land of the living, his or her body is buried (*mélaimekheté* 'they bury') in the land of the dead. The wailing that accompanies such burials can be heard in the land of the living as a prolonged whistling sound (*füponaup*). When this sound is heard just before or during the birth of a baby, the Korowai interpret it as a sign that a returning *yanopkhayan* is united with the baby about to be born.

Although much more research is needed, the notion of *yanopkhayan* might be the factor that connects the wide range of senses of the verb *khomi(lo)*: 'to die; to be unconscious; to be in deep sleep; to transform (into an animal)'. When someone is dizzy or faints, this is called *khomi afü lit.*, 'he wrestles with *khomi*'.

Dying and losing consciousness are both understood in terms of the *yanopkhayan's* leaving of the body.[66] We do not know enough about the idea of transformation, persons changing into animals and back (e.g., *benidaya khomi* 'to change into a bird of paradise'), but it might be that they are also understood in terms of the *yanopkhayan's* move into the body of an animal. The transformation-metamorphosis theme occurs in various totem stories (*laibolekha mahüon*), folktales (*wakhatum*),[67] and myths of origin (*lamolaup*).[68]

The shadow or ghost (*maf*) of a human being is distinguished from the *yanopkhayan*, or soul. In the time immediately after a death, the *maf* is the very last manifestation of the person who just died. Informants said that the *maf* goes into the body of a Torrent lark (*kham*), of which there are very many in Korowai land. In the form of the Torrent lark, the *maf* still dwells for some time around the grave and the house of the deceased person. The *maf* plays a role in divination techniques for the detection of *khakhua* witches (see below, Some central ideological notions). The noun *maf* 'shadow' denotes the shadow as cast by the sun of objects [e.g., *khaimaf* 'shadow of a treehouse' (< *khaim-maf*)]; the shadow reflects the form of that object and is some sort of picture or representation of it. Thus the noun *maf* is also heard to denote photographs of persons and, in a compound with *akh* 'water', to denote mirrors (*maf-akh*). The noun *khüfolun* 'shade' denotes the shadow, not as form cast by the sunlight but as a place where one is protected against the heat of the sunbeams.

The Korowai have a phenomenal knowledge of the anatomy of the human body and a rich vocabulary to denote its smallest details. The term *lokhül* 'body' can be used for the bodies both of living and of dead persons; for example, in *Mukhalé*, line (17) (chapter 6), we find *yanop-lokhül* 'person-body' for 'dead body'). The term *khal* 'skin', as *pars pro toto*, is also used very frequently to denote the body. In compounds with animal names, *khal* means 'meat', for example, *golkhal* 'pork'. Human flesh is usually denoted as *nop*, and the fat as *yabén* [cf. *Mukhalé*, lines (70), (71), (77), and (80) in chapter 6].

The most common term for bones is *kholol*, but sometimes the term *khokhukh* is used, which probably has 'hardness' or 'hard object' as its basic meaning. *Kholol* 'bone' seems to be used metaphorically in a number of compounds in Korowai, for example, *dukholol* 'tree trunk', *wola-kholol* 'earth' (lit. 'earth-bone'), and *kholol-anop* or *khokhukh-anop* 'enemy' (lit. 'bone-people). Words denoting specific parts of the skeleton are compounds with *kholol*, for example, *dénufekholol* 'pelvis (bone)', *gelifekholol* 'nose bone', *manggumkholol* 'cheekbone', and *menakholol* 'rib'.

When the body is functioning properly, this is called *khil* or *khitelo*, in opposition to *lép* or *léptelo*, which is the general term for the malfunctioning of the body or deficiencies in primary bodily needs (hunger or thirst; e.g., *nu maun-tép* 'I am thirsty'). The expression *lép* is also used to denote pain in specific body parts, as in *ne-mélol léptelo* 'my hand hurts'. The term *kelil-/kelitelo* 'zest for life' is used in expressions that denote mental well-being (cf. the experiential expression *ye kelil ütelo* 'he is depressed', *lit.* 'to him the zest for life is gone').

The human body is a rich source for the conceptualisation and expression of other, more abstract domains, such as number concepts (see the body-part tally system in chapter 3) and of mental and emotional states and processes.

The *khabéan* 'crown of the head' is considered a significant part of the body. It is, for example, one of the two places where the *yanopkhayan* 'soul' may leave the body (see below). *Khabéan* is metaphorically extended to leaders of groups and to the highest parts of certain objects.[69] In the numeral system, *khabéan* means 'thirteen'. *Main* 'shoulder' means 'ten' in the numeral system. The gesture of shrugging one's shoulders (*main gatakhmo* 'to shrug the shoulders') expresses uncertainty or not knowing something.

The human face is called *lulgelip*, a compound of *lul* 'eye' and *gelip* 'nose'. The usual term for eye is *lulop*.[70] Expressions of seeing and the eye are also used in the area of human relationships. The verb *imo* means 'to see, to look at' but may also mean 'to pay (positive) attention to someone with whom one has a relationship'. The Korowai discern something like the 'evil eye'; people with red eyes (*lulop khafümtelo*) are suspected of applying *ndafun* 'magic power' with bad intentions (see below, *ndafun*, in Some central ideological notions).

In various expressions, the face is viewed as reflecting emotions, for example, *ye-lulgelip khéntelo* 'his face is angry'; but the intestines (*khul, fimelon*), in combination with the gallbladder (*melun*), are seen as the seat of emotion and thought. This view is reflected in expressions of feeling and thinking, as in very many cultures of New Guinea. The standard expression for thinking is *ne-khul duelékha* or *ne-fimelon duelékha,* lit. 'I plant into my intestines, that . . .' or *ne khul-melun duelékha* 'I plant into in my intestines and gallbladder, that . . .' followed by a quotative complement that expresses the content of the thought (see Quote marking in chapter 3 and Subordinate linkage with *-kha* in chapter 4 for quotative complements of verbs of thought).

Not only thoughts but also emotions are linked to the belly. The following fragment of text describes the emotions of love and mutual attraction between a man and a woman:

(1) wa lal   ye-fimelon alo-melu   khenè wafil fimelon-an
    that female her-intestines stand-move.up.3SG.REAL next   man   intestines-LOC
    melé-ai-khai-do   wafil ye-khul-melun
    move-move.down-3SG.IRR-DS man   his-intestines-gall.bladder
    mesi alo-melu   khenè wa lal fimelon-an
    next stand-move.up.3SG.REAL next   that girl intestines-LOC
    melé-ai-khai-kha-fè   kholo-kholop momu-telo-kha-té
    move-move.down-3SG.IRR-CONN-TOP each-each   longing-be-IRR-3PL.REAL

'In case the woman's intestines will lift up themselves, and will get into the man's belly (intestines and gallbladder), and the man's intestines will lift up themselves and will get into the woman's intestines, they will long for each other . . .'

The liver (*üm*) occurs also in some expressions as the seat of emotions, again in combination with *khul* 'intestines' (cf. *ne-khul-üm guntelo* 'I am stressed', lit. 'my intestines-liver are short').

Concerning the ear (*khotop*)[71] and listening (*dai*), expressions of deliberation and consultation but also of obedience often refer to notions of hearing, for example, *kholokholop aup daibaté* 'to consult; to deliberate' (lit. 'to hear each other's voices/ words'), and *gekhenép anèdamén* 'you should be obedient!' (lit. 'you should hear'). Finally, *dai/daibo* 'to listen' is used with the meaning 'to understand; to know'.

Certain parts of the human body receive a special cultural significance because magic power is attributed to them. *Büngga* 'blood' is seen as a carrier of magic power (*ndafun*) in the sense of *mana* (van Baal 1981: 48; Trompf 1991: 13, 81).[72] Especially the blood of pregnant (*khondulmengga*) or menstruating (*wolop*) women is full of dangerous *ndafun*. Contact with such blood is lethal for men. Continuing emaciation (*afoptelo*) and coughing (*bokokhtelo*) in males are sometimes explained by contact with blood of women in childbirth. These views of female blood, including the relationship with symptoms of emaciation and coughing, are very common in the whole Upper Digul area.

Mukh 'hair' and *singga* 'nails' of both males and females are seen also as carriers of *ndafun* 'magic power'. This aspect of nails and hair comes to the fore in divination techniques, as well as in forms of harmful magic with bad intentions.[73] Hair, nails, and footprints (*bétom)* are seen as representations of a person that can be used in a type of harmful magic called *bendémekho* 'to hang'. For example, someone's hair, packed in leaves and hung in a nest of wasps, causes serious headaches. Similarly, footprints can be dug out and hung, which causes diseases of the feet.

The distinction between males and females is one of the themes in the origin myth *Ginol Silamtena* [lines (33)–(37), see chapter 6]. The first two people are two brothers, and the older brother, to facilitate procreation, cuts off the penis (*dul*) and the testicles (*lokhesukh-op* 'egg fruit') of the younger brother and turns him into a woman. He then has sex with her (*gomo* 'to have sexual intercourse with someone'; sometimes *lil gomo*, lit. 'to have sex with the vagina'), and she becomes pregnant. The verb *melu* 'to grow' is also used for 'to procreate' and, in *dul melu*, for 'erection'. The verb *melu* occupies a prominent position in the sacred fertility song *Gom*, which is sung during the closing ceremony of the sago grub feast (see above, Sago, and chapter 6). The noun *dul* 'penis' occurs also in *dul-e-khil* lit. 'penis health' or 'penis vitality' (perhaps 'penis life force'), the name of the special crowbar used in the sago grub feast to open the rotting sago trunks that contain the mature sago grubs ready to be harvested.

Korowai females wear short skirts (*sékh*) to cover their genitals; Korowai males use just a leaf wrapping to cover the glans of the penis. During feasts, a penis gourd (*mbayap, khawisip*) may be used, together with other adornments like rattan shingles (*lonoptabül*). Sexual relations between people are often phrased in terms of sharing food, especially sago (see, for example, *A Folktale about the Fofunonalin Brothers* in chapter 6). A strikingly explicit reference to sexual relations occurs in the real-life story *Mukhalé*, line (5) (see chapter 6). The nouns denoting male and female genitals are also used as abusive words.

Some central ideological notions

We mention in this section a number of key concepts that are part of major ideological structures and also play a role in the texts in chapter 6. Again, we do not pretend to give more than a first inventory of concepts, without placing them within wider ideological frameworks. Only when links between these concepts are very evident in our corpus of texts do we mention it. Kinship-related ideological notions of obligation and solidarity are not treated in this section.

Ayulekha

The noun *ayul* or *ayulekha* 'taboo; prohibition' is applied to words that are forbidden to pronounce and to things that are forbidden to do.[74] The term *ayulekha* can be replaced in all contexts with the term *masekha*. *Ayulekha* forms phrases with other words to denote specific types of taboos. For example, there are very many food taboos (*ayulekha lungga* 'forbidden food/food prohibition'), which restrict the use of food in a wide variety of ways.[75]

The term 'forbidden bamboo-tip arrow' (*ayulekha daup*), also called *khandin daup* 'secret bamboo-tip arrow', refers to the method of killing an entire clan by secretly putting a flat bamboo arrow tip (*daup, bumon*; see figure 1–17) into the fireplace of the house of the enemy clan, after having put a spell (*ayulekha mahüon*) on the arrow tip. When the arrow tip is burnt, destruction of the clan is inevitable.[76]

Figure 1–17   *Daup* arrowtips.
Gerrit van Enk, 1990.

The concept *ayul* comes close to the notion of *wol* 'sacredness; secret' when it is used in relation to risks associated with certain locations. In such contexts, the notions *ayulekha lop* 'taboo concerning a place' and *wo-top* 'sacred place' (from *wol-top* 'sacred place') can be used interchangeably. In other contexts, the notion *ayul* comes close to the notion *khandin* 'secret/sacred thing'; for example, the sacred central pole (see figure 1–18) of the ceremonial bivouac for the sago grub festival is called *ayulekha du* and also *khandin du*.

There is also a link with the notion *ndafun* 'power' (see below) since the presence of *ndafun* in places or activities or objects can be a reason to consider these *ayulekha*.

Mbolombolop

Mbolombolop is a noun used for the collectivity of both living and dead ancestors.[77] The *mbolombolop* form the highest ideological authority in the clan. The dead *mbolombolop* are associated with the holy places (*wotop*), which can be found in almost every clan territory. The pig sacrifice ritual, described from the Korowai perspective in chapter 6, has as its central thought that the *mbolombolop*, who receive the sacrificial pig, can guard and improve the well-being of the clan from their dwelling places in the vicinity. When hairs or nails or other things with 'power' (*ndafunmengga* 'with *ndafun*'; see below) are placed close to *wotop*, the fate of the

Figure 1–18   Sago grub festival bivouac (interior). Johannes Veldhuizen, 1986.

person whose nails or hair has been taken is put into the hands of the ancestors, often causing the death of that person.

The traditional account of the origin of the world (*lamolaup*), as well as the folktales (*wakhatum*) and the system of prohibitions (*ayulekha*), derive from the *mbolombolop*.[78] The living *mbolombolop* constantly refer to the authority of the dead *mbolombolop* when they warn the younger generation of the bad things that will befall them when they violate the rules laid down by the *mbolombolop*. The ultimate effect of violation and disobedience is the end of the world, or the world turned upside down (*wolalelokhai* or *lamotelokhai*; see below). In the first stage of acculturation, the threat of an imminent world end also serves to strengthen the authority of the *mbolombolop*, which itself is threatened by the new ideologies of the outsiders—the mission, the government, and others. In the text of *Khenil-khenil* [e.g., lines (81ff.) the relations among the three concepts of *mbolopmbolop*, *ayul*, and *wola* can be clearly observed in the context of acculturation problems.

Ndafun

The noun *ndafun* '(magic) power; mana' is very broadly applied. *Ndafun* can be both beneficial and destructive. When somebody is affected by destructive magic, it is called *ndafun üimbo* 'to be hit with *ndafun*'. Objects, words, people, actions—anything can be a carrier of *ndafun*, either because it is intrinsically full of *ndafun* or because people have magically 'put' *ndafun* on it (*ndafun fenè fu* 'to put *ndafun* on something/someone'). Important verbal means for putting on *ndafun* are *ndafun-mahüon* '*ndafun* word; spell'.[79]

The domains in which putting *ndafun* is most applied are health (*manopo, kholükhmo* 'to cure'), hunting (*ndafunto lungga ülmolekha* 'to kill game by *ndafun*'), sexual relations, and killing or damaging enemies. Intrinsically loaded with *ndafun* are, for example, hair, nails, menstrual blood, and blood of women in childbirth.

Tobacco has special 'power' (*dépo-ndafun*), which is used to cure illnesses. Headaches (*lokhutokhul*), for example, are cured by touching the head of the sufferer with the top (*bon*) of the bamboo pipe (*déponagél*) after the upper part of the pipe is moistened with spittle and the top part is warmed in the fire.[80]

The effect of *ndafun* can be diminished, be lost, or become dangerous when its beneficiaries violate one of the *ayul* 'taboo; prohibition' that accompany the use of specific kinds of *ndafun*. For example, when the pregnant or menstruating wife of a hunter eats from the animals killed by the hunter with the help of *ndafun*, the *ndafun* that accompanied the hunt and became associated with the game brought home by the hunter will turn against her and her children and kill them. Furthermore, her husband will loose his effectiveness as a hunter.

Finally, we mention a relationship between *ndafun* and 'the evil eye'. A person can by prolonged and silent staring at someone put destructive *ndafun* on the victim. The sign that someone is performing that kind of magic is the redness of the eyes caused by prolonged staring. Consider the expression *inè kilelobakhido yelulop khafümtelobakhi* lit., 'he kept staring at him silently for a long time and then his eyes turned red'.

Khandin

We encountered the concept *khandin* 'sacred; secret' in two contexts. The first is in the myths of the genre *lamolaup* 'story of the universe'. These texts are also called *khandin-mahüon* 'secret stories', where secret points to the secrecy distinctions that play a role in the differentiation of several genres of oral literature of the Korowai (see below, Oral tradition). The second context is the sago grub festival, more specifically the sacred part of the festival in which the *khandin-du* or the *khandin-fénop* 'sacred pole' occupies a central position, both literally (in the centre of the festival bivouac) and ritually. Around the sacred pole, there is a sacred fence (*khandin-damon*) that encloses the sacred fire (*khandin-melil*) (see above, Sago grub festival).

Khakhua

Death is very often ascribed to black magic practiced by male witches (*khakhua*) who 'eat' (*lé/fonolé*)[81] the vital organs of their victims in a magical way. When somebody is convinced that he or she is a victim of a *khakhua*, that person dies within a few days. Burials are quite often delayed to give relatives from other clan territories (especially maternal uncles) the opportunity to see the corpse and to carry out research to detect possible witchcraft and the witches responsible for the death. The destructive activities of the *khakhua* are seen as a horrible crime and as the result of an evil disposition.[82]

Witches (*khakhua*; Indonesian: *suangi*) use (invisible) arrows to shoot their victims in the heart. Sometimes, the arrows just brush (*khelilmekho*) the heart, and then the victim has a chance to survive. He or she can be treated by being hit (*bümaté/ yalombaté*) with irritating nettles (*yalün*).

The detection (*bilaimbaté* 'they search') and identification of the *khakhua* and the formal accusation (*falimekhobolekha mahüon*) that someone is a *khakhua*, and as such is responsible for the death of someone else, are the responsibility of the adult males of the victim's clan. To detect the *khakhua* responsible for a death, a variety of detection techniques is applied, including spiritualistic and divination techniques. We observed the following methods.

First, the victim may be asked (*laifaté* 'they interrogate') directly, just before his or her death, who was responsible. Second, immediately after the grave (*mébol*) has been closed, the deceased is asked this question in an indirect way, by posing closed questions about the circumstances in which the *khakhua* performed his crime. The answer takes the form of poltergeistlike rappings. Third, the *maf* 'shadow' of the deceased victim, considered to be present in the Torrent Lark (*kham*), is asked indirect closed questions in the vicinity of the grave. When this is done, pieces of the nails of the deceased are put into the bark of a tree close to the grave. Fourth, sharp things (*antabun*), such as arrow tips, are put halfway into the ground around the grave (*antabun duolaibaté* 'they have planted *antabun*) and covered with grass and leaves. The Korowai believe that the *khakhua* will return to the grave and hurt himself by walking on the sharp objects.[83]

According to reports of informants, the crimes of a *khakhua* are revenged by the death penalty, and his body is cut into pieces, distributed, and eaten.[84] We have never found any indications that the eating of human flesh occurs outside the *khakhua* context; that is, other crimes, like theft or adultery, are not punished in this way.[85]

When the *khakhua* is a member of the same clan as his victim, he is sent to an allied clan to be executed and eaten. Sometimes this is done in the framework of what seems to be a kind of exchange relationship between clans.

Kholofudamo and kholopamo

One of the most central principles governing social relationships in the Korowai community is that of *kholo-pa-mo* 'to reciprocate' (lit. 'each.other-also-do'): gifts received must in due time be balanced by a countergift; damage must be repaired by the party responsible for it; hostile acts demand hostile counteractions.

When in this framework of equivalence and parity (*kholopamo*), something valuable (women, pigs, axes, cowrie shells [figure 1–19], dogteeth, pig teeth [figures 1–20 and 1–21]), is given, it is called *kholofudamo* 'to give a replacement, replace'. The verb is a compound of *kholop*, denoting reciprocity (cf. *kholo-kholop* 'each other'), and *fu-damo*, which comprises *fu* 'to put' and *damo* 'similar.be/do'.

The context in which the verb *kholofudamo* is most often used is the traditional 'replacement' by a gift for a relative who died. The death-related recompensation gifts serve to maintain the ties among surviving relatives, who meet one another at the funeral.

The term *kholofudamo* is also used outside the context of death, for example, in marriage arrangements. The bride-giving clan is recompensated by the bride-taking

Figure 1–19 Saséan Khenei, adorned with cowrie shells. Name of child unknown.
Johannes Veldhuizen, 1987.

clan for the loss of the woman and her offspring in the form of bridal payments
(*monggo fenè fu* lit. 'unload put down') in pigs (*gol*), chains of dog teeth (*banggil*),
and shell money (*khül; malin*). (See figure 1–5 for a part of a bridal payment.) More
recently, steel axes (*khamba*) are also often requested. Asking recompensation (*gufu*
'to claim recompensation' or *misafilekhé nèkhmo* 'to ask for goods') can also be done
for damage. When a justified claim for recompensation is refused (*aündantelo*), it
can be the cause of prolonged conflicts between clans.

Related terms in the field of exchange and retribution (cf. Trompf 1991: 51–77)
are the verbs *abolo / abohüomo* 'to buy / sell / exchange goods' and the verb *fédo* 'to
give', used in expressions like *lal fédo* 'to give a woman' in the context of marriage
transactions and also in expressions like *bün fédo* 'to give *bün*', in which *bün* is the
recompensation given to the sorcerer for the magic aimed at harming a third party.
This practice of 'hiring harmful magic' is called *sewa* in (local) Indonesian.

Pigs play a central role in all major reciprocity arrangements (*fundam* 'arrangement'); because of this role, pigs are exclusively raised to serve as recompensation
goods to maintain and restore social relations, including the relationship with the
ancestors who receive sacrificial pigs (see below and chapter 6, *The Pig Sacrifice*).

People who refuse to reciprocate are bad (*lembul),* contrasting with cooperative
people who dutifully recompensate what was done or given to them (*manop* 'good').[86]
A clear example of a bad man in the texts is Mukhalé, who refuses to recompensate
the death of his brother [line (23); see chapter 6]; at the same time this man is a big
man (*letél-abül* 'strong man'), an aggressive leader of his clan who rose to a prominent position in his society. This story reveals the underlying tension of 'strength'/

Figure 1–20   Unknown Korowai man, adorned with pig teeth necklace. Johannes Veldhuizen, 1987.

coercion and consensus principles, so characteristic of many small-scale New Guinea communities without formal political structure (cf. Foley 1986: 15–19).

Laléo

Laléo 'demon; (bad) spirit' (pl.: *laléoalin*) differs from the spirits of the ancestors (*mbolombolop* 'ancestors; older people'). There is no kinship relation with the *laléoalin* and they are feared. Uninvited, nonrelated persons who enter the clan territory can be suspected *laléoalin*, and magic to repulse the intruders may be used. In *The Resurrection Story* [line (21), chapter 6], the people fear that the buried man who returns to them is a *laléo*.

The term *laléo* became the general term for outsiders who enter Korowai territories [cf. the text of *Khenil-khenil*, lines (1), (6), (7), etc.]. Initially, the Korowai did not believe that the white missionaries were *yanop* 'human person'; they were thought to be *laléoalin*. Words for new things associated with the outsiders often contain the noun *laléo*; for example:

laléo-aup	'Indonesian language'	< aup	'word; language'
laléo-ndaü	'bread'	< ndaü	'sago'
laléo-khal	'clothing'	< khal	'skin'
laléo-menil	'matches'	< menil	'fire(wood)'

The spirit with the name Sèifabül (lit. 'shiver-man') is sometimes called a *laléo*. Sèifabül plays a role in a kind of spiritistic séances, in which the woman who is the medium is called *sèip-engga lal* 'shiver-with woman'. The shiver element refers to the movements made by the medium when she has contacts with the spirit. The 'shiver-woman' plays a role in curing magic. We have a text in which an informant tells how a 'shiver-woman' removed a (magic) arrow from his body.[87]

Lamol/wola

The noun *lamol* is used to mean 'clan territory; ancestral land', as well as 'world; universe'. Another term for clan territory is *bolüp*, which also has a second sense of 'world (of the living)' (see above, Territories and treehouses of Korowai clans). The meaning of 'world' occurs in such contexts as *lamol-aup/wola-aup* 'story of the universe, myth of origin' and *khayolamol* 'arrows of the universe'.

Figure 1–21   Nailop Khawékh, wife of Sapuru Sendékh, adorned with pig teeth necklace. Rijke de Wolf, 1990.

In specific idioms, *lamol* and *wola* are used to denote the end of the world, that is, the expressions *wolamaman* and *wolalelokhai/lamotelokhai* 'the world will come to its destruction; the world will be destroyed'. The end of the world is thought of as the *bolübolüp* 'the land of the living' and the *bolüplefupé* 'the land of the dead' turned upside-down so that all beings succumb in the world-sea, the *méanmaél*, in which gigantic mythical fish (*ndewé*) live.[88] These fish devour all people and animals. The older people of the clan (*mbolombolop*) warn the young again and again that the end of the world is near, and these warnings are given in the context of exhortations to respect and obey the words of the ancestors (*mbolombolop mahüon; mülekha mahüon*). Pigs may be sacrificed to the ancestors (see *The Pig Sacrifice* in chapter 6) to fend off the danger of the end of the world.

The following phenomena are seen as signs that the end of the world is at hand: an extraordinary number of deaths, extreme droughts, extreme long periods of heavy rainfall, and solar eclipses. The solar eclipse of June 11, 1983, was seen as a threatening sign of the end of the world, and the people picked up bows and arrows to fend off the danger (Douma 1983: 138–139). Informants said that the arrows used on such occasions are called *khayo-lamol* 'arrow of the universe'. Arrows of the universe are arrows with *yelüp*, *fayan*, *mandil* and *mbonggon*, carved decorations at the top of the shaft. There are two *fayan* decorative motives, called the *yenal-fayan* 'female fayan' (see figure 1–3, arrow 1) and the *yum-fayan* 'male fayan' (see figure 1–3, arrow 2). Only the female *fayan* arrows are used as 'arrows of the universe'. For a *mandil*-like arrow, see Leroux 1950: plate 109, nos. 12 and 13.

Oral tradition

The Korowai culture is a primary oral culture in the sense of Ong (1982), that is, a culture untouched by writing, with a rich and fascinating oral tradition.[89] Thus far we have found four genres of oral traditional texts.

First, there are *wakhatum* 'folktales' or *wakhatum mahüon* 'folktale stories'. The tale about the Fofumonalin brothers in chapter 6 is an example of a *wakhatum* text. These *wakhatum* often give a popular explanation of the miraculous origin of some features in the flora or fauna or in the human world. These texts also frequently have etiological themes concerning the locations where people, animals, and spirits live (like turns of rivers). All members of the Korowai community may listen to and transmit these folktales. Typical characters with predictable behaviour are found in the various *wakhatum*. Because of their predictable and recognisable behaviour, they often cause the public to laugh.

Second, *ndafun-mahüon* 'magic sayings' can be applied either positively or negatively to change the course of events with respect to health, prosperity, relationships, sexuality, or success in hunting game. Literally, the compound *ndafun-mahüon* means 'power words'. These 'power words' may only be listened to and transmitted by adults. We have not yet been able to obtain examples of this kind of text since possessors of *ndafun mahüon* 'spells/magic sayings' keep them secret.

Third, *lamol-aup* 'history of the world' denote myths of origins. In *lamol-aup* the origin of the world is the main theme. Only male adults may listen to and trans-

Table 1–8 Totem animals

Clan		Totem Animal	Clan		Totem Animal
Dambol	abéap	'sand tortoise'	Khomei	bembüokh	'*bembüokh* lizard'
Gifanop	küal	'cassowary'	Manianggatun	kham	'Torrent lark'
Faülanop	kham	'Torrent lark'	Molonggai	dèkhlèkhalé	'fairy wren'
Khandunanop	khelé	'fish'	Nambul	béal	'sundbird/honey eater'
Khawékh	kèkèkh	'white cuckatoo'	Sendékh	mafom	'*mafom* snake'

mit these texts. It is not uncommon in New Guinea cultures to find secrecy distinctions that play a role in distinguishing indigenous genres of oral texts (cf. Wilson 1989 for the Yali of Irian Jaya). The *lamol-aup* stories are only recounted in exceptional situations, especially in times of crisis and threatening disaster. Informants mentioned the following examples of these circumstances: earthquakes, extremely long dry or wet spells, massive deaths, and solar eclipses. The Ginol Silamtena text in chapter 6 is an example of a *lamol-aup* text.

The fourth genre is the *laibolekha mahüon* 'words of descent'; these texts are the possession of the different clans and tell about the totem animal who was the first mythical ancestor of the clan. The *laibolekha mahüon* often present the background for (totem-related) food taboos. Interwoven with totemistic themes are etiological sections that refer to geographical features of the Korowai landscape and remarks about the origin of other clans and tribes. Even the youngest members know the taboos justified in the *laibolekha mahüon* of their clan. The story about the origin of the Khomei clan in chapter 6 exemplifies the *laibolekha-mahüon* type of text.

The totem stories found thus far have the following structure:[90]

1. Self-deliberation of the totemic animal
2. Hatching eggs or birth of first human beings
3. Growing up of first human (couple) to adulthood
4. Command to procreation
5. Instruction concerning food taboo
    a. Prohibition to kill/eat the totemic ancestor
    b. Exhortation to tradition of the taboo

In the majority of cases, it is forbidden to eat the totem animal. In some cases, like the *Khandunanop*, who have fish in general (*khelé*) as their totem animal, the totem story explicitly mentions the permission to eat the totem animal. To kill the totem animal on the clan territory may have fatal consequences for the clan. Thus far, we have noted the totem animals in table 1–8.

Phonemes and Morphophonemics

There are both segmental and suprasegmental phonemes in Korowai. The segmental phonemes can be divided into vowels and consonants on the basis of their function in syllables. Vowels function as the nuclei of syllables and can carry stress. Consonants form the periphery of syllables and cannot carry stress.

Consonants

Tables 2–1 and 2–2 illustrate consonant phonemes in Korowai.

Consonant allophones

We shall now describe the phonetic realization of the consonant phonemes given in table 2–1. The description is based on articulatory criteria of voicing, place of articulation, manner of articulation, and air mechanism (ingressive or egressive).

Voiced plosives

/b/: [b], a voiced bilabial plosive, with egressive lung air. Examples: [bɔːl] 'hole'; [dˀbɔ́ːp] 'heart'.

[ɓ], a voiced bilabial implosive, with ingressive pharynx air. Examples: [ɓai] 'bow'; [nˀɓáːn] 'my chest'.

[b] and [ɓ] seem to be freely varying allophones. Examples: [báːnun] 'back', [ɓáːnun] 'back'; [nˀbáːn] 'my chest', [nˀɓáːn] 'my chest'.

Table 2–1 Consonant phonemes

	Bilabial	*Alveolar*	*Palatal*	*Velar*
Voiced plosives	b	d	ɟ	g
Voiceless plosives	p	t		k
Prenasalised plosives	ᵐb	ⁿd		ⁿg
Nasals	m	n		
Fricatives	φ	s		x
Laterals	l			
Semivowels	w		j	
	ɥ			

/d/: [d], a voiced alveolar plosive, with egressive lung air. Examples: [du:p] 'banana'; [dᵊdíːl] 'root (of a tree)'.

[ɗ], a voiced alveolar plosive, with ingressive pharynx air. Examples: [ɗᵊbɔ́p] 'heart'; [daɗúː] 'to bathe'.

[d] and [ɗ] seem to be freely varying allophones. Examples: [diφɔ́:n] 'lake', [ɗiφɔ́:n] 'lake'; [nᵊdᵊbɔ́:p] 'my heart'.

/ɟ/: [ɟ], a voiced palatal plosive. Example: [laɟɔ́:] 'leech'.

/g/: [g], a voiced velar plosive. Examples: [gɔ:l] 'pig'; [igɔ́:] 'oar'.

Voiceless plosives

/p/: [p], a voiceless bilabial plosive. Examples: [pa:l] 'machete'; [xɔ:p] 'there'; [dé:pɔn] 'tobacco'.

Table 2–2 Distribution of consonant phonemes in words

Phoneme	*Word initial*	*Word medial*	*Word final*
b	+	+	−
d	+	+	−
ɟ	−	+	−
g	+	+	−
ᵐb	+	+	−
ⁿd	+	+	−
ⁿg	+	+	−
p	+	+	+
t	+	+	−
k	+	+	+
m	+	+	+
n	+	+	+
φ	+	+	+
s	+	+	−
x	+	+	+
l	+	+	+
w	+	+	+
ɥ	+	+	−
j	+	+	−

/t/:   [t], a voiceless alveolar plosive. Examples: [tɔ:p] 'place'; [atú:n] 'bow'.

/k/:   [k], a voiceless velar plosive. Examples: [kelɔ:] 'dugout'; [u:k] 'little cucumber'; [lᵊφu:kɔkɔ́:p] 'all kinds of'.

Prenasalised plosives

/ᵐb/: [ᵐb], a voiced bilabial prenasalized plosive. Examples: [ᵐba:m] 'child'; [gᵊᵐbᵊnú:l] 'short'.

/ⁿd/:   [ⁿd], a voiced alveolar prenasalized plosive. Examples: [ⁿdaü:] 'sago'; [maⁿdú:n] 'kind of fish'.

/ⁿg/:   [ⁿg], a voiced velar prenasalized plosive. Examples: [ⁿgeⁿgí:mexɔ:] 'to push'; [dɔⁿgɔ́:p] 'piece of wood'.

Nasals

/m/:   [m], a voiced bilabial nasal. Examples: [mɔ:m] 'uncle'; [mamá:p] 'a little'.

/n/:   [n], a voiced alveolar nasal. Examples: [nɔ:n] 'sago grub'; [nané:m] 'secretly'.

Fricatives

/φ/:   [φ], a voiceless bilabial fricative. Examples: [φɔ:] 'to marry'; [lɔ:φ] 'jungle'; [φaní:p] 'mountains'.

    [ß], a voiced bilabial fricative. [ß] varies with [φ] intervocalically. Examples: [diφɔ́:n] 'lake', [dißɔ́:n] 'lake'.

/s/:   [s], a voiceless alveolar fricative. Examples: [sɔ:l] 'new'; [xɔsüxɔ́:p] 'there'.

/x/:   [x], a voiceless velar fricative, and [γ], a voiced velar fricative. [γ] varies with [x] intervocalically. Examples: [mɔxᵊγú:p] 'true'; [la:x] 'poisonous snake'. Just as in Kombai (de Vries 1989: 130) there is lateralisation in Korowai. This affects /x/ also: [xl] and [x] vary freely with the lateralised allophone as the least frequent realisation. Examples: [xaxḻű:] 'to bite'; [xaxű:] 'to bite'; [xḻü:p] 'desire', [xü:p] 'desire'.

Laterals

/l/:   [l], a voiced lateral (unvelarised). Examples: [la:l] 'girl; daughter'; [xɔlɔ́:l] 'bone'.

Semivowels

/ɥ/:   [ɥ], a voiced rounded bilabial-palatal semivowel, as the first sound in French *huit* 'eight' but voiced. Examples: [ɥᵊté:] 'they killed'; [maɥɔ́:n] 'word'.

/w/:   [w], a voiced rounded labiodental semivowel, as the first sound of Dutch *wat* 'what' but more rounded. Examples: [wa:n] 'pig'; [gawí:l] 'stairs'; [na:w] 'my older sister'.

/j/: [j], a voiced unrounded palatal semivowel. Examples: [jabé:n] 'fat, bacon'; [wajɔ́:] 'thumb'.

Contrasts for consonant phonemes

/b/-/ᵐb/:	[lé:ᵐbate:]	'they are eating'	/d/-/ⁿd/:	[dᵊbɔ́:p]	'heart'
	[lé:bate:]	'they have eaten'		[ⁿdᵊmɔ́:p]	'swamp'
	[ᵐba:m]	'child'		[ɸudá:mɔp]	'I want to
	[ba:n]	'chest'			recompense'
	[ᵐbalá:mɔ:]	'share'		[ɸuⁿdá:m]	'arrangement;
	[balá:lmɔ:]	'rolling of			affair'
		thunder'		[dadü:]	'to swim'
				[dᵊⁿdü:]	'banana'
/g/-/ⁿg/:	[gɔlɔ́:lale:]	'I flee'	/ɟ/-/j/:	[baɟɔ́:m]	'kind of iguana'
	[ⁿgɔlɔ́:lale:]	'long, tall'		[bajɔ́:m]	'sandy lowland or
	[ge:l]	'species of *nibung*			swamp'
		palm tree'		[xaɟá:]	'lastborn'
	[ⁿge:l]	'old'		[xajá:n]	'very'
	[ge:n]	'name of river			
		spirit'			
	[ⁿge:n]	'kind of small			
		palm tree'			
/ᵐb/–/m/:	[ᵐbajá:p]	'penis gourd'	/ⁿd/-/n/:	[mí:ⁿda]	'do not drink'
	[mamá:p]	'little'		[miná:]	'lightning'
	[ᵐba:m]	'child'		[bá:nun]	'back'
	[ma:]	'also'		[xá:ⁿdun]	'stone'
	[á:limate:]	'they scooped'		[bᵊⁿdé:mekhɔ:]	'hang'
	[á:liᵐbate:]	'they start to		[bᵊné:nmukh]	'pubic hair'
		scoop'			
/p/-/b/:	[pɔ:l]	'two'	/t/-/d/:	[lefü:da:]	'not a day'
	[bɔ:l]	'hole'		[lefǘ:ta:]	'at noon'
	[pǘ:xmɔ:]	'throw'		[–dɔ:]	'DS'
	[bǘ:mɔ:]	'beat'		[–tɔ:]	'FOC'
				[leɸudé:p]	'pulling at one end'
				[lᵊnuté:p]	'sleepy'
/k/-/g/:	[kǘ:te:]	'finish'	/p/–/ɸ/:	[le:p]	'ill'
	[gǘ:le:]	'to become dark'		[le:ɸ]	'tongue'
	[ka:]	'call of the		[xɔpé:]	'the day before
		yearbird'			yesterday'
	[ga:]	'hard'		[xɔɸé:l]	'young male'
	[kᵊlᵊlǘ:xmɔ:]	'make noise'		[pᵊlí:]	'blunt'
	[gᵊlǘ:xmɔ:]	'graze'		[ɸᵊlí:]	'fall'
/k/–/x/:	[natexǘ:l]	'my fathers'	/t/–/s/:	[xá:sam]	'dance'
	[natekǘ:l]	'like my father'		[xá:ta:]	'toward'
	[kí:lᵊlɔ:]	'be silent'		[aüsɔ́:p]	'I will promise'
	[xí:telɔ:]	'strong'		[aütɔ́:p]	'place of whirlpool
					in the river'

/p/–/ᵐb/: [pa:n]   'self'   /t/–/ⁿd/: [xɔtú:]   'still'
           [ᵐba:m]   'child'   [xɔⁿdú:l]   'belly'
           [dé:pɔn]   'tobacco'   [atú:n]   'bow'
           [dé:ᵐbɔl]   'Dembol River'   [xaⁿdú:n]   'stone'

/k/–/ⁿg/: [lᵊɸú:kɔkɔ:p]   'all kinds of'
           [lᵊɸú:ⁿgɔⁿgɔ:p]   'some pieces of
                              wood'

/b/–/m/:   [be:l]   'foot'   /d/–/n/:   [du:p]   'banana'
           [me:l]   'hand'   [nu:p]   'I'
           [dé:pᵊbale:]   'I have smoked'   [mé:dap]   'palm of the hand'
           [dé:pᵊmale:]   'I usually smoke'   [né:nax]   'moisture of rotten
                                                                           corpse'

/ⁿg/–/x/: [ⁿge:l]   'old'   /ɸ/–/w/:   [ɸa:le:]   'to appear'
           [xe:l]   'flower'   [wá:le:]   '(morning) light'
           [maⁿgú:m]   'cheek'   [ɸɔtɔ́:p]   'he took and . . .'
           [waxú:m]   'wild chicken'   [wɔtɔ́:p]   'place where
                                                                           spirits live'
                                                          [ma:ɸ]   'shadow'
                                                          [na:w]   'my older sister'

/t/–/l/:   [aütɔ́:p]   'place of whirlpool   /d/–/l/: [de:p]   'cloud'
                              in the river'   [le:p]   'tongue'
           [aülɔ́:p]   'I want to close'   [ɸú:sada:]   'not an ironwood
           [atú:n]   'bow'   tree'
           [alú:n]   'fire'   [ɸú:sala:]   'to the ironwood
           [á:tᵊle:]   'I get'   tree'
           [á:lᵊle:]   'I build'

/ɸ/–/b/:   [ɸi:]   'name'   /b/–/w/:   [ba:n]   'chest'
           [bi:]   'swollen'   [wa:n]   'pig'
           [xɔɸé:manɔp]   'male youngster'   [be:l]   'leg'
           [xᵊbé:mɔ:]   'it tottered'   [we:l]   'torch'

Variation of consonant phonemes

In a number of words, the voiceless plosives vary with their homorganous fricative
counterparts.

/p/ AND /ɸ/ VARIATION

[lɔ:p]   'jungle'   [lɔ:ɸ]   'jungle'

[dᵊbű:p]   'way'   [dᵊbű:ɸ]   'way'

[pɔ́:ɸulᵊle:]   'to be silent'   [ɸɔ́:ɸulᵊle:]   'to be silent'

/t/ AND /s/ VARIATION

[jatí:m] 'garden'   [jasí:m] 'garden'

[tiⁿgá:] 'nail'   [siⁿgá:] 'nail'

/k/ AND /x/ VARIATION

[ku:l] 'thunder'   [xu:l] 'thunder'
[u:k] 'cucumber'   [u:x] 'cucumber'

Vowels

Vowel phonemes in Korowai are shown in table 2–3.

Vowel allophones

General rules of pronunciation

All vowels are lengthened in certain circumstances and reduced in other circumstances. Lengthening seems to occur in the following conditions: (a) in stressed syllables, for example, [φí:mᵊlɔn] 'intestines'; (b) in open final syllables, for example, [lé:ptᵊlɔ:] 'ill'. Weakening, or reduction, of vowel quality to the schwa [ᵊ], a neutral central vowel, occurs in unstressed, nonfinal open syllables. Examples: [maⁿdá:] 'not', [mᵊⁿdá:] 'not'; [lebí:l] 'tooth', [lᵊbí:l] 'tooth'; [lɛxí:ⁿga] 'far', [lᵊxí:ⁿga] 'far'; [dɔbɔ́:p] 'heart', [dᵊbɔ́:p] 'heart'; [lú:ⁿga] 'food', [maú:n–lᵊⁿga:] 'river food'.

Closed vowels

/i/:   [i], a closed unrounded front vowel. Examples: [φi:] 'name'; [mᵊsiⁿgá:] 'nail'.

/ü/:   [ü], a closed rounded front vowel. Examples: [bü:ⁿga] 'blood'; [á:ün] 'thorn'.

/u/:   [u], a closed rounded back vowel. Examples: [φu:p] 'wind'; [bá:nun] 'back'.

Half-closed vowels

/e/:   [e], a half-closed, unrounded, tense front vowel. Examples: [maé:l] 'river'; [me:] 'soil; earth'; [me:l] 'hand'.

       [ɪ], a half-closed, unrounded, lax front vowel. [ɪ] varies with [e] in unstressed syllables. Examples: [xá:le:] 'I went'; [xé:lɪ:] 'I went'.

Half-open vowels

/ɛ/:   [ɛ], a half-open, unrounded front vowel. Examples: [é:xmɔ] 'to cry, weep'; [ɛφɔ́:p] '*kenari* nut'.

/a/:   [a], an open central vowel; [æ], an open front vowel. [æ] occurs in variation with [a] in stressed vowels, [a] elsewhere. Examples: [ᵐba:m] 'child', [ᵐbæ:m] 'child'; [alű:] 'to burn'.

/ɔ/:   [ɔ], a half-open, lax, rounded back vowel. Examples: [ɔ:p] 'fruit'; [xɔtɔxá:l] 'ear'.

       [o], a half-closed, tense, rounded back vowel, occuring before [w]. Examples: [kow] 'Kouh' (name of village on the Digul).

Table 2–3 Vowel phonemes

	Front		Central	Back
	Unrounded	Rounded	Central	Back
Closed	i	ü		u
Half-closed	e			
Half-open	ε		a	ɔ

Contrasts for vowel phonemes

/i/-/ü/: [xi:p]   'sago beetle'   /i/-/e/: [di:l]   'beam'
    [xü:p]   'desiderative'   [de:l]   'bird'
    [li:l]   'vagina'   [atí:]   'catching'
    [lü:l]   'barricade'   [até:]   'he catches'

/e/-/ε/: [emɔ́:l]   'snake'   /ü/-/u/: [xü:l]   'beeswax'
    [εφɔ́:p]   *kenari* nut'   [xu:l]   'right side'
    [jalé:n]   'old man; sir'   [bú:ⁿga:]   'blood'
    [alé:p]   'canoe'   [bú:ⁿgul]   'rib of sago leaf'
    [xá:le:]   'I went'
    [xá:lε:]   'we went'

/u/-/ɔ/: [lu:l]   'eye'   /ɔ/-/a/: [la:l]   'girl'
    [lɔ:l]   'lizard'   [lɔ:l]   'lizard'
    [lu:p]   'I can enter'   [ba:n]   'chest'
    [lɔ:p]   'forest'   [bɔ:n]   'part of tobacco
    [bɔⁿgú:p]   'elbow'   pipe'
    [dɔⁿgɔ́:p]   'piece of wood'

/e/-/a/: [de:l]   'bird'   /e/-/ü/: [aφé:]   'repeatedly'
    [da:l]   'kind of *nibung*   [aφǘ:]   'fighting'
        palm'   [lé:ptᵊlɔ:]   'longing for'
    [le:l]   'roofing'   [lǘ:ptᵊlɔ:]   'heavy'
    [la:l]   'girl'

Stress

Stress is unpredictable and therefore phonemic:

    [dá:mɔ:]   'to say, to inform'
    [damɔ́:]   'to close'
    [laí:lφɔ:]   'to ask'
    [lá:ilφɔ:]   'to be broken'

Syllables

There is one syllable type: (C)V(C). Examples: [de:l] 'bird' (CVC); [a:m] 'breast; milk' (VC); [du:] 'tree' (CV); [εφɔ́:p] *kenari* nut' (V.CVC).

Table 2–4   Phonemes and graphemes

Phoneme	Grapheme	Phoneme	Grapheme
b	b	x	kh
d	d	l	l
ɟ	j	w	w
g	g	ɥ	hü
p	p	j	y
t	t	i	i
k	k	e	é
ᵐb	mb	ɛ	è
ⁿd	nd	ü	ü
ᵑg	ngg	a	a
m	m	u	u
n	n	ɔ	o
ɸ	f		
s	s	schwa	e

Syllables may be combined into words in such a way as to create VV (but not VVV) and (medial) CC clusters. Examples: [pɥ́xmɔ:] 'to throw' (CVCCV); [maé:l] 'river' (CVVC); [daé:] 'not' (CVV); [áɔ] 'to plant' (VV).

Morphophonemic changes

When phonemes become adjacent as a result of morpheme sequencing, they interact in several ways. We treat the most frequent morphophonemic changes in this chapter. Minor morphophonemic changes are not discussed in this chapter but when they occur in the examples or in the texts. The phonemes are represented by the graphemes in the table 2–4.

Assimilation

When two consonants (C1 and C2) become adjacent, the following types of assimilation have been found in the data.

The first is total progressive assimilation (C1 + C2 > C2). This type of assimilation has been found with the following consonants:

n + m > m: mén-main > mémain 'fifteen'
           other.side-shoulder

n + w > w: mén-wayo > méwayo 'twenty'
           other.side-thumb

n + l > l: mén-labul > mélabul 'sixteen'
           other.side-upper.arm

p + l > l: pinggup-lefül > pinggulefül 'Wednesday'
           third-day

p + t > t: gelip-top > gelitop 'nasal cavity'
nose-hole

p + mb > mb: mbolop-mbolop > mbolombolop 'forefathers'
forefather-forefather

p + d > d: alèp-debüp > alèdebüp 'by canoe'
canoe-way

l + b > b: melil-bol > melibol 'fireplace'
fire-hole

l + t > t: khonggél-telo > khonggételo 'it is big'
big-be.3SG.REAL

Regressive (total) assimilation (C1 + C2 > C1) is less usual than the progressive type. We have found it with the following consonants.

p + m > p: dup-mukh > dupukh 'banana leaf'
banana-leaf

wap-mengga > wapengga 'with that'
that-with

l + y > l: Manggél-yanop > Manggélanop 'people of Manggél'
Manggél-people Manggél'

p + y > p: Lelép-yanop > Lelépanop 'Lelép people'
Lelép-people

p + f > p: belüp-fekho > belüpekho 'under'
underside-CIRCUM

Partial assimilation of consonants has been found in the following cases.

AFFECTING POINT OF ARTICULATION

n + b > mb: mén-bonggup > mémbonggup 'seventeen'
other.side-elbow

AFFECTING MANNER OF ARTICULATION

p + l > pt: dép-lemül > déptemül 'cloud'
cloud-smoke

n + kh > ngg: dadun-kha > dadungga 'the swimming'
bathe.INF-CONN

non-khip > nonggip 'sago beetle'
sagogrub-beetle

In this case the velar fricative /kh/ and the preceding nasal fuse into the prenasalized velar plosive /ngg/.

Instead of total or partial assimilation, we have found insertion of a transitional schwa [ᵊ] between the adjacent consonants (C1 + C2 > C1 + [ᵊ] + C2):

(1) bol-khal > bolekhal 'lip'
   opening-skin

(2) alèp-khaup > alèpekhaup 'in the canoe'
   canoe-interior

(3) de-tél-kha > detélekha 'when he said . . .'
   say-3SG.REAL-CONN

Vowel harmony is widespread in Korowai. Vowel harmony affects the possessive pronouns most systematically (see chapter 3, Pronouns). Outside the realm of the possessive pronouns, vowel harmony also occurs frequently but optionally and unpredictably. It may affect suffixes on the basis of the vowels of the stems (see, e.g., possessive pronouns in chapter 3), but some suffixes exert assimilating influences on the stem vowels:

(4) kha-nè   > khenè 'going'
   go.STEM-SS

(5) fu-nè   > fènè 'putting'
   put.STEM-SS

(6) dodépo-nè   > dodépènè 'calling'
   call.STEM-SS

(7) lai-nè   > lenè 'coming'
   come.STEM-SS

Other stems, like *alü-* 'to burn; to cook', never seem to be affected by vowel harmony:

(8) alü-nè   > alünè 'cooking'
   cook.STEM-SS

Other processes

Dissimilation has been found in the following cases:

l + l > t: lafol-lefül > lafotefül 'Sunday'
         seventh-day

         melil-lemül > melitemül 'smoke'
         fire-smoke

         gil-lakhul > gitakhul 'an old bivouac'
         bivouac-used

However, this dissimilation does not always occur:

(9) wayafül-lefül > wayafülefül 'Thursday'
   fourth-day

When an /l/, in the process of morpheme sequencing, is placed after /n/, the /l/ changes into /t/:

(10) mén-lafol > méntafol 'eighteen'   gedun-lefül > geduntefül 'Saturday'
      other.side-lower.arm   sixth-day

This last process, exemplified by (10), might be viewed as partial dissimilation that consists of the devoicing of the second consonant in the nasal-lateral cluster (with the alveolar point of articulation remaining unchanged).

Lateralisation of /t/ always takes place when the /t/ in the process of morpheme sequencing is positioned intervocalically:

(11) sakhu-tena > sakhulena 'a little banana'
      banana-little

(12) khakhua-tale > khakhualalé 'a big witch'
      witch-big

(13) até-to > atélo 'father'
      father-FOC

(14) méan-tena-tena > méantenalena 'little dogs'
      dog-little-little

Fricativisation of /p/ takes place intervocalically:

(15) wap-e-kha > wafekha 'that'
      that-tr-CONN

(16) ip-e-kha > ifekha 'this'
      this-tr-CONN

Morphology

In the following outline of Korowai word classes, each section discusses a word category that seems relevant to the grammar of Korowai.[1] The word classes are first characterised by where and how they function in phrases and clauses and by the morphological categories they express. After this characterisation, derivational processes, if any, are discussed, followed by the inflectional aspects of that category.

Nouns

Nouns are words that may take possessive pronominal prefixes (see below, Pronouns). Their primary function is to be the head of a nominal phrase. Nouns may be modified by adjectives.

Plural forms

Nouns have no plural forms except for kinship terms and a few nonkinship nouns.

There are seven types of plural forms in our data on kinship nouns (see chap. 5): stem + -*dém,* stem + -*alin*, stem + -*khül*, stem + -*él*, stem + -*anggol*, special plural forms, and reduplicated forms. The plural forms are unpredictable and have to be specified per kinship noun:[2]

(1)	ni	'mother'	ni-khül	'mothers'
(2)	mom	'uncle'	mom-él	'uncles'
(3)	mbam	'child'	mba-mbam	'children'

(4) abül   'son'   abü-dem   'sons
                                mabün   'sons'

(5) mbolop   'husband's father'
    mbolof-alin   'husband's fathers'
    mbolo-mbolop   'husband's fathers'

(6) ban 'wife's parent'   ban-dém   'wife's parents'
                                ban-alin   'wife's parents'
                                bananggol   'wife's parents'

The plural suffixes *-dém* and *-alin* can be used interchangeably. The plural marker *-alin* occurs also with the following nonkinship nouns:

(7) laléo 'spirit'   laléo-alin 'spirit; white men'

    Lani   'Lani sister'   Lani-alin   'Lani sisters'

Reduplicated plural forms have been found with the following nonkinship nouns:

(8) khakhua 'witch'   khakhua-khakhua 'witches'

(9) mén   'side'   mé-mén   '(all) sides'

Compound nouns

There are two types of compound nouns. In the first type, a modifying noun stem precedes a modified noun stem in the compound noun:

(10) khawíl   'yearbird'
     sip   'beak'
     khawí-sip   '(penis gourd made of the) beak of the yearbird'

(11) kholól   'bone'
     yanop   'person'
     kholól-anop   'enemy'

(12) melíl   'fire'
     bol   'opening, hole'
     meli-ból   'fireplace'

(13) gelíp   'nose'
     bol   'opening, hole'
     geli-ból   'nostril'

The second type of compound noun comprises two equivalent noun stems:

(14) ati   'bow'
     khayó   'arrow'
     atí-khayo   'bow-and-arrows'

(15) yum   '(her) husband'
     defól   'wife'
     yum-defól   'couple'

(16) ni   'mother'
     até   'father'
     ni-até   'parents'

The accents indicate stress in examples (10)–(16). Stress, which is unpredictable in Korowai, is also unpredictable in the compound nouns.

Pronouns

Korowai has six personal pronouns:

(17) 1SG nup 'I'   1PL nokhup   'we'
     2SG gup 'you'   2PL gekhenép   'you'
     3SG yup 'he/she/it'   3PL yekhenép   'they'

The final /p/ is often dropped, especially in fast speech:

(18) nu maun mi-p
     I   water drink-1SG.INTENT
     'I want to drink water.'

When prefixed to nouns, the forms of (17) function as possessive pronouns. In that case, they never have final /p/ and the singular forms display vowel harmony:

(19) Possessive forms:
     1SG nV- 'my'   1PL nokhu-   'our'
     2SG gV- 'your'   2PL gekhené-   'your'
     3SG yV- 'his/her/its'   3PL yekhené-   'their'

The vowel harmony affects the vowel (V) of the possessive prefix as follows:

V = /a/ with central vowel in first syllable of noun stem.

V = /o/ with back vowel in first syllable of noun stem and before stem initial /w/.

V = /e/ with front vowel in first syllable of noun stem and before front consonants (bilabial and alveolar) regardless of the quality of the vowels in the following stem.

Because the possessive prefixes are unstressed, they often reduce to the neutral central vowel [ə]. When a noun has an initial vowel, the vowel of the possessive is elided. Examples of possessive pronominal prefixes follow:

(20) na-khabéan 'my head'
     my-head

(21) no-wayo 'my thumb'
     my-thumb

(22) ye-nop   'his meat'
      his-meat

(23) gekhené-sakhu 'your bananas'
      your-banana

(24) n-até   'my father'
      my-father

Independent possessive pronouns are formed by adding the connective -*kha* (see chapter 4) to the personal pronouns:

(25) INDEPENDENT POSSESSIVE PRONOUNS

1SG	na-kha	'mine'	1PL	nokhu-kha	'ours'
2SG	ga-kha	'yours'	2PL	gekhené-kha	'yours'
3SG	ya-kha	'his/hers/its'	3PL	yekhené-kha	'theirs'

(26) if-è   na-kha.
      this-CONN   mine-CONN

      'This is mine.'

Emphatic forms of the personal pronouns may be formed by adding the focus suffix -*to* (see chapter 4) to the forms of (17):

(27) EMPHATIC FORMS

1SG	nup-to	1PL	nokhup-to
2SG	gup-to	2PL	gekhenép-to
3SG	yup-to	3PL	yekhenép-to

(28) nu-da gup-to   mano-po-khai
      I-not you-FOC beautiful-SUPP-IRR.2SG

      'Not me but you will make it beautiful.'

The adverbial clitic -*pa(n)* 'also; self' is used with the possessive forms of the pronouns to form reflexive pronouns:

(29) REFLEXIVE FORMS

1SG	ne-pa	'myself'	1PL	nokhu-pa	'ourselves'
2SG	ge-pa	'yourself'	2PL	gekhené-pa	'yourselves'
3SG	ye-pa	'himself/herself/itself'	3PL	yekhené-pa	'themselves'

(30) nu ne-pa imo-p
      I my-self see-1SG.INTENT

      'I want to see myself.'

(31) ye-pan-to ye-pan ülmo
      he-self-FOC him-self kill.3SG.REAL

      'He killed himself.'

The reflexive meaning of -*pa(n)* is formally distinguished from its meaning, 'also'. When -*pa(n)* goes with the personal pronouns, it means 'also', but when it goes with the possessive forms it means 'self' (e.g., *nu-pa* 'I also' and *ne-pa* 'myself').

There are optional object forms of the personal pronouns:

(32) OBJECT FORMS

1SG	na-khata	'me'	1PL	nokhu-khata	'us'
2SG	ga-khata	'you'	2PL	gekhené-khata	'you (pl.)'
3SG	ya-khata	'him/her/it'	3PL	yekhené-khata	'them'

(33) yu na-khata khén-telo
he me-OBJ angry-be.3SG.REAL

'He is angry with me.'

(34) yu nu khén-telo
he me angry-be.3SG.REAL

'He is angry with me.'

The personal pronouns may take the connective *-è* and the topic marker *-(f)efè*:

(35) yuf-è   nggulun
he-CONN teacher

'He is a teacher.'

(36) nup . . . nuf-efè . . . nup mbakha-mo-n-alüp la-lé?
I   I-TOP   I   what-SUPP-TR-day   come-1SG.REAL

'I eh . . . I . . . eh . . . I, when did I arrive?'

Adjectives

Adjectives are words that function primarily as modifiers in noun phrases. Adjectives can be modified by the intensifying adverbial clitic *-khayan.* A list of some Korowai adjectives is presented in table 3–1. Adjectives can be used both attributively and predicatively. When used attributively, they precede the noun, but some adjectives like *khonggél* 'big; fat' and *hién* 'little' also occur after the noun:

(37) lembul nggulun   'a bad teacher'
bad   teacher

(38) manop khaim   'a good house'
good   house

(39) yanop khonggél-khayan[3]   'a very big person'
man   big-very

Table 3–1 Some Korowai adjectives

afop	'thin'	fékh	'wet'
khonggél	'big; fat'	finop	'sad'
anggokh	'slow'	fül	'sharp(ened)'
dialun	'clever; shining'	khokhukh	'strong'
manop	'good; beautiful; clean'	lembul	'bad; defective; ugly; dirty'

When used predicatively, the adjective is usually supported by the verb *-telo* 'to be', but the adjective may occur as a predicate without this verb:

(40) ife-kha   abül   khonggél-khayan
      this-CONN man   big-very

      'This man is very big.'

(41) yu mamün-telo
      he   hot-be.3SG.REAL

      'He is hot.'

(42) nu lép-telo
      I   ill-be.3SG.REAL

      'I am ill.'

The 3SG form of the verb in (42) is explained below, Verbs, where experiential predicates are discussed.

The use of *-telo* 'to be' is obligatory for the first member of a pair of coordinated adjectives:

(43) yu khokhukh-telo-dakhu dialun
      he   strong-be.3SG.REAL-SS clever

      'He is strong and clever.'

The adjectives *-talé* 'big' and *-tena* 'little' form a special pair. They cliticise to the nouns that they modify, and they function with other adjectives as intensifier (*-talé*) and diminutive (*-tena*):

(44) méan-talé   'a big dog'
      dog-big

(45) méan-tena   'a little dog'
      dog-little

(46) yanop khonggé-talé   'a very fat person'
      person big-very

(47) yanop khonggé-talé-khayan   'an extremely fat person'
      person big-very-very

(48) khofilun   'black'
      black

      khofilun-talé   'very black'
      black-very

      khofilun-tena   'a little black'
      black-little

(49) khokholun   'white'
      khokholun-talé 'very white'
      khokholun-tena 'a little white'

There is no morphological comparative or superlative form of the adjective. Comparatives are expressed as follows:

(50) if-e-kha   abül-efè khonggél-khayan waf-e-kha   abül be-khonggé-tebo-da
     this-tr-CONN man-TOP big-very   that-TR-CONN man NEG-big-be.3SG.REAL-NEG
     'This man is bigger than that man.'

Superlative meanings are expressed by choosing adjectives with strong meanings and by using intensifiers:

(51) yanop mup-khayan   'the best man'
     man   very.good-very

If the adjective *lekhingga* 'far' is intensified, the following conventional intensifying gesture usually accompanies its use: the left arm is raised, and with the right hand the speaker hits the left armpit rather hard while the head is moved down in the direction of the left armpit. Thus far we have seen this intensifying gesture only with *lekhingga*.
    Adjectives can be reduplicated to express plurality (reduplicated stems):

(52) khaim mano-manop   'good houses'
     house   good-good

(53) mbam afo-afop   'skinny children'
     child   thin-thin

(54) méan khofilun-khofilun   'black dogs'
     dog   black-black

Some adjectives have special plural forms:

(55) gol khonggél   'a fat pig'
     pig fat

     gol khongge-kél   'fat pigs'
     pig fat-PL

The intensifier *-talé* and the diminutive *-tena* can be reduplicated to produce plural forms: *-talélalé, -tenalena*:

(56) yanop wafi-talé-lalé[4]   'very big persons'
     person big-very(PL)

(57) méan-tena-lena   'little dogs'
     dog-little-little

Demonstratives

There are three basic place deictics:

(58) ip   'in proximity of speaker'
    wap   'in proximity of addressee'
    khop 'in proximity of neither speaker nor addressee'

The deictics of (59) are used adverbially, meaning 'here' (*ip*), 'there' (*wap*), and 'there (far away)' (*khop*). Furthermore, they are used as demonstratives (*ip* 'this', *wap* 'that', and *khop* 'that') and as markers of definiteness, for example, with proper nouns:

(59) nokhuf-è if-è   Didonalé lamé-mba-lè
      we-CONN this-CONN Didonalé   tie-PROGR-1PL.REAL
      'We are tying up Didonale.'

(60) waf-è   khülo   khe-nè Démbol khandun-ta-fekho   isila-ma-lè-dakhu⁵
      there-CONN upstream go-SS   Démbol   stonebank-at-CIRCUM pause-SUPP-1PL.REAL-SS
      beba-lè-fekho   wa-fosü khe-nè kho-sü kha-lé
      sit-1PL.REAL-until there-from go-SS   there-to go-1PL.REAL
      'And there we went upstream until we rested on the stones of the Dembol River and from there we went over there.'

When used adverbially, the place deictics take case suffixes like *-fekho* 'circumstantial/locative', *-è* 'connective', *-ta* 'locative', and *-fosü* 'from/to/via' (see below, Nominal case suffixes). Although the place deictics usually take one of these suffixes in the adverbial use, they may occur on their own. If so, they drop the final /p/:

(61) i   le-ba-lé
      here come-PERF-1SG.REAL
      'I have come here.'

(62) nggé, kho bau!
      Friend there be.3SG.REAL
      'Friend, there she is!'

We have found two other place deictics in the data, *dip* 'here' and the pair *khe* 'there' and *ye* 'here'. The final /p/ of *dip* does not occur when the form is used in isolation:

(63) di   ale-lé
      here stand-1SG.REAL
      'I stood here.'

(64) di-fosü   nu-fekho pendéta-fekho i-fekho   gülap   khe-méma-lè-do
      here-from I-and   pastor-and   here-CIRCUM upstream go-IMM-1SG.REAL-DS
      'From here the pastor and I went upstream and . . .'

(65) ye-sübo   '(to)here'
      here-to

(66) ye-mén 'this side'   khe-mén   'that side'
      this-side   that-side

(67) dif-akhüp   'here'
      here-place

The set *ip/wap/khop* is used for both dependent and independent demonstratives. When used as the latter, they may occur both with and without case suffixes:

(68) i   mbakha?
      this what
      'What is this?'

(69) wa ne-mom
      that my-uncle
      'That is my uncle.'

(70) khof-è   ne-mbam
      that-CONN my-child
      'That is my child.'

(71) if-è   mbakha?
      this-CONN what
      'What is this?'

(72) khof-efè n-até
      that-TOP my-father
      'That is my father.'

When used dependently, as demonstrative modifiers in noun phrases, the deictics almost always take the connective *-kha*:

(73) if-e-kha   abül   'this man'
      this-TR-CONN man

(74) khof-e-kha   abül   'that man'
      that-TR-CONN man

(75) wof-e-kha[6]   khaim 'that house (over there)'
      that-TR-CONN house

However, demonstrative modifiers have been observed without *-kha.* For example, in *a lal* 'that woman', the demonstrative *wap* occurs dependently in its shortened form *a.*

Occasionally, we find the forms *wofekha, ifekha,* and *khofekha* functioning independently:

(76) yakhof-e-kha-lo   wof-e-kha   amo-mémo?
      who-TR-CONN-FOC there-TR-CONN do-3SG.IMM.REAL
      'Who did that?'

Numerals

The Korowai counting system is a body-part tally system in which names of parts of the upper half of the body also signify numbers.[7] Such systems are common in New Guinea languages (see Laycock 1975). The verb *lamo* denotes the activity of counting.

The starting point of the body-part system is the little finger of the left hand (see table 3–2).

Counting is accompanied by touching the body parts involved with the middle and/or index finger, starting on the left side. When *khabéan* 'crown of the head'/ 'thirteen' is reached, counting on the right-hand side of the body begins with *mén* 'other side': Twenty-five is the logical end point of the system. However, for twenty-six and following numbers, one can start all over again by adding the word *laifu*, which (probably) means 'produce':

(77) laifu-senan   'twenty-six'
      produce-little.finger

      laifu-senanafül   'twenty-seven'
      produce-ring.finger

      laifu-khabéan   'thirty-eight'
      produce-head

When these numerals are used as modifying elements in noun phrases, the relational[8] noun *anop* 'amount' cliticises obligatorily to the numerators, signifying that the numerators are used as modifiers (MOD)[9]:

Table 3–2   The Korowai body-part system of counting

	Korowai numeral	*Corresponding body part*
1	senan	little finger
2	senanafül	ring finger
3	pinggu(lu)p	middle finger
4	wayafül	index finger
5	wayo	thumb
6	gédun	wrist
7	lafol	forearm
8	bonggup/lakha	elbow
9	labul	upper arm
10	main	shoulder
11	khomofekholol	neck
12	khotokhal	ear
13	khabéan	(crown of the) head
14	mén-khotokhal	ear on the other side
15	mén-khomofekholol	neck on the other side
16	mé-main	the other shoulder
17	mén-tabul	the other upper arm
18	mé-mbonggup	the other elbow
19	mén-tafol	the other lower arm
20	mé-nggédun	the other wrist
21	mé-wayo	the other thumb
22	mé-wayafül	the other index finger
23	mén-pinggu(lu)p	the other middle finger
24	mén-senanafül	the other ring finger
25	mén-senan	the other little finger

(78) pinggup   'three'
      middle.finger

(79) gol pinggu-anop   'three pigs'
      pig middle.finger-MOD

      gol wayafül-anop   'four pigs'
      pig index.finger-MOD

The relational noun *anop* also occurs in the following question word:

(80) mbakha-mo-n-anop   'how much/how many?'
      what-SUPP-INF-amount

The element *anop* cannot be added to *senan* 'little finger/one' and *senanafül* 'ring finger/two' to form modifying numerals:

(81) *gol senan-anop   'one pig'
      pig   one-MOD

Instead, *lidop* 'one' and *pol* 'two' are used as modifiers in noun phrases:

(82) gol lidop   'one pig'
      pig one

      gol pol   'two pigs'
      pig two

Lidop and *pol* are the only two numerals in Korowai that are not based on body parts. The word *pol* 'a pair/two' is used in combination with a word meaning 'just' to denote the concept of 'few':

(83) gol   pol-tanukh   '(a) few pigs'
      pig   pair-just

There are variations in the use of the body parts for counting. Some speakers skip the ear, in which case *khabéan* 'head' represents the number 'twelve'.
    The body-part/number noun stems form compound nouns with the noun stem *lefül* 'day' to indicate the days of the week (see table 3–3).[10] *Lidop* 'one' is used in combination with *-fekha* 'a certain' in indefinite-specific noun phrases:

(84) lido-fekha   abül   'a certain man'
      one-a.certain man

However, *-fekha* 'a certain' usually occurs without *lidop:*

(85) uma-té-do   abül-fekha   khomilo-bo
      tell-3PL.REAL-DS man-a.certain die.3SG.REAL-PERF
      'They told that a certain man had died.'

Table 3–3 Days of the week

senan-tefül little.finger-day	'Monday'
senanafü-tefül ring.finger-day	'Tuesday'
pinggu-lefül middle.finger-day	'Wednesday'
wayafü-tefül index.finger-day	'Thursday'
wayo-lefül thumb-day	'Friday'
gédun-tefül wrist-day	'Saturday'
lafo-tefül lower.arm-day	'Sunday'

(86) mül-ano-imban-pekha[11]   khomilo-do
       former-people-person-a.certain die.3SG.REAL-DS
       'Someone from the former people had died.'

Metaphorical idioms are derived from *lidop* 'one' and *pol* 'two' by reduplication, like *mahüon lido-lidop* 'a straightforward story' (lit. story one-one) and *ye-fimelon po-po-telo* 'he is in doubt' (lit. his-intestines two-two-be.3SG.REAL).

The number system is used in Korowai society especially in two contexts: first, in institutionalized payments in shell money and goods (bridal recompensation and payments; see chapter 1, Korowai views of universe and man); second, in the sago grub festival (see chapter 1, Sago), which also has a certain market function. In the counting of cowrie shells, pig teeth, dog teeth, and valued objects such as stone axes, the objects to be counted are positioned between the parties involved in the exchange.

Question words

A small, closed set of question words functions in question-word questions. They have the following characteristics.

First, there is a tendency for question words to function as modifiers in modifier-head noun structures. Second, question words are informationally salient and accordingly tend to take the focus suffix *-to*.[12] The following examples illustrate the modifier-head noun structure in which the question words tend to function:

(87) mbakha lekhén   'why?'
       what   reason

(88) mbakha top   'where?'
       what   place

(89) mbakha-mo-n-anop   'how much/how many?'
       what-SUPP-INF-amount

(90) mbakha-to-fosü   'from where?'
      what-place-from

(91) mbakha-mo-n-alüp   'when?'
      what-SUPP-INF-day

(92) mbakha debüf   'how?'
      what   way/road

The head noun *anop* 'amount' also functions as an attributive suffix with numerical modifiers (see above, Numerals).

We find the support verb *mo-* in (92) and (94). The main function of *mo-* is to be a verbaliser (see below, Derivation of verbs). It is not entirely clear what the function of *mo-* in these question words is.[13] Notice that the expression for 'how' is still fully verbal, with *mo-* as a verbalising support verb in reduplicated form:

(93) nggé, gu laléo lai-ati-bo-dakhu   lelé-mbol-e-kho-lo   tè
      friend you spirit come-hold-be.2SG.REAL-SS come-PROGR.2SG.REAL-TR-Q-FOC or
      mbakha-mol-mo-dakhu[14]   lelé-mbol-e-kho-lo?
      what-SUPP-SUPP.2SG.REAL-SS come-PROGR.2SG.REAL-TR-Q-FOC

      'Friend, are you coming as a spirit or how are you coming?'

In (92) and (94), the question word has the form of the nominal infinitive with the nominal infinitive suffix *-un* (with the /u/ elided).

The question words for 'who' and 'what' function independently:

(94) i   mbakha?
      this what
      'What is this?'

(95) yu mbakha i-mbo?
      he what   see-3SG.REAL.PROGR
      'What is he looking at?'

(96) yakhop-to nu ne-gol ülmo?
      who-FOC   I my-pig   kill.3SG.REAL
      'Who killed my pig?'

(97) yakhof-e-kha-lo   Didonale lamé-khai?
      who-TR-CONN-FOC Didonale   tie-3SG.IRR
      'Who shall tie Didonale?'

In possessive contexts *yakhop* functions as a modifier:

(98) wa yakho-sakhu?
      that whose-banana
      'Whose bananas are those?'

The second characteristic of question words is their informational saliency, which is expressed by intonational prominence and by the optional presence of the focus marker -*to* (see chapter 4, Focus clitics and interjections). This use of the focus marker is exemplified by (99) and (100). The use of focus markers or of an emphasis on words with question-word constituents also occurs in Kombai (de Vries 1993b: 42), in Wambon (de Vries and Wiersma 1992: 48), in both Awyu family languages, and in the neighbouring Asmat family (e.g., in the Flamingo Bay dialect; Voorhoeve 1965: 159, 168). The focus marker also always occurs on the question-marker -*kholo* (-*kho* + -*to* > -*kholo*). This question-marker occurs occasionally in question-word questions (especially in emphatic ones:

(99) mbakha-lekhé-nggo-lo? mbakha-lekhé lamé-ba-té-kho-lo?
      what-reason-Q-FOC   what-reason   bind-PERF-2PL.REAL-Q-FOC

      'Why? Why have you tied him up?'

Adverbs

As in other Awyu languages (see de Vries 1989: 174), adverbs are a marginal word category in Korowai because other word categories take over much of the functional load of adverbs (e.g., deictics as spatiotemporal adverbials and medial verb forms as manner adverbials). The list in table 3–4 presents the most important Korowai adverbs.

The adverbs do not have a fixed position in the clause. The adverb *pa(n)* 'also; self' cliticises to the word with which it has the closest association semantically. The adverb *mesendip* has several shortened forms: *sendip, mesé,* and *sé*. The adverb -*khayan* 'very' functions as an intensifier with adjectives (see above, Adjectives). The adverbs *mofu* and *tanu(kh)*, both meaning 'only', may co-occur.

(100) misafi sendip maun-an gilfo-do   yalin-mengga   walü-mengga
      thing   also   water-in disappear.3SG.REAL-DS   fishing.net-with peddle-with
      sendip khelé-mengga maun gilfo-do   khelé pol tanukh fe-nè
      also   fish-with   water disappear.3SG.REAL-DS fish two only   take-SS

      'Our things also fell into the water, the fishing net and the peddle and the fish, (these things) fell into the water, only two fish we could save'

(101) manderi-defol[15] alüm uma-lé
      health.worker-wife first tell-1SG.REAL

      'I told it first to the health worker's wife.'

Table 3–4 Korowai adverbs

menèl	'quickly'	lelip	'together'
alüm	'first'	mesendip	'again; also; next'
gülap	'upstream'	afé(n)	'usually'
süfap	'downstream'	naném	'hidden; illicitly'
khotu(l)	'still; not yet'	pa(n)	'also; self'
mofu	'only'	-khayan	'very'
tanu(kh)	'only, just'	-ma	'also'

(102) mülalüp nu-pa amo-ba-lé
       formerly I-also do.thus-PERF-1SG.REAL
       'I have also done things like that in former times.'

Nominal-case suffixes and the connective -è

Locative suffixes: *-ta, -an, -fosü, -ma, -pé*

The suffix *-ta* is a general locative case suffix meaning 'in, at, on'. Consider the following examples:

(103) nu amul-telo-do[16]   mamün-ta ba-lé
       I   malaria-be.3SG.REAL-DS sun-in   sit-1SG.REAL
       'I have malaria and (therefore) I sit in the sun.'

(104) khaim-ün-ta 'on top of the house'
       house-roofridge-on

The case suffix *-an* has a more specific locative meaning of 'in the interior of'. Consider the following examples:

(105) if-e-kha   khaim-khauf-an-è   yanop mafém
       this-TR-CONN house-inside-in-CONN people not.be
       'There are no people in this house.'

(106) nu pesau-khauf-an-fosü khosükhop ima-lé
       I   plane-interior-in-from   down.there see-1SG.REAL
       'I saw (it) down there from within the plane.'

(107) maun-an misafi gilfo-do
       water-in   things   vanish.3SG.REAL-DS
       '(Our) things vanished in the water.'

The case suffix *-fosü* (with a shorter allomorph *-sü)* marks a number of locative relations— source ('from') and destination ('to')—and it may mean 'through/via a certain space'. It is also used with reason phrases.

(108) kho-sü   kha-lé
       there-to/from go-1PL.REAL
       'We went there.' *or* 'We went from there.'

(109) bu-lelo-do   wa-sü   ibo-ba-lè
       tired-be.3SG.REAL-DS that-because sleep-stay-1PL.REAL
       'We were tired and therefore we slept.'

(110) gu mbakha-to-fosü le-bo?
       you what-place-from   come-2SG.PERF.REAL
       'Where have you come from?'

(111) nu yasim-fosü le-ba-lé
I   garden-from   come-PERF-1SG.REAL
'I have come from my garden.'

(112) bol-tena-sü   imo
hole-little-through look.3SG.REAL
'He looked through the little holes.'

(113) Lalop-fosü   le-nè
Lalop.river-via come-SS
'Coming via the Lalop river.'

The suffix *-ma* marks destination phrases[17]:

(114) yekhené kapolsek-ma kha-té
they   police.chief-to go-3PL.REAL
'They went to the police chief.'

The suffix *-pé(n)* has also been found to mark locative relations:

(115) gu anè   khe-mén-e-pé   fu-m!
you ADH/IMP there-side-TR-LOC put-IMP.2SG
'You must put it there on the side!'

Comitative suffixes: *-mengga, -alingga, -fekho*

The suffixes *-mengga* and *-fekho* can be used interchangeably in some contexts. Both have a basic comitative meaning ('accompanied by') and both are used as coordinators of nouns. But *-fekho* is also used as an interclausal conjunction in clause chains, as a general circumstantial postposition with noun phrases, and as a focus device (see chapter 4, Focus clitics and interjections). The postposition *-mengga* 'with' functions in opposition to the postposition *-alingga* 'without':

(116) yu lemup bokokhmo-do   büngga-mengga wakhali-mbo
he   cough   cough.3SG.REAL-DS blood-with   vomit-3SG.PROGR.REAL
'He is coughing up blood.'

(117) lebakhop Yalul-mengga-lo kho lakhi-nè alü   bante-té
old.woman Yalul-with-FOC   sago wrap-SS cook-SS distribute-3PL.REAL
'And together with the old lady Yalul they prepared sago in the fire and distributed it.'

(118) Saul-mengga mantri-mengga Sapuru-mengga melé-la-té
Saul-and   health.worker-and Sapuru-and   move-come-3PL.REAL
'Saul and the health worker and Sapuru went home.'

(119) yuf-è   mba-mengga[18] abül
he-CONN child-with   man
'He has children.'

(120) yuf-è   mbam-alingga abül
     he-CONN child-without   man

'He has no children.'

Compare now the following examples with *-fekho* and notice the wide range of circumstantial contexts in which it occurs, including instrumental, locative, and temporal:

(121) khakhul nu yekhené-fekho Manggél kha-lé
     yesterday I   them-with   Manggél   go-1SG.REAL

'Yesterday I went to Manggél with them.'

(122) yu pilin sabun-pekho[19] sukh-mbo
     he dishes soap-with   wash-3SG.PROGR.REAL

'He is washing the dishes with soap.'

(123) nu   maun-amin-ta-fekho ba-lé
     I   river-bank-on-CIRCUM sit-1SG.REAL

'I am on the riverbank.'

(124) lefül-ta-fekho   la-lé
     noon-at-CIRCUM come-1SG.REAL

'I arrived at noon.'

(125) khakhul-fekho   lép-telo
     yesterday-CIRCUM ill-3SG.REAL

'Yesterday he was ill.'

(126) nu-fekho gu-fekho
     I-and   you-and

'you and me'

(127) nu Yaniluma khambom-pekho[20] ba-lé
     I   Yaniruma   village-in   sit-1SG.REAL

'I live in the village Yaniruma.'

When *-fekho* links clauses in chains, it is used as a switch-reference neutral conjunction 'and'. Sometimes, the event expressed by the first verb has a certain duration and goes on 'until' the event of the next verb starts, for example, in (130):

(128) lamol   do-fo-dom-pekho   aful   amodo if-e-kha
     universe be.burnt-RESULT.3SG.REAL-DS-and wonder.3SG.REAL next   this-TR-CONN
     Ginol silam-tena   yu di-ati -afé lokhté   abul-khal
     Ginol mouse.like.animal-DIMIN he ? -hold-turn go.away.3SG.REAL treeswift-skin
     khomé-dakhu
     transform-SS

'The whole world burnt down and he was wondering, and then, Ginol—the little mouselike—he went away while looking around and then transformed (himself) in a moustached tree swift.'

(129) wai-dakhu-fekho   alo-bo-dom-pekho   khomolamol lekhüpwaila
   go.down.3SG.REAL-SS-and stand-be.3SG.REAL-DS-and all.kinds.of all.kinds.of
   bilamalin do-dél-e-kha-lalé   wai-mo-dom-pekho
   all.kinds.of burn-tear.off.3SG.REAL-TR-CONN-INTNS go.down-SUPP.3SG.REAL-DS-and
   fo anol-mekho
   get.SS side-SUPP.3SG.REAL

   'He came down and stood still and a very large amount of all kinds of torn off and
   scorched (remnants of the fire) he moved downward and he shoved it aside.'

(130) lelip khami-ba-té-fekho ye-defol fo
   together stay-sit-3PL.REAL-until his-wife take.3SG.REAL

   'They stayed together until he married.'

Between noun and case suffix

-tekhé(n)

The element -tekhé(n) 'cause, reason, purpose' is a relational noun on its way to becoming a nominal case suffix with cause, reason, purpose, recipient, addressee, and beneficiary phrases. In Awyu languages, modifier-head connectives function in noun phrases to link prenominal constituents to the head noun. The behavior of such connectives is a possible diagnostic for the determination of the categorial status of relational nouns (noun or nominal case suffix; see de Vries 1989: 180). When the connectives are obligatory in all contexts, it is an indication that the noun status is still relevant. When they start to be dropped in certain contexts, especially when this is followed by clitisation, the categorial status is changing in the direction of a case suffix.

  The transitional nature of -tekhé(n) (between noun and case suffix) is shown by the fact that the connective -kha is dropped in several but not all contexts. Furthermore, -tekhé(n) is cliticising to the preceding noun phrase with the accompanying morphophonemic changes. Consider the following examples, which also show the range of semantic relations expressed by -tekhé(n):

(131) nu if-e-kha   misafi gup-tekhé fédo-p
   I this-TR-CONN thing you-to   give-1SG.INTENT

   'I want to give these things to you.'

(132) gu mbakha-lekhé wa-mol-mo?
   you what-reason   that-do-do.2SG.REAL

   'Why do you do that?'

(133) nokhup Lalop dad-ungga-lekhé   khai-mba-lé
   we   Lalop bath-INF.CONN-reason go-PROGR-1SG.REAL

   'We are on our way to bathe in the Lalop River.'

(134) nokhu-nggé abül-fekha olekhi-lekhén wai-mémo-kha
   our-friend male-one faeces-because go.down-IMM.3SG.REAL-CONN
   lu-mbo-bene?
   enter-PROGR.3SG.REAL-Q

   '. . . is one of our friends who went down to relieve himself, entering?'

(135) nu ne-defo-lekhé dodépa-lé
    I   my-wife-ADDR call-1SG.REAL
    'I called my wife.'

The element *-tekhé*, sometimes with final nasal, as (134) shows, cliticises to the preceding nominal constituent; only when this preceding constituent is a nominal infinitive is the connective *-kha* obligatory. In other contexts *-kha* is always absent (e.g., with personal pronouns; *gup-tekhé* 'to/for you'); the /t/ changes into /l/ intervocalically (see for this morphophonemic change, the lateralisation of /t/, chapter 2, Other processes).

    The element *-tekhé(n)* is also used quite often predicatively:

(136) yu ye-mo-ma kha-u-ngga-lekhé
    he his-uncle-to go-INF-CONN-purpose
    'He intends to go to his uncle.'

Literally, (136) says, 'He (has) the purpose to go to his uncle'. Sometimes *-tekhé* is verbalised with *mo-* (see below, Verbs) when it functions predicatively:

(137) nu u-ngga-lekhén-ma-té
    me kill-INF.CONN-purpose-SUPP-3PL.REAL
    'They want to kill me.'

Debüf

The noun *debüf* 'road, way' is used as a relational noun to mark noun phrases that express the means of transport or travel, the route of the travel, or the manner of going. *Debüf* as a relational noun can be glossed as 'by, via, by way of'.

    Debüf forms compound nouns of the modifier-modified type (see above, Compound nouns) in which *debüf* is the modified noun stem:

(138) alè-debüf   'by canoe' (lit. 'the canoe-way')
    canoe-way

(139) fium-debüf   'by foot; over land'
    land-road

(140) gabün-debüf   'on the knees'
    knee-way

(141) nenin-debüf   'via the sandbanks (in the river)'
    sandbank-road

(142) alè-debüf   kho-sübo   kha-fén
    canoe-way   there-downstream go-1PL.INTENT/ADH
    'Let us go down by the river.'

Debüf is also used in the question phrase *mbakha debüf* 'how':

(143) yu mbakha debüf lai?
    he what road come.3SG.REAL
    'How did he come?'

Dimensional nouns

A set of dimensional relational nouns is used to express locative relations[21]:

(144) mülgop   'front (side)'
      banun   'back (side)'
      khaup   'interior/inside'
      ün   'roof ridge'
      mén   'side'
      belüp   'space under the house'
      akhabop   'downside'

Consider the following examples:

(145) khaim-belü-fekho   bau
      house-under-CIRCUM   be.3SG.REAL
      'He is under the house.'

(146) pesau-ün-ta   'on top of the plane'
      plane-on-LOC

(147) alèp-khauf-an   'in the canoe'
      canoe-interior-in

(148) khaim-banun-e-pé   'behind the house'
      house-back-TR-LOC

(149) khaim-mén-e-pé   'beside the house'
      house-side-TR-LOC

(150) khaim-mülgop-pén-pekho   bau
      house-front-LOC-CIRCUM   be.3SG.REAL
      'He is in front of the house.'

The dimensional nouns form compound nouns in which they are the modified stems ('the house-front' and 'the house-back'; see above, Compound nouns, for this type). The compound noun takes locative, topical, and connective suffixes.

The connective clitic -*è*

Just as do nominal case suffixes, the connective -*è* expresses a relation between nominals and the verb within the clause; but whereas nominal case suffixes express various semantic roles of these nominals, the connective -*è* expresses the syntactic link between nominals and the verb in the clause.

Connectives play an important role in the syntax of the languages of the Awyu family. Connectives in these languages are semantically and pragmatically neutral clitics that create syntactic cohesion in various domains. For example, Wambon -*o* links modifiers to the head noun in noun phrases and Wambon -*e* links noun phrases to the verb in clauses (see de Vries 1986). Yonggom -*e* links both modifiers to head nouns and noun phrases to verbs (see Drabbe 1959: 118). In Korowai, the role of connectives is relatively modest. The connective -*è* is most often used with independent demonstratives and personal pronouns. We have found it also in locative phrases and in subject phrases in stative clauses:

(151) if-è   ne-mbam
      this-CONN my-child
      'This is my child.'

(152) waf-e-kha   yanof-è   manop yanop
      that-TR-CONN person-CONN good   person
      'That person is good.'

(153) khof-è   sol nggulun
      that-CONN new teacher
      'That is the new teacher.'

(154) nuf-è   lép-telo
      I-CONN ill-be.3SG.REAL[22]
      'I am ill.'

We have one case in the data in which -*è* links a dependent demonstrative to the head noun in a noun phrase:

(155) if-è   mahüon 'this message'
      this-CONN message

Verbs

Verbs are words that may express status, subject person-number, aspect, mood, temporality, and switch reference. They function as heads of clauses.

Derivation of verbs

The verb *mo-* means 'to do':

(156) gekhené mbakha mo-mba-té?
      you   what   do-PROGR-2PL.REAL
      'What are you doing?'

This verb is frequently used as a verbalising support verb that forms compounds with other stems. We do not have enough data to say anything definitive about the productivity of the various derivation processes with *mo-*. We have found stems of the following categories as input for verbalisation with *mo-*. With adjectives:

(157) leléal   'glad, pleased'
      leléal-mo- 'to be glad; to accept something'

(158) manop   'in order, good, nice'
      manopo-[23] 'to make in order; to beautify; to cure'

With demonstratives:

(159) wa   'that'
      wa-mo- 'to do that/thus'

(160) i   'this'
      i-mo- 'to do this/in this way'

The dependent form *imonè* (SS of *imo-*) has developed into a time adverb meaning 'now'.

Indonesian verbs are integrated into the Korowai lexicon with *mo-*[24]:

(161) INDONESIAN   KOROWAI

      beristirahat 'to pause'   isila-mo-   'to pause'
      berdoa   'to pray'   berdoa-mo-   'to pray'
      kembali   'to return'   kembali-mo-   'to return'

There are many verbs with *mo-* without a corresponding (verb) stem without *mo-*, for example, *imo-* 'to see', but there is no verb *i-*:

(162) yamo-   'to wail'
      umo-   'to tell'
      ülmo-   'to kill'
      gelümo-   'to travel'

Drabbe (1959: 126) observes that the majority of verbs in the Yonggom dialect of Wambon, also of the Awyu family, contain *mo-* (or one of the two other support verbs of Wambon), just like many Korowai verbs. In verbs like those of (162), the element *mo-* cannot be said to function (anymore) as a verbal derivation device but rather as a suffix *-mo*, indicating that the word is a verb.

When an event is presented as repeatedly occurring (e.g., due to habit), the verb stem is repeated (reduplication) and the support verb *mo-* is added. The habitual iterative meaning may be reinforced by using the adverb *afé(n)* 'usually'; this occurs also in reduplicated form (*afé-afé*) or with the connective *-kha* (*aféngga*):

(163) afé-afé   mi-mi-mo
      usually   drink-drink-HAB.3SG
      'He drinks habitually.'

(164) yu afén   khéntelo-khéntelo-mo
      he usually angry-angry-HAB.3SG
      'As a rule he is angry.'

When there is no reduplication (verb stem + *mo-*), the derived verb may express ability or knowledge to perform an action and sometimes also habituality. The support verb *mo-* takes the form *ma-* in this formation, and the final vowel of the verb stem preceding the support stem optionally but usually reduces to schwa:

(165) dépo- 'to smoke'

    1SG   dépe-ma-lé   'I can smoke / I know how to smoke / I smoke habitually'
    2/3SG dépe-mo
    1PL   dépe-ma-lè/tè
    2/3PL dépe-ma-té

Thus far we have found the following noun-based derivations:

(166) tekhén   'cause, reason'   tekhén-mo-   'to intend, to mean, to
                                                            want'
     khe-mén   'the opposite side'   khe-mén-mo- 'to cross the river'
     gol-sanip 'big game' (lit. pig-cassowary)   gol-sani-po   'to hunt for big game'

(167) nu khof-e-kha   abül u-ngga   lekhén-ma-lé
     I   that-TR-CONN man hit-INF.CONN purpose-SUPP-1SG.REAL

     'I meant to hit that man.'

The element *-tekhé(n)* is a relational noun discussed above.

    Finally, *mo-* occurs in a number of question words. In one case, *mbakhamomo* 'how', the question word still functions as a verb, comparable to the question-word verbs of Wambon (see de Vries 1989: 15). In two other cases, the question words with *mo-* do not function as verbs and *mo-* might be a residue from the verbal origin of these question words (see also above, Question words):

(168) mbakha-mo-n-anop 'how much/many'
     what-SUPP-INF-amount

(169) mbakha-mo-n-alüp 'when'
     what-SUPP-INF-day

A number of verbs that contain *mo-* have causative meanings and corresponding resultative-stative verbs containing *fo-*:

(170) verb stem + *mo-*: causative verb
     verb stem + *fo-*: resultative-stative verb

(171) lail-mo-   'to break'   lail-fo-   'to be broken'
     demé-mo- 'to open, to undo (a knot)'   demé-fo- 'to be open'

(172) bamol-mo- 'to break into pieces'   bamol-fo- 'to be broken'
     do-mo-   'to burn'   do-fo-   'to be burnt'

    Having discussed some of the functions of *mo-,* we now turn to the forms of *mo-.* The verbaliser mo- is a shortened form of *mekho-.* Some verbs have been observed with both forms:

(173) wé   'continuous'
     wé-mo-   'to do continuously'
     wé-mekho- 'to do continuously'

However, there is one occurrence in the data in which the opposition between *mo-* and *mekho-* seems to be semantically relevant:

(174) bilai-mo 'to look for'   bilai-mekho 'to search desperately'

The verbaliser *mo-* is generally dropped in dependent verb forms (see below) when unstressed:

(175) ül-mo-   'to kill'   ül-nè   'killing'
      dil-mo-   'to cut'   di^{25} 'cutting'
      yokhol-mo- 'to vomit'   yokhol-nè   'vomiting'

There are exceptions to the dropping rule:

(176) yol-mo-   'to whistle'

(177) yol-me-nè   'whistling'

In (177), the support verb *mo-* is retained in unstressed conditions in the dependent form. When *mo-* carries word stress (stress is phonemic in Korowai; see chapter 2, Stress), it is never dropped in dependent forms. Compare

(178) dil-mo- 'to close'   dil-mo   'closing'

Inflection

Korowai distinguishes among dependent, independent, and infinitival verb forms.

Dependent verb forms

Dependent verb forms express switch reference (see chapter 4, Chaining linkage); they do not express status, aspect, mood, and subject person and number. Dependent verb forms are restricted to medial clauses.

The dependent verb forms are formed as follows:

(179) Dependent verb form: verb stem -/+ -*nè*

Formation (220) expresses the switch-reference distinction SS, that is, that the subject (first argument) of the next clause has the same referent(s) as the subject of the clause that contains the SS form. The SS marking suffix -*nè* is optional.

(180) mébol damil-mo   le-nè   lu-ba-lé
      grave   open-SUPP.SS   come-SS   ascend-PERF-1SG.REAL
      'I opened the grave and came up (the stairs).'

(181) i-nè   khami-bo
      see.SS   stay-sit.3SG.REAL
      'He was looking.'

(182) dal-khal   lop-tena-lena fu   wap-ta ye-lè
     dal.tree-bark hole-little-little put.SS that-on sleep-1PL.REAL

     'We covered the little holes with tree bark and slept on that (tree-bark covered place).'

Dependently linked clauses [e.g., the clause *lenè* 'coming' in (184) is dependently linked to the next clause, *lubalé* 'I ascended'] should be distinguished from serial root constructions (see Bruce 1986; Foley 1986), in which two or more verb roots are juxtaposed to form one complex predicate that is the head of one clause. This serialisation of verb roots is a productive morphosyntactical process in Korowai, as in many other Papuan languages (see Foley 1986). Sometimes serial root constructions become lexicalised into compound verbs. Signs of lexicalisation are the reduction of productivity, semantic transparency, and analysability (Bruce 1986). Consider the case of the compound verb *é-fu-* 'to sleep':

(183) gülé-do   é-fu-méma-té-tofekho
     be.dark.3SG.REAL-DS sleep-put-IMM-3PL.REAL-DS

     'And at night, when they just were asleep . . .'

The contribution of the stem *fu-* 'to put' to the meaning of *éfu-* 'to sleep' is not transparant.

     Example (188) shows both a serial root construction (with the verb roots *alü* and *féda*) and dependent clause linkage (*lakhinè* is dependently linked to the clause *alüfédatédo*):

(184) kho lakhi-nè alü-féda-té-do
     sago wrap-SS cook-distribute-REAL.3PL-DS

     'They wrapped sago (in leaves), cooked it, and distributed it.'

Certain verb roots in serial root constructions function as aspectual markers. The verb root *khami* 'to stay', for example, functions to mark durative aspect in (185).

     In transcribing and analysing Korowai texts, the distinction between serial root constructions and chained dependent clauses that consist of just the verb root is hard to make on other then intuitive grounds. In some cases the presence of material between the verb-root form and the next verb makes it possible to prove that there is no serial root construction but instead a chained clause, for example, the presence of *wapta* in (182).

Independent verb forms

Independent verb forms express status, subject person-number, mood, and aspect. They are used in independent (final) clauses, subordinate clauses, and chained (medial) clauses.

     STATUS   The actuality status of the event is expressed in the opposition between realis forms (verb stem plus person-number) and irrealis forms (verb stem plus -*kha* plus person and number). Realis forms are used when the event denoted by the verb has been realised. Irrealis forms are used when the denoted event has not (yet) been realised.

The *realis* is formed as follows:

(185) verb stem + person-number.

The person-number suffixes in the realis are as follows:

(186) 1SG   -lé/-ndé   1PL   -lè/-tè/-ndè
      2/3SG 'zero'/-l   2/3PL -té(l)

This same set is used with small variations for the other statuses, moods, and aspects. Intentional and imperative mood take an entirely different set of person-number endings, distinguishing second from third person in both singular and plural.

The 'zero' ending (stem-only form) is the usual non-1SG realis form. Occasionally, we have found /-l/ added to the verb stem in the non-1SG forms. Similarly, there is an occasional addition of the /-l/ to the non-1PL forms. The endings -*ndé* and -*ndè* may sometimes substitute for -*lé* and -*lè* in the first person forms. Compare

(187) pofulele-ndé   'I am/was silent'

(188) pofulele-lé   'I am/was silent'

Korowai verb stems generally end in a vowel. This final vowel is subjected to laxation/reduction processes in unstressed conditions. These vowel reductions take the following form in the realis: the person-number endings in realis forms are stressed, and the stem final vowel is unstressed. Only in non-1SG forms (with the 'zero' ending) are the verb stems stressed, and only in these forms does the stem final vowel remain unchanged. In the other forms, the final vowel is reduced as follows: if it is a close vowel, it is reduced to the schwa [ə], the close lax central vowel. If it is a nonclose vowel, it is reduced to the open lax central vowel [a]. Verb stems ending in /o/ sometimes reduce to [ə] and sometimes to [a]:

(189) alo-   'to stand'
      REAL 1SG   ale-lé 'I stood/I stand'   1PL   ale-lè
           2/3SG alo   2/3PL ale-té

(190) yalido- 'to show'
      REAL 1SG   yalida-lé 'I show(ed)'   1PL   yalida-lè
           2/3SG yalido   2/3PL yalida-té

(191) ati- 'to take'
      REAL 1SG   ate-lé 'I take/took   1PL   ate-lè
           2/3SG ati   2/3PL ate-té

(192) alü- 'to cook'
      REAL 1SG   ale-lé 'I cook(ed)'   1PL   ale-lè
           2/3SG alü   2/3PL ale-té

(193) abolai- 'to chase, to hunt'

REAL	1SG	abola-lé	'I chase(d)'	1PL	abola-lè
	2/3SG	abolai		2/3PL	abola-té

The *irrealis* (IRR) is formed as follows:

(194) IRR: verb stem + *-kha* + person-number.

With verb stems ending in /i/ or /e/, the irrealis marker *-kha* takes the form *-akha*. With *ai* stems the irrealis marker takes the form *-khe*. The person-number endings in the irrealis are

(195) 1SG   -lé   1PL   -lè/-tè
      2/3SG -é   2/3PL -té

The 1 PL ending *-lè* is sometimes replaced by *-tè*.

The verb stems are not affected by stress-conditioned reductions since they take the main stress in irrealis forms. The verbs *lai-* 'to come' and *khai-* 'to go' have *la-* and *kha-* as irrealis stems. The following are examples of paradigms:

(196) lai- 'to come'

IRR	1SG	la-khe-lé	'I (shall) come'	1PL	la-khe-lè
	2/3SG	la-khé		2/3PL	la-khe-té

(197) mi-'to drink'

IRR	1SG	mi-akha-lé	'I (shall) drink'	1PL	mi-akha-lè
	2/3SG	mi-akha-é		2/3PL	mi-akha-té

An example of the use of irrealis forms follows:

(198) imonè kha-khe-tél-e-kha-fè   menèl lu-kha-té.
      now   go-IRR-3PL-TR-CONN-TOP quickly arrive-IRR-3PL
      'If they go now, they will arrive early.'

Impossibility status (IMPOS) is expressed as follows:

(199) IMPOS: *be-* + INFINITIVE + *-din* + *-da*.

Be- . . . *-da* is the negation marker (see below). The suffix *-din* is the marker of impossibility status:

(200) yu be-khomilo-n-din-da
      he NEG-die-INF-IMPOS-NEG
      'He cannot die/It is impossible that he dies.'

(201) nokhu be-khelép-telo-n-din-da
      we   NEG-clear-be-INF-IMPOS-NEG
      'We cannot know / It is impossible that we know.'

ASPECT   The *perfect* aspect forms are used in verbs that denote events which are presented as completed. The perfect (PERF) aspect is formed as follows:

(202) PERF: verb stem + *-ba* + person-number.

The person-number suffixes in perfect forms are the following:

(203) 1SG -lé   1PL   -lè
       2/3SG -o   2/3PL -té

The /a/ of the perfect marker *-ba* is elided before the /o/ of the 2/3SG ending (*-ba* + *-o* > *-bo*). The main stress in perfect forms of the verb is on the verb stem. When this stress falls on the last syllable of the stem, there are no reduction phenomena. When the stress does not fall on the last syllable, there is optional but usual reduction of the stem final vowel to the schwa [ᵊ]. Compound verb stems with *mo-* usually have *mo-* reduced to *m-*. The following are examples of paradigms:

(204) alo-   'to stand'
       PERF 1SG   alo-ba-lé   'I have stood'   1PL   alo-ba-lè
             2/3SG alo-bo   2/3PL alo-ba-té

(205) dépo- 'to smoke'
       PERF 1SG   dépe-ba-lé 'I have smoked'   1PL   dépe-ba-lè
             2/3SG dépe-bo   2/3PL dépe-ba-té

(206) imo-   'to see'
       PERF 1SG   i-m-ba-lé   'I have seen'   1PL   i-m-ba-lè
             2/3SG i-m-bo   2/3PL i-m-ba-te

The *progressive* aspect (PROGR) forms are used to denote events presented as incompleted. The progressive is formed by adding the progressive marker *-mba* to realis forms. Periphrastic constructions (see below) can be used to express the progressive aspect for future events. The progressive is formed as follows:

(207) PROGR: verb stem + *-mba* + person-number.

There are no reduction phenomena. The main stress is on the verb stem. The /a/ of the progressive suffix is elided before the /o/ of the 2/3SG ending. The person-number endings are

(208) 1SG   -lé   1PL   -lè/-tè
       2/3SG -o/-ol   2/3PL -té

(209) dépo- 'to smoke'
       PROGR 1SG   dépo-mba-lé 'I am/was smoking'   1PL   dépo-mba-lè
              2/3SG dépo-mbo   2/3PL dépo-mba-té

(210) imo-   'to see'
       PROGR 1SG   imo-mba-lé   'I am/was seeing'   1PL   imo-mba-lè
              2/3SG imo-mbo   2/3PL imo-mba-té

The progressive forms are sometimes used to express ingressive meanings (INGRES), especially in combination with the ingressive particle *lé:*

(211) yu lé   khomilo-mbo
      he INGRES die.3SG.REAL-PROGR
      'He begins to die.'

Two types of *periphrastic* constructions are used to express aspectual distinctions. The first comprises the infinitival verb + periphrastic verb; the second, the dependent verb + periphrastic verb. Consider the following examples of the first type:

(212) nu dépo-ngga   wé-ma-lé
      I   smoke-INF.CONN continuous-SUPP-1SG.REAL
      'I smoke continuously.'

(213) nu dépo-ngga   solditai-mo-mba-lé
      I   smoke-INF.CONN begin-SUPP-PROGR-1SG.REAL
      'I begin to smoke.'

(214) nu dépo-ngga   kemél-mo-mba-lé
      I   smoke-INF.CONN usual-SUPP-PROGR-1SG.REAL
      'I usually (habitually) smoke.'

(215) nu dépo-ngga   lefaf
      I   smoke-INF.CONN finished
      'I have finished smoking.'

Example (212) expresses continuative aspect, (213) inchoative aspect, (214) habitual aspect, and (215) completive aspect.

    The periphrastic verb *wémo-* is a *mo*-derived verb (see above, Derivation of verbs) that means 'to do continuously', and this verb takes the nominal infinitive as its complement ('I do the smoking continuously'). The periphrasis with *solditaimo-* 'to begin' and *kemélmo-* 'to do usually' in (213) and (214) can be analysed along the same lines. We have found the invariable element *lefaf* 'finished' only in the perfect periphrasis context exemplified by (215).

    The second type of periphrastic aspect construction is exemplified by (216) and (217):

(216) nu dépe-nè wé-ma-lé
      I   smoke-SS continuous-SUPP-1SG.REAL
      'I smoke continuously.'

(217) i-nè   khami-ba-lè
      look-SS stay-sit-1PL.REAL
      'We are looking.'

In these examples, a dependent verb form precedes a periphrastic independent verb. The compound verb *khamiba-* consists of the stem *khami-* 'to stay' and the stem *ba-*

'to sit/be/stay'. These two verbs may also be used independently to express durative aspect. Example (216) exemplifies the expression of continuative aspect and has the same meaning as example (212).

MOOD   The *intentional/adhortative/imperative mood* is formed as follows:

(218) INTENT/ADH/IMP: verb stem + person-number.

This mood has its own set of person-number suffixes, in which all three grammatical persons are distinguished:

(219) INTENT/ADH/IMP: 1SG -p   1SG -f-Vn
                        2SG -m   2SG -m-Vn
                        3SG -n   3SG -tin

The final nasal of the 3SG, 1PL, and 2PL endings is sometimes realised as nasalisation on the preceding vowel. There is vowel harmony in the plural marker *-Vn* in the 1PL and 2PL endings. The plural suffix is *-én* with verb stems that have /i/, /é/, and /è/ as the final vowel; *-un* with verb stems that have /ü/ and /u/ as the final vowel; and *-on* with verb stems that have /a/ and /o/ as the final vowel.

The final vowel of the verb stem is affected as follows by reduction and laxing in unstressed conditions in the ADH/INTENT paradigms. Stem final /ü/, /é/, and /è/ reduce to the lax central neutral vowel schwa [ə]. Stem final /o/, /au/, and /ai/ reduce and lax to the lax back neutral vowel [a]. The tense stem final vowel /u/ laxes to [ɔ] in the 1PL and 2PL forms and to [ə] in the 3PL forms.

The 2SG and 2PL forms are used as positive imperatives. Consider the following paradigms:

(220) lu- 'to enter'
       1SG lu-p   'I want to enter / let me enter'
       2SG lu-m   'you must enter / you want to enter'
       3SG lu-n   'he wants to enter / let him enter'
       1PL lo-f-un   'we want to enter / let us enter'
       2PL lo-m-un   'you must enter / you want to enter'
       3PL le-tin   'they want to enter / let them enter'

The stress is on the endings in the ADH/INTENT/IMP forms. This means that the verb stem receives stress in the singular forms and is unstressed in the plural forms. This stress pattern conditions the reduction and laxing in the plural forms. Notice that the plural marker in the 1PL and 2PL forms is *-un* and not *-on*: the process of vowel harmony takes place before the process of laxing or reduction of the verb stem final vowel. Other examples follow:

(221) dépo- 'to smoke'
       1SG dépo-p 'I want to smoke / let me smoke'   1PL dépa-f-on
       2SG dépo-m   2PL dépa-m-on
       3SG dépo-n   3PL dépa-tin

(222) lé-   'to eat'

1SG	lé-p	'I want to eat / let me eat'	1PL	le-f-én
2SG	lé-m		2PL	le-m-én
3SG	lé-n		3PL	le-tin

(223) dadü-   'to swim'

1SG	dadü-p	'I want to swim / let me swim'	1PL	dade-f-un
2SG	dadü-m		2PL	dade-m-un
3SG	dadü-n		3PL	dade-tin

(224) lai-   'to come'

1SG	lai-p	'I want to come / let me come'	1PL	la-f-én
2SG	lai-m		2PL	la-m-én
3SG	lai-n		3PL	la-tin

(225) woliolau-   'to write'[26]

1SG	woliolau-p	'I want to write / let me write'	1PL	woliola-f-on
2SG	woliolau-m		2PL	woliola-m-on
3SG	woliolau-n		3PL	woliola-tin

When expressing adhortative or imperative meanings, the modal adverb *anè* option-ally precedes the verb. When expressing intentional ('to want') or desiderative ('to wish, to desire') meanings, the modal adverb *kholüp* (or in shortened form *khüp)* optionally follows the verb. Consider

(226) anè   lai-m
      IMP/ADH   come-IMP.2SG
      'You must come!'

(227) anè   kha-fén
      IMP/ADH go-1PL.ADH
      'Let us go!'

(228) nokhu ima-fon   khüp
      we   see-1PL.INTENT INTENT/DESID
      'We wish to see.'

Interrogatives are characterised by a rising intonation and the optional presence of question clitics attached to the verb. There are two question clitics, *-kholo* and *-benè*. It seems that they can be used interchangeably, but further research is needed to establish the relationship between them.

(229) lu-mbo-benè?
      enter-PROGR.3SG.REAL-Q
      'Is he entering?'

(230) afü-mba-te-kholo?
      fight-PROGR-3PL.REAL-Q
      'Are they fighting?'

(231) mbakha-lékhé lamé-mba-te-kholo?
    what-reason   tie-PROGR-3PL-Q

'Why are they tying (him) up?'

(232) yu la-khe-bené   tè be-lai-da-bené?
    he come-3SG.IRR-Q or NEG-come.3SG.IRR-NEG-Q

'Will he come or not?'

(233) gu laléo lai-ati-bo-dakhu   lelé-mbol-e-kholo   tè
    you spirit come-take-be.2SG.REAL-SS come-PROGR.2SG.REAL-TR-Q or
    mbakha-mol-mo-dakhu   lelé-mbol-e-kholo?
    what-SUPP-SUPP.2SG.REAL-SS come-PROGR.2SG.REAL-TR-Q

'Are you coming with a spirit or how are you coming?'

(234) mbakha-lekhé-nggolo?
    what-reason-Q

'Why?'

We see -*kholo* in a disjunctive question in (233) and -*benè* in a disjunctive question in (232), with the disjunctive conjunction *tè* 'or'. Examples (229) and (230) show both clitics in polar questions. Example (231) shows -*kholo* in a question-word question, but we have not yet found examples with -*bèné* in such questions.

When the clitic -*tu* is attached to the clause in polar questions, a positive answer is expected by the speaker. The clitic -*tu* may co-occur with the question clitics and follows them:

(235) yu lokhté-tu?
    she go.home.2SG.REAL-POS.EXP

'She went home, isn't it?'

(236) wa-mo-ngga   lekhé-benè-tu?
    that-SUPP-INF.CONN reason-Q-POS.EXP

'In order to do that, isn't it?'

        EXPANSION WITH -*méma, -bakha,* AND -*(fe)lu/-lulo* Realis, irrealis, and intentional/adhortative/imperative forms may optionally be expanded with the suffixes -*méma* 'a moment ago / in a moment' and -*(fe)lu/-lulo* 'yesterday/tomorrow', indicating degrees of remoteness in time from the moment of speaking. The suffix -*bakha* can only be added to realis forms; it indicates that the event occurred (earlier) today (hodiernum, HOD).

These suffixes might be adverbials, incorporated into the verb.[27] They occur in the adhortative/imperative paradigms, where we would not expect regular tense suffixes. Furthermore, the same suffixes -*méma* and -*(fe)lu/-lulo* occur in both realis and irrealis forms, in the former with past interpretation ('a moment ago'; 'yesterday') and in the latter with future interpretation ('in a moment'; 'tomorrow'). It is not uncommon to find adverbials in Papuan languages with both past and future interpretations, depending on the context, for example, one expression for 'yesterday' and 'tomorrow'. In the Awyu family, we have found such use of adverbials in Wambon (de Vries 1989: 48):

(237) koiv-o   talom-e   'last/next year'
      last/next-CONN year-CONN

Depending on the tense of the verb, such expressions as *koivo talome* refer to the time before or after the time of the utterance:

(238) koiv-o   talom-e   Mboma ka-lepo
      last-CONN year-CONN   Boma   go-1SG.PAST
      'Last year I went to Boma.'

We have not found a relation between the suffixes *-mémo*, *-(fe)lu(lo)*, and *-bakha* and lexical elements like *lefül* 'day', *walelélekhu* 'tomorrow', *khakhul* 'yesterday', *alüp* 'period; day', and *gülnanggaup* 'night'.

When the *immediacy marker -méma* 'just' is used with realis forms, the forms denote events that took place just before the utterance. The immediacy marker occurs between the stem and the person-number slot:

(239) IMM/REAL: verb stem + *-méma* + person-number.

The first syllable of *-méma* attracts main stress within the verb form. This means that the verb stem final vowel is unstressed. Accordingly, there is occasional (optional) reduction of that vowel to the schwa [ə] in IMM/REAL forms. Compound verb stems with *mo-* undergo complete reduction of *mo-* (deletion) in the IMM/REAL.

The person-number endings in the IMM/REAL are

(240) 1SG   -lé   1PL   -lè
      2/3SG -o   2/3PL -té

The last vowel of the IMM marker *-méma* elides before the 2/3SG ending *-o*:

(241) imo- 'to see'
      IMM 1SG   i-méma-lé 'I just saw'   1PL   i-méma-lè
          2/3SG i-mémo   2/3PL i-méma-té

(242) khai- 'to go'
      IMM 1SG   khe-méma-lé 'I just went' 1PL   khe-méma-lè
          2/3SG khe-mémo   2/3PL khe-méma-té

(243) ati- 'to take'
      IMM 1SG   ati-méma-lé 'I just took' 1PL   ati-méma-lè
          2/3SG ati-mémo   2/3PL ati-méma-té

When the IMM marker is integrated in irrealis forms, these forms denote events that will take place shortly after the utterance. The IMM/IRR is formed as follows:

(244) IMM/IRR: verb stem + *-mémo* + *-kha* + person-number.

Reduction phenomena in the IMM/IRR are the same as in the IMM/REAL. The person-number endings are the same as in the IRR forms:

(245) dépo- 'to smoke'

  IMM 1SG   dépe-mémo-kha-lé   'I shall smoke   1PL   dépe-mémo-kha-lè/-tè
                                  in a moment'
        2/3SG dépe-mémo-kha-i   2/3PL dépe-mémo-kha-té

(246) bante- 'to divide'

  IMM 1SG   bante-mémo-kha-lé   'I shall divide   1PL   bante-mémo-kha-lè/-tè
                                  in a moment'
        2/3SG bante-mémo-kha-i   2/3PL bante-mémo-kha-té

The immediate intentional/adhortative/imperative is formed as follows:

(247) IMM INTENT/ADH/IMP: verb stem + -méma + person-number.

The person-number suffixes are the same as in the INTENT/ADH/IMP forms without expansion. The verb stems undergo the same reductions as in the other -méma paradigms (see IMM/REAL and IMM/IRR above). The marker -méma takes the form -mémo in the singular forms:

(248) dépo- 'to smoke'

  1SG dépe-mémo-p   'I want to smoke   1PL dépe-méma-f-on
                      in a moment'
  2SG dépe-mémo-m   2PL dépe-méma-m-on
  3SG dépe-mémo-n   3PL dépe-méma-tin

When the *hodiernum* (HOD) *marker -bakha* is used with realis forms, these forms denote events that took place before the utterance but on the same day. The hodiernum is formed as follows:

(249) HOD: verb stem + -bakha + person-number.

Reduction phenomena in the verb stem are limited to occasional weakening of the stem final vowel to [ə]; the support verb *mo-* is usually reduced to *m-*. The main stress in the hodiernum forms is on the person-number endings, which are as follows:

(250) 1SG   -li   1PL   -un
        2/3SG -i   2/3PL -ti

The hodiernum marker -*bakha* has its final vowel elided before person-number endings that start with a vowel:

(251) alü- 'to cook'

  HOD 1SG   alü-bakha-li   'I cooked   1PL   alü-bakh-un
                              (on this day)'
        2/3SG alü-bakh-i   2/3PL alü-bakha-ti

(252) dépo- 'to smoke'

HOD 1SG   dépe-bakha-li   'I smoked   1PL   dépe-bakh-un
                                     (on this day)'

        2/3SG dépe-bakh-i   2/3PL dépe-bakha-ti

(253) mbalamo-   'to share'

HOD 1SG   mbala-m-bakha-li   'I shared   1PL   mbala-m-bakh-un
                                     (on this day)'

        2/3SG mbala-m-bakh-i   2/3PL mbala-m-bakha-ti

We have found a time remoteness marker, *-(fe)lu/-lulo* 'one/a few days remote in time', optionally added to realis, irrealis, and intentional/adhortative/imperative forms.

When the marker *-(fe)lu* is used in realis forms, these forms denote events that took place 'yesterday' (the day before the utterance) or the day(s) before 'yesterday' (up to about a week). The NEAR/REAL is formed as follows:

(254) NEAR/REAL: verb stem + *-(fe)lu* + person-number.

The NEAR marker *-(fe)lu* attracts the main stress on its second syllable. When the marker occurs in its longer form, the verb stems usually remain the same (with an occasional weakening of the stem final vowel to the schwa [ə]). When the marker occurs in its shorter form *(-lu),* however, close stem final vowels always reduce to [ə] and nonclose stem final vowels always reduce to the open lax neutral vowel [a], with *o* stems (verb stems ending in /o/) reducing sometimes to [ə] and sometimes to [a]. The support verb *mo-* changes into *ma-* but is not further reduced.

The person-number suffixes in the NEAR/REAL are

(255) 1SG   -ndé   1PL   -ndè
        2/3SG -lo   2/3PL -té

Some examples follow:

(256) fo- 'to take'

NEAR 1SG   fa-lu-ndé   'I took (recently)'   1PL   fa-lu-ndè
         2/3SG fa-lu-lo   2/3PL fa-lu-té

(257) alo- 'to stand'

NEAR 1SG   alo-felu-ndé 'I stood (recently)'   1PL   alo-felu-ndè
         2/3SG alo-felu-lo   2/3PL alo-felu-té

(258) imo- 'to see'

NEAR 1SG   ima-lu-ndé 'I saw (recently)'   1PL   ima-lu-ndè
         2/3SG ima-lu-lo   2/3PL ima-lu-té

The NEAR marker has a slightly different form *(-lulo)* when it is used in irrealis forms. The NEAR/IRR forms denote events that will take place on the day after the utterance or two days after the utterance:

(259) NEAR/IRR: verb stem + -(fe)lulo + -kha + person-number.

The verb stems in the NEAR/IRR forms undergo the same reductions as those in the NEAR/REAL forms. The person-number endings in the NEAR/IRR are the same as in the IRR forms:

(260) dépo-   'to smoke'
      NEAR   1SG   dépa-lulo-kha-lé   'I shall smoke (tomorrow or the day(s)
              2/3SG   dépa-lulo-kha-i   after tomorrow)'
              1PL   dépa-lulo-kha-lè/-tè
              2/3PL   dépa-lulo-kha-té

(261) é-   'to sleep'
      NEAR   1SG   é-felulo-kha-lé   'I shall sleep (tomorrow or the day(s)
              2/3SG   é-felulo-kha-i   after tomorrow)'
              1PL   é-felulo-kha-lè/-tè
              2/3PL   é-felulo-kha-té

When the expanded realis and irrealis forms are used in medial clauses, they do not take the time of the utterance as their deictic point of reference; rather, they locate the events in time relative to a reference point in the context. Compare the following examples:

(262) yakhofekha-lo wofekha amo-mémo?
     who-FOC   that   thus.do-3SG.IMM.REAL
     'Who has just done that?'

(263) efu-méma-té-tofekho   yekhené-nggé melu
     sleep-IMM.REAL-3PL-DS their-friend   enter.3SG.REAL
     'They had just gone to sleep when their friend entered.'

In (262), the IMM/REAL form refers to the time just before the utterance (262). This time is the point of reference (262), an absolute tense in the sense of Comrie (1985: 125). But in (263) the IMM/REAL form is used as a relative tense; that is, the event of sleeping is located in time relative to the entering event (relative tense in the sense of Comrie).

    Finally, the NEAR marker can be added to intentional/adhortative/imperative forms, as follows:

(264) NEAR INTENT/ADH/IMP: verb stem + -lulo + person-number

The person-number suffixes are the same as in the INTENT/ADH/IMP forms without expansion. The marker -lulo reduces to -lule in the plural forms in which the final syllable is stressed. The verb stems undergo the same reductions as in the NEAR/ REAL forms (see above):

(265) dépo   'to smoke'
      NEAR INTENT/ADH/IMP:
      1SG dépa-lulo-p   'I want to smoke   1PL dépa-lule-f-on
                         tomorrow'

2SG	dépa-lulo-m		2PL	dépa-lule-m-on
3SG	dépa-lulo-n		3PL	dépa-lule-tin

NEGATION   Independent verb forms are negated as follows:

(266) *be-* + independent verb form + *-da*

The negation comprises the prefix *be-* and the suffix *-da*:

(267)

	REAL POSITIVE		REAL NEGATIVE	
1SG	dépale	'I smoke(d)'	be-dépale-da	'I do (did) not smoke'
2/3SG	dépo		be-dépo-da	
1PL	dépalè		be-dépalè-da	
2/3PL	dépate		be-dépate-da	

The intentional/adhortative/imperative forms show three peculiarities when negated. First, the negative forms also function as irrealis negative forms; that is, the opposition irrealis versus INTENT.ADH/IM is neutralised in the negative forms. Second, the negative INTENT/ADH/IMP forms have person-number suffixes different from the positive forms. Third, the negative imperative forms do not have the negative prefix *be-*, and the negative imperative adverb *belén* is added. Compare (268) and (269):

(268) dépo- 'to smoke'

INTENT/ADH/IMP positive:

1SG	dépo-p	'I want to smoke / let me smoke'	1PL	dépa-f-on
2SG	dépo-m		2PL	dépa-m-on
3SG	dépo-n		3PL	dépa-tin

(269) dépo- 'to smoke'

INTENT/ADH/IMP negative

1SG	be-dépo-pelé-da	'I do not want to smoke / I shall not smoke'	1PL	be-dépo-pelè-da
2/3SG	be-dépo-n-da		2/3PL	be-dépa-tin-da

The fact that in the negative the opposition between second and third person is neutralised brings these forms into line with all other independent verb paradigms. The 2/3SG forms mean 'you/he/she shall not smoke'. When the imperative meaning is relevant, the negative prefix *be-* is absent with the 2/3 forms and the negative imperative adverb *belén* is added:

(270) dépo-n-da   belén
      smoke-2SG.IMP-NEG NEG.IMP
      'Do not smoke!'

(271) dépa-tin-da   belén
      smoke-2PL.IMP-NEG NEG.IMP
      'Do not smoke! (PL)'

The finite negative forms of (270 and 271) may be replaced by infinitival forms optionally linked to *belén* by the connective *-kha*:

(272) dépo-n   belén
      smoke-INF NEG.IMP
      'Do not smoke!'

(273) dépo-ngga   belén
      smoke-INF.CONN   NEG.IMP
      'Do not smoke!'

The forms (272 and 273) are neutral in person-number. In (273), the fusion rule /n/ + /kh/ > /ngg/ is operative (*dépo-n-kha* > *dépongga*; see chapter 2, Morphophonemic changes).

Infinitival forms

Thus far we have found two infinitival formations. The first is formed as follows:

(274) verb stem + *-un.*

The final vowel of the verb stem is elided before the initial vowel of *-un* with some verbs, whereas with other verbs the /u/ of *-un* is elided after the final vowel of the verb stem. Consider

(275) lé- 'to eat'   INF: lun

(276) dépo- 'to smoke'   INF: dépon

(277) ate- 'to hold'   INF: atun

With *kha-* 'to go' there is no elision (INF: *khaun*). The following is an example of the use of the infinitive:

(278) nu kelaya at-ungga[28]   lefaf
      I work hold-INF.CONN finished
      'I finished working.'

The second type of infinitive is used in negative contexts and is formed as follows:

(279) verb stem + *-mVn*

Thus far we have found this type always with *-alingga* 'without' (see above, Comitative suffixes). The final vowel of the verb stem determines the quality of the vowel in the negative infinitive marker *-mVn* (vowel harmony), and the final vowel of the verb stem itself is optionally subjected to reduction to the schwa [ə]:

(280) lé-   'to eat'
      le-mén-alingga   'without eating'
      eat-INF-without

(281) leléalmo-   'to accept'
      leléalma-mon-alingga   'without accepting'
      accept-SUPP-INF-without

(282) dadü-   'to bathe'
      dade-mun-alingga   'without bathing'
      bath-INF-without

(283) nokhu kelambu   dimekho-mon-alingga efu-bakh-un
      we   mosquito.net use-INF-without   sleep-HOD-1PL

      'We slept today without using a mosquito net.'

The verb -*telo*

The verb -*telo* 'to be' functions in stative clauses cliticising to the constituent, which functions as the predicate:

(284) Yaniluman-telo
      Yaniruma-be.3SG.REAL

      'It is Yaniruma.'

(285) kelaya-alingga-lelo
      work-without-be.3SG.REAL

      'He is without work.'

The verb -*telo* is a fully inflected verb. For example, in (286) we see the 1SG.NEAR form of -*telo*:

(286) nokhu khakhul khén-telo-felu-ndé
      we   yesterday angry-be-NEAR-1SG.REAL

      'Yesterday we were angry.'

The verb -*telo* is optionally but usually present with adjectival predicates. With nouns as predicates in stative clauses, -*telo* is optionally but infrequently present:

(287) yu nggulun-benè?
      he teacher-Q

      'Is he a teacher?'

(288) yu nggulun-telo-benè?
      he teacher-be.3SG.REAL-Q

      'Is he a teacher?'

The progressive forms of -*telo* mean 'to become':

(289) khén-telo-mba-te
      angry-become-PROGR-3PL

      'They are becoming angry.'

The dependent SS form of *-telo* has a reduced stem *-te:*

(290) anggo-te-nè   'being slow'
      slow-be-SS

In independent verb forms we have sometimes found *-té* replacing *-telo:*

(291) nu ne khelép-té
      I   me clear-be.3SG.REAL
      'It is clear to me'

(292) wolakholol be-lembu-té-n-da
      earth   NEG-out.of.order-be-3SG.INTENT-NEG
      'The world will not get out of order.'

The verb *-telo* is often used with predicates that denote physical and psychological experiences (ill, hungry, cold) in so-called experiential constructions. In such constructions the verb is a third person singular form and does not agree with the experiencer. For example:

(293) nu lép-telo
      I   ill-be.3SG.REAL
      'I am ill.' [Lit. '(It) is ill (to) me'.]

The verb in (293) does not agree with the experiencer constituent *nu* 'I'.
    The verb *-telo* is also used in aspectual periphrasis:

(294) mbam-tena yamo-ngga   wé-lelo
      child-little   cry-INF.CONN continuous-be.3SG.REAL
      'The little child cries continuously.'

Semantically, (294) is closely related to (295) in which continuative aspect is expressed with a *mo*-derived verb (see above):

(295) mbam-tena yamo-ngga   wé-mo
      child-little   cry-INF.CONN continuous-do.3SG.REAL
      'The little child cries continuously.'

Quote marking; the verb 'to say'

We have not found quotative suffixes or quotative clitics. The verb *di-/de-* 'to say' is used as a quote-marking verb, especially its medial SS form *denè*. When it is used as a quote-marking device, forms of *di-/de-* cliticise to the last word of the quoted clause.
    Just as in Kombai and other Papuan languages (see de Vries 1990) the Korowai verb for 'to say' is used in a wide range of contexts. Drabbe (1955, 1957, 1959) has already noted that thought and motives are represented as quoted speech in languages of the Marind and Awyu families. Healy (1964: 29) describes the use of quotative

clauses in Telefol with 'to say, think, see, know, feel' and calls the use of direct speech forms for the expression of nonverbalised thought 'direct cerebration'. In (296) and (297), *de-* is used in intentional contexts, both in first and third person contexts.

The basis of this use of 'to say' in intentional expressions is the tendency to express intention and other mental or emotional states as a form of 'inner speech' or 'quoted thought'. Consider the following examples:

(296) yu Lalop   dadü-n-de-nè   khai-mbo
     he Lalop.River swim-3SG.INTENT-QUOTE-SS go-3SG.PROGR.REAL

     'Is he going to swim in the Lalop River?'

(297) nokhu Lalop   dade-fun-de-nè   khai-mba-lè
     we   Lalop.River swim-1PL.INTENT-QUOTE-SS go-PROGR-1PL.REAL

     'We are going to swim in the Lalop River.'

(298) yuf-efè nu lép-telo-bo   dé
     he-TOP I   ill-be-sit.3SG.REAL QUOTE.3SG.REAL

     'He said he was ill.'

(299) nup-to Banyo khelép-enè   féda-lé
     I-FOC   Banyo   clear-QUOTE.SS give-1SG.REAL

     'I have explained it to Banyo.'

(300) nu yu nèkhma-lé-kha   mbisi-fekha nu fédo-m de-lé
     I   him ask.for-1SG.REAL-CONN steel.axe-one   me give-2SG.IMP QUOTE-1SG.REAL

     'I asked him to give a steel axe to me.'

(301) nu yu lanu-ma-lé-kha   gu anè   lai-m   de-lé
     I   him command-SUPP-1SG.REAL-CONN you ADHORT come-2SG.IMP QUOTE-1SG.REAL

     'I commanded him to come quickly.'

(302) wé   if-e-kha   lal   wof-e-kha   Wokhemél Yambim
     EXCLM this-TR-CONN female that-TR-CONN Wokhemél   Yambim
     mambisi-kholo-tom-pekho baka[29] dé-dakhu-fekho
     uterus-bones-FOC-ATTENT   crackle QUOTE.3SG.REAL-SS-and

     'Hey, this woman, it was Wokhemél Yambim, her uterus inflamed and . . .'

4

Patterns of Coherence

To facilitate understanding of the texts of chapter 6, some of their major morpho-syntactic patterns of coherence are discussed in this chapter.

The texts have as their basic unit single-verb clauses. These are combined into chains of clauses. The clause chains in their turn are connected by devices like tail-head and generic 'do/be' verb linkage to form larger stretches of discourse. Although chaining is the dominant type of clause linkage in the texts, there are also other ways to combine clauses, such as subordinate linkage with the connective *-kha*.

Coherence is a matter not only of linking units such as clauses and clause chains but also of differentiating between kinds of information within those units. We first discuss patterns of clause linkage; then we turn to linkage of clause chains and to discourse-linkage verbs. Topical and focal kinds of information are followed by illustrations of some of the points made in this chapter through *The Pig Sacrifice* text in chapter 6.

Patterns of clause linkage

Before we proceed to some mechanisms of clause linkage, here are just a few remarks on the internal structure of clauses. The great majority of clauses in our corpus of oral texts has a very simple internal structure: just a verb or a verb preceded by one or at most two noun phrases. In turn, these noun phrases also tend to have a very simple internal structure: just a noun or a noun with one or two modifiers. The result is a rather sharp contrast in the texts between the relatively simple internal structure of clauses and phrases and the complex internal structure of words, especially of verbs.

Clauses like (1)–(3), with more than two nominal phrases, are infrequent:

(1) khakhul nu yekhené-fekho Manggél kha-lé
    yesterday I   them-with   Manggél go-1SG.REAL
    'Yesterday I went to Manggél with them.'

(2) yu pilin sabun-pekho[1] sukh-mbo
    he dishes soap-with   wash-3SG.PROGR.REAL
    'He is washing the dishes with soap.'

(3) nu if-e-kha   misafi gup-tekhé fédo-p
    I   this-TR-CONN thing you-to   give-1SG.INTENT
    'I want to give these things to you.'

Clauses with several nominal phrases occur especially in discourse-initial clause chains, where the speaker builds up the time, place, and participant framework.

Korowai clauses are strictly verb-final. In transitive clauses, the actor must precede the goal. Peripheral nominals that specify the time or place setting for the clause usually occur clause-initially, as in (1), but they may also occur after the actor, as in (4):

(4) nokhu khakhul khén-telo-felu-ndé
    we   yesterday angry-be-NEAR-1SG.REAL
    'Yesterday we were angry.'

Other peripheral nominals, like instrument and comitative, tend to occur between the actor and the verb, as in (1) and (2).

The two most important ways to combine clauses in our texts are chaining linkage and subordinate linkage. Consider the following examples:

(5) Faül   dadü-ai-tofekho
    name.of.mythical.pig swim-go.down.3SG.REAL-DS
    'Faül came swimming downriver and . . .'

(6) Faül   ül-nè
    name.of.mythical.pig kill-SS
    'he killed Faül and . . .'

(7) bul-mekho-kha-fefè
    slaughter-SUPP.3SG.REAL-CONN-TOP
    'after he had slaughtered (Faül) . . .'

(8) Faül   ba-nggolol yaüya-pé fe-nè fu
    name.of.mythical.pig chest-bone   under-LOC get-SS put.3SG.REAL
    'he put the chest part of Faül under . . .'

The clauses in (5)–(8), except the clause in (7), are connected by chaining linkage, a nonembedded type of linkage in which interclausal relations of switch reference are expressed by dependent verb forms and by switch-reference conjunctions. Chained clauses cannot take the topic marker *-(f)efè*. The clause in (7) is a subordinate clause that takes the subordinating connective *-kha*. Switch-reference relations cannot be expressed in *-kha*-linked clauses. In certain conditions, *-kha*-linked clauses may take the topic marker *-(f)efè*.

Chaining linkage is used in the overwhelming majority of cases, in contrast to the more marked linkage with *-kha*. We shall now discuss these two ways to combine clauses in more detail.

Chaining linkage

Longacre (1972: 2) describes clause chains of Papuan languages as structures with an engine at the end and, preceding it, a bunch of hooked-on cars. This comparison points to the essential division among the fully inflected distinctive verb forms of the last clause, the independent or final verbs, and the less finite or dependent verb forms that occur medially in the chain.

Besides this central final-medial verb characteristic, there are two other typical features of New Guinea clause chaining, switch-reference and temporality distinctions. Temporality marking pertains to interclausal relations of sequence and simultaneity of events. Switch-reference markings indicate whether the following clause has the same subject (SS) or a different subject (DS) from that of the preceding clause in the chain.[2]

Clause chaining in Awyu languages differs from the usual type of New Guinea clause chaining (see de Vries 1993a). Special medial or dependent verb forms are not highly elaborated in Awyu languages (see Wurm 1982: 139). All Awyu languages employ independent verbs both chain-medially and chain-finally, but they vary widely in the grammatical place they accord to chain-medial independent forms. For example, independent forms of Kombai, when occurring medially, function as different subject forms (see de Vries 1993b), but Korowai independent forms function as switch-reference neutral forms in the chain-medial position.

Chaining is a neutral type of nonembedded linkage in Korowai, and context and situation determine the interpretation of the relation between the chained clauses. For example:

(9) nu lép-telo-do[3]   yu be-lai-da
    I   ill-3SG.REAL-DS he NEG-come.3SG.REAL-NEG

    'I am ill and he does not come.'

Depending on the context, the two clauses of (9) may be interpreted as 'Because I am ill, he does not come' or as 'Although I am ill, he does not come' or as 'When I was ill, he did not come'.

In the following examples, the goal relation between perception-cognition clauses and the clauses that denote what was perceived or thought must be inferred from the context:

(10) Mukhalé yu imo-tofekho   y-afé   élo-bo
      Mukhalé he   look.3SG.REAL-DS his-brother sleep-be.3SG.REAL

      'Mukhalé saw that his older brother was asleep.' (Lit. 'Mukhalé he saw and his older brother was asleep.')

(11) yanop mbakha-monggol-tel-do   afe-tél   a-mo-dom-pekho
      people whatever-not-be.3SG.REAL-DS wonder-3PL.REAL that-SUPP.3SG.REAL-DS-until
      y-afé-lom-pekho   ye-mofekha   atilo   dul   lokhesukh-op
      his-brother-FOC-ATTENT his-younger.brother hold.SS penis egg-fruit
      lafil-mo-dakhu-fekho
      cut.off-SUPP.3SG.REAL-SS-and

      'They struggled with the problem that there were no other people until it was the older brother who seized the younger one, cut off the penis and the scrotum, and . . .' (Lit. 'There were no people and they wondered . . .')

The following is an example of the use of chaining linkage in which the relationship between the chained clauses is interpreted as a question-word question:

(12) yu mbakha-mol-mo-dakhu   khomilo?
      he what-SUPP-SUPP.3SG.REAL-SS die.3SG.REAL

      'Why did he die?' (Lit. 'What occurred to him and he died?')

Switch reference

The only special medial verb form of Korowai is the same-subject formation that comprises the verb stem plus the optional same-subject suffix *-nè* (see chapter 3, Dependent verb forms). Sequence/simultaneity is not a morphological category of the verb. An example of the dependent same-subject form is the following:

(13) mébol damilmo le-nè   lu-ba-lé
      grave open.SS   come-SS ascend-PERF-1SG.REAL

      'I opened the grave and came up (the stairs).'

When independent verb forms function medially in clause chains, in the great majority of cases a switch-reference conjunction is cliticised to the verb to indicate whether the next clause has the same or a different subject. If such a conjunction is absent, the independent form is switch-reference neutral.

The switch-reference conjunctions we found in the data are listed in (14):

(14) -do(n)   'DS'
      -dakhu(l)   'SS'
      -anggu   'SS/INTENT'
      -tofekho (*or* -top) 'DS/ADVERS'

The conjunctions -*do(n)* 'DS' and -*dakhu(l)* 'SS' are the most frequently used of the set (14). The conjunctions -*anggu* 'SS.INTENT' and -*tofekho* 'DS.but' have a more marked meaning and are accordingly more restricted in occurrence, with -*anggu* used in intentional contexts and -*tofekho* in adversative contexts.

Above we saw an example of -*do* 'DS' [see (9)]. Example (15) shows -*dakhu(l)* 'SS':

(15) nu khomile-lé-dakhu khosü kha-lé
      I   die-1SG.REAL-SS   there   go-1SG.REAL
      'I died and went there (= to the place of the dead).'

The marker -*anggu* is a same-subject clitic that we have found only in intentional contexts:

(16) ge-lal-to   fédo-m-do   fo-p-anggu   ne-mom
      your-daughter-FOC give-2SG.IMP-DS take-1SG.INTENT-SS my-uncle
      kholop-fuda-mo-p
      replace-compensate-SUPP-1SG.INTENT
      'You must give your daughter and I want to marry her and I want to replace my uncle [= You must give your daughter to me as a compensation gift for my (dead) mother's brother].'

The marker -*tofekho* 'DS.but' is a DS conjunction that occurs especially in adversative contexts (contraexpectation or contrast):

(17) khakhul nu ne-mom dodépa-lé-lofekho   be-lai-da
      yesterday I   my-uncle call-1SG.REAL-DS.but NEG-come.3SG.REAL-NEG
      'Yesterday I called my uncle but he did not come.'

The conjunction -*fekho* 'and', which cliticises to medially used independent verbs, is a (switch-reference) neutral additive conjunction, often used in contexts of sequentiality of events. It occurs sometimes with the implication that the first event has a prolonged duration and goes on until the second event begins:

(18) lelip   khami-ba-té-fekho   ye-defol fo
      together stay-sit-3PL.REAL-until his-wife take.3SG.REAL
      'They stayed together until he married.'

False SS and DS markings; skipping phenomena

Occasionally, there occur so-called 'false' SS and DS markings in our corpus of texts, when the next clause in the chain has a different subject, in spite of a preceding SS marked clause, or the same subject after a DS marked clause.

Some of these 'false' markings may have to do with 'improperly' broken off clause chains, when a new chain is started but the old is not concluded in the 'proper' fashion (i.e., with an independent verb clause without a switch-reference conjunction). Consider the following stretch of text in (19)–(21):

(19) yekhené-pan-è khabéan bonggol lakhup duo   lé-ma-té-dakhu
      they-self-CONN head   mouth   stone   put.into.SS eat-HAB-3PL.REAL-SS

      'They themselves prepare the head and the mouth with (burning hot) stones and eat
      it . . .'

(20) béto-pé   lép afü-ma-tél-e-kha   menèl khi-telo
      behind-LOC ill wrestle-SUPP-3PL.REAL-TR-CONN quickly healthy-be.3SG.REAL
      khil-telo
      healthy-be.3SG.REAL

      'afterward the very sick people quickly become healthy . . .'

(21) lu-ngga   gol-o   küal-o   füon-o   yafil-o-fekho
      eat-INF.CONN pig-COORD cassowary-COORD marsupial-COORD snake-COORD-COORD
      lu-ngga   lefugop   be-manda-da   menèl lé-lé lefaf
      eat-INF.CONN all.kinds.of NEG-not.being-NEG quickly eat-eat finished

      'concerning the food, pigs, cassowaries, lizards, snakes and all kinds of food, there is
      really not soon an end to the eating of it.'

Chain (19) is 'improperly' broken off (ends in an SS marked clause), and then the discourse continues in (20) with a new unit and a different subject. The 'false' SS marking in (19) is probably the result of the abrupt break in the chain.

In the next example, the chain is interrupted and broken after the falsely marked SS clause *fudakhu* in (22) to make room for a parenthetical section in (23)–(24) about the woman; the chain started in (22), with the creator Ginol as the main participant, continues in (25):

(22) mül-khuf-efè   afe-fè   lamol   fu-bo-kha   abül-fefè
      former-time-TOP there-TOP universe put-3SG.PERF.REAL-CONN male.person-TOP
      yu lamol   menil fe-nè   fu-dakhu
      he universe fire   get-SS   put-SS

      'In former times the one who created the universe set the universe on fire and . . .'

(23) a-la-tom-pekho   khejo   saukh-tamon-tefu khejo
      that-female-FOC-ATTENT sago.leaf.stem tobacco-bunch-end sago.leaf.stem

      'the woman (had placed) tobacco at the sago leaf stem, the top of a bunch of tobacco
      leaves at the leaf stem . . .'

(24) kho   ü-lamü-gele-té-dakhu-fekho   wap-ta   khejo
      sago.tree cut.down-pound-press-3PL.REAL-SS-and there-LOC sago.leaf.stem
      ao-dakhu-fekho   saukh-tamon inggenun   khabian-ta fu-dakhu-fekho
      plant.3SG.REAL-SS-and tobacco-bunch sago.leaf.stem head-LOC   put.3SG.REAL-SS-and
      babo-tofekho
      sit.3SG.REAL-DS.but

      'they had cut down a sago tree, pounded (the stem), and pressed (the flour out of the
      fibres) and she had set up the sago leaf stem (construction), and at the very end of the
      leaf stem she had attached the bunch of tobacco leaves and she stayed there but . . .'

(25) Ginol Silam-tena   yu khonai-mémo-fekho   wof-e-kha
      Ginol mouse.like.animal-DIMIN he go-3SG.IMM.REAL-until that-TR-CONN
      mangga   lai-duo-bakh-i   melél-mo   melil khe-nè
      dry.sago.leaves break(broken)-put.into-HOD-3SG.REAL finish-SUPP.3SG.REAL fire go-SS
      fumo-to   él ü-telo-dom-pekho
      blow.3SG.REAL-DS yes gone-be.3SG.REAL-DS-and

      'and he, Ginol, the Little Mouselike, just was walking around, and he had collected all
      the dry sago leaves and put them on a heap when he went to the fire and blew it, but yes
      it was dead and . . .'

Another category of 'false' switch-reference markings concerns skipping phenomena in clause chaining: in switch-reference marking languages, it is possible that either
clauses are skipped by the switch-reference system that 'should' not be skipped or
certain types of clauses are not skipped that 'should' have been skipped.

Chained temporal clauses and weather clauses (e.g., 'when it became day, when
the rain started to fall') are ignored in some Papuan languages by the switch-reference
system (see Longacre 1972: 10; Reesink 1983). In the Awyu family, Wambon has
been found to systematically skip temporal chained clauses (see de Vries 1989), in
the sense that the choice of a DS or SS form that precedes a temporal or meteoro-
logical clause is determined by the subject reference of the clause that follows the
temporal or weather clause. Korowai, in the great majority of cases, uses switch-
reference neutral clauses (i.e., without switch-reference conjunctions) before chained
temporal clauses. But Korowai speakers may also use a DS marked clause before a
temporal clause to mark the switch of subject in the transition to the latter. Both options
occur in examples (26)–(29):

(26) yu   wai   lokhté-do   gülé-do   khe-nè lu
      she go.down.SS go.away.3SG.REAL-DS be.dark.3SG.REAL-DS go-SS enter.3SG.REAL

      'She went away and when it became dark, she came and entered again.'

(27) khe-nè   lu-do   é-felu-té-fekho   walé-do   yu
      go-SS   enter.3SG.REAL-DS sleep-NEAR-3PL.REAL-until daybreak.REAL.3SG-DS she
      wai   lokhté
      go.down.SS go.away.3SG.REAL

      'She came and entered and they spent the night until the next morning she went away
      again.'

(28) yu   wai   lokhté   walé-do
      she go.down.SS go.away.3SG.REAL daybreak.REAL.3SG-DS

      'She went away the next morning . . .'

(29) yu   wai   lokhté   gülé-do   khe-nè lu
      she go.down.SS go.away.3SG.REAL be.dark.3SG.REAL-DS go-SS enter.3SG.REAL

      'she went out and at night she entered.'

In (26)–(29), there are several temporal clauses (the *gülé-do* and *walé-do* clauses),
all preceded by switch-reference neutral clauses, except for (26), where a DS clause
precedes the temporal clause *gülédo* 'when it became dark'.

Sometimes clauses are not skipped by the switch-reference system that 'should' have been skipped because they are, strictly speaking, not part of the chain. Quotation clauses fall in this category. These clauses are not chained and accordingly are normally skipped by the switch-reference system; but we have a number of cases in the data in which a quotation clause is treated as part of the chain and in which the clause that precedes the quotation clause has a different subject marking to anticipate the different subject of the quotation clause:

(30) yekhené-nggé mé-laimekho-bakha-til-e-kha melu-tofekho
     their-friend   earth-bury-HOD-3PL-TR-CONN   get.up.3SG.REAL-DS

     Their friend, whom they had buried that day, got up and . . .'

(31) wé   mé-laimekho-bakha-ti-do mbakha-mo-f-è
     EXCLM earth-bury-HOD-3PL-DS   what-SUPP-1SG.INTENT-EXCLM
     dé-dakhu
     QUOTE.3SG.REAL-SS

     'he wondered, "Well, now that they have buried (me), what can I do?" and . . .'

Literally it says, 'Their friend got up and "Oh, they have buried me and what can I do?" he said'. Notice that the quotation clause ("Oh, they have buried me") has a different subject than the preceding clause ('their friend got up') and that this difference is registered by the switch-reference markings, although the quotation clause is not a chained clause.

Subordinate linkage with *-kha*

Clauses linked with *-kha* to a head noun

The connective *-kha* functions within noun phrases to link prenominal modifiers to the head noun.[4] Consider the following:

(32) NP [(MODIFIER) *-kha* (HEAD NOUN)]

The modifier slot in (32) can be filled by modifier constituents of various categorial status, for example, numerals, (33); demonstratives, (34); infinitival clauses, (35); and finite clauses, (36–37):

(33) lidof-e-kha   abül   'one man'
     one-TR-CONN man

(34) if-e-kha   abül   'this man'
     this-TR-CONN man

(35) nokhup Lalop dad-ungga-lekhé[5]   khai-mba-lé
     we   Lalop   bath-INF.CONN-reason go-PROGR-1SG.REAL

     'We are on our way to bathe in the Lalop River.

(36) mül-khuf-efè   af-efè   lamol fu-bo-kha
     former-time-TOP there-TOP universe put-3SG.PERF.REAL-CONN

abül-fefè yu   lamol   menil   fe-nè fu-dakhu
man-TOP he   universe fire   get-SS put-SS

'The man who in former times created the universe there, set the universe on fire and . . .'

(37) abül-fekha khomilo-bo-kha   mahüon uma-té-do
      man-a.certain die-3SG.PERF.REAL-CONN story   tell-3PL.REAL-DS

      'the story of a man who died they told.'

When a clause is inserted in the modifier slot of (32), the result is a prenominal relative clause, as in (36)–(37).

-kha clauses without head noun

The head-noun slot in (32) may be left unspecified; in that case the result is a subordinate clause, which can pragmatically be interpreted in various ways.

The *-kha* clause is interpreted as a relative clause with a specific antecedent noun in (38):

(38) wa gol ülme-tél-e-kha-fè   nokhu-gol
      that pig kill-3PL.REAL-TR-CONN-TOP our-pig

      'The pig that they killed is our pig.'

The *-kha*-marked clause is interpreted as a relative clause with an implicit generic antecedent 'person' or 'thing' ('whoever, whatever') in (39):

(39) béto-pé lép afü-ma-tél-e-kha   menèl khil-telo
      behind-in ill   wrestle-SUPP-3PL.REAL-TR-CONN quickly healthy-be.3SG.REAL

      'Afterward whoever is very ill quickly becomes healthy.'

With verbs of speech, perception, and cognition, the *-kha*-marked clause is pragmatically interpreted as the 'main' clause, notwithstanding its subordinate syntactic status as a subject NP in an equation clause:

(40) nu dai-mba-lé-kha   Sentani-fosü pesahu fiüm
      I   hear-PROGR-1SG.REAL-CONN Sentani-from plane   many

      'I hear many planes from Sentani.' [Lit. 'What I hear (is) many planes from Sentani.']

(41) nu ima-lé-kha   wof-e-kha   gol pinggu-anop
      I   see-1SG.REAL-CONN that-TR-CONN pig three-MOD

      'I saw those three pigs.' [Lit. 'What I saw (is) the three pigs.']

(42) nu ne-khul   due-lé-kha   nu ne lép-telo-bo
      I   my-intestines put.into-1SG.REAL-CONN I me ill-be-stay.3SG.REAL

      'I think that I am ill.' [Lit. 'What I think (is) that I am ill.']

(43) nu yu nèkhma-lé-kha   mbisi-fekha nu fédo-m   de-lé
      I   him ask.for-1SG.REAL-CONN steel.axe-one me give-2SG.IMP say-1SG.REAL

'I asked him to give a steel axe to me.' [Lit. 'What I asked him (is), give me a steel axe, I said.']

The use of -*kha* clauses exemplified in (40)–(43) is unmarked and does not imply a special marked information structure. There is no pause or intonation break between the -*kha* clause and the remainder of the construction in (40)–(43). Further research is needed to find out what motivates the choice between chaining linkage ('I saw and he came') and -*kha* linkage ['What I saw (is) he came'] with perception and cognition verbs.

The role of pragmatic factors in the interpretation of -*kha* clauses is also evident from the fact that the same -*kha* clause can be interpreted both as a relative clause and as an adverbial clause, depending on the context. It is only on the basis of the context, the comment '. . . is our pig', that the pig is interpreted as the pragmatic antecedent of a relative clause in (38). In a different context the first clause of (38) may mean 'When/because/while they killed that pig . . .'.

Consider also these adverbial clause interpretations of preposed -*kha*-marked clauses without head noun:

(44) ne-fimelon lép-telo-bo-kha   kholüma-té-do
      my-intestines ill-be-stay.3SG.REAL-CONN treat.disease.with.magic-3PL.REAL-DS

      'Because my inner parts were ill, they treated (me) with magic and . . .'

(45) imonè kha-khe-tél-e-kha-fè   menèl lu-kha-té
      now   go-IRR-3PL-TR-CONN-TOP quickly arrive-IRR-3PL

      'If they go now, they will arrive early.'

(46) le-mén-dakhu nokhu lép-telo-khai-kha   nokhu mano-pa-mon-do
      eat-2PL.IMP-SS we   ill-be-3SG.IRR-CONN us   good-SUPP-2PL.IMP-DS
      khi-telo-fon-è
      healthy-be-1SG.INTENT-EXCL

      'You must eat it and in case we fall ill, you must cure us so we can be healthy!'

Such initial adverbials with -*kha* may also occur extraclausally, separated by pauses or speaker-continuation markers, like *khenè* in (47), from the clause for which they present the relevant frame or thematic setting:

(47) lefé-lelup   difo-kha-fè   khenè y-afé   du-lekhül
      kind.of.bananas-sprig be.pulled.out.3SG.REAL-CONN-TOP next his-older.brother tree-?
      alop   du-lekhül-fekho ao-top   di-pükh-mekho
      firstborn tree-?-CIRCUM   plant-place pull.loose-throw.away-SUPP.3SG.REAL

      'Because his bananas had been pulled out, next he went to his eldest brother's garden and pulled out his planting and threw it away . . .'

(48) sekhula lekhé . . . wé-ma-lé-kha . . .   èpalap anèl-é
      school   PURPOSE continue-SUPP-1SG.REAL-CONN all right go.ahead-EXCLM
      dé
      QUOTE.3SG.REAL

      'As far as the school goes, with respect to my continuing (school), he said, "All right, go ahead!"'.

The -*kha*-marked subordinate clause in (48) is an extraclausal constituent that specifies the relevant framework in which to understand the quote 'All right, go ahead'.

It is these initial -*kha* adverbials, both extraclausal and intraclausal, that optionally but often take the topic marker -*efè* to mark their specific informational role of setting or frame.[6]

A special type of -*kha*-marked initial adverbial is the 'although' form, with the relational verb *amokha* 'although'.

(49) nu fédo-ngga-fè[7]   amokha be-leléal-mo-da
      I   give-INF.CONN-TOP although NEG-glad-SUPP.3SG.REAL-NEG

'Although I gave it, he did not accept it.'

Amokha consists of the third singular realis form of the verb *amo*- 'to do/be thus'. The data on *amokha* all show an adversative sense ('although'); furthermore, *amokha* always follows infinitival subordinate clauses marked with -*kha* and -*efè* 'topic'. Literally, the form translates as 'given that it happened that way/given that it was that way'.

(50) nu kha-un-ngga-fè   amokha b-amo-n-din-da
      I   go-INF-CONN-TOP although NEG-do.thus-INF-impossible-NEG

'Although I tried to walk, it was impossible to do so.'

Bamondinda is a -*din* form of *amo*-. This verb is used twice in (50), first as a relational verb ('although') and then as a regular verb that means 'to do that/thus'. Notice the infinitival form of this type of adverbial -*kha* clause. The more usual form for initial or preposed adverbial -*kha* clauses is the finite form, whereas for noninitial clausal complements of verbs, the infinitival form is the usual one.

Clausal goal complements with -*kha* occur with certain verbs and adjectives used in aspect periphrasis and with the verb *lekhénma*- 'to intend, to want'. These -*kha*-marked goal clauses do not have the setting or framing role that initial finite adverbial clauses with -*kha* tend to have, and accordingly the topic marker -*efè* has not been found on such goal complements with -*kha*.

Compare, first, the use of -*kha*-marked goal complements with *lekhénma*-:

(51) nu khof-e-kha   abül u-ngga   lekhén-ma-lé
      I   that-TR-CONN man hit-INF.CONN purpose-SUPP-1SG.REAL

'I meant to hit that man.'

The verbalising support verb is used to verbalise the noun *lekhén* 'reason, purpose, goal' in (51). In the next example, this (relational) noun *lekhén* is the head noun of an adverbial purpose phrase in which an infinitival clause modifier is linked to the relational head noun with -*kha* (lit. 'We are going the reason of bathing in the Lalop').

(52) nokhup Lalop dad-ungga-lekhé   khai-mba-lé
      we   Lalop bath-INF.CONN-reason go-PROGR-1SG.REAL

'We are on our way to bathe in the Lalop River.'

The next examples show the use of *-kha* clauses as complements of periphrastic aspect verbs:

(53) nu dépo-ngga   wé-ma-lé
   I smoke-INF.CONN continuous-SUPP-1SG.REAL

   'I smoke continuously.'

(54) nu dépo-ngga   solditai-mo-mba-lé
   I smoke-INF.CONN begin-SUPP-PROGR-1SG.REAL

   'I am beginning to smoke.'

(55) nu dépo-ngga   kemél-mo-mba-lé
   I smoke-INF.CONN usual-SUPP-PROGR-1SG.REAL

   'I usually (habitually) smoke.'

(56) nu dépo-ngga   lefaf
   I smoke-INF.CONN finished

   'I have finished smoking.'

(57) nu fono-ndé-e-kha   lefaf
   I eat-1SG.REAL-TR-CONN finished

   'I already have eaten.'

The verbalising element *mo/a-*, glossed as a support verb in the examples, literally means 'to do/to be'. The periphrastic aspect verbs *wémo-* 'to do continuously', *kemélmo-* 'to do usually', and so on take infinitival complements ('I do the smoking continuously').

Both subordination with *-kha* and chaining linkage are used to connect the periphrastic aspectual verb clause and the preceding clause. Compare (58) and (59):

(58) nu dépe-nè wé-ma-lé
   I smoke-SS continuous-SUPP-1SG.REAL

   'I smoke continuously.' [Lit. 'I smoke and do (that) continuously.']

(59) nu dépo-ngga   wé-ma-lé
   I smoke-INF.CONN continuous-SUPP-1SG.REAL

   'I smoke continuously.' [Lit. 'I do the smoking continuously.']

Chaining linkage and subordinate linkage

To summarise, chaining linkage of clauses differs from subordinate linkage with *-kha*. Chained clauses cannot take the topic marker *-(f)efè*; *-kha* clauses can take the topic marker. Chained clauses express switch-reference relations with the next clause; *-kha*-linked clauses cannot take switch-reference conjunctions.

The fact that chained clauses cannot take the topic or setting marker *-(f)efè* does not mean that these clauses cannot present topical or setting information; in fact they often do (e.g., with chained counterfactual and temporal setting clauses). Chaining linkage being by far the most frequent way to connect clauses, it is not surprising that chained clauses can present a great variety of types of information (focal, topical/setting, recapitulative).

The fact that subordinate clauses with *-kha* may take the topic marker does not imply that these clauses tend to be topical or setting clauses. Only preposed and clause-initial 'adverbial' clauses with *-kha* show a strong tendency to attract the topic or setting marker in Korowai. In itself, subordinate linkage with *-kha* is, just like chaining linkage, a very neutral type of linkage that occurs in a wide range of contexts, which determine its interpretation. Within noun phrases, *-kha* clauses function as prenominal relative clauses. With perception and cognition verbs, *-kha* clauses, although formally subordinate, pragmatically function as main clauses that express the main assertion [see example (42) and (43) above]. With certain verbs and adjectives used in aspect periphrasis and with the verb *lekhénma-* 'to intend, to want', *-kha* clauses express the goal argument.

Linkage of clause chains

The process of clause chaining results in units that may be called clause chains. Boundaries between clause chains generally are well marked: chain-final clauses are clauses without switch-reference conjunctions and with a final (falling) intonation. In the majority of cases, the presence of specific chain-linking devices gives additional evidence for chain boundaries.

By far the most frequent chain-linking device in our texts is tail-head linkage, a recapitulative device. The term *tail-head linkage* (*t-h linkage*) is from Thurman (1975). It refers to a phenomenon that is 'extremely common in Papuan languages, especially in narrative texts. Such texts are littered with dozens of examples of this usage' (Foley 1986: 201).[8] Longacre (1972: 45) has described the phenomenon as follows: 'Commonly the function of the first base in such chaining units is to refer back to the last base of the previous chain. If the chain structures as a paragraph, then such back-reference or recapitulation joins paragraph to paragraph.' The final clause of the previous chain is the tail. The first clause of the new chain that recapitulates information from that final tail clause is called the head. The head clause in tail-head linkage is sometimes called paragraph setting (Longacre 1972: 47). Healy (1966), who describes the recapitulation phenomenon for the levels of sentence, paragraph, and discourse in the Ok language Telefol, uses the term *paragraph margin* for the recapitulated first clause of the paragraph.

Foley (1986: 200) suggests that tail-head recapitulation is linked up with (topical) subordination in Papuan languages, but in Korowai and in Awyu languages in general tail-head recapitulation strongly prefers (nonsubordinate) chaining linkage. Consider discourse (60)–(62), with three clause chains, linked by tail-head linkage:

(60) wof-è   gol ül-ma-té-dakhu   bando-lu   khaim-an   fe-nè fu
     there-CONN pig kill-SUPP-3PL.REAL-SS bring-enter.SS treehouse-LOC get-SS put.SS
     bume-ma-té
     slaughter-HAB-3PL.REAL

     'After they have killed a pig there, they usually bring it, and having put it into the house they slaughter it.'

(61) bume-ma-té-dakhu   ol   di   fe-nè fu-ma-té-do   ni-khü-to
slaughter-HAB-3PL.REAL-SS faeces get.out.SS take-SS put-HAB-3PL-DS mother-PL-FOC
bando-khe-nè ao-ma-té
bring-go-SS   cleanse-HAB-3PL

'They slaughter it and remove the feces and put it down and the women take (the intestines) and cleanse it.'

(62) Ao-leful-mekho   khaim   gilfo-ma-té-do   gol-e-khal di-fu-ma-té
cleanse-end-SUPP.SS treehouse go.away-HAB-3PL-DS pig-TR-meat cut-put-HAB-3PL

'When they have finished washing they go away to the treehouse and (the males) cut the pig meat out and put it down.'

The final clause of chain (61) is recapitulated in the dependent verb SS clause *aolefulmekho* 'having cleansed' in (62). Similarly, the tail of (60) is repeated verbatim in the head of (61), *bumematédakhu*, with the SS clitical conjunction -*dakhu* signalling the nonsubordinate chaining type of linkage.

Notice that by using switch-reference marked chained clauses in t-h linkage, the monitoring of participants is carried over chain boundaries and the event line of the preceding chain is continued without interruption in the new chain.

Of course, instead of repeating the last clause or verb by t-h linkage, speakers can connect clause chains by pointing back in the first clause of the new chain to the information of the last verb or clause of the preceding chain. This can be done, for example, with generic verbs of doing or being in which a deictic is integrated (e.g., see the use of *wamo-* 'do thus/that' as a discourse-linkage verb in the next section). But connecting clause chains by pointing back with deictic adverbs or deictic verbs is less frequent than t-h linkage.

Tentatively, we can say that tail-head linkage is a continuity device: it continues the event line and the participant line across chain boundaries. Given the high frequency of t-h linkage, its *absence* is a marked transition between chains and might indicate some sort of thematic discontinuity in the progression of the text. Consider (63)–(67):

(63) wo   lül   lai-bo-top-ta   ao-mekho   ye khülo
there fallen.down.tree broken-stay.3SG.REAL-place-LOC plant-SUPP.SS he upstream
ye-mom-él   bolüp   ye lokhté
his-mother's.brother-PL clan.territory he go.away.3SG.REAL

'There at the broken trees' place he planted (a banana sprig) and then he went away upstream to his mother's brothers' territory.'

(64) ye lokhté-do   walüp-ta   walüp-ta   makhaya au-pekho-do
he go.away.3SG.REAL-DS half.way-LOC half.way-LOC kind.of.bat voice-SUPP.3SG.REAL-DS
wa-fekho   ye khülo ye khe-bo-fekho   gup-to   anè
there-CIRCUM he upstream he go-stay.3SG.REAL-until you-FOC ADHORT
da-mo-m-é   dé
hear-SUPP-2SG.IMP-EXCLM QUOTE.3SG.REAL

'He went away and halfway a *makhaya* bat squeaked and there he went upstream and he commanded (the little bat): "You should let me know".'

(65) khe-nè da-mo-m-é   dé-do   ye lokhté
      go-SS   hear-SUPP-2SG.IMP-EXCLM   QUOTE.3SG.REAL-DS   he go.away.3SG.REAL
      khe-bo   khe-bo   khe-bo   khe-bo
      go-stay.3SG.REAL   go-stay.3SG.REAL   go-stay.3SG.REAL   go-stay.3SG.REAL
      khe-bo   ye lokhte-bo   lu   ye-mom-él
      go-stay.3SG.REAL   he   go.away-3SG.PERF.REAL   enter.SS   his-mother's.brother-PL
      bolü-fekho   babo   babo
      clan.territory-CIRCUM   stay.3SG.REAL   stay.3SG.REAL

      'And after he commanded, "You should let me know", he went away and he walked
      and walked a long time, and having gone and having entered his mother's brothers'
      territory, he lived there for quite a long time.'

(66) ye-lu-lo   walé-do   makhaya khe-nè mèkh-mo   él
      sleep-NEAR-3SG   daybreak.REAL.3SG-DS   kind.of.bat   go-SS   squeak-SUPP.SS   yes
      kü-té-kha   wof-ap   dé-kha-fè   wa-fosübo
      right-be.3PL.REAL-CONN   there-LOC   QUOTE.3SG.REAL-CONN-TOP   there-be.downstream
      wai   lai
      move.down.SS   come.3SG.REAL

      'One day he had slept and the next morning the *makhaya* bat came and squeaked: "It's
      all right over there!" and so he came downstream there.'

(67) wa-fosübo   wai   ale-bo-do   khai-tofekho
      there-be.downstream   move.down.SS   walk-stay.3SG.REAL-DS   go.3SG.REAL-DS.but

      'He went downstream there and he walked but . . .'

In this text, chain (63) is connected to the next chain, (64), by t-h linkage. Similarly,
chains (64) and (65) are linked by t-h linkage and the discourse-relational verb *khenè*
'next'. But chain (65) is not connected by t-h linkage or deictic linkage to the next
chain, (66). The story takes a new turn in (66) with the message of the *makhaya* bat.
It could be that the absence of tail-head linkage (or other overt recapitulative or
anaphoric linkage) correlates with the thematic discontinuity in (66); but of course
thematic (dis)continuity is difficult to establish independently. Chain (66) is again
linked to the following one by t-h linkage.

Discourse linkage verbs

Verbs of doing and going are often used as discourse conjunctions in texts of Awyu-
family languages to provide linkages between chunks of the discourse, both within
and between chains (e.g., Wambon: de Vries 1989; Kombai: de Vries 1993b: 59). In
the Korowai texts of chapter 6, the forms *khenè* (lit. 'going'), *anè/(w)amo(l)mo* ('thus
doing'), and *amodo* ('he did so and' / 'thus it happened and . . .') are frequently used
to link chunks of the discourse. They may be glossed as 'and', 'next', and 'furthermore'. They may have a recapitulative chain-linkage function, express speaker continuation ('the next thing I tell you is . . .'), or provide a pause. Consider the following examples from the texts:

(68) gekhené if-e-kha   gol-mél   bando-khe-nè le-mén-dakhu nokhu
     you   this-TR-CONN pig-forepaw bring-go-SS   eat-2PL.IMP-SS us
     im-ba-mon-è
     see-stay-2PL.IMP-EXCLM

'You should take this forepaw of the pig and eat it, and pay attention to us."

(69) wa-mol-mo   mamaf bau   énon-mekho
     thus-SUPP-SUPP.3SG.REAL a.little   stay.3SG.REAL prolonged-SUPP.SS

'Having done this way, they stay for a while.'

The generic verb of doing, *wamo-*, is used to link (68) and (69) in a recapitulative fashion.

In (70)–(74), *khenè* 'and/next' is repeatedly used to provide linkage between a related series of discourse chunks:

(70) lefé-lelup   difo-kha-fè   khenè y-afé
     kind.of.bananas-sprig be.pulled.out.3SG.REAL-CONN-TOP next   his-older.brother
     dulekhül alop   dulekhül-fekho ao-top   di-pükh-mekho
     garden   firstborn garden-CIRCUM plant-DS.but pull.loose-throw.away-SUPP.3SG.REAL

'As for the bananas being pulled out, he went to his eldest brother's garden and planted one but he (the eldest brother) pulled it out and threw it away.'

(71) khenè alüf-e-kha   dulekhül-fekho ao-top
     next   in.between.one-TR-CONN garden-CIRCUM plant-DS.but
     di-pükh-mekho
     pull.loose-throw.away-SUPP.3SG.REAL

'And having gone to the next brother's garden, he planted one but he (the next brother) pulled it out and threw it away.'

(72) khenè alüf-e-kha   dulekhül-fekho ao-top
     next   in.between.one-TR-CONN garden-CIRCUM plant-DS.but
     di-pükh-mekho
     pull.loose-throw.away-SUPP.3SG.REAL

'And having gone to the next brother's garden, he planted but he (the next brother) pulled it out and threw it away.'

(73) khenè khaja-lo   alüf-e-kha   dulekhül-fekho ao-to-fekho
     next   lastborn-FOC in.between.one-TR-CONN garden-CIRCUM plant-place-CIRCUM
     di-pükh-mekho-ta
     pull.loose-throw.away-SUPP.3SG.REAL-?

'And then the last born went to the next brother's garden and he planted, but he (the next brother) pulled it out and threw it away.'

(74) khenè ye-pa   lül   lai-bo-top-ta   ao-mekho
     next   him-self fallen.down.tree broken-stay.3SG.REAL-place-LOC plant-SUPP.SS

'And then he himself planted (a banana sprig) at a broken trees' place.'

Khenè in examples like (70)–(74) has the same general meaning, glossed as 'next', that the adverb *mesé* or *sé* 'again' often has in discourse [e.g., in text of *The Pig Sacrifice*, chapter 6, (11), (18), and (24)].

In (75) and (76), *amodo* is twice used to indicate speaker continuation ('and next I tell you'):

(75) senggile-lé   amo-do   mé-bol dami-mo   le-nè
      be.frightened-1SG.REAL do.3SG.REAL-DS earth-hole open-SUPP.SS come-SS
      lu-ba-lé   dé-do
      enter-PERF-1SG.REAL quote.3SG.REAL-DS

      '"I was frightened, and having opened the grave I came and entered", he reported and . . .'

(76) gele-tél   amo-do   lelip   khami-ba-té-fekho
      be.afraid-3PL.REAL do.3SG.REAL-DS together sit-stay-3PL.REAL-until

      'they were afraid and they stayed together until . . .'

Topical and focal kinds of information

-(f)efè: topic

There are three recurrent elements in notional definitions of topics in the literature. First, topics are discourse entities or discourse referents. Second, the speaker assumes that these entities are easily accessible for the addressee. Third, the speaker intends the addressee to attach incoming propositional information to these easily accessible entities ('aboutness').

A typical topic definition along these lines is that of Lambrecht (1988: 146), who defines topic as 'the relation of *aboutness* holding between a referent and a proposition in a particular context'. Although 'aboutness' is the central element in most topic definitions (see, e.g., Dik 1989: 266; Gundel 1988: 210; Lambrecht 1988: 146), it is the most elusive element and is usually posited without much explication.

With a few exceptions, this topic notion of propositional/clausal aboutness coincides with the subject in Korowai: the clause in the overwhelming majority of cases in Korowai texts is 'about' the subject, and subject-related morphology like switch reference and person-number agreements help the addressee to identify the referent 'about' which the clause communicates something.[9] Active and semiactive referents (in the sense of Chafe 1987), generally seen in the literature as the 'highest' on topicality scales or 'best' topics (see Lambrecht 1988), form the overwhelming majority of referents of the subjects in Korowai texts.

But this clausal/propositional 'aboutness' topicality is different from the kind of topicality marked by the Korowai topic marker *-(f)efè*. This marker seems to be a processual device (pause/hesitation), and a device to organise chunks of discourse 'into manageable units of material so strung together that all that precedes at any point is in a loose, cumulative sense of the word "topic" for what follows', to use the wording of Bromley (1981: 328).

Because of the parallels between the Korowai topic marker *-(f)efè* and the Dani topic marker *-he/-te*, it is worthwhile to consider the analysis of the latter by Bromley

(1981) in more detail. Dani is a Papuan language of the Balim valley of Irian Jaya, in the mountains northwest of the Korowai area. The Dani clitic *-he (-te* after vowels) occurs most frequently in the sentence-initial position, at points for possible pause; especially when speakers hesitatingly build up their sentence, the clitic is frequent. In the beginning of discourses, it is not uncommon to find multiple occurrences of *-he*, also within single-verb clauses. But *-he* may also occur sentence-medially and sentence-finally with 'afterthought topics'. If it does so occur, it always marks thematic material.

Here follows a typical example of a narrative sentence in Dani with eight occurrences of the topic marker *-he/-te* (Bromley 1981: 328):

(77) (a) lakakusik-he,
           we.went.up.long.ago.prior-TOP

      (b) ikke-pa   lakaku   lakaku lakaku lakaku lakaku lakaku-te
           plateau-on we.went.long.ago (repet.)   we.went.long.ago-TOP

      (c) Hvehenema   noko-isu-kusik-he
           Huehenema(place) we.slept.long.ago.prior-TOP

      (d) moso sit   appik-en-he
           rain drizzle much-source-TOP

      (e) we sit   appik-en-he
           idle drizzle much-source-TOP

      (f) we welakaku   welakaku welakaku-te
           idle we.were.long.ago (repet.)   we.were.long.ago-TOP

      (g) likke pvlem-at   kisukusik-he
           midday middle-PREDICATOR we.entered.long.ago-TOP

      (h) Jvkheakeima noko-usa'-mekke-te
           at.Jukeagima   sleep.ought.to-ADVERSATIVE-TOP

      (i) it, mel   lak,
           they,dummy and.associates

      (j) Waesom mel
           Waesom too

      (k) Wenakasvky mel,
           Wenakasugi   too

      (l) it pykkyt-at   lakoukwha.
           they directly-PREDICATOR they.went.long.ago

'After we climbed up, we kept going on and on along the plateau, and after we slept at Huehenema, because of the heavy drizzle, we just waited idly, waited and waited; we had gone in at midday and should have slept at Jukeagima, but they, what's-their-names, Waesom and Wenagasugi, they went straight on.'

In his comment on this example, Bromley (1981: 329) notes that some of the units in (77), segments (b) and (f), have finite verbs not marked for dependence on a following verb and that 'grammatically, the units marked with *-he/-te* are disparate, but the occurrence of this clitic has the effect of levelling them as units of information or text.' The following example illustrates the multiple occurrence of -*he* in a simple sentence with a single verb:

(78) nen hat-he   hamelaik-he   helan
     then you(sg)-TOP your.bailer.shell-TOP take.it.yourself
     'You take your bailer shell yourself!'

It seems to us that the topic clitic -*he* has both a speaker-oriented and an addressee-oriented function. The former is the processual function as a pause/hesitation marker. The latter is the thematic function, to signal to the addressee the units of information that form a framework for what follows.

On the basis of this analysis, one would predict a decrease of the use of the topic marker in written texts, where the processual pause/hesitation function of the marker is not relevant. It is interesting that Dani written texts show a sharp decrease in frequency of the marker -*he*; the multiplied occurrences of the marker especially prompt negative reactions from Dani readers, the tendency being not 'to eliminate all instances of -*he* but rather to limit them frequently to one per sentence, where the clitic occurs attached to an element that may be considered as topical for the sentence' (Bromley 1981: 329).

The Korowai -*(f)efè* has a double processual/thematic function that resembles the Dani -*he*. It occurs with all sorts of constituents (not just noun phrases that denote discourse referents), especially in contexts where the speaker builds up the world of discourse. The Korowai -*efè* shares with the Dani -*he* the connection with intonational breaks, hesitations, and pauses. Also the multiplied occurrences in the first sentence of a discourse are typical for the Korowai topic marker. The Korowai -*(f)efè* also occurs discourse-medially, but multiplied occurrences are rarer there, except where the narrator hesitates or has complex material to express.

Consider the following opening utterances of a Korowai myth of origin (see the *Ginol Silamtena* text in chapter 6):

(79) mül-khuf-efè af-efè   lamol fu-bo-kha   abül-fefè yu lamol
     former-time-TOP there-TOP universe put-3SG.PERF.REAL-CONN man-TOP he universe
     menil   fe-nè   fu-dakhu
     fire   get-SS   put-SS
     'In former times the one who had created the universe set the universe on fire.'

In this first clause of the text, the topic marker -*efè* occurs three times, the first two times with the typical pause-marking rise-fall-rise contour on the topic clitic. It occurs with constituents that denote the time, place, and participant framework. This framework in (79) is the setting not only for the immediately following clause ('he set the universe on fire') but also for the discourse as a whole.

Consider the following opening section of a totem story (see chapter 6, *The Origin of the Khomei Clan*):

(80) nokhuf-efè mül-khuf-efè buom   buom   buom-da-é   apa
     we-TOP   former-time-TOP kind.of.lizard kind.of.lizard kind.of.lizard-NEG-EXCLM only

ye-nggé bembüo-lo lai-dakhu-fekho
his-friend lizard-FOC   break.3SG.REAL-SS-and

'As for us, in former times, the white house lizard, the white house lizard ... not the house lizard, only its friend, it was the little brown wood lizard('s eggs) that hatched out and ...'

(81) lai-bando-khe-nè lefu-fefè wola -khip gil-bolüp   fu-dakhu
     come-bring-go-SS   some-TOP   earth-over   ceremonial.festival.place-place put.3SG.REAL-SS
     lefu-fefè bando-khe-nè nokhu dif-e-kha-la   fu-dakhu
     some-TOP bring-go-SS   our   this-TR-CONN-LOC put.3SG.REAL-SS
     wa-mo-bo-kha-fefè   wof-è   nokhup laibo-kha-fefè
     thus-SUPP-3SG.PERF.REAL-CONN-TOP that-CONN us   be.born.3SG.REAL-CONN-TOP

'some (of the result, i.e., lots of people) he brought away and put them on a festival place, others he transported and placed them in our area, and given that he has done so ... that is (the story of) our origin.'

(82) amo-do   mül-khuf-efè af-efè   du-lalé yakhuo-talé   alobo-dom-pekho
     do.3SG.REAL-DS former-time-TOP there-TOP tree-big yakhuo.tree-big stand-3SG.REAL-DS-and
     wap-ta-sü Khinggo-imban-tom-pekho mumengga fuai-mémo-tofekho   sé
     there-LOC-at Khinggo-member-FOC-ATTENT dog   hunt-3SG.IMM.REAL-DS next
     Khomey nokhu laibo-kha   abül khol-mémo
     Khomey   our   be.born.3SG.REAL-CONN   man   walk-3SG.IMM.REAL

'he did so, and in former times that big tree . . . the big *yakhuol* tree stood there, a member of the Khinggo clan together with a dog just was hunting, as the Khomey, namely, the man who brought us forth, was walking there . . .'

The topic marker occurs nine times in these utterances; and just like the Dani *-he*, the Korowai topic marker seems to be more connected with the online production of thematically coherent speech, with building up the world of the discourse in the initial paragraph, than with indicating which referents are the cognitive grounding points 'about' which propositions or clauses supply information.

Consider, finally, the following example:

(83) lamol fu   mano-mano-po-dakhu-fekho
     world   set.SS in.order-right-SUPP.3SG.REAL-SS-and

'He created the world and he made it very good . . .'

(84) fu   mano-manop-khayan-mekhol-e-kha-fè
     set.SS   right-right-very-SUPP.3SG.REAL-TR-CONN-TOP
     mbakha-mbonè   yano-fè   mbakha-mo-kha-té-kholo
     what-do.INTENT.PROGR.3SG people-TOP what-SUPP-IRR-3PL-Q
     de-mémo-tofekho
     QUOTE-3SG.IMM.REAL-DS.but

'but as he had created it and made it very very good he just wondered what should be done about humankind.'

The clauses in (83)–(84) communicate information 'about' the subject, the creator Ginol Silamtena, and contextual clues in combination with switch-reference and agreement morphology help the listener to identify this 'aboutness' topic. But again the contribution of *-(f)efè* is in the organisation of the speech in thematic chunks that provide the setting for the information to follow, as well as linkage to the information that was just given. For example, the recapitulated sentence ('given that he made it very good') in (84) provides the setting for the next information ('what about humankind?'), whereas the SS suffix and the 3SG agreement of (84) make it possible for the listener to infer 'about' whom the discourse continues to communicate information (i.e., the creator Ginol).

The initial constituents marked by *-(f)efè* may be both clause-external constituents, separated by a pause from the following clause, or they may occupy the first position in the clause, intonationally integrated in that clause. For example, in (79) above, the constituents *mülkhufefè* and *afefè* are intonationally integrated in the clause, but in (80) *nokhufefè* and *mülkhufefè* are clause-external. There are no other than intonational criteria for the clause-externality of these thematic constituents.

Focus-clitics, interjections, and expletive nouns

This section is a first and tentative inventory of attention and focus devices found in the texts. These attention devices may be speaker-, message-, or addressee-oriented; that is, the devices may be used to focus the attention on salient parts of the message, to attract the attention of the addressee, or to focus on the attitudes and emotions of the speaker.

Focus clitics

We start with two message-oriented attention devices, the focus clitics *-to* and *-é*, which can best be discussed in opposition to the topic clitic *-(f)efè*, just described. The topic clitic *-(f)efè* is used discourse- and chain-initially, with constituents that provide the setting or framework for the discourse. Having established the discourse setting, the speaker proceeds to make his or her point, and when the speaker wants to highlight parts of the message in doing so, he or she may use either *-to* or *-é*.

Consider again example (80), the opening sentence of a totem story; we find the topic clitic in the first two constituents, where the speaker builds up the setting or framework. When the speaker proceeds to make the point about the lizard, the totem animal, he uses both *-é* and *-to* to highlight crucial pieces of information.

Although there is some overlap in the use of both clitics, as in (80), they have a basic division of labour. The clitic *-é* usually occurs with predicates and has an exclamative-emphatic nature (rather strong intonational prominence). The clitic *-to* occurs in referring noun phrases, nonexclamative, with only slight intonational prominence, very often occurring in noun phrases that refer to human participants that have local or global importance in the text.

THE FOCUS CLITIC *-é*   The focus clitic *-é* cliticises to the last word of the predicate. The word that takes *-é* stands out intonationally since it is pronounced in an exclamative fashion with some lengthening of *-é*. Thus, *-é* is typically used when the speaker wants to assert or command something emphatically. Consider the following examples (from *The Pig Sacrifice* text, chapter 6):

(85) iè   wof-e-kha   mbolo-fekho   ge-mba-mbam-pekho ge-yano-fekho
    EXCLM there-TR-CONN ancestor-COORD your-child-child-COORD your-people-COORD

    'Oh, forefather over there, and your children and your people . . .'

(86) if-e-kha   gol-khobül bando-khe-nè le-mén-é
    this-TR-CONN pig-leg   bring-go-SS   eat-2PL.IMP-EXCLM

    '. . . you should take this leg of the pig away and eat it . . .'

(87) le-mén-dakhu mano-pa-mon-é
    eat-2PL.IMP-SS good-SUPP-2PL.IMP-EXCLM

    'you should eat it and help (us)!'

Examples (85)–(87) form part of a forceful address to the ancestors in the context of a pig sacrifice. The first attention device is the interjection *iè* preceding the vocative phrase, an addressee-oriented attention device to which we shall return below. The second is the exclamative focus clitic *-é* in the imperative predicates in (86) and (87). Notice that the exclamative vowel is absent when the first imperative verb is repeated in the tail-head recapitulation of (87).

We see the focus clitic *-é* with nominal predicates in (88):

(88) nu laléo-da-é   nu yanof-é   dé-to
    I bad.spirit-NEG-EXCLM I person-EXCLM say.3SG.REAL-DS

    '"I am not a spirit, I am a man", he said.'

We have (only) two examples in our data in which emphasis on predicates is marked with the element *-kha*:

(89) Naomi-lo   alé-kha
    Naomi-FOC make.3SG.REAL-EMPH

    'Naomi made it.'

(90) yu ülmekho-ngga kemél-e-kha
    he shoot-INF.CONN be.knowing-TR-EMPH

    'He knows how to shoot!'

THE FOCUS CLITIC *-to*   Consider the following examples of *-to* in narrative material:

(91) mül-alüp mbolo-mbolop-to   mbolo-mbolop mahüon uma-té-do
    former-time ancestor-ancestor-FOC ancestor-ancestor story   tell-3p.REAL-DS

    'In former days the forefathers told a story to the (next generations of) forefathers and . . .'

(92) abül-fekha khomilo-bo-kha   mahüon uma-té-do
    man-a.certain die-3SG.PERF.REAL-CONN story   tell-2PL.REAL-DS

    '. . . the story of a man who died they told . . .'

(93) n-até   dai-bo-fekho   n-até-lo   nu umo
     my-father hear-3SG.PERF.REAL-until my-father-FOC me tell.3SG.REAL

'. . . and my father heard it until it was my father who told it to me.'

Examples (91)–(93) form the introductory utterances of a story. In such introductions, the evidential sources for the story [in this case the (fore)fathers of the narrator] are in focus, and this is marked by -*to*. Sometimes -*to* is accompanied by -*fekho*, which is normally used as a coordinator or as a circumstantial case suffix (see chapter 3, Comitative suffixes) but which seems to have a attention-related function in these focal contexts:

(94) khol-mémo-do   fulo-dakhu-fekho mumengga-lom-pekho sé
     walk-3SG.IMM.REAL-DS   meet-SS-and   dog-FOC-ATTENT   next
     ye-mumengga-lena ülmo
     his-dog-little   kill.3SG.REAL

'He just walked there and they met each other and it was the dog that killed his little dog'.

In the following examples, we see -*to* (here in the variant -*tu*) with a nominal predicate in (95) and with an adjectival predicate in (96):

(95) nokhu-yanop-tu de-té
     our-people-FOC   say-3PL.REAL

'It is our people, they said.'

(96) a   nu bo-khofél-aup-da nu mokhefup-tu
     EXCLM I   NEG-lie-word-NEG I   true-FOC

'Ah, I don't lie, I speak the truth!'

On the basis of narrative occurrences, as in (91), it would be very hard to establish the focus nature of -*to* without circularity. But if we look at contexts that have some cross-linguistic validity as focality-inducing conditions (see Dik 1989), such as question-word questions and explicitly contrastive expressions, we indeed find -*to* in the constituents predicted by these tests to have informational saliency of focality:

(97) ne-mbam-o nuf-è   laléo-da yanop-tu
     my-child-VOC I-CONN spirit-NEG human-FOC

'My child, I am not a spirit but a human being.'

(98) yakhop-to nu ne-gol ülmo?
     who-FOC I   my-pig kill.3SG.REAL

'Who killed my pig?'

(99) nu gol-e-khal tanukh-to lé-akha-lé
     I   pig-TR-meat only-FOC eat-IRR-1SG

'I shall eat only pork.'

We see -*to* in (97) in a contrastive context, in (98) in a question word, and in (99) in a selective context (one of a set is selected)—three contexts generally associated with message-oriented focality (see Dik 1989: 277–288).

THE VOCATIVE CLITIC -*o*   The focus-clitics -*to* and -*é* are intraclausal focus devices, used to highlight parts of the message, but there is also a number of focus or attention devices that are used extraclausally: the vocative clitic -*o* and interjections. These extraclausal attention devices seem to be connected with the speaker and addressee rather than with parts of the message.

Vocative noun phrases are optionally but usually marked by -*o*. Vocative noun phrases are intonationally prominent, with the vowel of the vocative clitic usually lengthened:

(100) hey   n-até-o   golo-m-belén-é   nu kolufo-yanof-é
       EXCLM my-father-VOC be.afraid-2SG.IMP-NEG-EXCLM I   Korowai-person-EXCLM
       dé-to
       say.3SG.REAL-DS
       'He said, "Hey, my father, do not be afraid! I am a Korowai person."'

In (100), both the interjection *hey* and the vocative focus clitic have to do with the speaker-addressee relation: the focus is not so much on (a part of) the message but on (getting the attention of) the addressee. However, the use of the exclamative clitic -*é* in the predicates in (100) is message-related.

There are exceptions to the rule that the exclamative vowel clitic -*o* is restricted to vocative noun phrases. In songs, the exclamative vowels -*é* and -*o* cooccur in verbs, as in (101), and sometimes just -*o* is used with the verbs, as in (102):

(101) khofé   mano-pelu-m-é-o
       youngster well-grow-2SG.ADHORT-EXCLM-EXCLM
       'Boy, you should grow well!'

(102) khakhül   melu-m-o
       khakhül.sago grow-2SG.ADHORT-EXCLM
       'Khakhül sago, you should grow!'

Interjections

Korowai speakers may insert a number of extraclausal exclamative vowels and vowel combinations to express emotional reactions or attitudes of the speaker; to attract the attention of the addressee; or to reinforce speech actions such as assertions, denials, warnings, commands, and adhortations.

The following interjections occur in the texts in emotional reactions to unexpected, shocking, astonishing, or fearful events: *wé, ü, wü, aü, i, aiè*. Here are examples of each of these interjections:

(103) ima-té-tofekho wé   khofél-apa
       see-3PL.REAL-DS EXCLM boy.EXCLM-only.EXCLM
       'They looked but—oh, boy!—...'

(104) khof-e-kha   khomilo-do   mé-laimekho-bakha-ti-kha abül   lu
that-TR-CONN die.REAL.3SG-DS earth-bury-HOD-3PL-CONN   male.person   go.upward.SS
falé   wü   nggé gu laléo lai-ati-bo-dakhu
appear.3SG.REAL EXCLM friend you demon come-hold-2SG.stay.REAL-SS
lelé-mbol-e-kholo-tè
come-2SG.PROGR.REAL-TR-Q-or

'that man who had died and whom they had buried that day did appear right now!, hey, friend, are you coming as a bad spirit, or . . .'

In this stretch of discourse, (103)–(104), the interjections *wé* and *wü* are used to indicate the strong emotions of fear and surprise caused by the sudden reappearance of a man who was supposed to stay in his grave (in which he had just been buried). In (105), the interjection *ü* is used in a context of fear:

(105) ü   nokhu golo-demil-me-lè
EXCLM we   be.afraid-run-SUPP-1PL.REAL
'Wow, we fled in fear.'

In (106), *iii* expresses fear:

(106) iii   gu laléo-lu   de-té-dakhu   yekhené golo-demil-me-té
EXCLM you bad.spirit-FOC say-3p.REAL-SS they   be.afraid-run-SUPP-3PL.REAL
'"Hush, you are a spirit, aren't you!", they replied.'

The interjection *aü* expresses an emotion of disappointment in (107):

(107) yakhatimekho   khaim   tu   lakhi-nè alü   fédo-tofekho   aü
renounce.3SG.REAL treehouse enter.SS stew-SS   bake.SS give.REAL.3SG-DS.but EXCLM
yakhatimekho
abandon.3SG.REAL

'She renounced and having entered the treehouse she stewed (grubs), offered it, but, oh, he refused.'

In (108), the vowel combination *aiè* is used in a context of great fear and anxiety:

(108) mbolo-mbolop   b-aup-da   nokhu bolüp-ta   nn   nokhu
older.people-older.people NEG-word-NEG we   clan.territory-LOC PAUSE we
gele-lè-lofekho   ü   yalén   mé-la-mé-la-mo-do
be.afraid-1PL.REAL-DS EXCLM respected.man   move-come-move-come-HAB.3SG-DS
aiè   gele-lè
EXCLM be.afraid-1PL.REAL

'The older people replied, "Do not say that, on our territories we are afraid, oh, when the respected man comes hence and forth, my! we are afraid."'

The following interjections occur in the texts in vocative contexts in which the attention of the addressee is sought: *iè* in example (109), *hey* in example (100), and *èé* in example (110):

(109) manop woto-fekha   fo   fe-nè fu   iè   wof-e-kha   maun-makho-ta
chest sacred.place-a.certain get.SS get-SS put.SS EXCLM there-TR-CONN river-mouth-LOC
bau-kha   abül-è
live.3SG.REAL-CONN male.person-CONN

'The chest they put on another sacred place and (they say), "Oh, man who lives there
at the mouth of the river . . ."'

(110) alè-debüf la-té-to   èé   mo kholfe-té   mo kholfe-té-do
canoe-way come-3PL.REAL-DS EXCLM just meet-3PL.REAL just meet-3PL.REAL-DS
hèé   golo-deme-té-do   n-até-o   belén-è
EXCLM be.afraid-run-3PL.REAL-DS my-father-VOC do.not.need.to-EXCLM
gole-tin-d-é   nu yanop le-ba-lé   dé
be.afraid-3PL.INTENT-NEG-EXCLM I   person come-PERF-1SG.REAL say.3SG.REAL

'By canoe they came, hey!—they wanted to meet, they wanted to meet—hey!—they fled
in fear, my father, you don't, you don't have to be afraid! I have come as a human being!'

The interjections *o* and *a* occur in the texts as interjections that reinforce illocutions,
such as denials and adhortations, but also seem to indicate emotional reactions.

In example (111), *a* is used to reinforce an adhortation:

(111) mbolo-mbolop   lefu-lon a   ülmekho-fon   de-té
older.people-older.people some-FOC EXCLM shoot-1PL.ADHORT say-3PL.REAL
'Some of the older people proposed, well, let us just shoot him.'

In example (112), *o* is used to reinforce a denial:

(112) o   manda-é khésekhan-é manda-é   dé
EXCLM no-EXCLM no-EXCLM   no-EXCLM say.3SG.REAL
'"Oh, no, no way, no", he said.'

In example (113), *o* is used not to reinforce an illocution but to express emotions of
the speaker:

(113) o   nokhup ni-khül-fekho mba-mbam-pekho   nokhu
EXCLM we   woman-PL-and child-child-and   we
golo-demil-me-lè   nokhu golo-demil-me-lè-do
be.afraid-run-SUPP-1PL.REAL we   be.afraid-run-SUPP-1PL.REAL-DS
mbolo-mbolop-tanukh   alo-ba-té   ili   wai
older.people-older.people-only stand-stay-3PL.REAL helicopter move.down.3SG.REAL

'Oh, and we, the women and the children, we fled in fear. We fled, only the older stood
as the helicopter landed . . .'

Finally, we have found emphatic-exclamative forms for the word 'yes' to reinforce
the affirmation *bailé*, as in (114), and *éluwo*, as in (115):

(114) gu mo gu gu lilol-benè dé-tofekho   U   bailé
you? you you falsehood-Q QUOTE.3SG.REAL-DS EXCLM oh.yes

dél-e-kha-lekhé
QUOTE.3SG.REAL-TR-CONN-therefore

'but perhaps you tell me lies, but he replied, "oh yes!", and therefore . . .'

(115) yakhatimekho-tofekho él-uwo   dé-kha-fefè
abandon.3SG.REAL-DS   yes-EXCLM say.3SG.REAL-CONN-TOP

'He refused and after she said, "Okay" . . .'

To reinforce the affirmation of *él* 'yes', the following nonverbal signs very often accompany the verbal affirmation: the chin is raised and the eyes open wide. Instead of using the verbal affirmation with *él* 'yes', a soft ingressive whistling sound may be produced, accompanying the raising of the chin and the widening of the eyes.

Spirits and friends: expletive nouns

Korowai has a closed class of expletive words that derive from nouns but function as interjections: semantically, they have no referents; syntactically, they do not have valency; and phonologically, they are always pronounced with intonational prominence.[10] For ease of reference, I call them expletive nouns.

The expletive nouns in our texts come from two sources: proper names of supernatural beings and nouns denoting 'dearness' relations (friend, companion, dear).

SPIRITS   The Korowai avoid personal names of people, let alone of supernatural beings. But as in so many other speech communities, it is words of taboo and avoidance that are used as expletives. We have found the following proper names of supernatural beings used as expletives: Ginol, the creator-spirit; Khufom, a water spirit; Gén, a river spirit; and Faül, a mythical pig.

Khufom and *gén* can be heard daily in Korowai conversations; they are popular expletives for everyday use. The use of names of spirits as swear words is subject to restrictions. For example, the name Gén, very often used in contexts of strong amazement, should not be used as a swear word close to the turn of the river Nailop, where this spirit lives. That could cause accidents and mishap.

As far as Faül goes, there is a myth of origin (see chapter 6) in which Faül occurs, first, to refer to the mythical pig, and much later in the same text, as an expletive noun. Consider first its nonexpletive use:

(116) meli-to ye mül-khup meli-to ye dofo-dakhu   sé   ap-ta
fire-with he former-time fire-with he be.burnt.RESULT.3SG.REAL-SS next there-LOC
maé-takhefi-mekho-do   khe-nè lokhté-do
water-open-SUPP.3SG.REAL-DS go-SS go.away.3SG.REAL-DS

'In former times with fire he had . . . with fire he had burnt and then there he had opened the (streams of) waters and it ran away.'

(117) ap-ta   alo-bo-dakhu-fekho   fo-ngg-alingga   lu-nè
there-LOC stand-stay.3SG.REAL-SS-and take-INF.CONN-without move.up-SUPP.SS
be-bakh-i   be-bakh-i   be-bakh-i   be-bakh-i
sit-HOD-3SG sit-HOD-3SG sit-HOD-3SG sit-HOD-3SG.REAL

'There he stood and he kept shoving aside (all of it) for a long time . . .'

(118) énonte-bo-tofekho   énonte-bakh-i-tofekho
      of.a.long.duration-stay.3SG.REAL-DS of.a.long.duration-HOD-3SG.REAL-DS

      'it had taken quite a period, but after a long time . . .'

(119) Faül dadü-ai-tofekho   Faül ül-nè bul-mekho-kha-fefè
      Faül swim-go.down.3SG.REAL-DS Faül kill-SS slaughter-SUPP.3SG.REAL-CONN-TOP
      Faül ba-nggolol yaüya-pé fe-nè fu   müf-e-kholol wola-khi-pé
      Faül chest-bone under-LOC get-SS put.3SG.REAL back-TR-bone world-over-LOC
      fe-nè fu-tofekho
      get-SS put.3SG.REAL-DS

      'Faül came swimming downstream, after having killed and slaughtered Faül, he put
      his chest-bone part (of meat) beneath (i.e., on the ground), his backbone part he placed
      toward the sky . . .'

In a much later episode of this text we meet the Original Couple, two brothers. The
older turns the younger brother into a woman by cutting off his penis and scrotum.
The older brother then has sex with his brother-turned-sister, but it does not feel good:

(120) khayal-yabén di-lu-dakhu   gomo-tofekho
      kind.of.fish-fat get.out-rub.3SG.REAL-SS have.sex.3SG.REAL-DS
      be-sikh-té-da-lelo-tofekho   malan-yabén di-lu-dakhu
      NEG-delicious-be.3PL.REAL-NEG-be.3SG.REAL-DS kind.of.snake-fat get.out-rub.3SG.REAL-SS
      gomo-tofekho   be-sikh-té-da-lelo-tofekho
      have.sex.3SG.REAL-DS NEG-delicious-be.3PL.REAL-NEG-be.3SG.REAL-DS

      'he rubbed with the fat of the *khayal* fish and had sex again, but it still did not feel
      good, so with the fat of the *malan* snake he rubbed, had sex again but still it was not
      nice and . . .'

(121) wap-ta milon   sip   non   dé-dakhu-fekho
      there-LOC kind.of.sago root.end sago.grub get.out.3SG.REAL-SS-and
      lu-lu-dakhu-fekho   gomo-tofekho
      rub-rub.3SG.REAL-SS-and have.sex.3SG.REAL-DS

      'there he got out a sago grub out of the root end of a *milon* tree, rubbed repeatedly
      (with the fat of it), and then he had sex another time and . . .'

(122) nggé faül sikh-ayan-telo
      friend faül delicious-very

      'Oh dear, Faül!, this feels very good!'

In (122), a 'dearness' expletive (*nggé*) and a 'supernatural' expletive (*faül*) are combined to express the feelings of the older brother. Faül as a mythical being does not
play a role in this episode, (116)–(122); in fact, having been killed by the creator-
spirit, his role as a mythical participant ended in (119).

   DEARNESS EXPLETIVES   Other 'dearness' expletives besides *nggé* are *mayokh*
'friends, dear people' and *khofélapa* 'boy'. Cross-linguistically, relationship terms
with strong connotations of helpfulness (*friend, dear, mother, brother*) are often used
as expletives of distress but may also be connected with other emotions such as surprise and amazement.

Example (123) is taken from the same myth of origin as examples (116)–(122). Ginol, the creator spirit, discovers that his fire has died:

(123) wé   mayokh dé-dakhu   meli-tekhé di-ati-afé-mémo-tofekho
      EXCLM friends   QUOTE.3SG.REAL-SS fire-purpose ? -hold-turn-3SG.IMM.REAL-DS
      '"Oh help", he said and wandered around looking for fire and . . .'

In the context there is no one else around to whom *mayokh* could have been addressed; it is safe to interpret example (123) as a case of a 'dearness' relationship term used as an expletive noun. This analysis is strengthened by the presence of another expletive phenomenon in (123): the interjection *wé*.

Example (125) illustrates the use of *khofélapa* 'boy' in a context of fear and shock, following the exclamative interjection *wé*:

(124) khala yafin-bo-ta   dal-mekho-do
      up   stairs-opening-LOC appearing-SUPP.3SG.REAL-DS
      'and upstairs in the stairs' entrance he appeared, and . . .'

(125) ima-té-tofekho   wé   khofél-apa
      see-3PL.REAL-DS EXCLM boy-only.EXCLM
      'they looked but—Oh boy!—. . .'

(126) khof-e-kha   khomilo-do   mé-laimekho-bakha-ti-kha   abül
      that-TR-CONN die.REAL.3SG-DS earth-bury-HOD-3PL.REAL-CONN male.person
      lu   falé   wü   nggé gu laléo lai-ati-bo-dakhu
      go.upward.SS appear.3SG.REAL EXCLM friend you demon come-hold-stay.2SG.REAL-SS
      lelé-mbol-e-kholo-tè
      come-2SG.PROGR-TR-Q-or
      'that man who died and who they had buried earlier today did appear right now! "Hey, friend, are you coming as a bad spirit, or . . ."'

(127) mbakha-mol-mo-dakhu   lelé-mbol-e-kholo   de-té-tofekho
      what.Q-SUPP-do.2SG.REAL-SS come-2SG.PROGR-TR-Q QUOTE-3PL.REAL-DS.but
      '"How are you coming?", they asked, but . . .'

(128) mayokh manda nu khomile-lé-dakhu kho-sü kha-lé-lofekho
      friends no   I   die-1SG.REAL-SS there-to go-1SG.REAL-DS.but
      'No, friends, I died and went there, but . . .'

The expletive use of *khofélapa* 'boy!' in (125) is strikingly similar to the use of the English exclamation *oh, boy* and the Dutch *tjonge* or *tsjonge-jonge*. The Korowai noun *khofé(l)* 'young man, boy', if it is used as an interjection, always occurs with the exclamative *-apa*. This *-apa* literally means 'just, only'. Notice that when Dutch speakers use *jongen* ('boy') as an expletive, it also tends to receive the special exclamative form *t(s)jonge!*

The context for (125) is a text (from the oral tradition) about a man who was buried but who, to the shock of those who buried him, came back to the land of the living (see chapter 6 for the whole text). In (124), the 'resurrected' suddenly appears in the treehouse entrance: it is the climax of the story.

Notice that in (126) and (128) the 'dearness' terms seem to be used as forms of address (and not as interjections) in the dialogue between the 'resurrected' man and the people who had buried him. 'Dearness' terms like *nggé* and *mayokh* are frequently used as forms of address, also between relatives, replacing kinship terms. This vocative use of 'dearness' terms, in extraclausal position, comes formally very close to the use of exclamative interjections. For example, the use of *nggé* in (126), following the interjection of fear and shock, *wü*, can be analysed both as an interjection and as a form of address. Since *khofé(l)* 'boy' receives a special exclamative form in expletive usage, this ambiguity does not play a role with the *khofélapa* 'oh, boy' expletive. Compare the vocative use in (129) with the expletive use in (125):

(129) khofé   mano-pelu-m-é-o
      youngster well-grow-2SG.ADHORT-EXCLM-EXCLM
      'Boy, you should grow well!'

Many languages use kinship terms with strong connotations of solidarity, such as *mother* or *brother*, as expletives [see the Italian *mamma mia!* and the Kannada *amma* (Bean 1981)], but we have not found that Korowai speakers do so. Instead, Korowai uses nonkinship 'dearness' terms for expletive purposes.

More research is needed to establish in which contexts the Korowai use 'supernatural' expletives (power/taboo) and in which contexts they use the 'dearness' expletives (solidarity). Notice that we have examples, such as (125), in which expletive nouns from both sources are combined in one expression.

Linkage and continuity in *The Pig Sacrifice* text

To illustrate some of the points mentioned in this chapter consider *The Pig Sacrifice* text (see chapter 6).

Status-mood-aspect continuity

This text is a procedural exposition on pig sacrifices presented in narrative form, following the chronological protocol for the pig sacrifice ceremony. Embedded in that framework are sections representing the *doleli* calls to the ancestral spirits. The use of habitual forms of the verb throughout the text contributes to its cohesion as a procedural discourse.

The habitual forms are repeatedly discontinued when the *doleli* calls to the ancestral spirits are quoted. In such compulsory addresses, these spirits are summoned to give health and food. We find imperative forms of the verb in these sections. Exclamative interjections and exclamative verb clitics also function to set these sections apart:

(130) kül-mekho-ma-té-do   ailo-fekho   khobül-fekho fe-nè fe-nè
      in.order-SUPP-HAB-3PL-DS kidney-COORD leg-COORD   get-SS get-SS
      woto-fekha   doleli-ma-té
      sacred.place-a.certain call-HAB-3PL

'When they have prepared (all of it), they usually put the kidneys and the leg down and they call a certain sacred place (on the clan territory).'

(131) iè   wof-e-kha   mbolo-fekho   ge-mba-mbam-pekho ge-yano-fekho
      EXCLM there-TR-CONN ancestor-COORD your-child-child-COORD your-people-COORD

'Oh, forefather over there, and your children and your people . . .'

(132) if-e-kha   gol-khobül bando-khe-nè le-mén-é
      this-TR-CONN pig-leg   bring-go-SS   eat-2PL.IMP-EXCLM

'you should take this leg of the pig away and eat it.'

(133) le-mén-dakhu mano-pa-mon-é
      eat-2PL.IMP-SS good-SUPP-2PL.IMP-EXCLM

'You should eat it and help (us)!'

(134) mesé   khobül-fekho woto-fekha   fo   fe-nè fu-ma-té-dakhu
      next   leg-COORD   sacred.place-a.certain get.SS get-SS put-HAB-3PL-SS

'And then they usually take another leg and put it down on another sacred place . . .'

The last verb of (130) is a habitual form of the speech-act verb *doleli-* 'to call/summon ancestral spirits'. The quoted content of the 'call' starts with an exclamative interjection in (131) and ends with an exclamative verb clitic, with imperative verb forms between them. Note that within the reported *doleli* call, tail-head linkage connects (132) and (133), with the recapitulation of the imperative verb form *leméndakhu*. The adverb *mesé* 'again' in (134) is used as a discourse connective ('next') between the different *doleli* calls at the various sacred spots in the clan territory.

The habitual forms are also discontinued in the section where the women are summoned to stay clear of the ceremony now that the preliminaries are done with and the proper sacrifical ceremony begins [see line (6)]. This aspect discontinuity correlates with a major break in participant continuity: since women have no place in the pig sacrifice ceremony, the women are very markedly introduced on stage and then removed in the preliminary part of the text [see lines (1)–(7)].

Participant continuity: switch reference and agreements

The central participants in a pig sacrifice ceremony are the adult, male clan members, as those who give the pig; the ancestral spirits, as those who receive the pig; and the pig, as the goal of the transaction. The agents of the transaction, the adult males of the clan, are never identified by full noun phrases. They are highly topical, presupposed from the beginning to be given to the addressee, and they are tracked by subject person-number agreements in the verbs and by switch reference. Consider their first introduction in (135), the first chain of the text, and the way in which they are tracked:

(135) wof-è   gol ülma-té-dakhu   bando-lu   khaim-an   fe-nè fu
      there-CONN pig kill-3PL.REAL-SS bring-enter.SS treehouse-LOC get-SS put.SS
      bume-ma-té
      slaughter-HAB-3PL

'After they have killed a pig there, they usually bring it and having put it into the house they slaughter it.'

The third plural marking on the first verb of (135), the SS forms in between, and the third plural marking on the last verb of (135) are the only formal clues to the identity of the agents of the verbs. Of course, the narrator of (135) presupposes that the addressee has cultural knowledge that enables him to identify and track the adult males of the clan as the agents of the actions reported in (135) and to identify the clan territory as the referent of *wofè* 'there'.

In the preparation of the ceremony, before its actual performance, the women play a minor participant role in the cleansing of the intestines of the pig, this cleansing being a customary female task. The introduction of the women causes participant discontinuity, signalled by the prominent introduction of the females in (137) by full noun phrases, with a focus marker, preceded by a DS verb form that indicates the switch from the males to the females. Subsequently, the female participants are continued by SS forms, with tail-head linkage carrying over the SS monitoring clause across the chain boundary [(137)–(138)]. Finally the female participants are very explicitly removed from the stage in (138) by the verb *gilfo-* 'to go away; to vanish', which bears the DS clitic. This DS clitic signals the switch back to the major participants, the males who receive only minimal coding in the verb form. The male participant line simply continues in (138) after the short female interval:

(136) bume-ma-té-dakhu   ol   di   fe-nè   fu-ma-té-do
      slaughter-HAB-3PL.REAL-SS faeces get.out.SS take-SS put-HAB-3PL-DS

      'They usually slaughter, and get the intestines out of it and put it down . . .'

(137) ni-khü-to   bando-khe-nè ao-ma-té
      mother-PL-FOC bring-go-SS   cleanse-HAB-3PL.REAL

      'and the women take (the intestines) and cleanse them.'

(138) ao-leful-mekho   khaim   gilfo-ma-té-do   gol-e-khal di-fu-ma-té
      cleanse-end-SUPP.SS treehouse go.away-HAB-3PL.REAL-DS pig-TR-meat cut-put-HAB-3PL

      'When they have finished washing they go away to the treehouse and (the males) cut the pig meat out and put it down.'

The sacrificial pig is introduced by the patient NP in (135) and, being the predictable goal or patient participant, left implicit as the second argument of the verbs that have to do with butchering and offering pigs. Notice that the first introduction of *gol* 'pig' in (135) forms the pragmatic basis for the introduction of a number of inferrables (see Prince 1981) or subtopics (see Hannay 1985) that are inferentially related to the pig, like *ol* 'feces' in (136). Most subtopics of 'pig' are introduced by compound nouns, with the noun *gol* 'pig' as a modifying noun—for example, *gol-khobül* 'pig leg' in line (9)—and are thus formally linked to the major sacrificial pig topic.

The ancestral spirits, the recipient participants, are very explicitly and extensively introduced in the exclamative-vocative coordinate NP in the beginning of the *doleli* address. Noun phrases of complex categorial structure being rare, this form certainly is a salient introduction:

(139) iè   wof-e-kha   mbolo-fekho   ge-mba-mbam-pekho ge-yano-fekho
      EXCLM there-TR-CONN ancestor-COORD your-child-child-COORD your-people-COORD

      'Oh, forefather over there, and your children and your people . . .'

Thus introduced, the ancestral spirits are tracked as given participants by SS linkages and agreements.

Clause linkage and continuity

The overwhelming majority of clauses in the pig sacrifice text are of the chained type,
with switch-reference conjunctions connecting the clauses in the chain. Subordinate
linkage with -kha occurs only five times in the text. Consider the following example
of subordinate linkage:

(140) le-mén-dakhu nokhu lép-telo-khai-kha   nokhu mano-pa-mon-do
      eat-2PL.IMP-SS we   ill-be-3SG.IRR-CONN us   good-SUPP-2PL.IMP-DS
      khi-telo-fon-è
      healthy-be-1PL.INTENT-CONN

      'You should eat it and if we fall ill, you should cure us so we can be healthy.'

In (140), the 'you' are the ancestral spirits, the recipients of the pig sacrifice, and the
'we' are the agents of the sacrifice, both highly topical participants. The first clause
of (140) has the ancestral spirits as its subject, and the verb in that clause has an SS
clitic; but the next clause in linear order, *nokhu léptelokhaikha,* has a different subject, 'we'. Of course, since that clause is a *-kha*-marked clause, it does not count as
the 'next' clause for the switch-reference system, which is restricted to chained
clauses; the 'next' clause is a structural, not a linear, notion. The 'next' clause is the
clause with *manopamondo* as its verbal head, which has the ancestral spirits as its
subject; the subordinate clause is an NP within that clause, providing a conditional
frame, 'if we fall ill', for the clause *nokhu manopamondo* 'you must cure us', which
has a place in the chain that follows *leméndakhu* 'you must eat'. Thus this subordinate clause is an interruption with respect to the main event/participant lines expressed
in the chain, an interruption that presents background or setting information for the
events in the main line.

Chain linkage and continuity in *The Pig Sacrifice* text

Recapitulative chain links create continuity across the chain boundaries in this text.
There are eleven clause chains in the pig sacrifice text. Tail-head linkage occurs eight
times, and generic deictic verb linkage occurs once. The dominant linkage types of
clauses (chaining linkage) and of clause chains (tail-head linkage) combine to give
narrative and procedural texts typically a rather 'flat' structure, consisting, so to speak,
of a chain of clause chains.

Kinship Terminology

Korowai kinship nouns are a class of nouns with two characteristics. First, they have plural forms, whereas other Korowai nouns do not have plural forms. Second, they can be glossed in terms of the English nouns for relationships in the nuclear family ('father/mother, son/daughter, brother/ sister, husband/wife').[1]

This use of genealogical glosses needs to be qualified. First, not all meanings of kinship terms can be glossed genealogically (see Bean 1981). The Korowai term *ni* 'mother', for example, is also used in the following ways: 'wife', 'woman', 'Mrs.', part of the proper names of females, and part of the expression for 'coward'. Some of such nonkinship uses in Korowai are described below, Nonkinship expressions. Second, the status of the genealogical glosses is suspect because their use is based on the questionable assumption that the words for 'mother' and similar terms in all languages share a cross-cultural genealogical component of meaning (see Schneider 1984).

We assume that semantic representations of kinship nouns (just like those of other lexical items) can consist of a core and an extension. General extension processes, like metaphoric and metonymic extension, are central to both literary and ordinary language (see Lakoff and Johnson 1980) and also affect kinship terms (see Bean 1981; Turner 1987). In addition to such general extension processes, there are more domain-specific extension rules. In the domain of kinship nouns, for example, there is the generational extension rule, which extends the range of reference of a term collaterally to include all other kinsmen of the same generation and of the same sex (see below).

Notwithstanding the theoretical problems of both the core/extension assumption and the genealogical assumption, for reasons of clear presentation of the complex data, we describe the kinship nouns in an extensionist and genealogical framework. We review some Korowai evidence that may be relevant to the genealogical assumption in The status of geneological glosses, below.

As in many New Guinea communities, personal names are avoided when Korowai people address one another. Instead, they use kinship nouns or nonkin terms of friendship and companionship like *nggé* 'friend' and *mayokh* 'companions' or so-called joking address forms like *nokulekham* 'my sandcrab'. The general avoidance of personal names and the taboo on the use of the personal names of one's mother-in-law, brothers-in-law, and siblings make the use of kinship nouns very frequent.

An extensionist account of Korowai kinship nouns

In an extensionist account, the range of reference of kinship nouns can be extended in two ways: (1) by extension rules, which tend to have a certain cross-cultural generality, and (2) by equivalences of a more limited generality.

Extension rules extend the primary range of reference of a term to include other ranges. The generational extension rule, for example, extends the range of reference of a term collaterally to include all other kinsmen of the same generation and of the same sex (Merrifield 1983a: 182, rule G). This rule is operative in many kinship systems all over the world. The term *até* 'father' in Korowai has ego's father (F) as basic reference, but generational extension extends *até* to FB, FFBs, FFFBss, and so on. We shall call FB, FFBs, and others classificatory fathers of ego. Another extension rule is the half-sibling rule, according to which the terms for full siblings are extended to half-siblings (Fs = B, Fd = S, etc.; see Lounsbury 1964: 357). In addition to generational and half-sibling extension, there are self-reciprocal and affinal extension rules in Korowai. We shall use these well-known concepts of extensionist kinship theory as defined by Merrifield (1983a: 182–186) and Lounsbury (1964).

The second, far less general, way to extend the range of kinship terms is by equivalences, which may reflect specific cultural institutions. For example, de Vries (1987) linked the equivalence MB = MBs in Kombai to the avunculate in that society.

The Korowai kinship system is an Omaha system, in which Lounsbury (1964) has described the types of equivalences that occur. His Omaha Type I equivalence of . . . ♀Bs = . . . ♀B and . . . ♀Bd = . . . ♀S is operative in Korowai. In the words of Lounsbury (1964: 360), 'One's female linking relative's BROTHER'S CHILD is therefore to be regarded as structurally equivalent to that female linking relative's SIBLING.' This equivalence results in the 'skewing' of natural and terminological generations, and therefore Lounsbury (1964) has termed this equivalence the Skewing Rule. Table 5–1 displays the skewing patterns in Korowai filial kinship terms.

The last formal notion we shall need is the cross and parallel distinction, which is defined by Merrifield (1983b: 295) as follows:

> Parallel (Seneca): Within the genealogical chain that links ego to alter, the two kins-men of the first generation above that of the junior member of the ego-alter dyad are of the same sex. Cross (Seneca): Within the genealogical chain that links ego to alter, the two kinsmen of the first generation above that of the junior member of the ego-alter dyad are of the opposite sex.

This Seneca type of bifurcation occurs in quite a few languages of Irian Jaya. The cross and parallel distinction is morphologically expressed in Korowai by the prefix *sa-* 'cross' in the opposition *abül* 'male parallel child' and *sabül* 'male cross child' and in *lal* 'female parallel child' and *salal* 'female cross child'.

Kinship nouns

General remarks

Possessive prefixes are optionally but usually present with kinship nouns. Apart from a few exceptions, kinship nouns are the only category of nouns in Korowai that bear suffixes that express the plural. There are five plural forms of this type: stem + *-dém*, stem + *-alin*, stem + *-khül*, stem + *-él*, and special plural stem. Sometimes the plural is expressed by the reduplicated stem. Only the plural suffixes *-dém* and *-alin* can be used interchangeably. Since the plural formation is unpredictable, we shall give the plural forms for each kinship noun.

Thus far we have not found different forms for terms of reference and of address. Since the terms for adoptive relationships have not yet been examined thoroughly, we shall not discuss them in this book.[2]

Kinship terms are also used when people meet each other; in such greeting situations people shake hands, in a strong, rhythmic, cranking manner, and the appropriate kinship terms are uttered in the rhythm of the handshake.

The last general remark concerns order of birth. There are three modifiers of absolute seniority: *-alop* 'firstborn', *-khaja* 'last born,'[3] and *-alüfekha* 'born in between'.

(1) *ne-mom-khaja*   'my last-born uncle'
     my-uncle-lastborn

(2) *nemomalop*   'my first-born uncle'

(3) *nemomalüfekha* 'my middle-born uncle'

Filial terms

Parent generation

Korowai distinguishes fathers (parallel males), mothers (parallel females), uncles (cross males) and aunts (cross females) in the parent generation.

Até 'father' (PL: *atékhül*) primarily denotes ego's F. By generational extension, *até* is extended to ego's father's brothers and classificatory brothers (FB, FFBs, etc.). Affinally, *até* is extended to include the husbands of mother's sisters (MSH). There is a special affinal term for FSH, *sop* (see below).

Até is also extended affinally to MBdH. The background of this extension is the Omaha Type I equivalence ... ♀Bd = ... ♀S. This rule makes MBd structurally equivalent to MS and MBdH to MSH. Above we saw that *até* extends affinally to MSH. Similarly, *até* is extended to MBsdH and MBssdH. By Omaha Type I skewing, MBs = MB, and therefore MBsdH = MBdH (see table 5–1).

Ni 'mother' (PL: *nikhül*) primarily denotes ego's mother. By generational extension *ni* is extended to mother's sisters and classificatory sisters. Ego uses *ni* also for the cowives of his father. Affinaly, *ni* is extended to the wives of father's brothers (FBW) and of mother's brothers (MBW), thus neutralizing the cross and parallel distinction in these affinal relations. *Ni* is also affinally extended to MBsW. The background of this extension is the equivalence MBs = MB, which follows from the Omaha I skewing rule. If MBs = MB, then MBsW = MBW. Above we saw that *ni* extends affinally to MBW. Also based on Omaha Type I skewing is the extension of *ni* 'mother' to MBd; MBd = MS (Omaha Type I) and MS = M (generational extension). Similarly, because MBs = MB, MBsd = MBd and MBssd = MBd (see table 5–1).

Mul 'father's sister' primarily denotes the paternal aunt (FS). By generational extension, *mul* is extended to father's classificatory sisters. We have not found other extensions. *Sop* 'father's sister's husband' is the special affinal term for the husbands of father's sisters. The plural form of *mul* is *mulekhül*; of *sop*, *sopalin*.

Mom 'uncle' (PL: *momél*) primarily denotes the maternal uncle (MB). Generationally, *mom* is extended to the classificatory brothers of mother. By Omaha Type I skewing, *mom* is extended to MBs, MBss, and so on.

Child generation

In the child generation, Korowai distinguishes sons (parallel males), daughters (parallel females), nephews (cross males) and nieces (cross females).

Mbam 'child' (PL: *mbambam*) is the sex-neutral and bifurcation-neutral reciprocal term to the parent terms given above.

Abül 'son' (PL: *abüldém*) is the male reciprocal term to the parallel parent terms *ni* 'mother' and *até* 'father' in all their extensions. Primarily, *abül* denotes ego's son (s). Generationally, *abül* extends to male ego's (classificatory) brother's (classificatory) sons (e.g., FBss) and to female ego's (classificatory) sister's (classificatory) sons. Affinally, *abül* is extended to HSs, HBs, WSs, and WBs as reciprocal term to the affinal extensions of *até* 'father' and *ni* 'mother' and to the special affinal parent term *sop* (FSH). By Omaha Type I skewing, the parent term *ni* 'mother' is extended to MBd, MBsd, MBssd, and so on (see under *ni* and table 5–1 below). Being the male reciprocal to *ni*, *abül* is accordingly extended to female ego's FSs, FFSs, FFFSs, and so on. *Até* 'father' is affinally extended to MBdH, MBsdH, MBssdH, and so on (see under *até* above). Accordingly, *abül* 'son' as the reciprocal to *até* is extended to WFSs, WFFSs, and so on.

Lal 'daughter' (PL: *laldém*) is the female reciprocal term to the parallel parent terms *até* 'father' and *ni* 'mother' in all their extensions.

Primarily, *lal* denotes ego's daughter (d). By generational extension, *lal* is extended to male ego's (classificatory) brother's (classificatory) daughters and to female ego's (classificatory) sister's daughters.

Affinally, *lal* is extended to HSd, HBd, WSd, and WBd. By Omaha Type I skewing, *ni* 'mother' is extended to MBd, MBsd, MBssd, and so on. Being the female reciprocal to *ni*, *lal* is accordingly extended to female ego's FSd, FFSd, FFFSd, and so on. Similarly, since *até* 'father' is extended affinally to MBdH, MBsdH, MBssdH, and others (see under *até* above), *lal* as the reciprocal term to *até* is extended to WFSd, WFFSd, and so on.

Sabül 'nephew' (PL: *samabün*) is the male reciprocal term to the cross-parent terms *mom* MB and *mul* FS in all their extensions.

Sabül primarily denotes male ego's sister's son and female ego's brother's son (cross male child). By generational extension, *sabül* is extended to male ego's classificatory sister's son and female ego's classificatory brother's son.

By Omaha Type I skewing, MBss = MBs = MB = *mom*, and therefore *sabül* as the male reciprocal to the cross-parent terms is extended to male ego's FSs, FFSs, and so on.

Salal 'niece' (PL: *salaldém*) (cross female child) is the female reciprocal term to the cross-parent terms *mom* MB and *mul* FS in all their extensions. *Salal* primarily denotes male ego's sister's daughter and female ego's brother's daughter. By generational extension, *salal* is extended to male ego's classificatory sister's daughter and female ego's classificatory brother's daughter. By Omaha Type I skewing, *salal* is extended to male ego's FSd, FFSd, and so on. The opposition cross versus parallel is formally expressed by *sa-* 'cross' in the contrasts *lal* (parallel female child) and *salal* (cross female child) and in *abül* (parallel male child) and *sabül* (cross male child).

Grandparent generation

Andüop (or *ndaté*) 'grandfather' (PL: *andüofalin*) is used primarily for parent's male parent (FF, MF, FMB, MMB). Generationally, *andüop* is extended to parent's male classificatory parent (FFB, MFB, etc.). Affinally, *andüop* is extended to the husbands of parent's female parents (FMH, FMSH, FFSH, MMH, MFSH, MMSH).

When ego's parents call somebody *mom* 'uncle' or *até* 'father' because of Omaha I equivalence (see above, under *mom* and *até* for these extensions), ego calls that person *andüop* (PMBs, PMBss, PMBdH, PMBsdH, PMBssdH).

Makh 'grandmother' (PL: *makhdém* or *makhalin*) primarily denotes parent's female parent (FM, MM, MFS, FFS). By generational extension, *makh* is extended to ego's parent's classificatory female parents (MMS, FMS, etc.). Affinally, *makh* is extended to the wives of ego's parent's male parents (MMBW, MFBW, FMBW, etc.). By Omaha Type I skewing, *makh* is extended to PMBd and PMBsW, PMBssW, PMBsd, PMBssd, and so on, that is, to all those for whom ego's parent uses the parent term *ni* 'mother' on the basis of Omaha skewing (see table 5–1). Since marriage to MMBd is quite common and to a certain extent preferred, quite a few Korowai men are married to their *makh* 'grandmother'; in such cases, the man uses *makh* for his wife.

Grandchild generation

Khafun 'grandchild' (PL: *khafunalin* or *khafundém*) is the sex-neutral, reciprocal term to the grandparent terms *andüop* 'grandfather' and *makh* 'grandmother' in all their extensions. *Khafun* may be replaced by *lalkhafun* 'child of female (cross or parallel) child' and *abülkhafun* 'child of male (cross or parallel) child'.

Great-grandchild and great-grandparent

Yebom 'great-grandchild/great-grandparent' (PL: *yebomdém* or *yebomalin*) is the sex-neutral, self-reciprocal term for ego's child's child's child and ego's parent's parent's parent. Affinally, *yebom* is extended to spouse's CCC/PPP. By Omaha Type I skewing, male ego uses the child terms *sabül* 'cross male child' and *salal* 'cross female child' for his FSs and FSd who belong to his own natural generation (see under *sabül* and *salal* above). As a consequence, ego uses grandchild terms (*khafun*) for his FSss, FSsd, FSds, and FSdd and great-grandchild terms (*yebom*) for his FSsss, FSssd, FSsds, FSsdd, FSdss, FSdsd, FSdds, and FSddd, although these belong to ego's second descending natural generation. (For this skewing of natural and terminological generations, see table 5–1).

Ego's own generation

Afé 'elder brother' (PL: *afékhül*) primarily denotes ego's older brother (eB). By generational extension, *afé* is extended to the sons of ego's FB and MS (if older than ego). By Omaha Type I skewing, *afé* is extended to MBds and MBsds inasmuch as they are older than ego. (See table 5–1).

   Mofekha 'younger brother' (PL: *mofekhadém* or *anolél*) primarily denotes ego's younger brother (yB). By generational extension, the term is extended to the sons of FB and MS (if younger than ego). By Omaha I skewing, *mofekha* is extended to MBds and MBsds inasmuch as they are younger than ego.

   Aw 'elder sister' (PL: *awkhül*) primarily denotes ego's elder sister (eS). Generationally, *aw* is extended to the daughters of FB and MS. By Omaha I skewing, *aw* is extended to MBdd and MBsdd.

   Modol 'younger sister' (PL: *modoldém*) primarily denotes ego's younger sister (yS). By generational extension, *modol* includes the daughters of FB and MS (if younger than ego). By Omaha I skewing, *modol* is extended to MBdd and MBsdd.

Summary of filial terms

Table 5–1, which presents the skewing pattern of Korowai, ego being male, is based on Lounsbury (1964: 363). The vertical alignments represent the natural generations. The superimposed lines segregate the terminological generations (G^{+1}, G^0, etc.). The horizontal arrows (→) express the effects of the Omaha Type I equivalence FS . . . → S . . . (the corollary of this rule for the reciprocals was given above: . . .♀Bs → . . .♀B and . . .♀Bd → . . . ♀S), of the half-sibling rule (e.g., Fs → B), and of the generational extension rule (FB → F, MS → M, etc.). These rules form an unordered set: There is never more than one rule applicable at the same point (Lounsbury 1964: 364).

   We give only one example of a derivation:

MBsds → Mbds	(Omaha I, MBs = MB)
MBds → Mss	(Omaha I, second application, MBd = MS)
MSs → Ms	(generational extension, MS = M)
Ms → B	(half-sibling rule)

The rules predict that for MBsds the term is used that is also used for B; indeed, Korowai uses *mofekha* 'younger brother' for MBsds, as well as for yB.

Spouse terms

Um 'husband' and *defol* 'wife' are the Korowai spouse terms. First and second wife in polygynous marriages are distinguished as follows: *mülekha defol* 'first wife' and *bétopengga defol* 'second wife'. *Um* 'husband' is also used in the compound *lalum* 'daughter's husband' and in the compound *nggéyum* 'husband's sister's husband' (see below).

There are two other terms for husband, *wafil* and *yalén; wafil* has 'male person' as its basic meaning ('my man = my husband') and *yalén* has 'old man' as its basic meaning. Both *wafil* and *yalén* occur in Kombai, spoken to the southeast of Korowai, with the same meanings (de Vries 1987: 114). There are also two alternative terms for wife, *yaén* and *lebakhop,* not occurring in Kombai. *Lebakhop* seems to mean 'old woman,' and it is, just like *yalén,* a respectful term.

We noted above (see under *makh*) that when a man is married to a woman who is also a filial relative, the filial term for her takes precedence over the spouse term.

Affinal terms

When a man marries, his status in the clan does not change. In contrast, when a woman marries, she becomes to quite an extent a member of her husband's clan. For example, when her husband dies, his brothers have rights over her and her children, provided that the bridal payments have been completed. One of them may take her as his wife, or they may marry her to a different clan, receiving bridal payments.

These status differences between man and woman are reflected in two ways in the terminology for affinal relations. First, there is a special pair of terms, *khaimon* (HB) and *khamokh* (BW), rooted in the levirate. Second, whereas a man tends to use special affinal terms for his wife's relatives, a woman tends to use either filial terms, following her husband terminologically, or one of the following nonkinship terms. The term *nggé* 'friend' is used by women for HS. The term *mbolop* 'respected old man; ancestor' (PL: *mbolom-bolop, mbolofalin*) is used by women *for* HF and HMB (H male P). The term *lebakhop* (PL: *lebakhofalin, lebakhondém*) is used for husband's female parent (HM, HFS). *Lebakhop* is also used as a spouse term for ego's wife. The term *lebakhop* has '(respected) old woman' as its basic meaning.

Parent generation

Ban 'wife's parent' (PL: *bandém, banalin, bananggol*) is used by a man for all those for whom his wife uses a filial parent term (*até* 'father', *ni* 'mother', *mom* 'maternal uncle', *mul* 'paternal aunt') except WM(S). Primarily, *ban* denotes WP except WM(S), (WF, WMB, WFS). By generational extension, *ban* is extended to include wife's classificatory parents (e.g., WFB). Affinally *ban* extends to the spouses of WP except WFBW (because WFBW = WFW = WM).

By Omaha Type I equivalence, *ban* is extended to include WMBs, WMBd, WMBss, and WMBsd, that is, for those for whom ego's wife uses parent terms on the basis of the Omaha Type I skewing rule (see table 5–1, the G^{+1} terminological generation).

Bandakhhol (PL: *bandakholalin, bandakholdém*) primarily denotes WM. By generational extension, *bandakhol* is extended to WMS (WM classificatory S). We have found no other extensions.

Ego's own generation

Nabul 'wife's sibling' (PL: *nabuldém*) primarily denotes ego's wife's sibling (WB/WS). Generationally, the term is extended to include the classificatory siblings of ego's wife. *Nabul* is a self-reciprocal term and therefore also refers to SH. We have not found affinal extensions; the compound *nabuldefol* (*nabul* + *defol* 'wife') occurs in the data for WBW.

Khaimon 'husband's brother' and *khamokh* 'brother's wife' are a special pair of terms for the relationship between a man and his brother's wife: *khaimon* 'husband's brother' and *khamokh* 'brother's wife', with the last term presupposing a male ego. Generationally, these terms are extended to include husband's classificatory brother and male ego's classificatory brother's wife. *Khaimon* has *khaimonalin* and *khaimondém* as plural forms; *khamokh* has *khamokhdém* as a plural form. Because these terms express the levirate (with the wife of ego's brother being a potential wife for ego, and vice versa), some people are embarassed to use them and use descriptive terms instead, like *nafédefol* (*nafé* 'older brother' + *defol* 'wife') 'my older brother's wife'.

Nggé 'husband's sister' (PL: *nggékhül*) and *nokho* (PL: *nokhoalin*) both mean 'friend'. The terms are also used for husband's sister and husband's brother's wife. Generationally, these terms are extended to include H classificatory S and H classificatory BW. The terms *nggé* and *nokho* are self-reciprocal and therefore also refer to female ego's brother's wife. There is a compound term *nggéyum* (*nggé* + *ye* 'her' + *um* 'husband') for HSH.

Child generation

Nanü 'son's wife' (PL: *nanündém, nanüalin*) denotes the wives of ego's male parallel and cross children, that is, the wives of those whom ego calls *abül* 'male parallel child' or *sabül* 'male cross child'. Generationally the term extends to ego's classificatory male parallel and cross children. One informant insisted on including HMB and HFS in the range of *nanü* (husband's cross parents). Another informant consistently restricted the term to the child generation. Further research is needed with respect to *nanü*.

Lalum 'daughter's husband' (PL: *lalumalin, lalumdém*) denotes the husbands of ego's female parallel and cross children, that is, the husbands of those whom ego calls *lal* 'parallel female child' or *salal* 'cross female child'. *Lalum* is a compound term consisting of *lal* 'daughter' and *um* 'husband'.

Table 5-1 Omaha reductions, type 1 Ego being Male, in Korowai

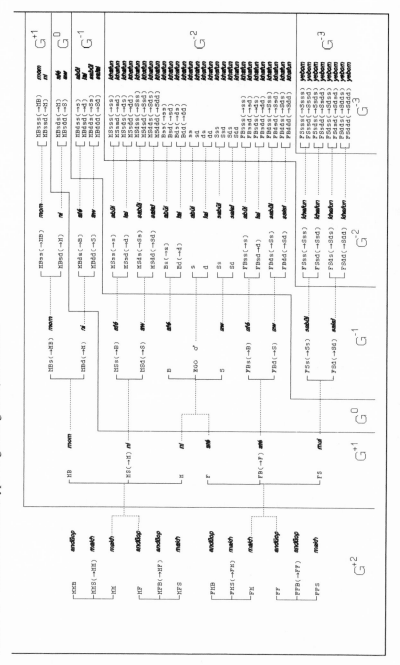

Adapted from F. G. Lounsbury, a formal account of the Crow- and Omaha-type kinship terminologies, *Explorations in cultural anthropology*, ed. Ward H. Goodenough (New York: McGraw-Hill, 1964), p. 363.

Grandparents

A woman follows her husband by using filial terms (*makh* 'grandmother', and *andüop* 'grandfather') for her HPP. A man either follows his wife by using filial terms or uses descriptive compound nouns. The following examples of these occur in the data:

> *banyaté* for WFF [*ban* (WP) + 'his' + *até* (F)]
>
> *banyeni* for WFM [*ban* (WP) + 'his' + *ni* (M)]
>
> *bandakholyeni* for WMM [*bandakhol* (WM) + 'her' + *ni* (M)]
>
> *bandakholyaté* for WMF [*bandakhol* (WM) + 'her' + *até* (F)] 5.4

Non-kinship extensions

We already discussed kinship-related extension rules, such as the generational extension rule. The work of Bean (1981) and Turner (1987) makes clear that there are also extension processes like metaphor and metonymy that may extend the use of kinship nouns to other domains. Thus far we found extensions to domains other than kinship with the parallell parent terms *ni* 'mother' and *até* 'father' and with the parallel child terms *abül* 'son' and *lal* 'daughter'.

The noun *ni* 'mother' occurs as part of certain proper names of females, as in (4):

(4) Afe-ni   'Afeni'
    Sife-ni   'Sifeni'
    Molofe-ni   'Molofeni'
    Piatu-ni   'Piatuni'

These proper names of females are compounds of the noun *ni* and other nouns. For two of the names, we can give the meaning of the other noun: *sip* means 'beak' and *piatu* is a loanword from Indonesian meaning 'orphan'.

Ni is also used in polite reference to married/adult women in general:

(5) bume-ma-té-dakhu   ol   di   fe-nè fu-ma-té-do
    slaughter-HAB-3PL-SS feces get.out.SS take-SS put-HAB-3PL-DS

'They usually slaughter, and get the intestines out of it and put it down . . .'

(6) ni-khü-to   bando-khe-nè ao-ma-té
    mother-PL-FOC bring-go-SS   cleanse-HAB-3PL

'the women take (the intestines) and cleanse it.'

(7) ao-leful-mekho   khaim   gilfo-ma-té-do   gol-e-khal di-fu-ma-té
    cleanse-end-SUPP.SS treehouse go.away-HAB-3PL-DS pig-TR-meat cut-put-HAB-3PL

'When they have finished washing they go away to the treehouse and (the men) cut the pig meat out and put it down.'

In the above example the term *ni-khü-to* 'mothers' is used to refer to adult women in general, in opposition to men. The context is the division of labor between male and female adults in the procedure for pig sacrifices.

The terms *ni* 'mother' and *até* 'father' are used for politely addressing adults unrelated to the speaker by kinship. We and our wives, for example, were addressed with these terms. These metaphorical extensions of the mother and father terms to 'woman, politely' and 'man, politely' are widespread in speech communities where adulthood, marriage, and parenthood , are inseparable [e.g., Indonesian, Kannada (Bean 1981)]. Unmarried Korowai males are vulnerable to witchcraft accusations and unmarried females to sexual abuse. Adults gain a respectable place in society through marriage and parenthood, and it is this element of respectability that provides the similarity between the primary referents of the parent terms and the nonkin referents to which the terms are metaphorically transferred for politeness (see Bean 1981).

In the following example, the term *até* 'father' is used as a polite form of address to an adult male who is not related to the speaker by kinship:

(8) hey   n-até-o   golo-m-belén-é   nu kolufo-yanof-é
     EXCLM my-father-VOC be.afraid-2SG.IMP-do'nt-EXCLM   I   Korowai-person-EXCLM
     dé-to
     say.3SG.REAL-DS

     'He said, "Hey, Sir, do not be afraid! I am a Korowai person."'

We have thus far not found any other non-kin uses of *até* 'father'.

The term *ni* is also used to refer to the wives of other people. The combination of respectability and sexual inaccessibility as connotations of the primary referent of the term *ni* 'mother' makes it suitable for politely referring to the wives of other men. Consider the following example:

(9) khain-khaja   ye-pan ye-ni-khül-fekho yo-Kolufo ni-khül-fekho tanukh khe-ne
     Khain-last.born him-self his-wives-PL-with   his-Korowai mother-PL-with only   go-SS
     khe-mén   tu
     the.other-side cross.SS

     'Khain's lastborn himself, with his wives, with just his Korowai wives, crossed (the river) to the other side.'

In the following example, *ni* is used to refer to the wives of the ancestral spirits to whom sacrificial pork is offered:

(10) damol fo   fe-nè fu   woto-fekha   mbolo-fekho ge-mambüm-pekho
     back   get.SS get-SS put.SS sacred.place-a.certain ancestor-and   your-children-and
     ge-yano-fekho ge-ni-khül-fekho if-e-kha   bando-khe-nè le-mén-é
     your-people-and your-mother-PL-and here-TR-CONN bring-go-SS   eat-2PL.IMP-EXCLM

     'And having put the back part (they say), "You forefathers of that certain sacred place, and your children, your people and your wives, you should take this and eat it!"'

We have found one use of *ni* 'mother' for nonkin referents in which the politeness dimension is absent: a man who behaves cowardly is called *golo-ni* 'fear-woman'. In such cases the speaker puts the male referent in a false category and in doing so indirectly performs an evaluative speech act (see Casson 1981b: 240).

Finally, we turn to non-kinship uses of the terms *abül* 'son' and *lal* 'daughter'. These terms are often used with the general meaning 'man, (male) person' / 'woman, (female) person'. Consider the following examples:

(11) lesukh abül   'a brave man'
     brave man

(12) wofekha abül-efè khokhukh-tebo   gol khakho gol-e-khén kül
     that   man-TOP aggressive-be.3SG.REAL pig like   pig-TR-angry like
     'As for that man, he is angry like a (wild) pig—, it is like the anger of a wild pig.'

(13) abül-fekha abül   'someone'
     man-a.certain man

(14) gu yafin tamélo-m-é   dé-do   i lal   yo él
     you stairs tie-2SG.IMP-EXCLM QUOTE.3SG.REAL-DS this woman yes yes
     dé-dakhu
     QUOTE.3SG.REAL-SS
     '"You must fasten the stairs"', he said, and the woman agreed and . . .'

(15) i lal   bepé-do   walelé-do   if-e-kha   abül i Mukhalé
     this woman blow.3SG.REAL-DS be.light.3SG.REAL-DS this-TR-CONN man this Mukhalé
     yu imo-tofekho   y-afé   élo-bo
     he look.3SG.REAL-DS his-older.brother sleep-stay.3SG.REAL
     'The woman blew (the fire) and it lighted up and the man Mukhalé saw that his older brother was asleep.'

The non-kinship use of the child terms does not have the politeness dimension that non-kinship uses of the parent terms have; rather it is a very neutral way to refer to people.

There are two kinds of non-kin extensions of kinship terms that are cross-linguistically quite common but which we have not found in our data. The first is the kind of figurative extension discussed by Turner (1987). The second is the use of kinship terms as expletives, as cries of distress (see Bean 1981).

To start with the latter, many languages use kinship terms like *mother* or *brother*, often together with interjections, as expletives to express emotional states of the speaker, like distress, shock, and fear. Bean (1981) has described the expletive use of the 'mother' term by the Kannada of south India. In certain varieties of English (*oh brother!*) and in Italian (*mamma mia!*), kinship nouns are used in very similar ways. The basis for such use is probably metonymic association with the help and solidarity dimension of kinship terms: children cry for their mother or (big) brother to help them in distress. The same dimension of solidarity is the basis for the use of 'dearness' terms as cries of distress (e.g., in English 'Oh dear!').

Korowai does not use kinship terms as distress cries, but it does use other relationship terms with connotations of solidarity in such circumstances, that is, terms of friendship and dearness, especially the nouns *mayokh* 'friends' and *nggé* 'friend' (see chapter 4, Focus clitics, interjections, and expletive nouns).

(16) wé   mayokh dé-dakhu   meli-tekhé di-ati-afé-mémo-tofekho
     EXCLM friend   say.3SG.REAL-SS fire-purpose get.out-hold-turn-3SG.IMM-DS
     '"Oh, help," he said and wandered around looking for fire.'

The second type of cross-linguistically common extension of kinship terms occurs in figurative language. Turner (1987) describes the pervasive use of kinship
metaphors in English (e.g., 'Death is the mother of beauty'). We have not yet found
this type of metaphorical extension of Korowai kinship nouns. Notice that it is not at
all clear whether the notions of biological progeneration, which Turner views as
central to English kinship concepts and which are the basis for many metaphorical
extensions in English, are central to Korowai concepts of kinship. This point brings
us to the complex problems of cross-cultural comparability and universality of (kinship) concepts that also underlie the problem of the status of glosses.

The status of genealogical glosses

Schneider has observed,

> In the field we must not translate or gloss every relationship between a woman and
> what appears to be the child she has borne as a mother-child relationship until that
> translation or gloss has been fully explored by examining in detail how the natives
> themselves conceptualize, define, or describe that relationship and their construc-
> tion of just where it stands in the context of their culture. (1984: 200)

This observation must be understood in the context of Schneider's lucid critique of
what he calls the Doctrine of the Genealogical Unity of Mankind. This doctrine consists of three interrelated axioms: first, that kinship is a natural and vital institution
or domain of all human societies; second, that kinship has to do with the reproduction of human beings and the relations between human beings that are the concomi-
tants of reproduction; and finally, that sexual reproduction creates biological links
between persons, and these have important qualities apart from any social or cultural attributes.

The use of the gloss 'mother' for the Korowai *ni* seems to presuppose a comparability of the Korowai and English concepts based on the assumption that such
genealogically defined categories, in their primary meaning, have a cross-cultural
validity; in the words of Schneider (1984: 120), 'A mother is a mother the world over,
even if mothers vary in certain ancillary aspects.'

This last point, that mothers the world over have something in common, is precisely
what Wierzbicka (1992: 337) wants to argue. She formulates the hypothesis that the
concepts of biological mother and father are lexicalised in all languages and accordingly can be used as universal semantic primitives of kinship terminologies. 'Lexicalised'
means that all languages have lexical items that have 'biological mother' and 'biological father' as their meanings or as one of their meanings. It is, of course, this last stipu-
lation ('or as one of their meanings') that makes this hypothesis so difficult to test.

Not surprisingly, Wierzbicka (1992) fully agrees with the following observation by Scheffler:

> Contrary to the fantasies of some Western observers, Australian concepts of kinship are rooted in concepts of bisexual reproduction. As understood in Australian cultures, fertile sexual intercourse is necessary and sufficient to produce an animate human being. The man and woman who produce such a being are known as his or her 'father' and 'mother'. (Scheffler 1978: 515)

Schneider objects to the use of terms like 'rooted in', 'constrained by', or 'based on' to describe the relationship between the biology of human reproduction and kinship notions on these grounds:

> The notion of a 'base in nature' creates a self-justifying and untestable definition of kinship: 'kinship' as a sociocultural phenomenon is, in the first instance, defined as entailing those 'natural' or 'biological' facts which it is at the same time said to be 'rooted in' or 'based on'. (1984: 138)

It is not difficult to find indications in Korowai texts that sexual intercourse between a male and a female is seen as necessary for pregnancy and procreation. Consider for example sections (32)–(38) of the *Ginol Silamtena* text, a myth of origin presented in chapter 6. In that fragment, it is clear that in order to bring forth other people, a man and a woman are needed; since the original couple are both males, the older one turns the younger one into a woman by removing his penis and scrotum and applying all sorts of animal fat until the sexual intercourse is satisfying and results in birth. This animal fat magic reveals that sexual intercourse is not the only thing needed for procreation: fertility magic is also crucial.

The presence of Korowai beliefs about bisexual reproduction in itself does not tell us anything about the significance of such biological links in the Korowai conceptualisation of genealogical relationships. Schneider (1984) has convincingly argued that not all genealogies are equal: the defining elements do not have the same place or significance in all cultures, and the nature and content of genealogical relationships vary from culture to culture. We simply do not know enough to say anything definitive about the nature and contents of Korowai genealogical relations.

It has been reported that some languages have words denoting classificatory parents, as opposed to 'biological' parents (e.g., Dyirbal; see Dixon 1989). We conclude this section by just mentioning some Korowai data that seem relevant in this context, leaving the complex issue of Korowai biological parenthood to future research.

First, there are the Korowai loan phrases *bapa sungguh* 'true father' and *mama sungguh* 'true mother' from local varieties of Indonesian, to distinguish one's 'own' father and mother from classificatory fathers and mothers. In other Awyu languages, with similar kinship terminologies, these same Indonesian expressions also have been loaned. Of course, the mere presence of a loan does not imply that the concept denoted by the loan was absent in precontact days, but we have the impression that these loans for 'true parents' are a response to the fact that outsiders in the area—for example, when they are informed that someone's parent has died—always want to know whether the deceased was a 'true' parent (*mama/bapa sungguh*).

Second, there are modifiers of absolute seniority, which perhaps imply a distinction between ego's classificatory parents and ego's 'own' parents: *-alop* 'first-born', *-khaja* 'last born', and *-alüfekha* 'born in between':

(17) naté-khaja   'my father's youngest brother'
      my.father-lastborn

(18) naté-alüfekha   'my father's in-between-born brother'
      my.father-in.between born

(19) naté-alop   'my father's oldest brother'
      my.father-firstborn

If classificatory are distinguished from nonclassificatory parents in the Korowai language, it remains to be determined by future research how that notion of 'biological' parenthood is construed in Korowai culture.

6

Korowai Texts

The texts in this chapter function as evidence for the grammatical statements in this book but also as illustrations of discourse patterns and of genres within the oral tradition. Furthermore, the texts are selected for the way in which they are windows to aspects of Korowai culture.

There are nine texts in this chapter. The texts were produced by six different speakers, all from different clans, including one female narrator. Four texts are narratives from the oral tradition, one text is an exposition on the procedure followed when pigs are sacrificed, three texts are real-life stories, and one text is a song.

Embedded in the texts are long sections with dialogues; the *Khenil-khenil* and the *Mukhalé* texts are especially rich in dialogue material.

The real-life narratives are the easiest to follow. The texts from the oral tradition, especially the myth of origin, *Ginol Silamtena*, are much harder to understand. Such texts are part of a whole tradition of stories and themes, the knowledge of which is presupposed.

Each text is preceded by a short introduction on its type and contents, the narrator, and the cirumstances of the recording.

Both the more esoteric, mythological texts from the oral tradition and the more transparant texts from real life are important for the ways in which they reflect aspects of Korowai culture. In the endnotes, we have tried to indicate where and how the texts reflect crucial concepts and conventions of Korowai culture, as discussed in chapter 1.

To underline the oral character of the texts, speech errors, hesitation phenomena, repetitions, false starts, and the like have not been edited out. For ease of reference, the texts have been given titles.

The following texts are presented:

1. *The Resurrection Story*. This text is from oral tradition about a man who was buried but came back to the land of the living. Themes: *khomilo* concept ('death'; cf. chapter 1, Mankind), *yanop-khayan* concept ('soul'; cf. chapter 1, Mankind), and *debüloptalé* ('road to the land of the dead'; cf. chapter 1, Universe).

2. *The Pig Sacrifice*. This is a procedural text about sacrificing pigs to ancestral spirits on *wotop* (sacred) spots on the clan territory. Themes: *mbolombolop* concept ('ancestors'; cf. chapter 1, Some central ideological notions) and *kholopamo* concept ('recompensation'; cf. chapter 1, Some central ideological notions).

3. *Ginol Silamtena*. This is a myth of origin of the *lamolaup* genre (cf. chapter 1, Oral tradition). Themes: destruction of the first creation by fire, primordial deluge, construction of the present universe out of the bones of the mythical pig Faül, the original human couple (two brothers, the older turning the younger into a woman to facilitate procreation), taboo concerning certain forms of sexual intercourse, common origin of celestial bodies and mankind, and animal food originating from the first woman.

4. *The Origin of the Khomei Clan*. The text belongs to the genre of *laibolekha mahüon* 'words of descent', totemistic stories about the origin of clans, in this case the origin of the Khomei people who live at the banks of the Fukh River. Themes: totem origin of Khomei people, distribution of covers for male and female private parts, and common origin of the Citak tribe and Khomei people.

5. *A Folktale about the Fofumonalin Brothers*. Text (by female narrator) of a *wakhatum* story, that is, a kind of Korowai folktale (see chapter 1, Oral tradition on Korowai genres). The actors presented in this story can be described as typical characters with stereotyped behaviour, who also play a role in other Korowai folktales. Themes: first appearance of the *beni* 'bird of paradise', preparation and celebration of a sago grub festival (cf. chapter 1, Sago), and metamorphosis of human beings in animals and vice versa (cf. chapter 1, Mankind).

6. *Khenil-khenil*. This is a real-life narrative. In this important ethnohistorical document, the story of the development of contacts between the Downstream Korowai and people of the outside world is told from the perspective of the Korowai people, starting with a report about the first encounter with the Dutch missionary Veldhuizen and the deliberations of the older Korowai concerning the completely new experiences. Since the missionaries in Yaniruma also wrote detailed reports on the first contacts (see appendix 4), the whole stage of first contact is richly documented for this recently contacted community. Themes: *mbolombolop* concept ('ancestors'; cf. chapter 1, Some central ideological notions), *kampung* formation (cf. chapter 1, Recent history of contact and Korowai villages: settlement and housing patterns), *laléo* concept ('bad spirit'; cf. chapter 1, Some central ideological notions), and *lamol/wola* concept ('universe'; cf. chapter 1, Universe).

7. *Aibum*. This text is a real-life narrative. The narrator gives an account of his attendance at several sago grub festivals. Theme: sago grub festival (cf. chapter 1, Sago).

8. *Mukhalé*. This is a real-life narrative. It is fascinating for the way in which it reflects the Korowai obsession with (magic) cannibalism connected with the *khakhua* concept, for the way in which the surgery to remove arrowtips from a wounded Korowai man by a Dutch nurse is told, and finally for the way in which the killings performed by Mukhalé are told. Themes: strong-man concept (cf. chapter 1, Cultural relations, under social and political organisation; kinship), *khakhua* concept ('witchcraft'; cf. chapter 1, Some central ideological notions), *khomilo* concept ('death'; cf. chapter 1, Mankind), and encounter between Korowai and outside world (cf. chapter 1, Recent history of contact).

9. *The Gom Song*. *Gom* is the name of the sacred song sung during the final stage of the sago grub feast, when the sacred fence (*khandin damon*) is removed (see Table 1–7, H: 38). Theme: growth and multiplication of the sago and the (young men of the) clan.

The Resurrection Story

The narrator was Fénélun Molonggai, a male, about 25 years of age. The text was recorded on November 1, 1989, when the narrator was asked to tell a traditional story about the resurrection of the deceased, in the context of a discussion of the issue of life after death.

This story about a man who has been buried but came out of his grave takes the form of a quotation from (4) until (31). The narrator quotes his father, who had heard the story from his father. Since prolonged unconsciousness is one of the most important criteria for establishing whether someone is dead, in Korowai society an apparently dead, living person may indeed be buried.

(1) mül-alüp   mbolo-mbolop-to[1] mbolo-mbolop mahüon uma-té-do
    former-time ancestor-ancestor-FOC ancestor-ancestor story tell-3PL.REAL-DS
    'In former days the forefathers told a story to the (next generations of) forefathers,'

(2) abül-fekha khomilo-bo-kha   mahüon uma-té-do
    man-a   die-3SG.PERF.REAL-CONN story tell-2PL.REAL-DS
    'the story of a man who had died they told,'

(3) n-até   dai-bo-fekho   n-até-lo   nu umo
    my-father hear-3SG.PERF.REAL-until my-father-FOC me tell.3SG.REAL
    'and my father heard it until it was my father who told it to me,'

(4) ne-mbam-o   mül-alüp[2] mül-ano-imban-fekha khomilo-do
    my-child-VOC former-time former-people-individual-a die.REAL.3SG-DS
    '"My child, once upon a time some person of the former people died, and . . ."'

(5) fe-lu-té   walé-do   debünenul[3]   mé-laimekhe-té-dakhu[4]
    put-NEAR-3PL.REAL early.in.the.morning daybreak.REAL.3SG-DS earth-bury-3PL.REAL-SS
    '"they put down (his corpse) and early the next morning they buried him, and . . ."'

(6) yekhené khaim[5] lu[6] é-fu-be-bakha-ti
    they   treehouse enter.SS sleep-put-sit-HOD-3PL.REAL
    '"having entered the treehouse they slept,"'

(7) güle-do   é-fu-méma-té-tofekho
     be.dark.3SG.REAL-DS sleep-put-IMM-3PL.REAL-DS
     "'and at night, when they just were asleep,'"

(8) yekhené-nggé mé-laimekho-bakha-til-e-kha   melu-tofekho[7]   wé[8]
     their-friend   earth-bury-HOD-3PL.REAL-TR-CONN get.up.3SG.REAL-DS EXCLM
     "'their friend, whom they had buried that day, got up and'"

(9) mé-laimekho-bakha-ti-do   mbakha-mo-f-è   dé-dakhu
     earth-bury-HOD-3PL-DS   what-SUPP-1SG.INTENT-EXCLM QUOTE.3SG.REAL-SS
     "'he wondered, 'Well, now that they have buried (me), what can I do?' and ...'"

(10) baul   amo-do   mé-laimekho-bakha-til-e-kha
     stay.3SG.REAL do.3SG.REAL-DS earth-bury-HOD-3PL.REAL-TR-CONN
     damil-mo-dakhu[9]
     open-SUPP.3SG.REAL-SS
     "'thus he stayed, the buried one, and then he opened (the grave), and'"

(11) mé   bul-mekho-bol-e-kha[10]
     earth covered-SUPP-stay.3SG.REAL-TR-CONN
     "'because of being covered with mud,'"

(12) anggo-te-nè khaim   khe-bakh-i   khe-bakh-i   khe-bakh-i[11]
     slow-be-SS   treehouse go-HOD-3SG.REAL go-HOD-3SG.REAL go-HOD-3SG.REAL
     "'he walked to the treehouse just slowly'"

(13) khe-nè yafin   anggo-te-nè[12] lu-bakh-i
     go-SS treehouse.stairs slow-be-SS   go.upward-HOD-3SG.REAL
     lu-bakh-i   lu   lu
     go.upward-HOD-3SG.REAL go.upward.3SG.REAL go.upward.3SG.REAL
     lu   lu   lu
     go.upward.3SG.REAL   go.upward.3SG.REAL go.upward.3SG.REAL
     lu   lu   lu-dom-pekho[13]
     go.upward.3SG.REAL   go.upward.3SG.REAL go.upward.3SG.REAL-DS-and
     "'then just slowly he went upstairs, going up and up and up and up,'"

(14) yafin   khala-kho   lefu khebé-mo-khebé-mo-mo[14]
     treehouse.stairs be.on.top-there end totter-SUPP-move.to.and.fro-SUPP-SUPP.3SG.REAL
     "'he caused the top of the stairs to move to and fro ...'"

(15) khebé-mo-khebé-mo-mo-do[15]
     totter-SUPP-totter-SUPP-SUPP.3SG.REAL-DS
     "'He caused it to move to and fro, and'"

(16) i-mbakha[16] nokhu-nggé abül-fekha   ol-ekhi-lekhén-tè dul-ekhi-lekhé
     this-what.Q   our-friend male.person-a.certain faeces-?-reason-or penis-?-reason
     wai-mémo-kha   lu-mbo-benè   de-té-dakhu
     go.out-3SG.IMM.REAL-CONN go.upward-3SG.PROGR-Q QUOTE-3PL.REAL-SS
     lu-bakh-i   lu
     go.upward-HOD-3SG.REAL go.upward-SS
     "'they wondered, 'What is this? Is one of our friends, who just had gone out for relieving himself or for urinating, entering this moment?' and'"

(17) i-nè khami-bo-do
look.at-SS sit-stay.3SG.REAL-DS

"'they were watching, and'"

(18) wof-e-kha abül lu-bakh-i
that-TR-CONN male.person go.upward-HOD-3SG.REAL

"'that man went up and up and up'"

(19) khala yafin-bo-ta dal-mekho-do[17]
up treehouse.stairs-opening-LOC appearing-SUPP.3SG.REAL-DS

"'and upstairs in the stairs' entrance he appeared, and'"

(20) ima-té-tofekho wé khofél-apa
see-3PL.REAL-DS EXCLM boy-only.EXCLM

"'they looked but—Oh boy!—...'"

(21) khof-e-kha khomilo-do mé-laimekho-bakha-ti-kha abül lu
that-TR-CONN die.REAL.3SG-DS earth-bury-HOD-3PL.REAL-CONN man go.upward.SS
falé wü nggé gu laléo[18] lai-ati-bo-dakhu
appear.3SG.REAL EXCLM friend you demon come-hold-be.2SG.REAL-SS
lelé-mbol-e-kholo-tè
come-2SG.PROGR-TR-Q-or

"'that man who died and whom they had buried earlier that day, did appear right now, 'Hey, friend, are you coming as a bad spirit,''"

(22) mbakha-mol-mo-dakhu lelé-mbol-e-kholo de-té-tofekho
what.Q-SUPP-do.2SG.REAL-SS come-2SG.PROGR-TR-Q QUOTE-3PL.REAL-DS.but

"'or how are you coming?', they asked, but'"

(23) mayokh manda nu khomile-lé-dakhu[19] kho-sü[20] kha-lé-lofekho
friends no I die-1SG.REAL-SS there-to go-1SG.REAL-DS.but

"''No, friends, I passed away and went there, but''"

(24) debülop-talé[21] walüp-ta lül aüle-té-do
way-big half.way-LOC barrier close-3PL.REAL-DS

"''halfway the big road they had made a barrier''"

(25) sé wokhelimekho lailo la-lé-lofekho
next return.SS return.SS come-1SG.REAL-DS.but

"''and I returned and came back but ...''"

(26) gekhené nu mé-laimekho-bakha-ti-do
you me earth-bury-HOD-3PL.REAL-DS

"''you already had buried me, and ...''"

(27) senggile-lé amo-do mé-bol dami-mo le-nè
be.frightened-1SG.REAL do.3SG.REAL-DS earth-hole open-SUPP.SS come-SS
lu-ba-lé dé-do
enter-PERF-1SG.REAL quote.3SG.REAL-DS

"''I was frightened, and having opened the grave I came and entered", he reported, and'"

(28) gele-tél   amo-do   lelip   khami-ba-té-fekho
      be.afraid-3PL.REAL do.3SG.REAL-DS   together sit-stay-3PL.REAL-until

      "'they were afraid and they stayed together until'"

(29) ye-defol fo-dakhu   ye-mba-mbam laifu-dakhu
      his-wife   marry.3SG.REAL-SS   his-child-child   bring.forth.3SG.REAL-SS

      "'he married a wife, and he got children and'"

(30) babo   babo   babo-fekho
      live.3SG.REAL   live.3SG.REAL   live.3SG.REAL -until

      "'he lived his life until'"

(31) nggé-telo-dakhu   khomilo-bo
      old.man-be.3SG.REAL-SS   die-3SG.PERF.REAL

      "'he became an old man and then he died,'"

(32) dé-dakhu-fekho[22]   n-até-lo   wa-mo-nè   umo-do   dai-ba-lé
      quote.3SG.REAL-SS-and   my-father-FOC thus-SUPP-SS tell.3SG.REAL-DS   hear-PERF-1SG.REAL

      'he said, it was my father who told it this way and I heard it.'

The Pig Sacrifice

Another discourse produced by narrator Fénélun Molonggai[23] was recorded on June 10, 1990, during a conversation about a pig sacrifice.

The text is an exposition on pig sacrifices in general and accordingly is told in the habitual mood.

The Korowai perform pig sacrifices in certain circumstances in which there is a general feeling that the well-being of the clan is seriously threatened, for example, when many people are ill [cf. (28)] or when food is scarce [cf. (29)]. In 1989, five pigs were sacrificed to the ancestors by the Khaul-Nandup people after an expedition of outsiders had crossed their territory. When outsiders enter clan territories, this is perceived as a serious threat (see chapter 1, Territories and treehouses of Korowai clans).

Pig sacrifices are performed by the male adults of a single clan. A pig is slaughtered, and the pieces of meat are located at several spots within or close to a *wotop* (a sacred clearing on the clan territory). While allocating the pieces, the participants in the ceremony call the spirits of the ancestors who live in the neighbourhood, urging them to consume the meat and to repay the sacrifice with their helpful mediation. After the ceremony is over, including a pause in which the ancestors are supposed to take the meat, the pieces are collected and distributed among the relatives who are attending the ceremony and consumed by them.

The morphosyntactical patterns of linkage and continuity in this text have been analysed in chapter 4.

(1) wof-è[24]   gol ülma-té-dakhu
     there-CONN   pig   kill-3PL.REAL-SS

     'After they have killed a pig there,'

(2)   bando-lu   khaim-an   fe-nè fu   bume-ma-té[25]
      bring-enter.SS treehouse-LOC get-SS put.SS slaughter-HAB-3PL

      'they bring it and having put it into the house they slaughter it . . .'

(3)   bume-ma-té-dakhu   ol[26] di   fe-nè   fu-ma-té-do
      slaughter-HAB-3PL-SS feces get.out.SS take-SS put-HAB-3PL-DS

      'They usually slaughter, and get the intestines out of it and put it down,'

(4)   ni-khü-to   bando-khe-nè   ao-ma-té[27]
      mother-PL-FOC   bring-go-SS   cleanse-HAB-3PL

      'and the women take (the intestines) and cleanse (them).'

(5)   ao-leful-mekho   khaim   gilfo-ma-té-do[28]   gol-e-khal di-fu-ma-té
      cleanse-end-SUPP.SS treehouse go.away-HAB-3PL-DS   pig-TR-meat cut-put-HAB-3PL

      'When they have finished washing, they go away to the treehouse and (the males) cut
      the pig meat out and put it down.'

(6)   di-fu-leful-mekho él gekhené khaim-khaup gübole-mon-é
      cut-put-end-SUPP.SS yes you(PL)   treehouse-inside come.together-2PL.IMP-EXCLM
      de-di-ma-té[29]
      QUOTE-QUOTE-HAB-3PL

      'They cut it and when they have put it down, "Yes, you should come together in the
      treehouse', they say.'

(7)   kül-mekho-ma-té-do[30]   gailo-fekho   khobül-fekho fe-nè fe-nè woto-fekha[31]
      in.order-SUPP-HAB-3PL-DS kidney-COORD leg-COORD   get-SS get-SS sacred.place-a
      doleli-ma-té[32]
      call-HAB-3PL

      'When they have prepared (all of it) they usually put the kidneys and the leg down and
      they call a certain sacred place (on the territory),'

(8)   iè   wof-e-kha   mbolo-fekho   ge-mba-mbam-pekho ge-yano-fekho
      EXCLM there-TR-CONN ancestor-COORD your-child-child-COORD your-people-COORD

      '"Oh, forefather over there, and your children and your people,'

(9)   if-e-kha   gol-khobül bando-khe-nè le-mén-é
      this-TR-CONN pig-leg   bring-go-SS   eat-2PL.IMP-EXCLM

      '"you should take this leg of the pig away and eat it.'

(10) le-mén-dakhu mano-pa-mon-é[33]
      eat-2PL.IMP-SS good-SUPP-2PL.IMP-EXCLM

      '"You should eat it and help (us)!"'

(11) mesé khobül-fekho woto-fekha[34]   fo   fe-nè fu-ma-té-dakhu
      next leg-COORD   sacred.place-a.certain get.SS get-SS put-HAB-3PL-SS

      'And then they usually take another leg and put it down on another sacred place, and . . .'

(12) wof-e-kha   mbolo-wè   ge-mba-mbam-pekho if-e-kha   bando-khe-nè
      there-TR-CONN ancestor-VOC your-child-child-COMIT this-TR-CONN bring-go -SS
      lé-m-é
      eat-2SG.IMP-EXCLM

      '"Oh, forefather over there, with your children, you should take this and eat it!"'

(13) lé-m-dakhu   nokhup dél-o   füon-o   gol-o
     eat-2SG.IMP-SS us   bird-COORD marsupial.species-COORD pig-COORD
     fédo-m-do   le-fén-è
     give-2SG.IMP-DS eat-1PL.INTENT-EXCLM

'"You should eat and give us birds and lizards and pigs, so we can eat it!"'

(14) damol fo   fe-nè fu   woto-fekha mbolo-fekho ge-mambüm-pekho
     back   get.SS get-SS put.SS sacred.place-a ancestor-COORD your-children-COORD
     ge-yano-fekho   ge-ni-khül-fekho   if-e-kha   bando-khe-nè
     your-people-COORD your-mother-PL-COORD here-TR-CONN bring-go-SS
     le-mén-é
     eat-2PL.IMP-EXCLM

'And having put the back part (they say), "Hey, you forefather of that certain sacred place, with your children, your people and your wives, you should take this and eat it!"'

(15) le-mén-dakhu nokhu lép-telo-khai-kha   nokhu mano-pa-mon-do
     eat-2PL.IMP-SS we   ill-be-3SG.IRR-CONN us   good-SUPP-2PL.IMP-DS
     khi-telo-fon-è
     healthy-be-1PL.INTENT-CONN

'"You should eat it and if we fall ill, you should cure us so we can be healthy."'

(16) manop woto-fekha   fo   fe-nè fuiè   wof-e-kha
     chest sacred.place-a.certain get.SS get-SS put.SS.EXCLM there-TR-CONN
     maun-makho-ta bau-kha   abül-è
     river-mouth-LOC live.3SG.REAL-CONN man-CONN

'The chest they put on another sacred place and (they say), "Oh, man who lives there at the mouth of the river . . ."'

(17) gu if-e-kha   manop gol-manop bando-khe-nè lé-m-é
     you this-TR-CONN chest pig-chest bring-go-SS eat-2SG.IMP-EXCLM
     de-di-ma-té
     QUOTE-QUOTE-HAB-3PL

'"you should take this chest, this pig chest and eat it," they say.'

(18) sé khabéan fo   fe-nè fu   wof-e-kha   du-dül-fekho
     next head   get.SS get-SS put.SS there-TR-CONN tree-crown-CIRCUM
     bau-kha   mbolop
     live.3SG.REAL-CONN ancestor

'Next they take the head and put it down, (and then they say), "Oh, forefather that lives in the crown of that tree over there,"'

(19) gu if-e-kha   gol-khabéan bando-khe-nè lé-m-è
     you this-TR-CONN pig-head   bring-go-SS eat-2SG.IMP-EXCLM

'"you should take this pig head and eat it."'

(20) lé-m-dakhu   nokhu imbo-m-è   de-dil-ma-té
     eat-2SG.IMP-SS us   pay.attention-2SG.IMP-EXCLM QUOTE-QUOTE-HAB-3PL

'"You should eat it and pay attention to us!"'

(21) khamon fo   fe-nè fu   wof-e-kha   du-dül-fekho   ba-té-kha
forepaw   get.SS get-SS put.SS there-TR-CONN tree-crown-CIRCUM live-3PL.REAL-CONN
yanop
people

'After having put down a forepaw, (they say), "Oh, people that live there in the top of the trees,"'

(22) gekhené if-e-kha   gol-mél   bando-khe-nè le-mén-dakhu nokhu
you   this-TR-CONN pig-forepaw bring-go-SS   eat-2PL.IMP-SS us
im-ba-mon-è
see-stay-2PL.IMP-EXCLM

'"you should take this forepaw of the pig and eat it, and pay attention to us."'

(23) wa-mol-mo   mamaf bau   énon-mekho[35]
thus-SUPP-SUPP.3SG.REAL a.little stay.3SG.REAL prolonged-SUPP.SS

'Having done this way, they stay for a while'

(24) sé gol-khal fo   gübo-nè   fu-ma-té   fu-leful-mekho gol-khal dil-ma-té
next pig-meat get.SS collect-SUPP.SS put-HAB-3PL put-end-SUPP.SS pig-meat cut-HAB-3PL

'and then they collect the pig meat and put it down; having finished this they cut it into pieces.'

(25) di-leful-mekho-ma-té-dakhu
cut-end-SUPP-HAB-3PL-SS

'When they have finished cutting,'

(26) mom[36]   sabül[37] afé   aw   modol   mofekha   ni[38]
mother's.brother nephew older.brother older.sister younger.sister younger.brother mother
sendip bante-nè   leful-mekho-ma-té-dakhu
next   distribute-SS end-SUPP-HAB-3PL-SS

'they distribute (the pieces) all of it among the mother's brothers, the nephews, the brothers and the sisters, and the mothers and . . .'

(27) yekhené-pan-è khabéan bonggol lakhup duo   lé-ma-té-dakhu
they-self-CONN head   mouth   stone put.into.SS eat-HAB-3PL.REAL-SS

'they themselves prepare the head and the mouth with (burning hot) stones and eat it and'

(28) béto-pé   lép afü-ma-tél-e-kha   menèl khi-telo   menèl
behind-LOC ill wrestle-SUPP-3PL.REAL-TR-CONN quickly healthy-be.3SG.REAL quickly
khi-telo
healthy-be.3SG.REAL

'afterward the very sick people quickly become healthy.'

(29) lu-ngga   gol-o   küal-o   füon-o   yafil-o-fekho
eat-INF.CONN pig-COORD cassowary-COORD marsupial-COORD snake-COORD-COORD
lu-ngga   lefugop   be-manda-da   menèl lé-lé lefaf
eat-INF.CONN all.kinds.of NEG-not.being-NEG quickly eat-eat finished

'Concerning the food, pigs, cassowaries, marsupials, snakes, and all kinds of food, there is really not soon an end to the eating of it.'

Ginol Silamtena

The narrator, Dofualé, an 18-year-old male member of the large Khomei (Khayak-hatun) clan produced the *Ginol Silamtena* text in the missionary's office in Yaniruma in May 1991.

In 1989, the narrator already had given some fragmentary information on this subject, namely, the story of the creation of the universe according to the oral tradition of his clan. At that time there was no opportunity to tape the spoken text.

Presently the narrator was asked to tell the whole story again in front of the tape recorder. He asked us to handle the information with care because of its secret character; the story forms part of the larger corpus of the *lamolaup* 'the stories of the universe', the contents of which are not allowed to be known by women, children, or outsiders (see chapter 1, Oral tradition).

The story contains three episodes: (1) the creator-spirit Ginol Silamtena setting the former universe afire; (2) creation of a new world and humankind; (3) origin of the various kinds of food.

(1)   mül-khuf-efè   af-efè   lamol   fu-bo-kha   abül-fefè[39]   yu
       former-time-TOP there-TOP universe put-3SG.PERF.REAL-CONN male.person-TOP he
       lamol   menil fe-nè fu-dakhu[40]
       universe fire get-SS put-SS

       'In former times the one who created the universe set the universe on fire and . . .'

(2)   a   la-tom-pekho[41]   khejo[42]   saukh-tamon-tefu khejo
       that female-FOC-ATTENT sago.leaf.stem tobacco-bunch-end sago.leaf.stem

       'the woman (placed) tobacco at the sago leaf stem, the top of a bunch of tobacco leaves at the leaf stem,'

(3)   kho   ü-lamü-gele-té-dakhu-fekho[43]   wap-ta   khejo
       sago.tree cut.down-pound-press-3PL.REAL-SS-and   there-LOC sago.leaf.stem
       ao-dakhu-fekho   saukh-tamon inggenun[44] khabéan-ta fu-dakhu-fekho[45]
       plant.3SG.REAL-SS-and   tobacco-bunch sago.leaf.stem head-LOC put.3SG.REAL-SS-and
       babo-tofekho
       sit.3SG.REAL-DS.but

       'they had cut down a sago tree, pounded (the stem), and pressed (the flour out of the fibres) and she had set up the sago leaf stem (construction) and at the very end of the leaf stem she had attached the bunch of tobacco leaves and she stayed there but . . .'

(4)   Ginol[46] Silam-tena[47]   yu khonai-mémo-fekho wof-e-kha   mangga[48]
       Ginol   mouse.like.animal-DIMIN he go-3SG.IMM.REAL-until that-TR-CONN dry.sago.leaves
       lai-duo-bakh-i   melél-mo   melil khe-nè
       break(broken)-put.into-HOD-3SG.REAL finish-SUPP.3SG.REAL fire go-SS
       fumo-to   él ü-telo-dom-pekho[49]
       blow.3SG.REAL-DS yes gone-be.3SG.REAL-DS-and

       'Ginol, the Little Mouselike, he just was walking around and he had collected all the dry sago leaves and put them on a heap and he went to the fire and blew it, but yes it was dead and'

(5)   wé   mayokh[50] dé-dakhu   meli-tekhé di-ati-afé-mémo-tofekho[51]
       EXCLM friends   QUOTE.3SG.REAL-SS fire-purpose get(?)-hold-turn-3SG.IMM.REAL-DS

       '"Oh, dear", he said and wandered around looking for fire . . .'

(6)   wé   if-e-kha   lal   wof-e-kha   Wokhemél Yambim[52]
       EXCLM this-TR-CONN female that-TR-CONN Wokhemél Yambim
       mambisi-kholo-tom-pekho baka   dé-dakhu-fekho[53]
       uterus-bone-FOC-ATTENT   sound.of.inflaming QUOTE.3SG.REAL-SS-and

       'Hey, this woman, it was Yokhemel Yambin, her uterus inflamed and . . .'

(7)   dali saukh-tamon ülfo-dakhu[54]   wa-sü   lamol
       there tobacco-bunch gone.RESULT.3SG.REAL-SS there-from universe
       do-fo
       be.burnt-RESULT.3SG.REAL

       'from there the bunch of tobacco immediately was gone and from there the whole world
       burnt down.'

(8)   lamol do-fo-dom-pekho   aful[55]   amodo if-e-kha
       universe be.burnt-RESULT.3SG.REAL-DS-and wonder.3SG.REAL next   this-TR-CONN
       Ginol Silam-tena   yu di-ati-afé lokhté   abul-khal[56]
       Ginol mouse.like.animal-DIMIN he? hold-turn go.away.3SG.REAL moustached.treeswift-skin
       khomé-dakhu[57]
       transform-SS

       'The whole world burnt down and he was wondering, and then, Ginol, the Little Mouselike,
       looking around, he went away, then transformed (himself) into a moustached tree swift.'

(9)   di-ati-afé khe-bakh-i   khe-bakh-i   khe-bakh-il-fekho   kha-nè
       ?-hold-turn go-HOD-3SG.REAL go-HOD-3SG.REAL go-HOD-3SG.REAL-until go-SS
       kho-sü   kül-mo-dakhu-fekho   do   be-bakh-i-do
       there-from in.order-SUPP.3SG.REAL-SS-and burn.SS stay-HOD-3SG.REAL-DS
       kül-mekho-do
       in.order-SUPP.3SG.REAL-DS

       'Looking around he walked for quite a long time until he had finished (his job) there,
       until he had burnt, so that all had been finished and'

(10)   alif-e-kha[58] Wolop-akhol[59] laünkhul   laünbün[60]   khakholo-bol
       this-TR-CONN Wolop.river-mouth freshwater.fish.species freshwater.fish.species mouth-opening
       melé-ai-to   él falép   mén-e-pé
       move-go.down.3SG.REAL-DS yes side.of.upper.chest side-TR-LOC
       do-demé-mo-do[61]
       burn-tear.open-SUPP.3SG.REAL-DS

       'at the mouth of the Wolop River he landed into the mouth of a laünkhul, of a laünbün
       fish, and then he discovered that his flank had been burnt through,'

(11)   khalilmekho abul-khal   khomilo   bedi-lokhte-bakh-i sé
       be.frightened.SS moustached.treeswift-skin transform.SS fly-go.away-HOD-3SG next
       wai-dakhu
       go.down.3SG.REAL-SS

       'so he was frightened and then he transformed himself into a moustached tree swift and
       flew away after which he came down and'

(12) wai-dakhu-fekho   alo-bo-dom-pekho khomolamol lekhüpwaila   bilamalin[62]
go.down.3SG.REAL-SS-and stand-be.3SG.DS-and all.kinds.of   all.kinds.of   all.kinds.of
do-dél-e-kha-lalé[63]   wai-mo-dom-pekho   fo
burn-tear.of.3SG.REAL-TR-CONN-INTENS go.down-SUPP.3SG.REAL-DS-and get.SS
anol-mekho
side-SUPP.3SG.REAL

'He came down and stood still and a very large amount of all kinds of torn off and scorched (remnants of the fire) moved downward and he shoved it aside.'

(13) fo-anol-mekho-nè be-bakh-i   yu-fè wai   du-lefu-la
get-side-SUPP-SS   sit-HOD-3SG.REAL he-TOP go.down.SS tree-end-LOC
alo-bo-dakhu
stand-stay.3SG.REAL-SS

'He kept shoving it aside and then he came down, stood still on the end of a tree (branch) and'

(14) meli-to[64] ye mül-khup meli-to[65] ye dofo-dakhu   sé ap-ta
fire-with he former-time fire-with he be.burnt-RESULT.3SG.REAL-SS next there-LOC
maé-ta hefi-mekho-do[66]   khe-nè lokhté-do[67]
water-open-SUPP.3SG.REAL-DS go-SS   go.away.3SG.REAL-DS

'In former times with fire he had . . . with fire he had burnt and then there he had opened the (streams of) waters and it ran away and . . .'

(15) ap-ta   alo-bo-dakhu-fekho   fo-ngg-alingga   lu-nè[68]
there-LOC stand-stay.3SG.REAL-SS-and take-INF.CONN-without move.up-SUPP.SS
be-bakh-i   be-bakh-i   be-bakh-i   be-bakh-i   be-bakh-i
sit-HOD-3SG.REAL sit-HOD-3SG sit-HOD-3SG sit-HOD-3SG sit-HOD-3SG.REAL

'There he stood and he kept shoving aside (all of it) for a long time,'

(16) énonte-bo-tofekho   énonte-bakh-i-tofekho
of.a.long.duration-stay.3SG.REAL-DS of.a.long.duration-HOD-3SG.REAL-DS

'it had taken quite a period, but after a long time,'

(17) Faül[69]   dadü-ai-tofekho   Faül   ül-nè
name.of.mythical.pig swim-go.down.3SG.REAL-DS name.of.mythical.pig kill-SS
bul-mekho-kha-fefè[70]   Faül   ba-nggolol yaüya-pé fe-nè
slaughter-SUPP.3SG.REAL-CONN-TOP name.of.mythical.pig chest-bone   under-LOC get-SS
fu   müf-e-kholol wola-khi-pé fe-nè fu-tofekho
put.3SG.REAL back-TR-bone world-over-LOC get-SS put.3SG.REAL-DS

'Faül came swimming downstream, after having killed and slaughtered Faül, he put his chest- bone part (of meat) beneath (i.e., on the ground), his backbone part he placed toward the sky and'

(18) méan[71] dadü-ai   méan ül-nè bul-fo-kha-fè[72]
dog   swim-go.down.3SG.REAL dog   kill-SS slaughter-RESULT-CONN-TOP
méan-manop-yabén-tom-pekho[73] di-béa-mo-dakhu[74]   i-fekho
dog-chest-fat-with-ATTENT   get.out-rub-SUPP.3SG.REAL-SS here-CIRCUM
wola-khip wola-khif-e-kha   Faül   müf-e-kholol di
world-over world-over-TR-CONN name.of.mythical.pig back-TR-bone cut.SS
lamé-abo-lu[75]
play-chase-move.up.3SG.REAL

'when the dog came swimming downstream, and having killed and slaughtered the dog, with the fat of the dog's chest, which he had cut, he rubbed the backbone parts of Faül to the sky, to the sky upward he played, chasing it upward quickly . . .'

(19) lamé-abo-lu-dakhu-fekho   yelüp[76]   fayan
     play-chase-move.up.3SG.REAL-SS-and kind.of.arrow kind.of.arrow
     mandi-mbonggon-tamon[77]   dilmekho lu
     kind.of.arrow-kind.of.arrow-bunch grip.SS   move.up.3SG.REAL

     'playing he chased it up and then he gripped a bunch of *yelüp*, *fayan*, *mandil*, and *bonggon* arrows and moved it up'

(20) lé-mu-kailon[78]   mayu-mu-kailon[79]   wof-e-kha
     sago.tree-leaf-arrow.made.of.rib mayu.sago-leaf-arrow.made.of.rib that-TR-CONN
     kamèn-mu-kailon-tamon-talé-lom-pekho duo-lai-lu-bo[80]
     long.grass-leaf-arrow-bunch-big-with-ATTENT shoot-come-move.up-stay.3SG.REAL

     'and with a large bunch of small arrows made of the ribs of leaves of *lé* and of *mayu* sago trees long grass he shot continuously.'

(21) lu   khalakh-mekho-dom-pekho lu   khalakh-mo-do[81]
     move.up.SS up-SUPP.3SG.REAL-DS-and   move.up.SS up-SUPP.3SG.REAL-DS
     bebal-yabén   di-béal-fo wa méan-manop-yabén di-béal-fo-mo-do
     centipede.species-fat cut-rub-?   that dog-chest-fat   rub-?-SUPP.3SG.REAL-DS
     lu   khalakh-mekho-do imo-dakhu   mesé melé-ai-dakhu
     move.up.SS up-SUPP.3SG.REAL-DS look.3SG.REAL-SS next move-go.down.3SG.REAL-SS
     wa lamol fu[82]
     that world set.3SG.REAL

     'So it moved up, in upward direction it moved up and then with the fat of the *bebál* centipede, which he had cut out, he rubbed, with the fat of that dog's chest, which he had cut, he rubbed and it moved up, in upward direction, and when he had seen it, he came down again and thus he created the world.'

(22) lamol fu   mano-mano-po-dakhu-fekho
     world set.3SG.REAL in.order-right-SUPP.3SG.REAL-SS-and

     'He created the world and he made it very good and'

(23) fu   mano-manop-khayan-mekhol-e-kha-fè   mbakha-mbonè
     set.3SG.REAL right-right-very-SUPP.3SG.REAL-TR-CONN-TOP what-do.INTENT.PROGR.3SG
     yano-fè   mbakha-mo-kha-té-kholo de-mémo-tofekho
     people-TOP what-SUPP-IRR-3PL-Q   QUOTE-3SG.IMM.REAL-DS.but

     'when he had created it and made it very very good, he just wondered what should be done about mankind.'

(24) mbakha-mo-kha-tél-kho de-mémo-tofekho   él ali dabüp-tan-tena[83]
     what-SUPP-IRR-3PL-Q   QUOTE-3SG.IMM.REAL-DS.but yes this kind.of.rattan-rope-DIMIN
     pa   dé[84]
     crack QUOTE.3SG.REAL

     '"How about them?" he wondered and yes, (the seed of) a *dabüp* rattan burst . . .'

(25) dabüp-tan-tena   pa dé-do   wap-ta alo-bo-dakhu-fekho
     kind.of.rattan-rope-DIMIN crack QUOTE.3SG.REAL-DS there-LOC stand-stay.3SG.REAL-SS-and

     'a *dabüp* rattan burst and (the plant) stood there . . .'

(26) alo-bo-do[85]   énon-té-tofekho   pükh dé-dakhu[86]
stand-stay.3SG.REAL-DS of.a.long.duration-3PL.REAL-DS crack QUOTE.3SG.REAL-SS
lu   khala-khalakh-mekhol amo-do   sé walüp-ta-sü
move.up.SS up-up-SUPP.3SG.REAL do.3SG.REAL-DS next half.way-LOC-at
bi-lelo   pükh de-bo-tofekho
swollen-be.3SG.REAL crack QUOTE-3SG.PERF.REAL-DS

'it stood there for quite a certain period and then it burst open, that is to say, it grew up this way and then halfway (the rope of it) swelled up and burst'

(27) abül   pol monggo-felé-tofekho[87] ap-ta   mamün wakhol gun[88]
male.person two get.out-fall.3SG.REAL-DS there-LOC sun   moon   group
monggo-fele-té-to
get.out-fall-3PL.REAL-DS

'and two male persons fell out of it and also the sun and the moon all together fell out of it and . .'

(28) khami-bo   khami-bo   khamél   amo-do   i
sit-stay.3SG.REAL sit-stay.3SG.REAL sit.3SG.REAL do.3SG.REAL-DS this
ye naném-telo-tofekho   gekhené-fè i-mofu fele-tél-anop[89]   gekhenép-to
he secretly-be.3SG.REAL-DS you-TOP   this-only fall-3PL.REAL-people you-FOC
i-mofu nu wola-kholol[90] khendé-mba-mon-é[91]   dé
this-only me world-bone   care-INGR-IMP.2PL-EXCLM QUOTE.3SG.REAL

'they stayed (there) for some time, they stayed and then he (i.e., Ginol) had hidden himself and said to them, "You people who fell out, you have to care for the world."'

(29) khendé-mba-mon-é[92]   dé-do   wa khendé-mba-té-do
care-INGR-IMP.2PL-EXCLM QUOTE.3SG.REAL-DS there care-INGR-3PL.REAL-DS
Lefilkhei-imban-è[93]   yu di-ati-afé alo-bakh-i   di-ai
Lefilkhei.clan-individual-CONN he ?-keep-turn stand-HOD-3SG.REAL ?-go.down.SS
alolé-tofekho   gu-fala   dé-tofekho
stand.3SG.REAL-DS you-what.about QUOTE.3SG.REAL-DS

'"You people shall take care," he commanded, and they took care, and then some Lefilkhei person who had walked around there stood still and he (Ginol) asked, "Hey, what about you?" and'

(30) nu Lefilkhei-imban   wai   alo-ndé   dé-tofekho   gu Khufom[94]
I Lefilkhei.clan-individual go.down.SS stand-1SG.REAL QUOTE.3SG.REAL-DS you Khufom
Khufom wai   alo-ndé-fé   dé-tofekho
Khufom go.down.SS stand-1SG.REAL-EXCLM QUOTE.2SG.REAL-DS

'"I am a Lefilkhei man who came out and I stand here," he answered, but he said, "You are Khufom, Khufom, you (who) state 'having come out I stay here'"'

(31) gu mo gu gu lilol-benè dé-tofekho   u   bailé
you ? you you falsehood-Q QUOTE.3SG.REAL-DS EXCLM oh.yes
dél-e-kha-lekhé
QUOTE.3SG.REAL-TR-CONN-CAUSE

'"'but perhaps you tell me lies?' but he replied, 'Oh, yes!' and therefore"'

(32) gu a-mofu alo-bo-m-é   dél-e-kha-fé   wa-sü
you there-only stand-stay-IMP.2SG-EXCLM QUOTE.3SG.REAL-TR-CONN-TOP there-at

füboli felé-kha-fè   yu ye naném-telo-do   sé   af-e-kha
jump.SS fall.3SG.REAL-CONN-TOP he he secretly-be.3SG.REAL-DS next that-TR-CONN
yanop pol di-ai-feli-méma-tél-e-kha   ba-té   ba-tél-fekho[95]
person two ?-move.down-fall-IMM-3PL.REAL-TR-CONN stay-3PL.REAL stay-3PL.REAL-until

"'he commanded, 'You only stand there!', but having jumped down from there, he hid himself and next the two people who just had fallen out (of the rattan rope) stayed and stayed until'"

(33) yanop mbakha-monggol-telo-do afe-tél[96]   a-mo-dom-pekho
     people whatever-not-be-DS   wonder-3PL.REAL that.SUPP.3SG.REAL-DS-and
     y-afé-lom-pekho   ye-mofekha   atilo dul lokhesukh-op
     his-older.brother-FOC-ATTENT his-younger.brother hold.SS penis egg-fruit
     lafil-mo-dakhu-fekho
     cut.off-SUPP.3SG.REAL-SS-and

"'they struggled with the problem that there were no other people. Then it was the older brother who seized the younger one, cut off the penis and the scrotum and'"

(34) wof-e-kha   dabüp   dabüp-alop-tom-pekho   dabüp-efekha[97]
     that-TR-CONN kind.of.rattan kind.of.rattan-firstborn-FOC-ATTENT kind.of.rattan-lastborn
     lokhesukh lafé-dakhu-fekho   go-gomo-tofekho
     egg   cut.off.3SG.REAL-SS-and have.sex-have.sex-3SG.REAL-DS.but
     be-sikh-té-da-lelo-tofekho
     NEG-delicious-be.3PL.REAL-NEG-be-DS

"'the rattan rope . . . the rattan rope's firstborn cut off the rattan rope's lastborn's genitals and he had repeatedly sex with him but it did not feel good and . . .'"

(35) khayal-yabén[98] di-lu-dakhu[99]   gomo-tofekho
     fish.species-fat get.out-rub.3SG.REAL-SS have.sex.3SG.REAL-DS.but
     be-sikh-té-da-lelo-tofekho   malan-yabén[100] di-lu-dakhu
     NEG-delicious-be.3PL.REAL-NEG-be-DS snake.species-fat get.out-rub.3SG.REAL-SS
     gomo-tofekho   be-sikh-té-da-lelo-tofekho
     have.sex.3SG.REAL-DS.but NEG-delicious-be.3PL.REAL-NEG-be-DS

"'he rubbed with the fat of the *khayal* fish and had sex again, but it still did not feel good, so with the fat of the *malan* snake he rubbed, had sexual intercourse again but still it was not nice and'"

(36) wap-ta   milon-sip non[101] dé-dakhu-fekho   lu-lu-dakhu-fekho
     there-LOC sago-root sagogrub get.out.3SG.REAL-SS-and rub-rub.3SG.REAL-SS-and
     gomo-tofekho[102]
     have.sex.3SG.REAL-DS

"'there he got out a sago grub out of the root end of a *milon* tree, rubbed repeatedly (with the fat of it) and then he had sex another time and'"

(37) nggé Faül[103]   sikh-ayan-telo-tofekho
     friend name.of.mythical.pig delicious-very-be.3SG.REAL-DS
     pa i-mofu-bo-m-é   du-n-din-telo   dé-to
     also this-only-stay-2SG.INTENT-EXCL say-INF-POTENT-be.3SG QUOTE.3SG.REAL-DS
     ayul-é[104]   y-afé-mofekha   él dé
     taboo-EXCLM he-older.brother-younger.brother yes QUOTE.3SG.REAL

"''Oh dear, this is very nice, almost it could be said, you stay this way for ever!', he said but then he continued, 'It is certainly not allowed for male siblings to do so.'"

(38) y-anol-mekho-dom-pekho   mesé güli-mo-don-è
      him-side-SUPP.3SG.REAL-DS-and next   be.dark-SUPP.3SG.REAL-DS-EXCLM
      fekha-lalé-lo[105] gül-u-ngga-lekhé-mo-tofekho   fekha-lalé-lo khe-nè
      one-big-FOC   be.dark-INF-CONN-purpose-SUPP.3SG.REAL-DS one-big-FOC   go-SS
      dimekho-mo-do[106]   if-e-kha   khomolamol fu
      put.in-SUPP.3SG.REAL-DS this-TR-CONN all.kinds.of   bring.forth.SS
      ibe-lulo-ma-té   ibe-lulo-ma-té   ibe-lulo-ma-té
      lay.down-NEAR-HAB-3PL lay.down-NEAR-HAB-3PL lay.down-NEAR-HAB-3PL
      ibe-lulo-ma-té   ibe-lulo-ma-té-fekho
      lay.down-NEAR-HAB-3PL lay.down-NEAR-HAB-3PL-until

"'He put him aside and then, when it had become evening, it was a tall one, when it was going to become dark, it was a big one who came and penetrated (him) and, and, giving birth to all kinds of (creatures), they used to lay down all night until . . .'"

(39) nggaüm-ta[107] khondul afü[108] fü-pe-mo-kha   khejom[109]
      finish-LOC   belly   struggle yell-SUPP-SUPP.3SG.REAL-CONN morning.bird
      pi-pe-mol-e-kha   pi-pe-mol-e-kha-fè
      sound.of.khejom-SUPP-SUPP-TR-CONN sound.of.kheyom-SUPP-SUPP-TR-CONN-TOP
      wal-u-ngga-lekhé-mo-mol-é   dil-ma-tél-e-kha
      daybreak-INF-CONN-purpose-SUPP-SUPP.3SG.REAL-EXCLM QUOTE-HAB-3PL-TR-CONN
      khi-te-be-ma-té-do   wali-mo-kha   khondul afü
      alive-be-be.in.the.status.of-HAB-3PL-DS be.light-SUPP.3SG.REAL-CONN belly   struggle.SS
      fü-pol-é   de-di-ma-tél-e-kha-fè
      yell-SUPP.3SG.REAL-EXCLM QUOTE-QUOTE-HAB-3PL-TR-CONN-TOP
      énonté-mo-tofekho   waleli-mo-kha-fè
      of.a.long.duration-SUPP.3SG.REAL-DS become.day-HAB.3SG-CONN-TOP

"'in the end when (s)he yelled in labour pains, (at the time) when the brown-headed crow is crying, when it is crying, at the time when it is going to become light, at the time when people use to say . . . when they are awake, when it becomes light, when people use to say, 'She yells in labour pains', (at the time) it usually still lasts a certain period before it is really getting light,'"

(40) lu-ngga-o[110]   if-e-kha   kho-mol-a-mo-talé
      eat-INF.CONN-COORD this-TR-CONN that-SUPP-that-SUPP-a.lot.of
      fu-ba-lulo-mo   waleli-mo-tofekho   wof-e-kha
      bring.forth-stay-NEAR-SUPP.3SG.REAL become.day-SUPP.3SG.REAL-DS that-TR-CONN
      sol walél-e-khayan   fu-mémo-kha-fè   khal-fayup anol-è
      new be.light.REAL.3SG-TR-true put-3SG.IMM.REAL-CONN-TOP skin-supple snake-CONN
      yabén-mengga duo mayokh if-è   manop-khayan-khayan
      fat-with   mice friends   this-CONN good-very-very
      di-ma-tél-e-kha-fè   manda sol walél-e-khayan
      QUOTE-HAB-3PL-TR-CONN-TOP not   new daybreak.REAL.3SG-TR-really
      fu-mémo-kha   de-ba-té
      bring.forth-3SG.IMM.REAL-CONN tell-PERF-3PL.REAL

"'she (already) had kept on bringing forth this large amount of all kinds of food—then when it really became light, those ones she just given birth early in the morning, namely, the ones with their supple skins, snakes and the ones with fat, the rodents, (in short) the ones of whom people use to say: 'This is very nice! No, this is what she had given birth when it was really beyond daybreak', they told.'"

(41) nokhu-mbolo-mbolop-ton-è   wa-mo-nè   di-ba-té
      our-older.people-older.people-FOC-CONN thus-SUPP-SS say-PERF-3PL.REAL

      'It is our older people (forefathers) who have told it this way.'

The Origin of the Khomei Clan

The next story, which has the same narrator and time of recording as the preceding
text, belongs to the genre of *laibolekha mahüon* 'words of descent', totemistic stories about the origin of clans (see chapter 1, Oral tradition).

The narrator was asked to tell the story about the origin of his own clan, that is,
the Khomei people who live at the banks of the Fukh River.[111] The story was tape-
recorded in the missionary's office in Yaniruma while the narrator and his friend were
left alone. The friend of the narrator is addressed explicitly in (15).

The first part of the story gives a summarised report on the origin of the Khomei
people in general, namely, in (1), (2), and (3). In the second part, (4)–(15), the first
(totemic) ancestor of the Khomei people is said to have determined the living places
of the respective subclans of the Khomei, namely, the Walüfekhatun, Walofekhatun,
and Khayakhatun, in (11) and (12) (see chapter 1 for such subclan divisions). Assumed kin relationships between Khomei people and the Citak and Kombai tribes
are explained within the framework of the ancestor's instructions to his first descen-
dants, namely, in (13).

(1) nokhuf-efè mül-khuf-efè buom   buom   buom-da-é   apa
     we-TOP   former-time-TOP lizard.species lizard.species lizard.species-NEG-EXCLM only
     ye-nggé bembüo-lo[112]   lai-dakhu-fekho[113]
     his-friend lizard.species-FOC break.3SG.REAL-SS-and

     'As for us, in former times, the white house lizard, the white house lizard . . . not the house
     lizard, only its friend, the little brown wood lizard('s eggs) which hatched out and'

(2) lai-bando-khe-nè[114] lefu-fefè wola-khip[115] gil-bolüp   fu-dakhu   lefu-fefè
     come-bring-go-SS   some-TOP earth-over   festival-place put.3SG.REAL-SS end-TOP
     bando-khe-nè nokhu dif-e-kha-la   fu-dakhu
     bring-go-SS our   this-TR-CONN-LOC put.3SG.REAL-SS
     wa-mo-bo-kha-fefè   wo-fè   nokhup laibo-kha-fefè[116]
     thus-SUPP-3SG.PERF.REAL-CONN-TOP that-TOP us   be.born.3SG.REAL-CONN-TOP

     'some (of the result, i.e., lots of people) he brought away and put them on a festival
     place; others he transported to our area, and given that he did so, that is (the story of)
     our origin.'

(3) amo-do   mül-khuf-efè af-efè   du-lalé yakhuo-talé
     do.3SG.REAL-DS former-time-TOP there-TOP tree-big yakhuo.tree-big
     alo-bo-dom-pekho   wap-ta-sü Khinggo-imban-tom-pekho[117] mumengga
     stand-stay.3SG.REAL-DS-and here-LOC-at Khinggo-member-FOC-ATTENT   dog
     fuai-mémo-tofekho   sé Khomei nokhu laibo-kha   abül
     hunt-3SG.IMM.REAL-DS next Khomei our   be.born.3SG.REAL-CONN man
     khol-mémo
     walk-3SG.IMM.REAL

'He did so, and in former times the big tree, the big *yakhuol* tree stood there, a member of the Khinggo clan together with a dog just was hunting, when the Khomei, namely, the man who brought us forth, was walking there.'

(4) khol-mémo-do   fulo-dakhu-fekho[118] mumengga-lom-pekho sé
    walk-3SG.IMM.REAL-DS meet-SS-and   dog-FOC-ATTENT   next
    ye-mumengga-lena[119] ülmo
    his-dog-little   kill.3SG.REAL

'He just walked there and they met each other and it was the dog (of the Khinggo man) which killed his (i.e., the Khomei man's) little dog,'

(5) Khailfüoalop-tena[120] fuai-mémo-do[121]   fuai-mémo-dom-pekho
    Khailfüoalop-DIMIN   hunt-3SG.IMM.REAL-DS hunt-3SG.IMM.REAL-DS-and
    sé   kheyop kha-lulo-kha   ye khai-tofekho   é   y ai
    next house go-3SG.NEAR.REAL-CONN he go.3SG.REAL-DS EXCLM he move.down.SS
    kha-lulo-fekho   khenè kheyop lu   é-felulo   sé   khai-tofekho
    go-3SG.NEAR-until next house move.up.SS sleep-3SG.NEAR next go.3SG.REAL-DS
    amomengga ü-felulo-kha   abül[122] y ébo-top   yakhuo-talé
    this.way kill-3SG.NEAR-CONN man   he sleep.3SG.REAL-place yakhuol.tree-big
    kholükh-mo-lulo[123]
    break.down-SUPP-3SG.NEAR

'he just had hunted with the little (dog called) Khail-füoalop, he just had put it down and then he went the way he had gone home the day before, yes, he had gone out, and then he walked and having entered the house he slept, then he went that way to the place of the man who had killed (his dog), and where the enormous *yakhuol* tree had broken down the day before,'

(6) kholükh-mo-lulo-do[124]   khenè imo-tofekho   kha-nggo-fekho[125]
    break.down-SUPP-3SG.NEAR-DS next   look.3SG.REAL-DS top-there-CIRCUM
    daüm-ta-fekho[126] bau[127]   siop-ta-fekho   bau
    end-LOC-CIRCUM be.3SG.REAL lower.end-LOC-CIRCUM be.3SG.REAL
    mekhe-té-dom-pekho walüpi-nè gun-telo-bo
    SUPP-3PL.REAL-DS-and half.way-SS group-be-stay.3SG.REAL

'he had broken it down and now he looked and in the top of it was a man, and in the lower end was a man and halfway there were lots of people.'

(7) gun-telo-bo-dom-pekho   aful[128]   a-mo-dom-pekho
    group-be-stay.3SG.REAL-DS-and think.3SG.REAL that-SUPP.3SG.REAL-DS-and
    kheyop gelü-nè   khenè mbayap fo-dakhu   sékh fo-dakhu
    house run-SUPP.SS next penisgourd get.3SG.REAL-SS skirt get.3SG.REAL-SS
    wai   lai
    move.down.SS come.3SG.REAL

'Masses of people there were and he worried and ran home and took penis gourds and took skirts and came out again and arrived.'

(8) wai   le-nè   mbayap mbala-mo-dakhu   sékh
    move.down.SS come-SS penisgourd distribute-SUPP.3SG.REAL-SS skirt
    mbala-mo-dakhu   afü-be-bakh-i   melél-mo-tofekho
    distribute-SUPP.3SG.REAL-SS think-stay-HOD-3SG.REAL finish-SUPP.3SG.REAL-DS
    di-lelo-tofekho   sé   khaim gelü-nè khe-bakh-i   lu
    lacking-be.3SG.REAL-DS next house run-SS go-HOD-3SG.REAL move.up.SS

fo-dakhu
get.3SG.REAL-SS

'He came out and arrived and dispensed the penis gourds, and he dispensed the skirts and then still was worried for a while and there still was a shortage, so he ran to the treehouse, entered it, and got (some things, i.e., penisgourds and skirts)'

(9) wai le-nè mbala-nè alo-bakh-i melél-mo-tofekho
move.down.SS come-SS distribute-SUPP.SS walk-HOD-3SG finish-SUPP.3SG.REAL-DS.but
di-lelo-tofekho sé mesip lu fo-dakhu wai le-nè
lacking-be.3SG.REAL-DS next again move.up.SS get.3SG.REAL-SS move.down.SS come-SS
mbala-nè alo-bakh-i melél-mo-tofekho di-lelo-tofekho
distribute-SUPP.SS walk-HOD-3SG.REAL finish-SUPP.3SG.REAL-DS.but lacking-be-DS

'and he came down, arrived, and walked around while distributing until it was finished, but still it was not enough, so he entered again, took (of those goods), came down, arrived, and while dispensing he walked around until it was finished, but still it was insufficient.'

(10) aful amo-do kheyop gelü-nè khai gelü-nè
think.3SG.REAL do.3SG.REAL-DS house run-SS go.3SG.REAL run-SS
khe-bo-tofekho[129] sé mesip lufo-dakhu wai khenè
go-3SG.PERF.REAL-DS next again move.up.SSget.3SG.REAL-SS move.down.SS next
mbala-mo-tofekho di-lelo-do
distribute-SUPP.3SG.REAL-DS.but lacking-be.3SG.REAL-DS

'He wondered (what to do) and then again he ran away, he ran away and then again entered and collected (goods) and came down again, and arrived and distributed, but still it was not enough and'

(11) lefu-fefè[130] gekhenép dip-ta ba-mén-é dé
some-TOP you. PL here-LOC stay-2PL.IMP-EXCLM QUOTE.3SG.REAL

'to some (of them all) he said, "You should stay here."'

(12) mesé lefu-fefè gekhené yaüap[131] ai kha̜-mén-é
next others-TOP you(PL) downstream move.down.SS go-2PL.IMP-EXCLM
dé
QUOTE.3SG.REAL

'Another group he commanded, "You should move downstream,"'

(13) lefu-fefè Banam-telo-mon-é[132] dé-dom-pekho alèp tamükh
others-TOP Citak.people-be-2PL.IMP-EXCLM QUOTE.3SG.REAL-DS-and canoe hew.out.SS
duobo-mekhe-té-dakhu-fekho wa Kuakhil-akh-to-debüf sü kha-té-dakhu-fekho
pull-put.in-3PL.REAL-SS-and there Kuakhil-river-by-way through go-3PL.REAL-SS-and
kha-nè Lemé-lo-fosü[133] i-fekho[134] sübap gelilfo-do[135] lefu-fefè
go-SS Lemé-FOC-through here-CIRCUM downstream go.away.3SG.REAL-DS some-TOP
i-fekho yaüp wai-la-tél-e-kha-fè
here-CIRCUM downstream move.down-come-3PL.REAL-TR-CONN-TOP
if-e-kha-la-khayan ba-té-dakhu
here-TR-CONN-LOC-INTNS live-3PL.REAL-SS

'another group he adressed, "You should become Citak people," and they hew dug-outs, and they pulled them into the water and there via the Kuakhil River they departed and going through the Lemé River they went downstream, and some of them, moving downstream, came and here they settled,'

(14) ip-ta   ba-tél   amodo   dife-nè   mé-na-fekha-fekho[136] ba-tél
here-LOC live-3PL.REAL thus.be.and.DS withdraw-SS side-LOC-one-CIRCUM live-3PL.REAL
amodo   dife-nè   lu   khala-khop khame-té-dakhu wof-ap
thus.be.and.DS withdraw-SS move.up.SS high-there   sit-3PL.REAL-SS there-LOC

'here they settled thus and they withdrew themselves to the other side (of the river) and there they stayed, and they withdrew again and they moved up to the higher grounds and there they live now,'

(15) wa-mo-do   sé if-e-kha   if-e-kha-la   yanof-efè a-fè
thus-SUPP.3SG.REAL-DS next here-TR-CONN here-TR-CONN-LOC people-TOP there-TOP
ye-pan dip-ta   khai-bo-kha   yanop mé-na[137] lu   ye-mén
his-self here-LOC sit-stay.3SG.REAL-CONN people side-LOC cross.SS here-side
lu-nè   khai-bo-kha   yanof-efè a-fè   gu[138]
cross-SUPP.SS sit-stay-3SG.REAL-CONN people-TOP there-TOP you
ge-mo-mengga   wof-e-kha   Mbulul Yalul-mengga[139] wof-e-kha   ye
your-mother's.brother-with that-TR-CONN Mbulul Yalul-with   that-TR-CONN his
gunop wof-ap   wa khame-té   fap
clan   there-LOC there sit-2PL.REAL that

'it happened that way and then here, as for the people who (live) here, who live there on themselves, and with respect to the people who have crossed (the river) to the other side and live there, where you with your mother's brother, Mbulul with Yalul, your clan, live.'

A Folktale about the Fofumonalin Brothers

The narrator, Menggél Khandunanop, a woman about 20 years old, was asked to tell a so-called *wakhatum* story, that is, a kind of Korowai folktale (see chapter 1, Oral tradition, on Korowai genres). While she told the story, she was helped by her husband, Fénélun Molonggai, through his sustaining communication.

Some of the main themes in this tale are the first appearance of the *beni* 'bird of paradise' [see (79), (80), (85), and (86)] and the preparation and celebration of a sago grub festival.[140]

The actors presented in this story can be described as typical characters with stereotyped behaviour, who also play a role in other Korowai folktales. Their experiences and activities are, for the Korowai audience, predictable.

(1) Fofumon-alin tonggo lé-khami-bo-kha[141]   yekhené-mofekha Khondubidop[142]
Fofumon-PL   many   eat-sit-stay.3SG.REAL-CONN their-younger.brother Khondubidop
lefé-lelup   lefé-lelup   de-té
banana.species-sprig banana.species-sprig pull.out-3PL.REAL

'When the majority of the Fofumon brothers once were together, they pulled out banana sprigs of their younger brother Khondulbidop.'

(2) yasim y-afé-khül   kholo-kholop yasim fiüm
garden his-older.brother-PL each-each   garden many

'As for gardens, his brothers all of them had many gardens.'

(3) y-afé-khül   kholo-kholop yasim fiüm-telo-do
his-older.brother-PL each-each   garden many-be.3SG.REAL-DS

'His brothers all of them had many gardens and'

(4) lefé-lelup   difo-kha-fè   khenè y-afé   dulekhül
     banana.species-sprig be.pulled.out.3SG.REAL-CONN-TOP next   his-older.brother garden
     alop   dulekhül-fekho ao-top   di-pükh-mekho[143]
     firstborn garden-CIRCUM   plant.3SG.REAL-DS.but pull.loose-throw.away-SUPP.3SG.REAL

     'as for the bananas being pulled out, he went to his eldest brother's garden and planted
     one but he (the eldest brother) pulled it out and threw it away.'

(5) khenè alüf-e-kha   dulekhül-fekho ao-top
     next   in.between.one-TR-CONN garden-CIRCUM plant.3SG.REAL-DS.but
     di-pükh-mekho
     pull.loose-throw.away-SUPP.3SG.REAL

     'And having gone to the next brother's garden he planted one but he (the next brother)
     pulled it out and threw it away.'

(6) khenè alüf-e-kha   dulekhül-fekho ao-top
     next   in.between.one-TR-CONN garden-CIRCUM plant.3SG.REAL-DS.but
     di-pükh-mekho
     pull.loose-throw.away-SUPP.3SG.REAL

     'And having gone to the next brother's garden he planted but he (the next brother) pulled
     it out and threw it away.'

(7) khenè khaja-lo   alüf-e-kha   dulekhül-fekho ao-tofekho
     next   lastborn-FOC in.between.one-TR-CONN garden-CIRCUM plant.3SG.REAL-DS.but
     di-pükh-mekho-ta
     pull.loose-throw.away-SUPP.3SG.REAL-?

     'And then the last born went to the next brother's garden and he planted, but he (the
     next brother) pulled it out and threw it away.'

(8) khenè ye-pa lül   lai-bo-top-ta   ao-mekho
     next   him-self fallen.down.tree broken-stay.3SG.REAL-place-LOC plant-SUPP.SS

     'And then he himself planted (a banana sprig) at a broken tree's place.'

(9) wo lül   lai-bo-top-ta   ao-mekho ye khülo
     there fallen.down.tree broken-stay.3SG.REAL-place-LOC plant-SUPP.SS here-upstream
     ye-mom-él[144]   bolüp   ye lokhté
     his-mother's.brother-PL clan.territory he go.away.3SG.REAL

     'There at the broken tree's place he planted (a banana sprig) and then he went away
     upstream to his mother's brothers' territory.'

(10) ye lokhté-do   walüp-ta   walüp-ta   makhaya au-pekho-do
     he go.away.3SG.REAL-DS half.way-LOC half.way-LOC bat.species voice-SUPP.3SG.REAL-DS

     'He went away and halfway a *makhaya* bat squeaked and'

(11) wa-fekho   ye-khülo   ye khe-bo-fekho   gup-to anè
     there-CIRCUM here-upstream he go-3SG.PERF.REAL-until you-FOC ADHORT
     da-mo-m-é[145]   dé
     hear-SUPP-2SG.IMP-EXCLM QUOTE.3SG.REAL

     'there he went upstream and he commanded (the little bat), "You should let me know."'

(12) khe-nè da-mo-m-é   dé-do   ye lokhté
     go-SS   hear-SUPP-2SG.IMP-EXCLM QUOTE.3SG.REAL-DS he go.away.3SG.REAL

khe-bo   khe-bo   khe-bo   khe-bo   khe-bo
go-be.3SG.REAL go-be.3SG.REAL go-be.3SG.REAL go-be.3SG.REAL go-be.3SG.REAL
ye lokhte-bo   lu   ye-mom-él   bolü-fekho
hego.away-3SG.PERF.REAL enter.SS his-mother's.brother-PL clan.territory-CIRCUM
babo   babo
stay.3SG.REAL stay.3SG.REAL

'And after he commanded, "You should let me know," he went away and he walked and walked a long time, and having gone and having entered his mother's brothers' territory he lived there for quite a long time.'

(13) ye-lu-lo   walé-do   makhaya khe-nè mèkh-mo   él
sleep-NEAR-3SG daybreak.REAL.3SG-DS bat.species go-SS squeack-SUPP.SS yes
kü-té-kha   wof-ap[146] dé-kha-fè   wa-fosübo
right-be.3PL.REAL-CONN there-LOC QUOTE.3SG.REAL-CONN-TOP there-be.downstream
wai-lai
move-come.3SG.REAL

'One day he had slept and the next morning the *makhaya* bat came and squeaked, "It's all right over there!" and so he came downstream there.'

(14) wa-fosübo   wai   ale-bo-do   khai-tofekho
there-be.downstream move.down.SS walk-stay.3SG.REAL-DS go.3SG.REAL-DS.but

'He went downstream there and he walked but'

(15) ye-sübo   i-pén-efè   y-afé   alop-to   khe-nè imo-tofekho
here-be.downstream here-LOC-TOP his-older.brother firstborn-FOC go-SS look.3SG.REAL-DS

'(in the meantime) here downstream at this place his oldest brother came and saw,'

(16) y-afé   alop-to   khe-nè imo-tofekho   aw-alop[147]
his-brother firstborn-FOC go-SS look.3SG.REAL-DS older.sister-firstborn
lu-bendé-bo[148]
move.up-hang-stay.3SG.REAL

'his oldest brother came and saw the firstborn older (Lani) sister hanging (in the banana tree).'

(17) lu-bendé-bo-tofekho   ülmekho-ngga lekhé-mo
move.up-hang-stay.3SG.REAL-DS shoot-INF.CONN purpose-SUPP.3SG.REAL

'She hung and he wanted to shoot her.'

(18) ülmekho-ngga lekhé-mo-tofekho   ülmekho-n-da dé
shoot-INF.CONN purpose-SUPP.3SG.REAL-DS.but shoot-INF-NEG QUOTE.3SG.REAL

'He wanted to shoot her, but "Do not shoot," she said.'

(19) ülmekho-n-da dé-do   melé-ai[149]
shoot-INF-NEG QUOTE.3SG.REAL-DS move-move.down.SS

'"Do not shoot me," she said and coming down,'

(20) melé-ai-do   yekhené gilfo[150]
move-move.down.3SG.REAL-DS they go.away.3SG.REAL

'she came down and they departed.'

(21) yekhené khaim-pé   gilfo   yekhené khaim-pé
they   treehouse-LOC go.away.3SG.REAL they   treehouse-LOC

gilfo-do   alüf-e-kha   walé-do   khai
go.away.3SG.REAL-DS   in.between.one-TR-CONN daybreak.REAL.3SG-DS go.3SG.REAL

'They went home, they went home and the second brother the next morning came'

(22) mo[151]   alüf-e-kha   lu-bendé-bo-tofekho
     he.saw.that in.between.one-TR-CONN move.up-hang-stay.3SG.REAL-DS

'and the second sister hung (in the banana tree) and'

(23) ülmekho-ngga   lekhé-mo-tofekho
     shoot-INF.CONN   purpose-SUPP.3SG.REAL-DS.but

'he wanted to shoot (her) but'

(24) ülmekho-n-da dé   melé-ai   yekhené gilfo
     shoot-INF-NEG QUOTE.3SG.REAL move-move.down.3SG.REAL they   go.away.3SG.REAL

'"Do not shoot me," she said and she come down and they went away.'

(25) mo alüf-e-kha   bendé-bo   ülmekho-n-da dé
     ? in.between.one-TR-CONN hang-stay.3SG.REAL shoot-INF-NEG QUOTE.3SG.REAL
     melé-ai-do   walé-do   yekhené gilfo
     move-move.down.3SG.REAL-DS daybreak.REAL.3SG-DS they   go.away.3SG.REAL

'The second sister hung (in the banana tree), "Do not shoot me," she said and she came down and the next morning they went away.'

(26) wa   yu alo-bakh-i   alo-bakh-i   khai-tofekho   khaü-fekho[152]
     there he walk-HOD-3SG.REAL walk-HOD-3SG.REAL   go.3SG.REAL-DS   down-CIRCUM
     khaja-lena   khaü-fekho   khaja-lena   amo-bo-do[153]   bendé-bo
     lastborn-DIMIN down-CIRCUM   lastborn-DIMIN do-stay.3SG.REAL-DS hang-stay.3SG.REAL

'There he walked for a long time and (at the place he went to) at the lower end (of the banana tree) the youngest sister hung, at the lower end the youngest sister hung.'

(27) ülmekho-n-da dé-tofekho   ülmekho
     shoot-INF-NEG QUOTE.3SG.REAL-DS.but shoot.3SG.REAL

'"Do not shoot me!," she said but he shot (her).'

(28) ülmekho-do   ülmekho-do   melé-ai
     shoot.3SG.REAL-DS shoot.3SG.REAL-DS move-move.down.3SG.REAL

'He shot, he shot and she came down.'

(29) melé-ai-do   khaim   gilfo
     move-move.down.3SG.REAL-DS treehouse go.away.3SG.REAL
     ye-khul-wakhai-telo   yu nggu-telo[154]
     his-intestines-discontented-be.3SG.REAL he discontented-be.3SG.REAL

'She came down and he went home but in his heart he was discontented, discontented was he.'

(30) yu nggu-telo-do   yu nggu-telo-do   khaim
     he discontented-be.3SG.REAL-DS he discontented-be.3SG.REAL-DS treehouse
     gelil-mo   khaim ba-té   beba-té-fekho
     go-SUPP.3SG.REAL treehouse stay-3PL.REAL stay-3PL.REAL-until

'He was discontented, he was discontented and they went to the treehouse and stayed there, they lived there until'

(31) gu ne nau-ma-tél-e-kha   no no no khosül tu-n-da-é
you my eat-SUPP-3PL.REAL-TR-CONN my my my sago   eat-INF-NEG-EXCLM
dé
QUOTE.3SG.REAL

'"You, my food, you should not eat my sago!," he said.'

(32) no khosül tu-n-da-é   dé-do   él dé
my sago   eat-INF-NEG-EXCLM QUOTE.3SG.REAL-DS yes quote.3SG.REAL

'"My sago you should not eat," he said and she answered, "All right."'

(33) a   gu ne-maun mu-n-da-é   dé   él dé
EXCLM you my-water drink-INF-NEG-EXCLM QUOTE.3SG.REAL yes QUOTE.3SG.REAL

'"You should not drink my water', he said, and she answered, "All right."'

(34) gu ne gèkh   tu-n-da-é   dé   él dé
you my sago.grub eat-INF-NEG-EXCLM QUOTE.3SG.REAL yes QUOTE.3SG.REAL

'"You should not eat my sago grubs," he said. She answered, "All right."'

(35) melé-babo   babol-fekho   melé-babo   babol-fekho
be.in.motion-sit.3SG.REAL sit.3SG.REAL-until move-sit.3SG.REAL sit.3SG.REAL-until
yakhatimekho babo   babol-fekho   yakhatimekho
renounce.SS   stay.3SG.REAL sit.3SG.REAL-until renounce.3SG.REAL

'Thus she lived a long time and renounced.'

(36) mesé y-um   yu wafil   mesendi-mesendi-po
next   her-husband her husband prepare-prepare-SUPP.3SG.REAL

'And for her man, for her husband she usually prepared (food).'

(37) y-um   mesendi-mesendi-pe-nè gu maun guf-efè mesendi-po-do
her-husband prepare-prepare-SUPP-SS you water you-TOP prepare-SUPP.3SG.REAL-DS
lé   babo-fekho   lé   babo-fekho   y-aw-khü-to   khosü-gaul
eat.SS sit.3SG.REAL-until eat.SS sit.3SG.REAL-until her-older.sister-PL-FOC sago-second.layer
fédo-ma-té   lé-mo   fonolé
give-HAB-3PL eat-SUPP.SS eat.3SG.REAL

'Preparing (food) for her husband, (saying:), "Here is yoúr water," she served and he ate
and stayed until her older sisters regularly provided pieces of baked sago and she ate.'

(38) y-aw-khü-to   maun fédo-fédo-ma-té
her-older.sister-PL-FOC water give-give-HAB-3PL

'Her older sisters regularly provided water.'

(39) fédo-fédo-ma-té-do mi-mekho y-élo-mo
give-give-HAB-3PL-DS drink-fill.SS she-sleep-HAB.3SG

'They usually provided and she, having drunk, slept.'

(40) y-élo-do   y-é-felulo-mo   waleli-mo-do   è
she-sleep.3SG.REAL-DS she-sleep-NEAR-HAB.3SG be.light-HAB.3SG-DS PAUSE
y-um-pekho   ye-wafil-fekho   wai   khe-nè
her-husband-COMIT her-husband-COMIT move.down.SS go-SS

'She slept, she slept and usually when it became morning, ah, with her man, with her
husband she went out,'

(41) y-um-pekho   wai   khe-nè yekhené kholmbekho-ma-tél-e-kha
       her-husband-COMIT move.down.SS go-SS   they   take.a.walk-HAB-3PL-TR-CONN

       'she went out and given that she and her husband usually went out for a walk,'

(42) yekhenép kholmbekho-ma-tél-e-kha   lu   indo   fédo-mo-tofekho
       they   take.a.walk-HAB-3PL-TR-CONN enter.SS bake.SS give-HAB.3SG-DS.but
       a-nè   gu lu-n-da-é   de-di-mo
       that-SUPP.SS you eat-INF-NEG-EXCLM QUOTE-QUOTE-HAB.3SG

       'after their walk she entered (the house) and she baked (food) and gave it but always he
       said, "You should not eat."'

(43) lu-n-da-é   de-di-mo-do   él di-mo-dakhu   ye-wafil
       eat-INF-hear-EXCLM QUOTE-QUOTE-HAB.3SG-DS yes QUOTE-HAB.3SG-SS her-husband
       ye-pa   wa-mo-nè babo   babo
       him-self that-SUPP-SS sit.3SG.REAL sit.3SG.REAL

       '"you should not eat," he always said and she answered, "Yes, okay" and her husband,
       thus doing, he himself lived for a long time.'

(44) wa-mo-nè   babo   babo   babo-fekho   gu khul-wakhél
       that-SUPP.SS-SS sit.3SG.REAL sit.3SG.REAL sit.3SG.REAL-until you stone.axe-handle
       takhebé-m-akhu-fekho ne gèkh   ü-m-é   dé
       make-2SG.IMP-SS-and my sago.grub cut.down-2SG.IMP-EXCLM QUOTE.3SG.REAL

       'Thus doing he stayed until he commanded, "You should make a handle for the stone
       axe and cut down trees for breeding my sago grubs."'

(45) ne gèkh   ü-m-é   dé-do   él dé
       my sago.grub cut.down-2SG.IMP-EXCLM QUOTE.3SG.REAL-DS yes QUOTE.3SG.REAL

       '"You should cut down trees for breeding my sago grubs," he commanded and she re-
       plied, "All right."'

(46) él dé-do   khul-wakhél   takhebé-dakhu-fekho y-é-lu-lo
       yes quote.3SG.REAL-DS stone.axe-handle make.3SG.REAL-SS-and she-sleep-NEAR-3SG.REAL
       walé-do   wai   khe-nè khelélmekho
       daybreak.REAL.3SG-DS move.down.SS go-SS cut.down.3SG.REAL

       'She said, "All right" and made a handle for the stone axe and having slept the next
       morning she went out and cut trees for breeding sago grubs.'

(47) khelélmekho   khelélmekho-do   aun   aun
       cut.down.3SG.REAL cut.down.3SG.REAL-DS sago.tree.marrow sago.tree.marrow
       sél   di   la-ngga-mo-ngga   lekhé-mo-mo-tofekho
       crispy.sago.marrow cut.SS eat-INF.CONN-SUPP-INF.CONN purpose-SUPP-HAB.3SG-DS.but
       fonolu-ngga lekhé-mo-mo-tofekho
       eat-INF.CONN purpose-SUPP-HAB.3SG-DS.but

       'She cut down (sago trees) and cut sago tree marrow . . . that crispy marrow and wanted
       to eat of it, she wanted to eat it but'

(48) ü   gu wa-fefè   i-mba-lé   de-di-mo-dakhu   ye
       EXCLM you there-TOP watch-PROGR-1SG QUOTE-QUOTE-HAB.3SG-SS he
       khén-telo-mo-do   él di-mo
       angry-be-HAB.3SG-DS yes QUOTE-HAB.3SG

"'Hey, I am watching you there," he then used to say and was angry at her and she used
to reply with, "All right.'"

(49) él di-mo-dakhu-fekho   nnn   él di-mo-dakhu-fekho   ye yu-pé ye
    yes QUOTE-HAB.3SG-SS-and PAUSE yes QUOTE-HAB.3SG-SS-and he he-?   he
    gol-sani-pe-nè   wai   khe-bo-mo-kha   ye gol ülmekho-bo-mo-kha
    pig-cassowary-SUPP-SS go.out.SS go-be-HAB.3SG-CONN he pig shoot-be-HAB.3SG-CONN

"'"All right," she then said, "all right" she then replied, and when he went out for hunting big game, every time he went and shot a pig,'

(50) khul   ao[155]   lu   fe-nè fu   lawa   duo   fe-nè fu è
    intestines cleanse.SS enter.SS get-SS put.SS food.wrapped.in.leaves stew.SS put-SS put PAUSE
    yu lu-ngga   lekhé-mo-mo-tofekho
    she eat-INF.CONN purpose-SUPP-HAB.3SG-DS.but

'she cleansed the intestines and entered and put it down, stew it with stones and put it
down and then wanted to eat of it but'

(51) gup belén-é   de-di-mo   él mofu y-élo
    you do'nt-EXCLM QUOTE-QUOTE-HAB.3SG yes only she-sleep.3SG.REAL

'then he always said, "You should not!" and then she just slept.'

(52) mofu y-é-bo-mo-do   mesendi-mesendi-pekho fe-nè fu
    only she-sleep-be-HAB.3SG-DS prepare-prepare-SUPP.SS get-SS put
    y-élo-bo-mo-do   é-felulo-mo   wali-mo-mo-do
    she-sleep-be-HAB.3SG-DS sleep-NEAR-HAB.3SG daybreak-SUPP-HAB.3SG-DS
    gil[156]   ayan è   wof-e-kha   gèkh
    ceremonial.festival.place ?   PAUSE that-TR-CONN sago.grub
    ü-bekho-mo-kha-lalé[157]   aun-talé-lalé
    cut.down-INTNS-SUPP.3SG.REAL-CONN-INTNS sago.tree.marrow-big-INTNS
    aun-talé-lalé   a-nè khandü   fe-nè fu
    sago.tree.marrow-big-INTNS that-SS stew.on.hot.stones.SS get-SS put
    é-bekho-mo-kha   ye é   y-um   khén-telo-mo-do
    sleep-INTNS-HAB.3SG-CONN her PAUSE her-husband angry-be-HAB.3SG-DS

'She usually slept, after serving the food she usually only slept, and one morning when
she had slept, at the ceremonial festival place she cut a large amount of (trees for breed-
ing) sago grubs and lots of sago tree marrow, lots of it she stew with hot stones and
served it and then slept like a log, and her husband still was angry and'

(53) wa-mo-nè   babol-fekho   wap-ta-fekho   gèkh   tamé-dakhu-fekho[158]
    thus-SUPP-SS sit.3SG.REAL-until there-LOC-CIRCUM sago.grub tie.3SG.REAL-SS-and

'thus doing she stayed until she tied the sago grubs (in leaves) and'

(54) gèkh   tamé leful-mekho-dakhu-fekho wap-ta-fekho   tamé
    sago.grub tie.SS end-SUPP.3SG.REAL-SS-until there-LOC-CIRCUM tie.SS
    leful-mekho-kha-fefè   wap-ta-fekho   nau-ma-tél-e-kha[159]   khosül
    end-SUPP.3SG.REAL-CONN-TOP there-LOC-CIRCUM eat-SUPP-3PL.REAL-TR-CONN sago
    ülmo[160]
    cut.3SG.REAL

'she finished tying the sago grubs and . . . there the food, sago trees she cut.'

(55) khosül ülmo-dakhu-fekho é   khosül ülmo-kha-fefè
sago   cut.3SG.REAL-SS-and PAUSE sago   cut.3SG.REAL-CONN-TOP
walé-do   khoülmo-kha-fefè   kha-nè balin tamélo balin
daybreak.REAL.3SG-DS sago.treecut.3SG.REAL-CONN-TOP go-SS rack tie.SS   rack
ali   fe-nè fu[161]
build.SS get-SS put.3SG.REAL

'Sago she cut, after having cut sago trees the next morning she cut sago trees, and she tied a rack, she built a rack.'

(56) balin ali   fe-nè fu-dakhu-fekho   lu   ye-lu-lo   walé-do
rack build.SS get-SS put.3SG.REAL-SS-and enter.SS sleep-NEAR-3SG daybreak.REAL.3SG-DS
walüp nau-ma-tél-e-kha   ülmo
half.way eat-SUPP-3PL.REAL-TR-CONN cut.3SG.REAL

'She built a rack and having entered she slept and the next morning she cut the second food stock.'

(57) khosül ülmo-do   lamü   khamil-mo balin lu   monggo fe-nè
sago   cut.3SG.REAL-DS pound.SS stay-SUPP.SS rack move.up.SS take.out.SS get-SS
fu
put.3SG.REAL

'Sago she cut and she kept pounding, and having ascended the rack she took it out of the net bag and put it down and'

(58) walé-do   walüp nau-ma-tél-e-kha   ülmo[162]
daybreak.REAL.3SG-DS half.way eat-SUPP-3PL.REAL-TR-CONN cut.3SG.REAL

'the next morning she cut the third food stock.'

(59) ülmo lamü   geli be-bakh-i   bando-nè fe-nè fu   walé-do
cut.SS pound.SS go sit-HOD-3SG bring-SS   get-SS put.3SG.REAL daybreak.REAL.3SG-DS
lefaf   dé
finished QUOTE.3SG.REAL

'She cut and pounded and kept transporting and putting it at its place (the rack) and the next morning he said that it was ready.'

(60) lefaf   dé-dakhu   banibol nau-ma-tél-e-kha-lanukh   lamü
finished QUOTE.3SG.REAL-SS leaf.stem eat-SUPP-3PL.REAL-TR-CONN-only pound.SS
be-bakh-i-fekho   bando-le-nè banibol[163] di   fe-nè fu
stay-HOD-3SG-until bring-come-SS leaf.stem   pull.loose.SS get-SS put.3SG.REAL

'"It is ready," he said and the sago for immediate consumption she continued to pound and . . . she transported it and having pulled loose the leaf stems they put it on its place.'

(61) banibol di   fe-nè fu-do   ye-lu-lo   ye-lu-nté
leaf.stem pull.loose.SS get-SS put.3SG.REAL-DS sleep-NEAR-3SG sleep-NEAR-3PL.REAL
walé
be.light.REAL.3SG

'Having pulled loose leaf stems she put it on its place and then she slept, they slept until daybreak.'

(62) ye-lu-nté   walé-do   lul   di   ai   kha-té[164]
sleep-NEAR-3PL.REAL daybreak.REAL.3SG-DS leaves cut.SS move.down.SS go-3PL.REAL

'They slept and the next morning they went out for picking leaves.'

(63) lul   di   ai   khe-bakha-ti la-té-dakhu   ibe-lu-té
      leaves cut.SS move.down.SS go-HOD-3PL   come-3PL.REAL-SS sleep-NEAR-3PL.REAL
      walé
      daybreak.REAL.3SG

      'They went out for picking leaves, came back and slept till the next morning.'

(64) é-felu-nté   walé-do   wai   khe-nè gèkh
      sleep-NEAR-3PL.REAL daybreak.REAL.3SG-DS move.down.SS go-SS   sago.grub
      do-ma-té[165]
       cleave-SUPP-3PL.REAL

      'They slept and the next morning they went out and split (the trees for picking) sago
      grubs.'

(65) gèkh   do-ma-té-dakhu-fekho   lu   khe-nè gil-fekho
      sago.grub cleave-SUPP-3PL.REAL-SS-until enter.SS go-SS   ceremonial.festival.place-CIRCUM
      ye-té
      sleep-3PL.REAL

      'They split (the trees for picking) sago grubs and having entered the festival place they
      slept there.'

(66) gil-fekho   ibe-lu-té-fekho   walé-do
      ceremonial.festival.place-CIRCUM sleep-NEAR-3PL.REAL-until daybreak.REAL.3SG-DS
      walü   da-té
      half.way split-3PL.REAL

      'They slept in the festival bivouac and the next morning they split the second stock.'

(67) do-nè ai   kha-té   do-nè ai   khe-bakha-ti-fekho mo khenè
      split-SS move.down.SS go-3PL.REAL split-SS move.down.SS go-HOD-3PL-until   just next
      lu-n-da-é di-mo
      eat-INF-NEG-EXCLM QUOTE-HAB.3SG

      'They went out splitting, they went out splitting and he said as usual, "You should not
      eat!"'

(68) él dél-e-kha-fè   do-nè fu leful-mekho-kha-fè
      yes QUOTE.3SG.REAL-TR-CONN-TOP split-SS put end-SUPP.3SG.REAL-CONN-TOP
      lamo   fu   leful-mekho-kha-fè[166]   ne-yanop-tekhé lamo
      wrap.in.leaves.SS put.SS end-SUPP.3SG.REAL-CONN-TOP my-people-for   wrap.in.leaves.SS
      fu-m-é   dé
      put-2SG.IMP-EXCLM QUOTE.3SG.REAL

      '"All right," she said and when she had finished splitting, putting down, wrapping and
      putting (the grubs on the racks) when she had finished it, he commanded, "You should
      wrap for my family."'

(69) él dél-e-kha-fè
      yes QUOTE.3SG.REAL-TR-CONN-TOP

      'Given that she said, "All right,"'

(70) él dé-dakhu   a-mol-mo
      yes QUOTE.3SG.REAL-SS that-SUPP-SUPP.3SG.REAL

      '"All right," she said and thus . . .'

(71) él dé-dakhu   lamo   fu   leful-mekho-dakhu-fekho
     yes QUOTE.3SG.REAL-SS wrap.in.leaves.SS put.SS end-SUPP.3SG.REAL-SS-until
     walé-do   yanop gübo-mo¹⁶⁷
     daybreak.REAL.3SG-DS people come.together-SUPP.SS

     '"All right," she said and she wrapped (the grubs) until finished and the next morning
     the people came together.'

(72) yanop gübo-mo-dakhu-fekho
     people come.together-SUPP.3SG.REAL-SS-and
     khasa-khasam-tu-dakhu-fekho¹⁶⁸
     khasam.dance-khasam.dance-enter.3SG.REAL-SS-and

     'The people came together and while *khasam* dancing they entered and . . .'

(73) é-felu-nté   lefu ai   geli-mo-do   lefu
     sleep-NEAR-3PL.REAL end move.down.SS go-SUPP.3SG.REAL-DS end
     é-felu-nté-fekho   walé-do   yè lefu ai
     sleep-NEAR-3PL.REAL-until daybreak.REAL.3SG-DS again end move.down.SS
     geli-mo¹⁶⁹
     go-SUPP.3SG.REAL

     'they spent the night and some left, others slept and the next morning again some departed.'

(74) walé-do   yekhené ai   gilfo-do
     daybreak.REAL.3SG-DS they   move.down.SS go.away.3SG.REAL-DS
     gil   dayabél-é   dé-dakhu
     ceremonial.festival.place exhausted-EXCLM QUOTE.3SG.REAL-SS

     'The next morning they departed and he said, "I am exhausted of the feast" and'

(75) ibo-ibo-nè   fu-bakh-i   dé-dakhu   ibofe-nè fu-bakh-i-do
     sleep-sleep-SUPP.SS put-HOD-3SG QUOTE.3SG.REAL-SS sleep put-SS put-HOD-3SG-DS

     'having slept he said so,'

(76) ibo fu-bakh-i-fekho walé-do
     sleep put-HOD-3SG-until daybreak.REAL.3SG-DS

     'he slept until the next morning.'

(77) é-felu-té   walé-do¹⁷⁰   yekhené ai   gilfo
     sleep-NEAR-3PL.REAL daybreak.REAL.3SG-DS they   move.down.SS go.away.3SG.REAL

     'They slept, and the next morning they went out.'

(78) yekhené gèkh   khelèl-nè ai   khe-bakha-ti-fekho dif-e-kha   lal   yu
     they   sago.grub split-SS move.down.SS go-HOD-3PL-until this-TR-CONN female she
     bandüp¹⁷¹   sékh   laimofo-kha¹⁷²
     kind.of.sago.tree raw.material.for.skirt break.loose.3SG.REAL-CONN

     'They went out splitting (trees for picking) sago grubs until the woman, having broken
     loose the grain from the top of a *bandüp* sago tree,'

(79) mofu sékh   laimofo-kha   ye-sékh
     only raw.material.for.skirt break.loose.3SG.REAL-CONN her-raw.material.for.skirt
     taimekho   fe-nè fo-dakhu-fekho   a-nè   i-mo   fubo-khai
     break.loose.SS get-SS take.3SG.REAL-SS-until that-SUPP.SS this-SUPP.3SG.REAL fit-3SG.IRR
     dé-tofekho¹⁷³   beni   daya kü-telo
     QUOTE.3SG.REAL-DS bird.of.paradise feather like-be.3SG.REAL

'having broken loose the grain, she broke loose her skirt grain and put it down and she thought, "Does it fit this way?" and it looked like the feather of a bird of paradise.'

(80) beni   khal kü-telo   mm   güme-nè
bird.of.paradise skin same-be.3SG.REAL PAUSE play-SS
da-da-mo-tofekho[174]   kü-telo   dé-kha-fè   kha-nè
similar-similar-SUPP.3SG.REAL-DS like-be.3SG.REAL QUOTE.3SG.REAL-CONN-TOP go-SS
y-um   gèkh   do-mo
her-husband sago.grub split-SUPP.3SG.REAL

'It looked like a bird of paradise's skin, eh, and playing she imitated (a bird of paradise) and having thought, "very fitting" she walked while her husband split (sago trees for picking) grubs.'

(81) y-um   gèkh   do-mo-do   do-mo-do   khe-nè
her-husband sago.grub split-SUPP.3SG.REAL-DS split-SUPP.3SG.REAL-DS go-SS
bon-ta-fekho   a-nè   bon-ta-fekho   fekha monggo   fono-ndé
end-LOC-CIRCUM that-SUPP.SS end-LOC-CIRCUM one   take.out.SS eat-1SG.REAL
dé-tofekho   ye khén-telo
QUOTE.3SG.REAL-DS.but he angry-be.3SG.REAL

'Meanwhile her husband split (sago trees for picking) grubs, he split, and at the end, at the end she took one (grub) out and she said, "I eat" but he went angry.'

(82) ye khén-telo-do   yakhatimekho
he angry-be.3SG.REAL-DS renounce.3SG.REAL

'He went angry and she renounced.'

(83) yakhatimekho   khaim tu   lakhi-nè   alü   fédo-tofekho
renounce.3SG.REAL treehouse enter.SS stew.with.leaves-SS bake.SS give.REAL.3SG-DS.but
aü   yakhatimekho
EXCLM abandon.3SG.REAL

'She renounced and having entered the treehouse she stewed (grubs) offered it but, oh, he refused.'

(84) yakhatimekho-tofekho él-uwo   dé-kha-fefè
abandon.3SG.REAL-DS.but yes-EXCLM QUOTE.3SG.REAL-CONN-TOP

'He refused and after she said, "All right"'

(85) yakhatimekho ndalif-e-kha ye beni   daya khomi
abandon.SS   this-TR-CONN her bird.of.paradise feather transform.SS

'and after she renounced, she transformed (herself) into a bird of paradise and'

(86) ye beni   khal fo dimekho-kha-fefè   i-fekho   mé-nggop
her bird.of.paradise skin take put.on.3SG.REAL-CONN-TOP here-CIRCUM side-there
ya-khaim-pé   bedi ai   lokhté
her-treehouse-LOC fly.SS move.down.SS go.away.3SG.REAL

'her bird of paradise skin she took and put it on and here on this side she flew out of the treehouse and went away.'

(87) if-e-kha   mé-nggop ye bedi ai   lokhté
this-TR-CONN side-there   she fly.SS move.down.SS go.away.3SG.REAL

'Here at this side she flew out of the treehouse.'

(88) ye bedi ai   lokhté-do   y-um   él kho-fè   y-um   ye
she fly.SS move.down.SS go.away.3SG.REAL-DS her-husband yes there-TOP her-husband he
ba-melé-bo   ye bau   melél   amo-do
sit-be.in.motion-stay.3SG.REAL he stay.3SG.REAL move.3SG.REAL do.3SG.REAL-DS
y-um   bétop wai   khai
her-husband behind move.down.SS go.3SG.REAL

'She flew out and went away and her husband said, "Well, that's it," her husband stayed, he stayed and thus he did and her husband afterward also went out.'

(89) wai   alobo-do   khai-tofekho
move.down.SS walk.3SG.REAL-DS go.3SG.REAL-DS

'He went out and walked.'

(90) [mofu wai   khai   di-m   wai   alobo-do
only   move.down.SS go.3SG.REAL say-2SG.IMP move.down.SS walk.3SG.REAL-DS
du-n-da   gu anè]
say-INF-NEG you ADHORT

[(intervention language helper:) 'You should just say, "He went out". Don't say, "He went out and walked", right go on.']

(91) wai   khai   wai   khai-tofekho   khaim[175] alobo
move.down.SS go.3SG.REAL move.down.SS go.3SG.REAL-DS treehouse stand.3SG.REAL

'. . . he went out, he went out and there stood a treehouse,'

(92) khaim alobo-do   khaim alobo-do   khaim alobo-do
treehouse stand.3SG.REAL-DS treehouse stand.3SG.REAL-DS treehouse stand.3SG.REAL-DS
melé-lu
move-enter.3SG.REAL

'the treehouse stood there, the treehouse stood there, and he moved up and entered.'

(93) melé-lu-tofekho   be-babo-da
move-enter.3SG.REAL-DS.but NEG-sit.3SG.REAL-NEG

'He moved in but she was not there.'

(94) be-babo-da-lelo-do   babo   babo
NEG-sit.3SG.REAL-NEG-be.3SG.REAL-DS sit.3SG.REAL sit.3SG.REAL
y-énon-té-do   khe-nè lu
he-of.a.long.duration-3PL.REAL-DS go-SS   move.up.3SG.REAL

'She was not there, and he stayed, a pretty long time he stayed, and then she came in.'

(95) khe-nè lu-do   lelip[176] é   fe-nè fe-té
go-SS   enter.3SG.REAL-DS together sleep get-SS put-3PL.REAL

'She came in and they spent the night together.'

(96) yekhené é-felu-té   walé-do   yu wai
they   sleep-NEAR-3PL.REAL daybreak.REAL.3SG-DS she move.down.SS
lokhté
go.away.3SG.REAL

'They spent the night and by daybreak she went out.'

(97) yu wai   lokhté-do   gülé-do   khe-nè lu
she go.down.SS go.away.3SG.REAL-DS be.dark.3SG.REAL-DS go-SS   enter.3SG.REAL

'She went away and at night she came and entered again.'

(98) khe-nè lu-do é-felu-té-fekho walé-do mo yu
go-SS enter.3SG.REAL-DS sleep-NEAR-3PL.REAL-until daybreak.REAL.3SG-DS just she
wai lokhté
go.down.SS go.away.3SG.REAL

'She came and entered and they spent the night until the next morning she went away again.'

(99) yu wai lokhté walé-do
she go.down.SS go.away.3SG.REAL daybreak.REAL.3SG-DS

'She went away and the next morning . . .'

(100) yu wai lokhté gülé-do khe-nè lu
she go.down.SS go.away.3SG.REAL be.dark.3SG.REAL-DS go-SS enter.3SG.REAL

'She went out and at night she entered.'

(101) gülé-do khe-nè lu-do ibo é-felu-té yu
be.dark.3SG.REAL-DS go-SS enter.3SG.REAL-DS sleep sleep-NEAR-3PL.REAL she
wai lokhté
go.down.SS go.away.3SG.REAL

'At night she came and entered, and they spent the night and then she went out again.'

(102) khom-u-ngga lekhé-mo khom-u-ngga lekhé-mo-do
die-INF-CONN purpose-SUPP.3SG.REAL die-INF-CONN purpose-SUPP.3SG.REAL-DS
lamül-fekho[177] ukh-ma[177] bando-lu fédo[178] fonolé
green.cucumber-COORD small.cucumber-also bring-enter.SS give.REAL.3SG eat.3SG.REAL

'He was to die, he was to die and she brought a *lamül* cucumber and an *ukh* cucumber and she gave it to him and he ate.'

(103) fonolé-do é-felu-nté walé-do è i-fekho
eat.3SG.REAL-DS sleep-NEAR-3PL.REAL daybreak.REAL.3SG-DS pause here-CIRCUM
mén-ap yekhené ai gilfo lelip yekhené ai
side-LOC they go.down.SS go.away.3SG.REAL together they go.down.SS
gilfo-tofekho
go.away.3SG.REAL-DS

'He ate of it and they slept and the next morning they went out to this side (of the river), together they went away and'

(104) yekhené gilfo-do nn yekhené be-bakha-ti-fekho gülé-do
they go.away.3SG.REAL-DS pause they stay-HOD-3PL-until be.dark.3SG.REAL-DS
yekhené ye-mén yekhené lu é-felu-té-fekho yekhené gol
they this-side they enter.SS sleep-NEAR-3PL.REAL-until they pig
üe-té
kill-3PL.REAL

'they went away and they stayed (there the whole day) until darkness fell and they crossed the river and spent the night in (her) treehouse and the next morning they killed a pig.'

(105) yekhené gol khedi-bakh-i mo khedi-bakha-ti
they pig kill-HOD-3SG just kill-HOD-3PL

'They killed another pig.'

(106) üe-té-dakhu-fekho khedi-bakha-ti melél-me-té-dakhu-fekho
kill-3PL.REAL-SS-and kill-HOD-3PL finish-SUPP-3PL.REAL-SS-and

'And when they had finished slaughtering,'

(107) khedi-bakha-ti melél-me-té-dakhu-fekho   mekho   leful-me-té-dakhu-fekho
　　　 kill-HOD-3PL   finish-SUPP-3PL.REAL-SS-and   put.into.SS end-SUPP-3PL.REAL-SS-and
　　　 yekhené le-ba-té-to-pé   kha-té
　　　 they   come-PERF-3PL.REAL-place-LOC go-3PL.REAL

'when they had finished slaughtering, they put the meat in a bag and they went to the
place where they had come from.'

(108) [mofu difo-difo]
　　　 only   arrive-arrive

[(intervention language helper:) 'Only to arrive (at the place from where they had
come)'.]

(109) kha-té-do   kha-té-dom-pekho khe-nè yekhené khaim-pekho lu
　　　 go-3PL.REAL-DS go-3PL.REAL-DS-and go-SS they   treehouse-in   enter.SS
　　　 é-felu-té-fekho   walé-dom-pekho   mmm ye-lu-nté
　　　 sleep-NEAR-3PL.REAL-until daybreak.REAL.3SG-DS-and PAUSE sleep-NEAR-3PL.REAL
　　　 walé-do   wai   khe-nè gèkh   khelèl-nè   fédo
　　　 daybreak.REAL.3SG-DS go.down.SS go-SS   sago.grub split-SUPP.SS give.REAL.3SG

'They went on until they arrived at his treehouse, they entered and slept (there) and the
next morning they collected sago grubs and he gave them to his wife.'

(110) fédo-do   fonolé
　　　 give.REAL.3SG-DS eat.3SG.REAL

'He gave them and she ate.'

(111) khaim   lu   fonolé   khaim-pekho   lu   lé
　　　 treehouse enter.SS eat.3SG.REAL treehouse-CIRCUM enter.SS eat.REAL.3SG.

'Having come home they ate.'

(112) é-felu-nté   walé-do   yekhené lé   khami-ba-té[179]
　　　 sleep-NEAR-3PL.REAL daybreak.REAL.3SG-DS they   eat.SS sit-stay-3PL.REAL
　　　 de-ba-té-kha
　　　 tell-PERF-3PL.REAL-CONN

'They slept and the next day they were eating (together in peace), they told.'

Khenil-khenil

In this important ethnohistorical document, the story of the development of contacts
between the downstream Korowai and people of the outside world is told from the
perspective of the Korowai people, starting with a report about the first encounter with
the Dutch missionary Veldhuizen and the deliberations of the older Korowai people
concerning their completely new experiences. A second part concerns the building up
of the first Korowai village, Yaniruma. The end of the story gives an impression of the
recent developments in opening up the Korowai tribal area and a short evaluation.

　　　The narrator is Labülun Sendékh, a young man who acted as one of the first
intermediaries between the mission and the Korowai. The text was recorded in May
1991 in the office of the missionary in Yaniruma. The narrator was asked to tell about
the feelings of the Korowai people of the Becking River's downstream banks when

they experienced the first contacts with the outside world, the mission and particularly the first missionary in the area, Johannes Veldhuizen (see figure 6–1). The narrator told his story to the tape recorder while alone in the missionary's office.

(1) beba-lè-fekho[180]   kheni-khenil   khotu khenil-e-khayan[181] khotu laléo[182]
    stay-1PL.REAL-until beginning-beginning still   beginning-TR-very   still   bad.spirit
    la-mén-alin-alüp[183]   beba-lè-fekho   naném alè-debüf melé-la-té
    come-INF-without-time stay-1PL.REAL-until secretly canoe-way   move-come-3PL.REAL

    'We stayed, in the beginning when still . . . in the very beginning, at the time when the spirit not yet had come, we lived until secretly they came by canoe.'

(2) alè-debüf melé-la-té-do   nokhu khai-ba-lè[184]   bil   ai
    canoe-way move-come-3PL.REAL-DS we   stay-stay-1PL.REAL stone move.down.SS
    lu-fa-lè-dakhu
    cross-?-1PL.REAL-SS

    'They arrived by canoe and we stayed, we had come down to the stone banks and crossed (the river) and'

(3) ilol-debüf ai   lu-fe-nè   ye-mén[185] meléle-bakh-un
    stone-way   move.down.SS cross-?-SS this-bank   move-come-HOD-1PL

    'along the stone banks coming down, having crossed to this side, we had arrived,'

(4) nokhu-mbolo-mbolop   bétop nokhu-mbolo-mbolop   bétop la-té-tofekho
    our-older.people-older.people behind our-older.people-older.people behind come-3PL.REAL-DS
    mé-le-bakha-ti   kha-té   gol ü-nè   abé-mekho[186]
    move-come-HOD-3PL   go-3PL.REAL pig   kill-SS carry.on.the.back-put.into.3SG.REAL

Figure 6–1 Katüal Lén and his daughter. Johannes Veldhuizen preparing an injection with antibiotics. George Steinmetz, 1995.

'our older people behind, our older people came behind, having killed a pig, they carried it on their back.'

(5) gol bu   feli-bo-do   ü-nè   abé-mekho   alo-bakha-ti
pig pitfall fall-3SG.PERF.REAL-DS kill-SS carry.on.the.back-put.into.SS walk-HOD-3PL
ilo-ta   bu-ma-fon   de-té
stone-LOC slaughter-SUPP-1PL.ADHORT QUOTE-3PL.REAL

'The pig had fallen into a pitfall and they had killed it and carrying it on their back, they
had walked, "Let us slaughter it on the stone banks," they said.'

(6) de-té-do   ilo-ta   bu-ma-té-do   ilo-ta
QUOTE-3PL.REAL-DS stone-LOC slaughter-SUPP-3PL.REAL-DS stone-LOC
bu-ma-té-dom-pekho   nokhu kha-lè-do   bu-méma-lè-lofekho   alèp
slaughter-SUPP-3PL.REAL-DS-and we   go-1PL.REAL-DS slaughter-IMM-1PL.REAL-DS canoe
sübap   gelelukh-mo-gelelukh-mo-mo-do[187]   ima-lè-lofekho   wé
downstream splash-SUPP-splash-SUPP-SUPP.3SG.REAL-DS see-1PL.REAL-DS EXCLM
laléo-mengga alèp melé-le-bakha-ti
bad.spirit-with canoe move-come-HOD-3PL.REAL

'They said (so) and they slaughtered it at the stones, at the stones they slaughtered and
then we arrived, when we just were slaughtering it, downstream there was the repeti-
tive noise of a splashing canoe (= canoe did 'splash' repeatedly), and we looked at it
but, wow, people had arrived with a canoe containing a bad spirit.'

(7) o   ne-mba-mbam i-mol-alüp   laléo   khop
EXCLM my-child-child this-SUPP.3SG.REAL-time bad.spirit there
melé-le-bakh-i   de-té
move-come-HOD- say-3PL.REAL

'"Oh, my children, now the bad spirit has arrived over there," they said.'

(8) de-té-tofekho   Él de-nè nokhu golo-ai-demil-me-lè
say-3PL.REAL-DS yes say-SS we   be.afraid-go.out-run-SUPP-1PL.REAL

'They said and we, affirming this, ran away full of fright.'

(9) khebüm-ta-da kembakhi-la-da   nokhu golo-demil-me-lè
wasp-LOC-NEG aggressive.ant.species-LOC-NEG[188] we   be.afraid-run-SUPP-1PL.REAL

'As if there were no wasps or ants, we fled in agony.'

(10) mbolo-mbolop   a   gol-e-khal ati-sasi-po-do
older.people-older.people EXCLM pig-TR-meat hold-QUICK-SUPP.3SG.REAL-DS
golo-demil-me-té
be.afraid-run-SUPP-3PL.REAL

'The older people snatched the pig meat together and fled away.'

(11) gol-e-khal ati-sasi-po-do   golo-demil-me-té-tofekho   e
pig-TR-meat hold-QUICK-SUPP.3SG.REAL-DS be.afraid-run-SUPP-3PL.REAL-DS PAUSE
lefu-lon de-té   gol-e-khal bando-khe-nè baja-mekhe-té
some-FOC say-3PL.REAL pig-TR-meat bring-go-SS hidden.place-SUPP-3PL.REAL
bai-mekhe-té[189]   bajam   lefu-lon bai-mekhe-té-do   de-té
hide-SUPP-3PL.REAL hidden.place some-FOC hide-SUPP-3PL.REAL-DS say-3PL.REAL
anè   khe-nè ülmekho-fon   de-té
ADHORT go-SS shoot-1PL.ADHORT say-3PL.REAL

'The pig meat they snatched together and fled away, but some of them proposed to bring the pig meat and hide it, yes, to hide it, others said, "Come on, let us shoot him."'

(12) sé mbolo-mbolop   lefu-lon de-té   Él nokhu ülmekho-ngga-da
next older.people-older.people some-FOC say-3PL.REAL yes we   shoot-INF.CONN-NEG
nokhu wola-lelo-lelo-khai[190] de-nè de-té   wola-lelo-khai   de-nè
us   universe-be-3SG.IRR say-SS say-3PL.REAL universe-be-3SG.IRR say-SS
de-té-tofekho
say-3PL.REAL-DS

'And then some of the older people said, "We should not shoot him, otherwise the world will come to its end," they said, "the universe will come to its end."'

(13) sé kholo-kholo-aup da-té-dakhu   kholo-kholo-aup da-té-dakhu   Él
next each-each-talk   hear-3PL.REAL-SS each-each-talk   hear-3PL.REAL-SS yes
bo-khofél-aup-da nokhu belén de-té
NEG-lie-word-NEG we   do'nt say-3PL.REAL

'Next they listened to each other's arguments, they listened to each other's arguments and they concluded, "Yes, this is true, we should not do that."'

(14) sé nokhu nokhu golo-demil-me-lè   golo-demil-me-lè-do   ü
next we   we   be.afraid-run-SUPP-1PL.REAL be.afraid-run-SUPP-1PL.REAL-DS EXCLM

'And then we fled in fear, we fled in fear, and wow,'

(15) hey n-até-o   golo-m-belén-é   nu kolufo-yanof-é
EXCLM my-father-VOC be.afraid-2SG.IMP-do'nt-EXCLM I Korowai-person-EXCLM
dé-to[191]
QUOTE.3SG.REAL-DS

'he said, "Hey, my father, do not be afraid! I am a Korowai person."'

(16) ü   nokhu golo-demil-me-lè
EXCLM we   be.afraid-run-SUPP-1PL.REAL

'Wow, we fled in fear.'

(17) nokhup mbolo-mbolo-fekho   golo-demil-me-lè-do   é
we   older.people-older.people-COMIT be.afraid-run-SUPP-1PL.REAL-DS EXCLM
yekhenép nokhu alèf-e-khaup kuasél fikh   fo   fe-té
they   our   canoe-TR-inside fish.hook razor.blade take.SS put-3PL.REAL

'With our older people we fled, and they took out of their luggage fishhooks and razor blades and put it in our canoes.'

(18) kuasél fikh   fo   fe-té-tofekho   walé-do   khe-nè
fish.hook razor.blade take.SS put-3PL.REAL-DS daybreak.REAL.3SG-DS go-SS
ima-té-tofekho[192]
see-3PL.REAL-DS

'They took out fishhooks and razor blades and put it down and the next morning they came and had a look and'

(19) ü   nokhu-alèf-e-khaup maf-akh   kuasél fikh   laléo-melil a-mofu
EXCLM our-canoe-TR-inside   picture-water fish.hook razor.blade bad.spirit-fire that-only
ibo-ibo
be-be.3SG.REAL

'Oh, my!, in our canoes were only mirrors, razor blades, and matches.'

(20) i-mba   fa-fon
    this-what get-1PL.INTENT
    "'What is this? Let us take it!'"

(21) fo-n-è-tè   belén de-nè a-me-tél   amo-do
    take-INF-CONN-DISJNCT not   say-SS that-SUPP-3PL.REAL do.3SG.REAL-DS
    b-i-nè[193]   nè[194]   fa-té
    EFFORT-see-SS SUPP.SS get-3PL.REAL
    "'Take it or not?', thus they deliberated and having inspected they took it.'

(22) nè   fa-té -do   tè   kho-sübo   gilfa-té   tè   lefül
    SUPP.SS get-3PL.REAL-DS PAUSE there-be.downstream go.away-3PL.REAL PAUSE day
    po-té-do mesé alè-debüf la-té
    two-be-DS next canoe-way come-3PL.REAL
    'They took it and they had departed downstream but . . . after two days they came again
    by canoe.'

(23) alè-debüf la-té-to   èé   mo kholfe-té   mo kholfe-té-do
    canoe-way come-3PL.REAL-DS EXCLM just meet-3PL.REAL just meet-3PL.REAL-DS
    èé   golo-deme-té-do   n-até-o   belén-è
    EXCLM be.afraid-run-3PL.REAL-DS my-father-VOC do.not.need.to-EXCLM
    gole-tin-da-é   nu yanop le-ba-lé   dé
    be.afraid-3PL.INTENT-NEG-EXCLM I   person come-PERF-1SG.REAL say.3SG.REAL
    'By canoe they came, "Hey!"—they wanted to meet, they wanted to meet—"Hey!"—
    they fled in fear, "My father, you don't, you people don't have to be afraid! I have come
    as a human being!"'

(24) nu laléo-da-é   nu yanof-é[195]   dé-to
    I   bad.spirit-NEG-EXCLM I   person-EXCLM say.3SG.REAL-DS
    "'I am not a spirit, I am a man," he said.'

(25) iii   gu laléo-lu   de-té-dakhu   yekhené golo-demil-me-té
    EXCLM you bad.spirit-FOC say-3PL.REAL-SS they   be.afraid-run-SUPP-3PL.REAL
    "'Hush, you are a spirit, aren't you!" they said and they fled.'

(26) gu laléo-lu   de-té-dakhu   golo-demil-me-té-do   wof-e-kha
    you bad.spirit-FOC say-3PL.REAL-SS be.afraid-run-SUPP-3PL.REAL-DS that-TR-CONN
    alèf-e-khaup kuasél-o   fikh-o   melil-o   fo-nè
    canoe-TR-inside fish.hook-COORD razor.blade-COORD fire-COORD take-SUPP.SS
    fu   maf-akh   fo-nè   fu
    put.3SG.REAL image-water take-SUPP.SS put.3SG.REAL
    "'You are a spirit for sure!' they said and they fled in fear but he unpacked fishhooks,
    razor blades, matches and put it in the canoes, mirrors too he unpacked and put it
    down.'

(27) fo-nè   fu   lokhte-lu-lo   le-nè   ima-té-tofekho él
    take-SUPP.SS put.3SG.REAL go.away-NEAR-3SG come-SS see-3PL.REAL-DS yes
    fo-benè-ngga[196]   alèf-e-khaup b-ibo-da
    take-HAB-INF.CONN canoe-TR-inside NEG-be.3SG.REAL-NEG
    'Having unpacked all of it and put it down he left and then they came and looked, and
    yes, all the things he had unpacked, in the canoe there was nothing more left.'

(28) sé   wekhelimekho fium-debüf e   sé   wekhelimekho lai   Ü
next return.SS   land-way   PAUSE next return.SS   come.3SG.REAL EXCLM
ülmekho-fon   de-té-tofekho   Ü   belén nokhu nokhu wola-lelo-khai
shoot-1PL.ADHOR QUOTE-3PL.REAL-DS EXCLM do'nt to.us   to.us   universe-be-3SG.IRR

'Next he returned and came by foot, when he came back, (there were) people (who) said, "Hey, let us shoot him," but (other) people (said), "Oh, don't do that, otherwise our world will get out of order."'

(29) nokhu-laléo ülmekho-kha-té-kha nokhu-laléo ü-bo-kha-tél-e-kha   nokhu
our-spirit   shoot-IRR-2PL-CONN   our-bad.spirit kill-?-IRR-2PL-TR-CONN us
wola-lelo-khai   nokhu belén   de-té
universe-be-3SG.IRR we   do.not.need.to QUOTE-3PL.REAL

'"If you shoot our spirit, if you kill our spirit, our universe will get out of order, so we are against it," they said.'

(30) mbolo-mbolop   lefu-lon a   ülmekho-fon   de-té
older.people-older.people some-FOC EXCLM shoot-1PL.ADHORT QUOTE-3PL.REAL

'Some of the older people said, "Well, let us just shoot him."'

(31) ülmekho-fon   de-té-tofekho   lefu-lo mmm belén
shoot-1PL.ADHORT QUOTE-3PL.REAL-DS   some-FOC PAUSE not
nokhu-wola-mama   nokhu-wola-lelo-khai nokhu belén   de-té
our-universe-out.of.orderness our-universe-be-3SG.IRR us   do.not.need.to quote-3PL.REAL

'"Let us shoot him," they said, but others said, "No, our universe will get out of order, our universe will come to its end, as for us, we are against it," they said.'

(32) nokhu-laléo ülmekho-ngga-da   de-té   de-té-do   Él
our-bad.spirit shoot-INF.CONN-NEG QUOTE-3PL.REAL QUOTE-3PL.REAL-DS yes
de-nè   gele-té   gele-té-fekho   ü   khobo-mo
QUOTE-SS be.afraid-3PL.REAL be.afraid-3PL.REAL-until EXCLM come.and.go-HAB.SS
melé-lai
move-come.3SG.REAL

'"Do not shoot our spirit," they said, thus they said, and agreeing they feared, they were afraid until—Wow!—on patrol he once came.'

(33) mo melé-lai-do   ü   b-aup-da[197]   kholfe-fun
just move-come.3SG.REAL-DS EXCLM NEG-word-NEG meet-1PL.ADHORT
de-té
QUOTE-3PL.REAL

'He came, ah, nothing to refuse, they proposed to meet with him.'

(34) kholfe-fun   de-té-dakhu   la-la-mo-do   mo kholfe-té
meet-1PL.ADHORT QUOTE-3PL.REAL-SS come-come-HAB.3SG-DS just meet-3PL.REAL

'"Let us meet," they said and when he kept coming they met.'

(35) kholfe-té-do   nokhup ni-khül mba-mbam-è   nokhup golo-ba-lè
meet-3PL.REAL-DS we   woman-PL child-child-EXCLM we   be.afraid-stay-1PL.REAL

'They met, but we, the women and the children, we were afraid.'

(36) mbolo-mbolop-tanukh   fulo-fulo-ma-té   mbolo-mbolop-tanukh
older.people-older.people-only meet-meet-HAB-3PL older.people-older.people-only

fulo-fulo-ma-té-do
meet-meet-HAB-3PL-DS

'Only the older people usually met with them, only the older people used to meet with them.'

(37) é   sé   a-nè   sé   ili-debüf   la-la-mo   ili-debüf
EXCLM next that-SUPP.SS next helicopter-way come-come-HAB.3SG helicopter-way
la-lai-dakhu   lai-dakhu   khai   i   yanop[198] kuasél-o
come-come.3SG.REAL-SS come.3SG.REAL-SS go.3SG.REAL this people   fish.hook-COORD
fikh-o   maf-akh   fédo   wa-mo-a-mo-mo
razor.blade-COORD image-water give.REAL.3SG thus-do-that-do-SUPP.3SG.REAL

'Yes, and next he used to come by helicopter, he came and went by helicopter and the people he gave fishhooks, razor blades, mirrors, this doing all the time.'

(38) wa-mo-a-mo-mo-mémo-fekho   gekhené khop-ta[199] khaü
thus-do-that-do-SUPP.3SG.REAL-IMM-until you(PL) there-LOC bivouac
ale-mén-é   dé
build-2PL.INTENT-EXCLM QUOTE.3SG.REAL

'Thus he did all the time until he urged, "You should make a bivouac over there."'

(39) khaü   ale-mén-é   dé-do   Él de-nè   khaü
bivouac build-2PL.INTENT-EXCLM QUOTE.3SG.REAL-DS yes QUOTE-SS bivouac
ale-té
build-3PL.REAL

'"You should make a bivouac," he said, and they agreed and made a bivouac.'

(40) khaü   ale-té-dakhu   khai-ba-té-do   alè-debüf lai
bivouac build-3PL.REAL-SS stay-stay-3PL.REAL-DS canoe-way come.3SG.REAL

They made a bivouac, stayed and then he came by canoe.'

(41) alè-debüf lai-dakhu   é   é   yano-fè   ye-té   bahüo
canoe-way come.3SG.REAL-SS PAUSE PAUSE people-TOP sleep-3PL.REAL sugar.cane
a   dufol-o   ndaü-o   non-o   folapé folapé bando-khe-nè
EXCLM banana-COORD sago-COORD sago.grub-COORD bring   bring bring-go-SS
fu-fu-ma-té
put-put-HAB-3PL

'By canoe he came and eh . . . eh . . . the people spent the night and brought sugar cane, bananas, sago and sago grubs and put it in front of him.'

(42) folapé bando-khe-nè fu-ma-té-do   yalén   yu abolo-abolo-mo
bring   bring-go-SS   put-HAB-3PL-DS respected.man he buy-buy-HAB.3SG
abolo-abolo-mo-do ya . . .   ya . . .   él yano-fekho[200] khofu
buy-buy-HAB.3SG-DS people.INTRUP people.INTRUP yes people-COMIT be.with.all
lé-lé-ma-té   lé-lé-ma-té-dakhu sé   kho-sübol   gilfo
eat-eat-HAB-3PL eat-eat-HAB-3PL-SS next there-be.downstream go.away.3SG.REAL

'Bringing it they put it down, and the respected man bought all of it. He bought all of it and they, yes with all the people, ate it. They ate and then they departed in downstream direction.'

(43) sé   if-e-kha-p-ta   a   mbelüp di-méma-mon-é
next here-TR-CONN-there-LOC EXCLM clearing open-IMMP-2PL.INTENT-EXCLM

i-mbelüp-ta   ili-debüf   le-nè   wai-kha-lè-fé   dé
here-clearing-LOC   helicopter-way come-SS   move.down-IRR-1PL-EXCLM QUOTE.3SG.REAL

'And then he said, "You should open a clearing here at this place, and I will come and land with a helicopter."'

(44)   nokhu ili-debüf   nokhu belén   nokhu wola-lelo-khai   de-té-tofekho
      to.us   helicopter-way to.us   do.not.need.to to.us   universe-be-3SG.IRR say-3PL.REAL-DS
      o   o   manda-é   khésekhan-é manda-é dé
      EXCLM EXCLM no-EXCLM   no-EXCLM   no-EXCLM QUOTE.3SG.REAL
      bu-wola-lé-n-da-é   khésekhan-é dé
      NEG-universe-be-3SG.INTENT-NEG-EXCLM no-EXCLM   QUOTE.3SG.REAL

'"As for us, by helicopter, we are against it, the world will get out of order," they said, but he said, "Oh, no, that is not the case, the world will not get out of order, no way!"'

(45)   ip-ta   mbelüp di-felule-mon-do   lai-p-akhu   khamba
      here-LOC clearing open-NEAR-2PL.INTENT-DS come-1SG.INTENT-SS steel.axe
      mbala-mo-f-é   dé
      distribute-SUPP-1SG.INTENT-EXCLM QUOTE.3SG.REAL

'"If you soon will have made a clearing at this place, I will come and distribute axes," he said.'

(46)   él de-té-dakhu   de-té   di-felu-té-do   do y-aup
      yes QUOTE-3PL.REAL-SS   open-3PL.REAL   open-NEAR-3PL.REAL-DS   DS his-word
      uma-lulo-kha   kü-telo   dai-ba-té-tofekho
      speak-3SG.NEAR-CONN   just-be.3SG.REAL   hear-PERF-3PL.REAL-DS
      ili-bü-mo-n-aup-elu[201]
      helicopter-beat-SUPP-INF-sound-?

'They agreed and when they had opened a clearing—the promise he had done a couple of days before appeared to come true they heard the humming of a helicopter.'

(47)   o   nokhup ni-khül-fekho   mba-mbam-pekho nokhu
      EXCLM we   woman-PL-COORD child-child-COORD   we
      golo-demil-me-lè   nokhu golo-demil-me-lè-do
      be.afraid-run-SUPP-1PL.REAL we   be.afraid-run-SUPP-1PL.REAL-DS
      mbolo-mbolop-tanukh   alo-ba-té   ili   wai
      older.people-older.people-only stand-stay-3PL.REAL   helicopter move.down.3SG.REAL

'Oh, and we, the women and the children, we fled in fear. We fled, only the older stood as the helicopter landed.'

(48)   ili   wai-dakhu   i   ye-mbolo-mbolop   i   yanop
      helicopter move.down.3SG.REAL-SS   here his-older.people-older.people this people
      kholfu-bo-kha   mbisi   mbala-mo
      meet-3SG.PERF.REAL-CONN   steel.axe distribute-SUPP.3SG.REAL

'The helicopter landed and his people distributed steel axes among the people they met here.'

(49)   mbisi   mbala-mo-dakhu-n   dé   gekhené ip-ta   kelaja[202]
      steel.axe share-SUPP.3SG.REAL-SS-?   QUOTE.3SG.REAL you   here-LOC settlement
      de-mén-é   dé
      open-2PL.IMP-EXCLM QUOTE.3SG.REAL

'He distributed steel axes and said, "You should open up a settlement here."'

(50) kelaja   de-mén-é   dé-tofekho   Ü   kelaja   mbakha-mo-nè
settlement open-2PL.IMP-EXCLM QUOTE.3SG.REAL-DS EXCLM settlement what-do-SS
dil-ma-té-kholo   mbolo-mbolop   ii   nokhu wola-lekhén-è
open-SUPP-3PL.REAL-Q older.people-older.people EXCLM we   universe-for-CONN
de-té-dakhu   mbolo-mbolop   wola-lekhé manda gele-té-tofekho
QUOTE-3PL.REAL-SS older.people-older.people universe-for no   be.afraid-3PL.REAL-DS
o   dé   bu-wola-fè   bu-wola-lé-n-da-é
EXCLM QUOTE.3SG.REAL NEG-universe-TOP   NEG-universe-be-3SG.INTENT-NEG-EXCLM
dé
QUOTE.3SG.REAL

'"You should open up a settlement," he said, but the older men said, "Oh, how to open
up a settlement? Oh, for our world! No, for our universe not that way," the older people
said and were afraid but he said, "With respect to the universe . . . the universe will not
get out of order," he said.'

(51) khésekhan-è bu-wola-lé-n-da-é   dé   wola-fè
no-EXCLM   NEG-universe-be-3SG.INTENT-NEG-EXCLM QUOTE.3SG.REAL universe-TOP
wola-lekhé gele-tin-da-é   gekhenép kelaja
universe-for be.afraid-3PL.INTENT-NEG-EXCLM you(PL)   settlement
de-mén-é   dé
open-2PL.INTENT-EXCLM QUOTE.3SG.REAL

'"Oh, no, the universe will not vanish," he said, "concerning the universe, about the
universe you should not be afraid, so you can open up a settlement," he said.'

(52) él de-nè   de-té   de-té-tofekho   ye alè-debüf lai
yes QUOTE-SS open-3PL.REAL open-3PL.REAL-DS he canoe-way come.3SG.REAL
alè-debüf Banam[203] Banam-tom-pekho   alèf ali-mekhe-té-do
canoe-way Citak.people Citak.people-FOC-ATTENT canoe row-put.in-3PL.REAL-DS
ye-gülol   la-la-ma-té
here-upstream come-come-HAB-3PL

'They said they would agree, thus they spoke, and then he came by canoe, by canoe—
Citak people, it were Citak people who rowed the canoe and they came here several
times upstream.'

(53) alè-debüf le-nè   imonè if-è   balüm-takh-telo   ndemop ip-ta-da
canoe-way come-SS now   here-CONN mud-LOC-be.3SG.REAL swamp   here-LOC-NEG
dé   gülaf-e-kha   fiu-ma-la-kholo dé
QUOTE.3SG.REAL upstream-TR-CONN land-also-LOC-Q   QUOTE.3SG.REAL

'By canoe they came and now he said, "It is muddy here, a swamp, not here . . ." and he
asked, "Perhaps there upstream are also higher grounds?"'

(54) dé-do   Nggop-engga[204] khofu-la-té   le-nè
QUOTE.3SG.REAL-DS Nggop-with   be.with.all-come-3PL.REAL come-SS
Banam-imban Kualégofalé-fekho la-té
Citak-person   Kualégofalé-COMIT come-3PL.REAL

'Thus he asked and with Nggop they all came. With the Citak man Kualégofalé they
came.'

(55) le-nè   if-e-kha   khop-ta-sü alè yaüyaf-e-kha   Yaniluman
come-SS this-TR-CONN there-LOC-at canoe downstream-TR-CONN Yaniruma.river

makho-ta[205] difa-té-dakhu   anggo-te-nè bi-ai-ma-té
mouth-LOC   arrive-3PL.REAL-SS   slow-be-SS   look.for-move.down-HAB-3PL
Bi-bi-bi-bi   bi-kha-té-fekho
look.for-look.for-look.for-look.for look.for-go-3PL.REAL-until

'Coming here, at the canoe (landing place) down there, at the mouth of the Yaniruma River, they arrived and made a thorough and long inspection until'

(56) él lapangga[206] fu-n-din   mo ip-ta   mo fium-telida khambom[207]
     yes air.strip   put-INF-POTENT just here-LOC just land-nice   village
     du-n-din-telo   él gekhené ip-ta   khambom
     open-INF-POTENT-be.3SG.REAL   yes you   here-LOC village
     de-mén-é   dé
     open-2PL.INTENT-EXCLM QUOTE.3SG.REAL

'"Yes, possible to make an airstrip, here at the nice high ground a village can be opened, yes, here you should open a village!" he said.'

(57) ip-ta   khambom de-mén-é   dé-tofekho   Él de-nè
     here-LOC village   open-2PL.INTENT-EXCLM QUOTE.3SG.REAL-DS yes open-SS
     khaüo-kho-fekho[208] hièn khaü   lidop ali-fe-té
     down-there-CIRCUM   small bivouac one   build-set-3PL.REAL

'"Here you should open a village," he said, and they agreed and built one small bivouac down there.'

(58) khaü   lidop ali-fe-té-tofekho   e   yalén   lai
     bivouac one   build-set-3PL.REAL-DS PAUSE respected.man come.3SG.REAL

'One small bivouac they built and the respected man came again.'

(59) lai-dakhu   yo nu   khala-khof-akhüp[209] khelé-pa-mon
     come.3SG.REAL-SS yes to.me high-there-place   plain-SUPP-2PL.INTENT
     dé
     QUOTE.3SG.REAL

'He came and said, "Yes, as for me, you should clear up the higher places over there."'

(60) khala-khof-akhüp khelé-pa-mon   dé-do
     high-there-place plain-SUPP-2PL.INTENT QUOTE.3SG.REAL-DS
     khelé-pa-té-do
     plain-SUPP-3PL.REAL-DS

'"The higher places over there you should make plain," he said and they cleared it up and . . .'

(61) nu menèl nggulun[210] fédo-kha-lé-fé   de-do   è
     I quickly evangelist give-IRR-1SG.REAL-EXCLM QUOTE.3SG.REAL-DS PAUSE
     yalé   Kris-fekho[211] yalé   Kelaja-khabéan-alé-fekho[212] mm
     respected.person Kris-COORD   respected.person work-head-respected.person-COORD PAUSE
     bando-ai   bando-ai-dakhu   gekhené ne-nggulun
     bring-move.down.3SG.REAL bring-move.down.3SG.REAL-SS   to.you   my-evangelist
     if-é   dé   ne-nggulun if-é   ne-nggulun-pekho
     this-EXCLM QUOTE.3SG.REAL my-evangelist this-EXCLM my-evangelist-COMIT
     khai-ba-mon-é   dé   nu khe-nè le-nè
     live-stay-2PL.INTENT-EXCLM QUOTE.3SG.REAL I go-SS   come-SS
     mo-kha-lé-fé   dé
     do-IRR-1SG.REAL-EXCLM QUOTE.3SG.REAL

'He promised, "I will give you an evangelist quickly," and eh . . . Mister Kris and Mister Kelajakhabianalé he brought, he brought them and said, "For you, this is my evangelist—my evangelists are these, you should live together with them," he said, "I (myself) will come and go regularly," he said.'

(62) dé-tofekho   Él de-nè   khai-ba-lè   sé khe-mé-nggof-e-kha
     QUOTE.3SG.REAL-DS yes QUOTE-SS live-stay-1PL.REAL next there-side-there-TR-CONN
     wotan[213] khami-ba-tél-anop   de-té   ya nokhu
     forest   stay-stay-3PL.REAL-people QUOTE-3PL.REAL yes us
     wola-maman-é
     universe-out.of.order-EXCLM

     'He said so, and then they agreed and stayed, and then, the people at the other side of the river, the people who stay in the forests, said, "Yes, as for us, the end of the world is there."'

(63) nokhu if-e-kha   khambom di-mba-tél-é   nokhu
     to.us here-TR-CONN village   open-PROGR-3PL.REAL-EXCLM us
     wola-maman-é   nokhu yanop khedi-ül-fa-fon
     universe-out.of.order-EXCLM us   people terminate-kill-?-1PL.ADHORT
     de-té
     QUOTE-3PL.REAL

     '"As for us, they are opening this village, to us this means the end of the world, so let us kill the people," they said.'

(64) nokhu yanop khedi-fa-fon-dakhu   laléo-ma   ül-me-fon
     we   people terminate-?-1PL.ADHORT-SS bad.spirit-also kill-SUPP-1PL.ADHORT
     de-té
     QUOTE-3PL.REAL

     '"Let us finish off the people and kill the bad spirit too," they said.'

(65) de-té-tofekho   sé lefu-lo   aa mayokh nokhu-mayokh nokhu-mayokh
     QUOTE-3PL.REAL-DS next some-FOC ah friends   our-friends   our-friends
     belén   de-té   nokhu-mayokh belén de-té-do   Él nokhu
     do.not.need.to QUOTE-3PL.REAL our-friends   don't QUOTE-3PL.REAL-DS yes we
     wof-è   wola-mama   wola-maman-tu
     that-CONN universe-out.of.orderness universe-out.of.order-FOCUS
     khambom di-mba-tél-e-kha-fefè
     village open-PROGR-3PL.REAL-TR-CONN-TOP

     'They said so, but others said, "Ah, friends, our friends, don't do that, our friends, don't do that!" they said, "Yes, as for us, it means the end of the world, because they are opening a village."'

(66) é   nokhu wola-mama   ye-pa bolü-fekha
     EXCLM we   universe-out.of.order it-self place-some.far.away
     bolü-fekha-lon-è   khambomdi-ma-té   nokhup ip-ta-fè
     place-some.far.away-FOC-CONN village open-SUPP-3PL.REAL we   here-LOC-TOPIC
     belén de-té
     don't QUOTE-3PL.REAL

     '"Yes, as for us, the universe will get to its end, so at a distant place, on a distant territory, they might open a village but at this place, we should not do," they said.'

(67) nokhu ip-ta   wola-lelo-khai   de-nè   wof-e-kha   yanop
we   here-LOC universe-be-3SG.IRR QUOTE-SS that-TR-CONN people
khedi-fa-fon-dakhu   laléo-fekho   khedi-fa-fon-do
terminate-?-1PL.ADHORT-SS bad.spirit-COMIT terminate-?-1PL.ADHORT-DS
khedi-fa-fon-dakhu   de-té
terminate-?-1PL.ADHORT-SS QUOTE-3PL.REAL

'They said, "Here we will get the end of the world" and proposed, "let us terminate those people, with the bad spirit, let us terminate them."'

(68) sé   lefu-lo   khai-ba beba-té-fekho-n   de-té   e   mm   mayokh
next some-FOC stay-stay stay-3PL.REAL-until-? QUOTE-3PL.REAL PAUSE PAUSE friends
nokhu-yanop belén nokhu-yanop-tu de-té   nokhu-yanop-tu
our-people   don't our-people-FOC QUOTE-3PL.REAL our-people-FOC
de-té-tofekho   a-mo-nè   khai-ba-té   khai-ba-té
QUOTE-3PL.REAL-DS that-SUPP-SS stay-stay-3PL.REAL stay-stay-3PL.REAL
khai-ba-té
stay-stay-3PL.REAL

'And then others proposed not to do anything, "Eh friends, it is our people, don't do that, it's our own people," they said and thus they just stayed.'

(69) sé   le-nè   imo-ngga-lo-ma   golole-té   le-nè
next come-SS look-INF.CONN-FOC-also be.afraid-3PL.REAL come-SS
imo-ngga-lo-ma   golole-té-do   gekhené-palap de-té
look-INF.CONN-FOC-also be.afraid-3PL.REAL-DS you-do.not.matter QUOTE-3PL.REAL

'And then, having come, they also had a look and they were afraid—having coming they also had a look and then they were afraid and (the others) said, "You do not need to do so!"'

(70) de-té-tofekho   mbolo-mbolop   b-aup-da   nokhu-bolüp-ta
QUOTE-3PL.REAL-DS older.people-older.people NEG-word-NEG our-clan.territory-LOC
nn   nokhu gele-lè-lofekho   ü   yalén
PAUSE we   be.afraid-1PL.REAL-DS EXCLM respected.man
mé-la-mé-la-mo-do   aiè   gele-lè   gele-lè-lofekho
move-come-move-come-HAB.3SG-DS EXCLM be.afraid-1PL.REAL be.afraid-1PL.REAL-DS
yalén   mé-la-mé-la-mo-kha   lekhé khofe-lè
respected.man move-come-move-come-HAB.3SG-CONN cause meet-1PL.REAL
de-té
QUOTE-3PL.REAL

'They said so, but the older people replied, "Do not say that, on our territories we are afraid, oh when the respected man comes hence and forth, my! we are afraid," but they said, "Because he usually comes here, we meet him."'

(71) khofe-lè-kha-fè   b-aup-da   nokhu yalén   ip-ta   khambom
meet-1PL.REAL-CONN-TOP NEG-word-NEG our   respected.man here-LOC village
de-mén   dé-do   nokhu di-m
open-2PL.INTENT QUOTE.3SG.REAL-DS we   open-SUPP.SS
di-mba-lè-kha-fè   ip nokhu nggulun-pekho i   khame-lè
open-INGR-1PL.REAL-CONN-TOP here we   evangelist-COMIT here stay-1PL.REAL

'When we met him, really, our respected person urged, "You should open a village," and we started to open (a village) and here we stay with our evangelist.'

(72) b-aup-da   nokhu bo-golo-pelè-da   de-té
    NEG-word-NEG we   NEG-be.afraid-1PL.INTENT-NEG QUOTE-3PL.REAL
    "'So, don't say that, we will not be afraid," they said.'

(73) nokhu bo-golo-pelè-da   sé   wotan-anop gekhenép gé gekhenép nokhu
    we   NEG-be.afraid-1PL.INTENT-NEG next forest-people you   ? you   us
    u-ngga   belén e   laléo   ülmekho-ngga belén gekhenép naném
    kill-INF.CONN do'nt PAUSE bad.spirit shoot-INF.CONN do'nt you   silently
    khami-ba-mon
    stay-stay-2PL.INTENT

    "'We will not be afraid, and then, forest people, you should not kill us! Eh, you should
    not shoot the spirit, you should keep quiet."'

(74) nu nokhup na   naném khai-bo-kha-lè   nokhu i   laléo-aup²¹⁴
    I we   PAUSE   silently stay-stay-IRR-1PL we   this bad.spirit-language
    kü-kül-ma-lèl-anof-è   nokhu kha-bo-kha-té   de-té
    adopt-adopt-HAB-1PL-people-CONN   we   stay-stay-IRR-3PL.REAL QUOTE-3PL.REAL

    "'On the other hand, we of our side will stay calmly too and we will live here as people
    who use the spirit's language," they said.'

(75) de-té-dakhu   beba-té   beba-té   beba-té   me-té-tofekho
    QUOTE-3PL.REAL-SS stay-3PL.REAL stay-3PL.REAL stay-3PL.REAL do-3PL.REAL-DS
    ü   nggé khambom di   khe-nè khaü khaü a-me-té-dakhu
    EXCLM friend village   open.SS go-SS house house that-make-3PL.REAL-SS
    Aim-talé   gübol-o   Kolufo-é   diof-è   mayokh
    Kombai-a.lot.of come.together-EXCLM Korowai-EXCLM quickly-EXCLM friends
    Kolufo-é   mayokh if-è   nokhu-pa nokhu-bolüp-ta-tu   Kolufo
    Korowai-EXCLM friends   here-CONN our-self   our-clan.territory-LOC-FOC Korowai
    nokhu-bolüp-ta   khambom di-fu-lu   yo gübo-ma-mon
    our-clan.territory-LOC village   open-set-FOC yes come.together-SUPP-2PL.IMP
    anè   la-mén-o   de-lè   da de-té-dakhu
    IMP/ADHORT come-2PL.IMP-EXCLM QUOTE-1PL.REAL NEG QUOTE-3PL.REAL-SS
    mbolo-mbolop   a-me-té-tofekho   ya <clic>²¹⁵ nokhu ayul
    older.people-older.people that-do-3PL.REAL-DS yes <clic>   to.us prohibition
    de-té
    QUOTE-3PL.REAL

    'They said so and lived for quite a period and did thus, and, when they had opened a
    village and had built many houses, they complained, "Lots of Kombai people came
    together! Hey, Korowai, come on! Korowai friends, come on, here at our own territo-
    ries, here at our own grounds, a village they have made. Yes, you should come together,
    come on!" we said, not we, it were them who said, and the older people did this way,
    "Oh, yes, but we are not allowed to do so," they said.'

(76) nokhu khambom nokhu be-khai-pelè-da   nokhu
    we   village   we   NEG-go-1PL.INTENT-NEG   to.us
    ayul   de-té
    prohibition QUOTE-3PL.REAL

    "'We will not go to the village, we are not allowed to do so," they said.'

(77) mofu le-nè   kelaja ati-ma-té-dakhu   selèn-bayu-kha-khokha²¹⁶ kuasél
    only come-SS work   get.hold.of-HAB-3PL-SS shorts-shirt-CONN-sort.of fish.hook

fikh maf-akh fo-ma-té-dakhu lokhté-lokhté-ma-té
razor.blade picture-water take-HAB-3PL-SS depart-depart-HAB-3PL

'They only come for working and for taking some things like shorts and shirts, fish-hooks, razor blades, mirrors, and then they usually leave again.'

(78) nokhu-mbolo-mbolop de-té mayokh a-me-tin-da i
our-older.people-older.people QUOTE-3PL.REAL friends that-do-3PL.INTENT-NEG here
khambom-ta khaü ale-mén-dakhu lelip khai-ba-fon-dakhu lelip
village-LOC bivouac build-2PL.IMP-SS together live-stay-1PL.ADHORT-SS together
beba-fon-dakhu-fekho kelaja ati-ma-fon-dakhu e kuasél-o
stay-1PL.INTENT-SS-and work get.hold.of-HAB-1PL.INTENT-SS PAUSE fish.hook-COORD
fikh nggalam-o sabu-ngga-khokha molo-kha-khokha²¹⁷
razor.blade salt-COORD soap-CONN-sort.of diving.glasses-CONN-sort.of
fo-fo-ma-fon-o de-té-tofekho mbolo-mbolop
get-get-HAB-1PL.INTENT-EXCLM QUOTE-3PL.REAL-DS older.people-older.people
wa-me-té-tofekho nn nokhu ayul de-té
thus-do-3PL.REAL-DS PAUSE we prohibition QUOTE-3PL.REAL

'Our older people said, "Friends, do not do that! At this village you should build houses and we could live here together, stay together in order to work, and to get, eh, fish-hooks, razor blades, salt, things like soap, diving glasses," they said and the older people did so but they concluded, "to us it is taboo."'

(79) nn nokhu mofu kelaja ati-ma-fon-dakhu fo-fo-ma-fon-dakhu
PAUSE we only work get.hold.of-HAB-1PL.INTENT-SS get-get-HAB-1PL.INTENT-SS
nokhu khai-khai-ma-fon de-nè de-té sé mbolo-mbolop
we go-go-HAB-1PL.INTENT QUOTE-SS QUOTE-3PL.REAL next older.people-older.people
de-té gekhené alümenèle-fè gekhenép nokhu ül-nè
QUOTE-3PL.REAL you in.former.times-TOP you.PL us kill-SS
dife-ba-tél-e-kha gekhenép mbakha-lekhé laléo
be.almost-PERF-2PL.REAL-TR-CONN you.PL what-cause bad.spirit
lepé-mekhe-té
meet-SUPP-2PL.REAL

'"We only want to do work and to get things and to come and go," they said, and then the older people said, "You, in former times you who almost had killed us, wherefore do you have contact now with the spirit?"'

(80) if-è laléo lepé-mekhe-tél-ano-fè é laléo-fekho i
this-CONN bad.spirit meet-SUPP-3PL.REAL-people-TOP EXCLM bad.spirit-with this
yano-fekho khedi-fa-fon-dakhu de-té-do nokhu
people-with terminate-?-1PL.INTENT-SS QUOTE-3PL.REAL-DS we
golo-ba-lèl-e-kha gekhené imolalü-fè gekhené
be.afraid-PERF-1PL.REAL-TR-CONN you.PL now-TOP you
misafia-fo-m-ba-té de-té
things that-take-SUPP-PERF-2PL.REAL QUOTE-3PL.REAL

'"As for the people who got in touch with the spirit, eh, the spirit and with the people, let us terminate them," they said and to us who were afraid they said, "Now you take things."'

(81) de-té-dakhu khu-laimekhe-té²¹⁸ mayokh mbolo-mbolop
QUOTE-3PL.REAL-SS intestines-hide.thoroughly-3PL.REAL friends older.people-older.people
de-té mayokh anggufa i nokhu-pa nokhu-bolüf-u nokhu-pa
QUOTE-3PL.REAL friends why this our-self our-clan.territory-EXCLM our-self

bolüp-ta   khambom di-fe-lè-fo   la-mén-do   leli-kha
clan.territory-LOC village   open-set-1PL.REAL-? come-2PL.IMP-DS together-CONN
khai-ba-fon-o   de-té-dakhu   mbolo-mbolop
stay-sit-1PL.ADHORT-EXCLM QUOTE-3PL.REAL-SS older.people-older.people
a-me-té-tofekho   wé-ma-té   uma-té-tofekho   wé
that-SUPP-3PL.REAL-DS continue-SUPP-3PL.REAL speak-3PL.REAL-DS EXCLM
golole-té   nokhu ayul²¹⁹ de-té   nokhu khambom
be.afraid-3PL.REAL to.us   prohibition QUOTE-3PL.REAL we   village
be-lu-pelè-da   de-té   mbolo-mbolop   b-aup-da
NEG-enter-1PL.INTENT-NEG QUOTE-3PL.REAL older.people-older.people NEG-word-NEG
gekhené-palap de-té   nokhu ba-lè   de-té
you-do.not.matter QUOTE-3PL.REAL we   stay-1PL.REAL QUOTE-3PL.REAL

'So they said and hid their thoughts and the older people said, "Friends, why we our-selves, our grounds, why did we on our own territory open a village? You should come and together we could live here," they said and the older people insisted to do so, and talked this way but, oh, they were afraid, they said, "It is forbidden to us, we cannot enter to live in the village," they said and the older people said, "All right, as for you, it doesn't matter, but as for ourselves, we stay here," they said.'

(82) beba-té-fekho   mbolo-mbolop   khomi-khaü-fo-do yekhené i
     stay-3PL.REAL-until older.people-older.people dead-INTNS-?-DS   they   this
     Aim-kho-pén-to   mé-la-té
     Kombai-there-LOC-FOC move-come-3PL.REAL

'They stayed until the older people, all of them, had died, and they, the Kombai people came here.'

(83) Aim-kho-pé   yekhené è   khambom a   aturan²²⁰ lé
     Kombai-there-LOC they   PAUSE village   EXCLM rules   ?
     dai-dife-ba-tél-e-kha-lelo-dakhu   a   Ugo
     hear-be.almost-PERF-3PL.REAL-TR-CONN-be.3SG-SS EXCLM Ugo.village
     Boman-o   Uni-o   wokaka Khawagé-o
     Boma.village-COORD Uni.village-COORD all.kinds Kawagit.village-COORD
     Kow-o   wof-e-kha   udediop²²¹
     Kouh.village-COORD that-TR-CONN situation
     dai-ba-té-kha-lelo-dakhu   yekhené mè   if-e-kha   khambom
     hear-PERF-3PL.REAL-CONN-be.3SG.REAL-SS they   SUPP.SS this-TR-CONN village
     di-fu-tofekho menè mé-la-té
     open-set-DS   quickly move-come-3PL.REAL

'The Kombai people, they already know a little about the village rules, of Ugo, Boma, Uni etc., of Kawagit and Kouh, about the situation of those (villages) they already heard and they opened this village and quickly they moved in.'

(84) yekhené menè mé-la-té   è   Kolufo-pén-è   ü
     they   quickly move-come-3PL.REAL PAUSE Korowai-LOC-CONN EXCLM
     kheni-telo-dakhu   yekhené golole-té   nokhu khambom-è kholfunè
     beginning-be.3SG.REAL-SS they   be.afraid-3PL.REAL we   village-CONN all
     fono-mé-lu-kha-lè-kha-fè   nokhu   wola-lekhén-è   de-té-dakhu
     ?-move-enter-IRR-1PL-CONN-TOP to.us   universe-benefit-CONN QUOTE-3PL.REAL-SS
     wof-e-kha   wola-lekhé   gele-té-dakhu   golole-té
     that-TR-CONN universe-benefit be.afraid-3PL.REAL-SS be.afraid-3PL.REAL

'They quickly moved in, eh as for the Korowai people, my! in the beginning they were afraid, and they said, "In case all of us will move into the village, our world will get out of order," and for the universe's (end) they were afraid.'

(85) wola-lekhén de-té-dakhu golole-té-tofekho gekhené-palap
universe-benefit QUOTE-3PL.REAL-SS be.afraid-3PL.REAL-DS you-do.not.matter
de-té
QUOTE-3PL.REAL

'"For the world('s end)," they said and they feared, but they said, "as for you, it doesn't matter."'

(86) alüm-efè imonè-ta-fè nokhu-mbolo-mbolop khemi-khaü-fo-do sé nokhu
before-TOP now-?-TOP our-older.people-older.people dead-INTNS-?-DS next we
mba-mbam-tanukh khame-lè-kha-ma
child-child-only stay-1PL.REAL-CONN-also

'Now, when first our older people, all of them, are dead, then we, only the children, stay too.'

(87) yo mayokh i khambom khonggé-telo-tu anè la-mén-do
yes friends this village big-be.3SG.REAL-FOCUS IMP/ADHORT come-2PL.IMP-DS
leli khai-ba-fon a tokop-khop mbisi pal selèn-bayu
together stay-stay-1PL.ADHORT EXCLM store-there steel.axe machete shorts-shirt
bolkhop a kuasél fikh mayokh tokop-khop alo-lo-kha
place EXCLM fish.hook razor.blade friends store-there stand.3SG.REAL-?-CONN

'"Yes, friends, this village is a big one, isn't it, so come in, and we can stay together—there is a store, a place where there are axes, machetés, clothing, well, there are fishhooks, razor blades, friends, since there is a store."'

(88) kelaja lapanggan[222] kho ibol-o mayokh gübo-ma-mon-do
work air.strip there be.3SG.REAL-EXCLM friends come.together-SUPP-2PL.IMP-DS
lelip sama-sama[223] lelip khofu khambom-ta beba-fon lelip
together together together be.with.all village-LOC stay-1PL.ADHORT together
la-mén-do kholfunè beba-fon-o de-lè-lofekho nokhu
come-2PL.IMP-DS all stay-1PL.ADHORT-EXCLM QUOTE-1PL.REAL-DS.but our
mayokh nokhu ayul de-té
friends to.us prohibition QUOTE-3PL.REAL

'"There is work at the airstrip, friends, so come together and we all can live together in the village, together you must come and all of us can live together," we said, but our friends said, "No, we are not allowed to."'

(89) mbam mbolo-mbolop kheme-khaü-fè mba-mbam gekhené-pa
child older.people-older.people dead-INTNS-TOP child-child you-self
khami-ba-mon nokhu ayul de-té nokhu ayul
stay-stay-2PL.IMP to.us prohibition QUOTE-3PL.REAL to.us prohibition
de-té-do khai-ba-té khai-ba-té khai-ba-té
QUOTE-3PL.REAL-DS stay-stay-3PL.REAL stay-stay-3PL.REAL stay-stay-3PL.REAL

'"Children, when all the older people have died, children, you yourselves can live there, we are not allowed to," they said, "we are not allowed to," they said and they stayed where they were.'

(90) sé yekhené-pa lefu-lefu é khambom khol-ma-lè-lofekho bail-é
next they-self some-others PAUSE village ?-SUPP-1PL.REAL-DS oh.yes-EXCLM

de-tél-ano-fè   wap Manggél[224]   de-té
QUOTE-3PL.REAL-people-TOP   there Manggél.village open-3PL.REAL

'And then they themselves, some of them, the people who had agreed upon coming together in villages, opened Manggél village.'

(91) Yaniluma   khol-ma-lè-lo   nokhu bail-él-ano-fè   Yafufla
Yaniruma.village ?-SUPP-1PL.REAL-DS   we   oh.yes-yes-people-TOP Yafufla.village
de-té   Mabül   de-té   sé sol Félman   wa
open-3PL.REAL Mabül.village open-3PL.REAL next new Ferman.village there
de-té-fap[225]
open-3PL.REAL-that

'We who came together in Yaniruma village, namely, the people who agreed, opened up Yafufla village, opened Mabül village and recently Férman village, they opened there.'

(92) m   wé   mayokh i   khalu-khalu-fefè mayokh kholfunè i   khambom
PAUSE EXCLM friends   this near-near-TOP   friends   all   this village
gübole-mon   de-lè-lofekho   nn   yanop aündan-tele-té
come.together-2PL.IMP QUOTE-1PL.REAL-DS.but PAUSE people resisting-be-3PL.REAL
nokhu ayul   de-té-do   gekhené-palap de-nè   nokhup
to.us   prohibition QUOTE-3PL.REAL-DS you-do.not.matter QUOTE-SS we
mba-mbam nokhu-pan-tanukh nokhu Aim-pekho   khai-ba-lè-do
child-child   we-self-only   we   Kombai-COMIT stay-stay-1PL.REAL-DS

'"Oh, my! Friends, close to this place, friends, in this village, all of you should gather together," we said, but the people did not want to and they stated they were not allowed to, and then we said, "All right it is up to you," and we, the children, stay on ourselves, together with the Kombai people and'

(93) sé nokhu-mayokh a   Filuf-e-khambom-fekha   Filup
next our-friends   EXCLM Firu.village-TR-village-some.far.away Firu.village
de-ba-tél-e-kha   ye-pa Nabékha[226] sé   a   siama-ton[227]
QUOTE-PERF-3PL.REAL-TR-CONN it-self Nombéakha next EXCLM head.of.district-FOC
dé   gekhenép khambom-tena belén   gekhenép ye-gülo
QUOTE.3SG.REAL you   village-DIMIN do.not.need.to you.PL   here-upstream
Yaniluman   melé-la-mén   dé
Yaniruma.village move-come-2PL.IMP QUOTE.3SG.REAL

'then our friends, as for the village Firu which was a bit far away, the so-called Firu village, (the people) themselves (call it:) Nombéakha, and then it was the head of the district who said, "You should not live in a little village, you must go upstream there and join the people of Yaniruma."'

(94) dé-do   sé a   Él de-té-dakhu   melé-la-té[228]
QUOTE.3SG.REAL-DS next EXCLM yes QUOTE-3PL.REAL-SS move-come-3PL.REAL

'Thus he said, and then they agreed and entered.'

(95) melé-la-té   if-è   Kolufo-khambom de-tél-e-kha-lo
move-come-3PL.REAL this-CONN Korowai-village   open-3PL.REAL-TR-CONN-FOC
Kolufo mo golole-té   aündan-te-té-do   a   Aim-Nabékha-lo
Korowai just be.afraid-3PL.REAL refusing-be-3PL.REAL-DS EXCLM Kombai-Nombéakha-FOC
melé-la-té-do   mesé nokhu Kolufo-mba-mbam po-tanukh
move-come-3PL.REAL-DS next   we   Korowai-child-child   a.couple.of-only
khame-lè
stay-1PL.REAL

'They entered, at the place where people had opened a Korowai village, the Korowai people shrunk back and resisted, but the Kombai and Nombéakha people came in, and then we, children of the Korowai, only a couple of us live here.'

Aibum

The Aibum text was tape-recorded in March 1989 in van Enk's house in Manggél. The narrator is Bailumalé Dajo, at that time around 16 years old and a permanent inhabitant of Manggél. He gives a short account of his attendance at several sago grub festivals.

(1) aibum[229]   gil   non   u-tofekho[230]
stepbrother ceremonial.festival.place sago.grub cut.3SG.REAL-DS

'Younger stepbrother organised a sago grub festival and'

(2) khenè non   ü   . é-ba-lé
next   sago.grub cut.down.SS sleep-stay-1SG.REAL

'I assisted in the preparations and I slept (there).'

(3) ye-sü   melé-la-lu-ndé-lofekho
here-from move-come-NEAR-1SG.REAL-DS

'From here we had arrived'

(4) Sékh-Tabul[231]   gil   üop[232] tai-do
Sékh.clan-Tabul.clan sago.grub.festival message come.3SG.REAL-DS

'and there came an invitation for a feast at the the Sékh and Tabul . . . .'

(5) khenè afé-ngga   nokhup gil   op   nokhup lanol   tokhül
next   usually-CONN we   festival.place house we   tree.species stem
o-fekho   ye-lu-ndè-fekho
house-CIRCUM sleep-NEAR-1PL.REAL-until

'then, as we usually do, at our festival bivouac, in our shelter of *lanol* stems, we slept until'

(6) walé-do   khülo ai   kha-lè   khenè walü-fekho
daybreak.REAL.3SG-DS upstream descend.SS go-1PL.REAL next   half.way-CIRCUM
aibum   Géla-lo mil-fekha   ao-bol-e-kha
stepbrother Gela-FOC banana.species-one plant-3SG.PERF.REAL-TR-CONN
lembu-telo-do   lai-lu   fu-bol-e-kha   walü-fekho
bad-be.3SG.REAL-DS break-NEAR put-3SG.PERF.REAL-TR-CONN half.way-CIRCUM
lu-alü-lé-khami-ba-lè-fekho
enter-bake-eat-sit-stay-1PL.REAL-until

'the next morning we came downstream at a place halfway—and some *mil* bananas planted by stepbrother Gela, which proved to be not so good, which we had cut and collected— halfway we entered (a house) prepared (the bananas), ate (them) and sat together until'

(7) walé-top   walé-do   folé-top   if-è
daybreak.REAL.3SG-DS daybreak.REAL.3SG-DS be.afternoon.3SG.REAL-DS here-CONN
khosükhop khe-nè dokhon[233] külo-nè[234]   mekhe-lè
there   go-SS   small.bivouac do.külo.dancing-SUPP.SS do-1PL.REAL

'at daybreak the next day . . . in the afternoon we went there and dancing in the *külomo* way we entered a small bivouac.'

(8) Lefilkhei   dokhon külo-nè   Sabül   amin-ta Sabül   amin-ta
Lefilkhei.clan bivouac külo.dancing-SUPP.SS Sabül.River bank-LOC Sabül.River bank-LOC
dokhon külo-nè   mekho
bivouac külo.dancing-SUPP.SS do.SS

'We entered a Lefilkhei people's halting bivouac while *külomo* dancing, a bivouac at the Sabül banks we entered in the *külomo* way,'

(9) é-felu-ndè   walé-do   khasam[235] külo-nè
sleep-NEAR-1PL.REAL daybreak.REAL.3SG-DS khasam.dance külo.dancing-SUPP.SS
wai   kha-mén   de-té-tofekho   nu nokhup ayul[236]
move.down.SS go-1PL.ADHORT QUOTE-3PL.REAL-DS I us   prohibition
de-ba-lè-lofekho   khasam   tamé-mekho[237]   lamé
QUOTE-PERF-1PL.REAL-DS khasam.dance tie-SUPP.SS   tie.SS
khami-bakh-un-tofekho
stay-HOD-1PL-DS

'and we slept and the next day they said, "Let us go out in the *khasam* combined with *külomo* way of dancing," but we said, "No, we are not allowed," so we (only) kept dancing in the *khasam* way,'

(10) du mofu khe-nè oldintai   la-lé   mofu khonggekél
tree only go-SS notch.at.both.sides.and.break come-1SG.REAL only big
mofu du olai-bo-ma-lè[238]   fu-do-DS   ma-lè-do
only tree break.off.both.sides-stay-SUPP-1PL.REAL put.3SG.REAL do-1PL.REAL-DS

'we just danced and notched down trees at both sides of the path and'

(11) kholükh-nè   khenè lakhato-mo-do   lamé khami-bakh-un-tofekho
break.down-SUPP.SS next   down-SUPP.3SG.REAL-DS dance stay-HOD-1PL-until
khe-nè dife-lé-lofekho
go-SS be.almost-1SG.REAL-DS

'(trees) broke and then went down and we kept dancing and we almost arrived and . . .'

(12) apafu   manop bolüf-khayan   bolüp   ye-pa khof-e-kha   mofu kelaja[239]
EXCLM nice   clan.territory-real clan.territory his-self that-TR-CONN just settlement
kü-te-bol-e-kha   nè lamé-digeli-nè   khami-ba-lè-lofekho
like-be-3SG.be.REAL-TR-CONN ? tie-hip.with.feet-SUPP.SS sit-stay-1PL.REAL-DS

'My, what a nice place, a real place itself, it was like a village, with hipping movements of our feet we kept dancing until'

(13) khaü wai   khaü ü-lelo[240] kho ale-té   kho alü   mbala-mekho
bivouac go.out.SS bivouac Ow!-be sago bake-3PL.REAL sago bake.SS distribute-SUPP.SS
lakhup   di-èi[241]   lail-me-té-do
packet.with.grubs take-bring.down.SS cut-SUPP-3PL.REAL-DS

'we came out from the bivouac (there) while shouting "*Üüüü!*"—Ow!—they baked sago, sago they baked and distributed, leaf packets (with sago grubs) they got down and opened (the packets) and'

(14) aibum-khül ye-sübo[242]   wai   melé le-nè   dokhom-pekho
stepbrother-PL here-downstream move.down.SS move come-SS small.bivouac-CIRCUM

wai   ye-té-tofekho   lé   nuf-è   ye-lé
move.down.SS sleep-3PL.REAL-DS presently I-CONN sleep-1SG.REAL

'the stepbrothers came here downstream, moved out and in the small halting bivouac to sleep, where I slept at the same time,'

(15) a   nokhup kheyop é-fu-ba-lè-lofekho   sü-lekhé   ne
     EXCLM we   house   sleep-make-stay-1PL.REAL-DS tobacco-purpose me
     bu-lelo-ba-lé
     tease-be-stay-1SG.REAL

'in the house we slept, I was teasing (them) to get tobacco.'

(16) amo-kha-tél-e-kha   minya[243] alip-ta   alü-kha-lé-fé
     do-IRR-2PL.REAL-TR-CONN fuel   here-LOC burn-IRR-1SG-EXCLM
     de-ba-lé-lofekho   lakhelilo-lakhelilo-ma-lé wa   ni   sü
     QUOTE-PERF-1SG.REAL-DS pour-pour-HAB-1SG   there woman tobacco
     Minu-lom-pekho[244] sü-fekha   abolo sü   lamon Kolufo sü   lamon-tena
     Minu-FOC-ATTENT   tobacco-one buy.SS tobacco bunch Korowai tobacco bunch-DIMIN
     fédo-do
     give.REAL.3SG-DS

'"If you do so, I will raise a fire by means of petroleum," I said and I kept pouring down (the petroleum), and that woman's tobacco . . . it was Minu who had bought a bunch of tobacco, a small bunch of Korowai tobacco she had bought and she gave (it to me) and'

(17) dépe-nè é-felu-ndé-fekho   walé-do   khenè walü-fekho
     smoke-SS sleep-NEAR-1SG-and be.light.REAL.3SG-DS next   half.way-until
     é-ba-lé-fekho   ye-sübol   gilmambolüp[245] la-lè
     sleep-be-1SG.REAL-until here-be.downstream old.festival.bivouac come-1PL.REAL

'I smoked and slept, the next day halfway we slept again, and downstream we arrived at the festival place.'

(18) gilmambolüp   la-lè   nokhup le-nè   é-fu-ba-lé-fekho   wa
     old.festival.bivouac come-1PL.REAL we   come-SS sleep-put-stay-1SG.REAL-until that
     gil   alü-dilme-té-do[246] nokhup ai   melé-la-lè-dakhu
     festival.place bake-finish-3PL.REAL-DS we   move.down.SS move-come-1PL.REAL-SS
     nokhup nana-fa-lè
     we   do.nothing-?-1PL.REAL

'At the next festival place we came, we came, slept until at that festival they finished celebrating grub feasts, then we went out and finally we did not attend feasts anymore.'

Mukhalé

The narrator of the following real-life narrative is Labülun Sendékh, a young man who also related the text about the first contacts with missionaries. The text was recorded on November 1987 in van Enk's office in Yaniruma. The narrator was asked whether he could tell something about the background of the attempt to kill Didonalé Lemakha. The attempt failed, but Didonalé had to be flown out of Yaniruma to the nurse in Boma, who removed the arrowtips from his body.

The text begins with the story of the fratricide by Mukhalé Manianggatun (see figure 6–2) because of a young woman and the complications that result from a series of witchcraft accusations and concomitant revenge actions. In the context of these revenge actions Didonalé becomes a captive of the Manianggatun clan, who wants to send him to an allied clan to be executed.

In a succesful attempt to escape, Didonalé is hit by arrows. The events of his arrival in Yaniruma, badly wounded; of the flight to Boma; and of the operation by the nurse are recounted in a very lively manner by the narrator, who went with Didonalé to Boma and witnessed the operation.

Figure 6–2   Mukhalé Manianggatun with his youngest son. Johannes Veldhuizen, 1986.

(1) Mukhalé-fekho Mukhalé y-afé
Mukhalé-COMIT Mukhalé his-older.brother
'With Mukhalé, Mukhalé's older brother,'

(2) Mukhalé y-afé-lo   Dajo-menél fe-nè fo-dakhu
Mukhalé his-older.brother-FOC Dajo-young.girl get-SS marry.3SG.REAL-SS
'it was Mukhalé's older brother who married a young girl from the Dajo clan,'

(3) Dajo-menél   fe-nè fo-do   wof-e-kha   Dajo-menél   ye-fimelon[247]
Dajo-young.girl get-SS marry.3SG.REAL-DS that-TR-CONN Dajo-young.girl her-intestines
nu if-è   Mukhalé duo-tofekho   él y-afé-da-é
I this-CONN Mukhalé think.3SG.REAL-DS yes his-older.brother-NEG-EXCLM
nu Mukhalé-lo fo-p-khelüf-é   dé
I Mukhalé-FOC marry.SS-1SG.INTENT-DESID-EXCLM QUOTE.3SG.REAL

'a young Dajo girl he married and that Dajo girl said by herself, "Yes, for me Mukhalé's older brother is not the one, oh I might have Mukhalé himself as my man."'

(4) dé-dakhu   mofu fimelon duo-fu-dakhu   babo-fekho
QUOTE.3SG.REAL-SS only intestines put.in-set.3SG.REAL-SS stay.3SG.REAL-until
Mukhalé if-e-kha   lal   khai   alo-bo-top
Mukhalé this-TR-CONN woman go.3SG.REAL stand-stay-3SG.REAL-place

'Thus she said, she only thought so and stayed until Mukhalé once came to the place where this woman lived.'

(5) lal   alo-bo-top   khai-do   ya gu-fè lai-m-do
female be-stay-3SG.REAL-place go.3SG.REAL-DS yes you-TOP come-2SG.IMP-DS
goma-fon   dé-do   goma-té-dakhu   if-e-kha   lal
have.sex-1PL.INTENT QUOTE.3SG.REAL-DS have.sex-3PL.REAL-SS this-TR-CONN woman
taifo   nu-fè mo go fo-kha-lé   dé
ask.3SG.REAL I-TOP just you marry-IRR-1SG QUOTE.3SG.REAL

'To the woman's living place he came and she said, "Come and let us have sex!" and they had sex and the woman asked, "Shall I marry you?"'

(6) nu ne-Mukhalé go fo-kha-lé   dé-do   sé Mukhalé yu-pa él
I my-Mukhalé   you marry-IRR-1SG QUOTE.3SG.REAL-DS next Mukhalé he-also yes
dé
QUOTE.3SG.REAL

'"I will marry you, my Mukhalé," she said and then Mukhalé also agreed.'

(7) g-afé   lekhén-o dé-tofekho   n-afé   lé   ü-kha-lé
your-older.brother for-EXCLM QUOTE.3SG.REAL-DS my-older.brother presently kill-IRR-1SG
dé
QUOTE.3SG.REAL

'"And what about your older brother?" she said and he said, "My older brother, I am going to kill him."'

(8) n-afé   lé   ü-kha-lé   dé-do   él g-afé
my-older.brother presently kill-IRR-1SG QUOTE.3SG.REAL-DS yes your-older.brother
ü-m-do   gu-fekho   nu-fekho fa-fon   dé
kill-2SG.IMP-DS you-COORD I-COORD marry-1PL.INTENT QUOTE.3SG.REAL

'"My older brother, I am going to kill him," he said and she agreed, "Yes, you should kill your brother, so you and me, we can marry," she said.'

(9) nu nu-fè wof-e-kha   lefül-efè gülnanggaup nu lu-kha-lé-fé
    I I-TOP   that-TR-CONN day-TOP   night   I   ascend-IRR-1SG-EXCLM
dé
QUOTE.3SG.REAL

"'As for me, I will come in tonight," he said.'

(10) gu yafin tamélo-m-é   dé-do   i   lal   yo él
    you stairs tie-2SG.IMP-EXCLM QUOTE.3SG.REAL-DS this woman yes yes
dé-dakhu   éba-té-fekho   gülé-do   i   lal   yu nu
QUOTE.3SG.REAL-SS sleep-3PL.REAL-until be.dark.3SG.REAL-DS this woman she I
ol-ekhi-é   dé-dakhu   yafin[248] tamélo
faeces-?-EXCLM QUOTE.3SG.REAL-SS stairs   tie.3SG.REAL

"'You must fasten the treehouse stairs," he said and the woman agreed, and they slept
until it became night, and the woman, she said, "I have to relieve myself," and she fastened the stairs.'

(11) yafin   tamélo-dakhu lu-do   élo-ba-té-do   i
    treehouse.stairs tie.3SG.REAL-SS move.up.3SG.REAL-DS sleep-stay-3PL.REAL-DS this
Mukhalé naném alo-lulo   gülnanggaup alo-lulo   alo-lulo
Mukhalé   silently walk-3SG.NEAR night   walk-3SG.NEAR walk-3SG.NEAR
lu   lu-tofekho   él nggé mo é-fe-nè   fu-ba-té   i
move.up.SS move.up.3SG.REAL-DS yes friend just sleep-take-SS put-stay-3PL.REAL this
lal   khafén-telo-bo   i   wafil élo-bo
woman awake-be-3SG.stay.REAL this man   sleep-stay.3SG.REAL

'She fastened the treehouse stairs and entered again and they slept and Mukhalé secretly
walked in the night, he walked and walked, and moved up into the treehouse, and oh
dear, yes, they lay asleep, the woman was awake, the husband slept.'

(12) élo-bo-do   i   lal   y   imo-tofekho   i[249] Mukhalé lu
    sleep-3SG.stay.REAL-DS this woman him see.3SG.REAL-DS this Mukhalé   move.up.SS
aloli-mémo   lu   abüokh-bo-ta   lu   melil bepé[250]
stay.on-3SG.IMM.REAL move.up.SS door-opening-LOC move.up.SS fire   blow.3SG.REAL
melil alolé-tofekho   i   lal   bepé-de   walelé-do
fire   stand.3SG.REAL-DS this woman blow.3SG.REAL-DS be.light.3SG.REAL-DS
if-e-kha   abül i   Mukhalé yu imo-tofekho   y-afé
this-TR-CONN man   this Mukhalé he look.3SG.REAL-DS his-older.brother
élo-bo
sleep-stay.3SG.REAL

'He was asleep and the woman saw him, Mukhalé who just had come and having moved up
now was standing in the opening of the treehouse entrance, and the woman blew the fire,
she blew the fire so it shone and the man, Mukhalé, he saw that his older brother was asleep.'

(13) élo-bo-do   ülmekho duol-mo
    sleep-stay.3SG.REAL-DS shoot.SS   put.into-SUPP.3SG.REAL

'While he slept, he shot him.'

(14) ülmekho duol-mo-tofekho   gebelipekho-dakhu   melil-an
    shoot.SS   put.into-SUPP.3SG.REAL-DS start.from.sleep.3SG.REAL-SS fire-LOC
felé
fall.3SG.REAL

'He shot him so he started from his sleep and he fell into the fire.'

(15) melil-an felé-tofekho   i   la-to   ye-wafil   atilo
     fire-LOC   fall.3SG.REAL-DS   this   female-FOC   her-husband   get.hold.of.3SG.REAL
     'He fell into the fire and the woman got hold of her husband.'

(16) atilo-dom-pekho   lelip   ati-ba-té-dakhu   ül-me-té-dakhu   mintafi
     hold.3SG.REAL-DS-and   together   hold-stay-3PL.REAL-SS   kill-SUPP-3PL.REAL-SS   goods
     laifa-té-dakhu   bando   ai-lofekho   fe-nè   fe-té-dakhu   lu   khaim
     get.out-3PL.REAL-SS   bring   move.down-DS   take-SS   put-3PL.REAL-SS   move.up.SS   treehouse
     melil dimekhe-té
     fire   put.on-3PL.REAL
     'She got hold of him, and then together they held and killed him, got the (household) goods out, brought it downstairs, put it down there, moved up (again), and incensed the treehouse with fire.'

(17) melil dimekhe-té-do   yanop lokhül-fekho dofo
     fire   put.on-3PL.REAL-DS   person corpse-COMIT   be.burnt.3SG.REAL
     'They put it on fire and with the corpse it burnt down.'

(18) yanop lokhül-fekho dofo-do   wa-fekho   melil di-atimekho[251]
     person   corpse-COMIT   be.burnt.3S.REAL-DS   there-CIRCUM   fire   pull.out-hold.SS
     yekhené kheyop gilfo
     they   house   go.away.3S.REAL
     'With the human corpse it burnt down, and from there they took fire and went home.'

(19) kheyop gilfo-dakhu   wof-e-kha   Mukhalé ülmol-e-kha-fè   yu
     house   go.away.3SG.REAL-SS   that-TR-CONN   Mukhalé   kill.3SG.REAL -TR-CONN-TOP   he
     mbam lidop wafi-mbam waf-è   wafi-mbam e   o   Bafén[252]
     child   one   man-child   there-CONN   man-child PAUSE   EXCLM Bafén
     yu wafi-mbam ati-bol-e-kha   ye-alé   sol ye-alé
     he male-child   hold-3SG.stay.REAL-TR-CONN   her-husband   new   her-husband
     Mukhalé-fekho wai-gilfo
     Mukhalé-COMIT   go.down-go.away.3SG.REAL
     'They went to (Mukhalé's) house. The one whom Mukhalé shot, he had one boy, Bafén, after she had taken her boy, she got out of there with her new husband Mukhalé.'

(20) sol ye-alé   Mukhalé-fekho wai-gilfo-do   a   khaim   meli-to
     new her-husband Mukhalé-COMIT   go.down-go.away.3SG.REAL-DS EXCLM treehouse fire-with
     dofo   yanop lokhül-fekho dofo-do   o walé-do
     be.burnt.3SG.REAL person corpse-COMIT be.burnt.3SG.REAL-DS oh daybreak.REAL.3S-DS
     ü   i   fala   de-té-tofekho   aja   Mukhalé khe-bo-tofekho
     Ow! this what.about? QUOTE-3PL.REAL-DS EXCLM Mukhalé travel-3SG.PERF.REAL-DS
     ye-mofekha   Nènèp-tekhén[253] dé   nggé-lowe
     his-younger.brother   Nènèp-PURPOSE   QUOTE.3SG.REAL friend-EXCLM
     ne-mofekha-lowe   nokhu-afé   ülme-lé-fé   dé
     my-younger.brother-EXCLM   our-older.brother   kill-1SG.REAL-EXCLM   QUOTE.3SG.REAL
     'With Mukhalé, her new husband she went out from there, and since the treehouse with the corpse had burnt down, the next morning people said, "Ow! What has happened here?" and when Mukhalé arrived, and his younger brother asked about Nènèp, he said, "Friend, my younger brother, I myself shot our older brother."'

(21) ü   dé-tofekho   a gu ü²⁵⁴ du-n-da   gu-pa   ü-akha-lé
Ow! say.3SG.REAL-DS ah you Ow! say-INF-NEG you-also kill-IRR-1SG.REAL
dé
QUOTE.3SG.REAL

'"Ow!" he said, but he said, "you should not say 'Ow!', or I will shoot you too."'

(22) dé-kha   lekhé lenggilé-dakhu   yakhatimekho
QUOTE.3SG.REAL-CONN CAUSE be.frightened.3SG.REAL-SS renounce.3SG.REAL

'Because he said that, he was frightened and renounced.'

(23) lenggilé-dakhu   yakhatimekho-do   é   yekhené lambi-lambil è
be.frightened.3SG.REAL-SS renounce-3SG.REAL.DS PAUSE they   family-family PAUSE
gufe-té-tofekho²⁵⁵   a gufe-tin-da   gekhené-afé
claim.for.goods-3PL.REAL-DS ah claim.for.goods-3PL.INTENT-NEG your-older.brother
fano nu ne-pa n-afé   ü-ba-lé   gekhené belén
NEG I I-self my-older.brother kill-PERF-1SG.REAL you.PL do.not.need.to
dé
QUOTE.3SG.REAL

'He was frightened and renounced and when their relatives claimed for recompensation,
he said, "You should not claim for anything, for it does not regard your older brother,
it was mine, and I myself have killed him, you should not ..."'

(24) gekhené gufe-tin-da   gekhené belén-è
you(PL) claim.for.goods-3PL.INTENT-NEG you(PL) do.not.need.to-EXCLM
dé-kha   lekhé é   lenggilé-té-dakhu
QUOTE.3SG.REAL-CONN REASON PAUSE be.frightened-3PL.REAL-SS
yakhatimekhe-té
renounce-3PL.REAL

'Because he said, "You should not claim, you should not! ..." they were frightened
and renounced.'

(25) lenggile-té-dakhu   yakhatimekhe-té-do è   babo-fekho   ye-pa
be.frightened-3PL.REAL-SS renounce-3PL.REAL-DS PAUSE sit.3SG.REAL-until he-self
fe-nè fo-dakhu   babo-fekho   mbam-tena-ma bé-mo-dakhu
take-SS marry.3SG.REAL-SS stay.3SG.REAL-until child-DIMIN-also care-SUPP.3SG.REAL-SS
ye-laün-abül²⁵⁶ bé-mo-dakhu   khenè sé ye-pa mbam-pekha e
his-foster-son   care-SUPP.3SG.REAL-SS next next he-self child-one PAUSE
Mukhalé ye-pa ye fo-tofekhol-è   mbam wafi-mbam-pekha
Mukhalé he-self he marry.3SG.REAL-DS-EXCLM child male-child-one
wafi-mbam-efè Lonofalé²⁵⁷
man-child-TOP Lonofalé

'They were frightened and renounced, and he stayed until he himself married (another
woman), then he stayed, cared also for a little child, he cared for his little male foster
child, and then he himself, a child ... eh, Mukhalé himself married, (and out of this
marriage was born) a boy, (named) Lonofalé.'

(26) Lonofalé dé-dakhu   a   ye-pa a ye-pa-mam-pekho Mukhalé
Lonofalé say.3SG.REAL-SS PAUSE he-self PAUSE he-self-also-CIRCUM Mukhalé
ye-pa-mam-pekhol-è   y-abül lidop Lonofalé
he-self-also-CIRCUM-EXCLM his-son one   Lonofalé

'He called him Lonofalé, well, he himself, Mukhalé . . . for himself, his own one (and only) son was Lonofalé.'

(27) Lonofalé-lelo-do   khenè sé ye babo-fekho   wof-e-kha
Lonofalé-be.3SG.REAL-DS   next   next he stay.3SG.REAL-until that-TR-CONN
Dajo-menél   fe-nè   fo-dakhu   babo-fekho   sé Khawékh
Dajo.clan-young.girl take-SS marry.3SG.REAL-SS stay.3SG.REAL-until next Khawékh.clan
menél   Kaélfup-Khawékh   menél   fe-nè fo-dakhu   a
young.girl Kaélfup.subclan-Khawékh.clan young.girl take-SS marry.3SG.REAL-SS PAUSE
Dedilo-mam-pekhol-efè[258] wo-fè   y-abül a   e   Sèmbelèfalé y-abül
Dedilon-also-COMIT-TOP   that-TOP his-son PAUSE PAUSE Sèmbelèfalé his-son
lidop-kha-fè   Sèmbelèfalé lé   lekha-telo-mbol   amodo
one-CONN-TOP Sèmbelèfalé   presently tall-be.3SG.REAL-PROGR DS.and
khai-ba-té-fekho   mesé Faülanop khomile-khaü-té-do   Mafém[259] y-até
live-be-3PL.REAL-until next Faülanop die-INTNS-3PL.REAL-DS Mafém   her-father
khomilo-do
die.3SG.REAL-DS

'Lonofalé was there, and he (Mukhalé) stayed until he married the young Dajo woman, then he stayed until he married a Khawékh girl, a Kaélfup Khawékh girl, and (he married) with Dedilon also, the latter got her baby boy, Sèmbelèfalé, her only son, while Sèmbelèfalé was becoming a tall boy they lived, and then all the people of the Faülanop clan died; also Mafém her father died and'

(28) Mafém y-até   khomilo-do   a-è   mo wof-e-kha   Golokhofalé-lo
Mafém her-father die.3SG.REAL-DS EXCLM-EXCLM just that-TR-CONN Golokhofalé-FOC
nolél-è[260]   de-té
eat.3SG.REAL-EXCLM QUOTE-3PL.REAL

'Mafém's father died and they said, "It is Golokhofalé, who has eaten him."'

(29) Golokhofalé-lo nolél-è   de-té-dakhu   Golokhofalé
Golokhofalé-FOC eat.3SG.REAL-EXCLM QUOTE-3PL.REAL-SS Golokhofalé
lamé-lo   Didonalé lamé-lo   Didonalé y-afé
tie-CAUS.3SG.REAL Didonalé tie-CAUS.3SG.REAL Didonalé his-older.brother
lamé-lo[261]
tie-CAUS.3SG.REAL

'"It is Golokhofalé who has eaten him," they said and they tied Golokhofalé, and Didonalé's older brother they tied.'

(30) Golokhofalé lambil-efè Didonalé y-afé   fe-nè fe-té[262]
Golokhofalé   family-TOP Didonalé his-older.brother take-SS put-3PL.REAL

'To Golokhofalé's family they sent Didonalé's older brother.'

(31) Didonalé y-afé   lambil-efè Golokhofalé[263] fe-nè fe-té
Didonalé his-older.brother family-TOP Golokhofalé   take-SS put-3PL.REAL
Lemakha-bolüp fe-nè fe-té-do   ül-nè alü-no-nté-do[264]   khenè
Lemakha-land   take-SS put-3PL.REAL-DS kill-SS bake-eat-3PL.REAL-DS next
wof-e-kha   mbolop[265] ye-pa babo khomilo
that-TR-CONN old.man   he-also stay.SS die.3SG.REAL

'To Didonalé's older brother's family they sent Golokhofalé, to the Lemakha territory they sent him, and (the Lemakha people) killed, baked, and ate him and the old man stayed and died.'

(32) khomilo-do   béto-fekho   wa ye-mbam²⁶⁶ lamé-lo   fe-nè fe-té-do
     die.3SG.REAL-DS after-CIRCUM that his-child   tie-CAUS.SS take-SS put-3PL.REAL-DS
     ül-nè alü-no-nté-do   a   Faülanop khomi-khaülé-do²⁶⁷
     kill-SS bake-eat-3PL.REAL-DS PAUSE Faülanop dead-INTNS.3SG.REAL-DS

     'He died, and afterward his child they sent and they tied his child and they sent
     him, then they killed, baked, and ate him and the Faülanop people, all of them died
     and . . .'

(33) Faülanop khomi-khaülé-do   khai-ba-té-fekho²⁶⁸   yanop
     Faülanop   dead-INTNS.3SG.REAL-DS live-stay-3PL.REAL-until people
     dame-té-dakhu   è   khede-té-dakhu   Didonalé ülmekhe-té-do
     root.out-3PL.REAL-SS PAUSE terminate-3PL.REAL-SS Didonalé shoot-3PL.REAL-DS
     lebükh-ma-té-do   lai-mo   Yaniluma   melé-lai
     shoot-SUPP-3PL.REAL-DS hatch-SUPP Yaniruma.village move-come.3SG.REAL

     'All the Faülanop died and they kept rooting out people, they terminated them,
     and Didonalé they shot, they shot him, and he hatched (the arrows) and came to Yaniruma
     village.'

(34) nu²⁶⁹ yanop-to naném-anop-to²⁷⁰   ne-khaü demé-méma-té-do   lu
     for.me person-FOC illegal(ly)-person-FOC my-house open-IMM-3PL.REAL-DS move.up
     uma-lè-dakhu o   mayokh nu yanof-é   de-lé-do   gülnanggaup
     tell-1PL.REAL-SS EXCLM EXCLM I   people-EXCLM tell-1SG.REAL-DS night
     lu   uma-lè-dakhu-fekho²⁷¹ é-felu-ndè   walé-do
     move.up tell-1PL.REAL-SS-and   sleep-NEAR-1PL.REAL daybreak.REAL.3SG-DS
     u-méma-lé   yanop aup féde-méma-lé
     talk-IMM-1SG.REAL people word give-IMM-1SG.REAL

     'As for me, there were people, thieves, who just had broken into my house, and I went
     up and made it known, "Oh, friends, someone . . . " I made it known, that night I moved
     up and made it known and we slept, and the next morning I just told it, to the (village)
     people I just had announced,'

(35) nu na-khaim yanop lu-do   gülnanggaup abo-abo-la-lé-fè
     I my-house person enter.3SG.REAL-DS night   chase-chase-come-1SG.REAL-TOP
     abo-lail-me-lé-fè   de-lé-do   wof-e-kha   mahüon
     chase-come-SUPP-1SG.REAL-TOP tell-1SG.REAL-DS that-TR-CONN story
     uma-lé-do
     talk-1SG.REAL-DS

     'that someone had entered into my house that night, and that I had chased him, "I had
     chased him," I said, that story I was telling and'

(36) wof-e-kha   mahüon uma-lé-do   wé   Amosé²⁷² lai
     that-TR-CONN word   talk-1SG.REAL-DS EXCLM Amos   come.3SG.REAL

     'I told that story, when Amos came.'

(37) Amosé lai-do   él bétop ima-lè-lofekho yanop²⁷³ falé
     Amos come.3SG.REAL-DS yes behind see-1PL.REAL-DS person   crooked
     le-bol-e-kha   falé le-bol-e-kha   mé-lai
     come-be.3SG.REAL-TR-CONN crooked come-be.3SG.REAL-TR-CONN move-come.3SG.REAL

     'Amos came, and yes, behind him I saw a person with his body crooked, who came
     walking with his body crooked.'

(38) le-bo-tofekho   nggé nabul   nu ne-banun b-imo-m
come-be.3SG.REAL-DS friend brother.in.law I   my-back   EFFORT-look-2SG.IMP
dé
say.3SG.REAL

'He came and said, "Friend, brother-in-law, you try to look at my back."'

(39) dé-do   a   ati   wokhelimekho-do ü   yi   ye-pa   khayo
say.3SG.REAL-DS EXCLM hold.SS turn.3SG.REAL-DS Ow! EXCLM he-self arrow
baosa-m-bo   mé-lai
pierced-SUPP-be.3SG.REAL move-come.3SG.REAL

'So he said, and as they turned him around, "Ow, my!," he had come pierced with arrows!'

(40) nokhu lenggile-lè-dakhu   sé af-e-kha   mahüon a
we   be.frightened-1PL.REAL-SS next there-TR-CONN story   EXCLM
u-méma-lè-kha   melél-mo   mesé wof-e-kha   yanop yanop a
tell-IMM-1PL.REAL-CONN finish-SUPP.SS next that-TR-CONN people people there
ülmekhe-tél-e-kha   uma-lè-dakhu   è   mbakha-mol-mo
shoot-3PL.REAL-TR-CONN talk-1PL.REAL-SS PAUSE what-SUPP-HAB.3SG.REAL
mbakha-mol-mo   de-lè-lofekho
what-SUPP-HAB.3SG.REAL QUOTE-1PL.REAL-DS

'We were frightened, so the story I was telling, we interrupted and we talked about that person, about the person they had shot, we said, "what has happened . . . ?" and'

(41) él   manda[274]
yes it.is.not

'(he began) "Yes, no,"'

(42) a   Mafém y-até   khomilo-do   Golokhofalé lamé-lo
PAUSE Mafém her-father die.3SG.REAL-DS Golokhofalé   tie-CAUS.3SG.REAL
n-afé   laméle-té-dakhu nup pa lamé-lo   amo-méma-té-tofekho
my-older.brother tie-3PL.REAL-SS I   also tie-CAUS.3SG.REAL do-IMM-3PL.REAL-DS
nu golo-kha-lé-do   pükh-ma-té-do   nu pükh[275] ne alolé-do
I be.afraid-go-1SG.REAL-DS shoot-SUPP-3PL.REAL-DS I arrow   me hit.3SG.REAL-DS
le-ba-lél-è   n-afé-fè   Kolufo-bolüp   fe-nè
come-PERF-1SG.REAL-EXCLM my-older.brother-TOP Korowai-clan.territory take-SS
fe-té   dé   e   Golokhofalé-fè e   Bafé-yano-bolüp
put-3PL.REAL say.3SG.REAL PAUSE Golokhofalé-TOP PAUSE Eilanden.River-people-territory
Lemakha-bolüp take-SS fe-té   dé
Lemakha-territory fe-nè   put-3PL.REAL say.3SG.REAL

'"Mafém's father's died and then, having tied up Golokhofalé, they tied up my older brother, and since they also had handcuffed me, I fled, and then they shot me and the arrows hit me as I went, and as for my older brother, they have sent him to the Korowai territories, and Golokhofalé, they have sent to the territories where the Eilanden River people live, to the places of the Lemakha they have sent him," he said.'

(43) él de-nè mbakha-ma-fon   mbakha-ma-fon   de-nè manderi-manggaka[276]
yes say-SS what-SUPP-1PL.INTENT what-SUPP-1PL.INTENT say-SS health.worker-CIRCUM
duo gübo-ma-lè-dakhu   yakhatimekho ü ip-ta-da-lu   ip-ta
? come.together-SUPP-1PL.REAL-SS not.willing.SS Ow! here-LOC-NEG-FOC here-LOC

bumo-ngga-da[277]   mo Bomam-pekho[278]   anè   fo   fo-fun-do
incise-INF.CONN-NEG just Boma.village-CIRCUM ADHORT take.SS put-1PL.ADHORT-DS
khai-n-tu   de-té[279]
go-3SG.INTENT-EXCLM say-3PL.REAL

'After we had affirmed this and talked about what we should do, we came together at the health worker's (place), but he refused, saying "Ow!, not here, it cannot be operated surgically at this place, come on, we should send him to Boma," they said.'

(44) gekhené-fè nup-tekhé gup menèl uan-tekhé[280]   tyari-mo[281]
     you.PL-TOP I-for   you quickly money-purpose look.for-SUPP.SS
     bilai-mon-dakhu-fekho   uan   sia-pa-mon-do[282]   anè   abo pesau[283]
     look.for-2PL.INTENT-SS-and money keep.ready-SUPP-2PL.INTENT-DS do.SS buy aeroplane
     abole-mon-dakhu Boma   wa-té-lekhu   bu-ma-tin
     buy-2PL.INTENT-SS Boma.village move.down-3PL.REAL-IRR.DS incise-SUPP-3PL.INTENT
     de-té
     say-3PL.REAL

'"You, as far as I am concerned, you should quickly look for money and you should keep it ready in order to pay a plane and have a flight to Boma, so that they can do a surgical operation," they said.'

(45) él nokhu uan   manda-lu   de-lè
     yes we   money not.being-FOC say-1PL.REAL

'"Yes, but we have no money at all," we said.'

(46) nokhu uan   manda-lu   de-lè-lofekho   è   nokhu imban y-até-khül
     we   money not.being-FOC say-1PL.REAL-DS PAUSE our   member his-father-PL
     è   uma-té   è   amo-n-tekhu   kha-mén-dakhu
     PAUSE talk-3PL.REAL PAUSE do-INTENT-IRR.DS go-2PL.INTENT-SS
     la-mén-dakhu-to   béto-fekho   bayar-ma-mon-é[284]   de-té
     come-2PL.INTENT-SS-FOC after-CIRCUM pay-SUPP-2PL.INTENT-EXCLM say-3PL.REAL

'"We have got no money at all," we said, but our relative's "fathers" talked about it; they said, "When you do it this way, you can go and then come back, and afterward you can pay."'

(47) de-té-do   él de-nè yakhop-to yakhop-to yakhop-to yu-fekho kha-khe-té
     say-3PL.REAL-DS yes say-SS who-FOC   who-FOC   who-FOC   he-COMIT go-IRR-3PL.

'They talked and they reached agreement (and asked), "Who ... who ... who is the one to go with him?"'

(48) yanop menèl labode-mén   de-té-tofekho   mayokh nu-fekho la   mayokh
     people quickly join-2PL.INTENT say-3PL.REAL-DS friends   I-COMIT come.SS friends
     nu-fekho lé   de-lé
     I-COMIT presently say-1SG.REAL

'"Someone has to join him quickly," they said, and I said, "Friends, with me coming ... friends, with me it will be."'

(49) nup-to labode-lé   nup-to labode-lé-do   wa lefül lidop pesahu
     I-FOC join-1SG.REAL I-FOC join-1SG.REAL-DS that day one   aeroplane
     wai
     move.down.3SG.REAL

'I was the one who joined him, it was me that joined, and that day there was only one aeroplane that landed.'

(50) wa lefül lidop pesau   wai-do   wa pesahu-debüp-to alo-bakh-un i
that day one aeroplane move.down.3SG.REAL-DS that aeroplane-way-with go-HOD-1PL this
Boma   khe-nè wa-lè
Boma.village go-SS   move.down-1PL.REAL

'That day only one aeroplane landed, and with that plane we went to Boma and landed there.'

(51) Boma   khe-nè wa-lè-dakhu-fekho[285]   manderi-manderi
Boma.village go-SS   move.down-1PL.REAL-SS-and health.worker-health.worker
Map[286] khaü khaü-bo-ta-fekho   khai-bo
M.A.F. bivouac bivouac-opening-LOC-CIRCUM sit-be.3SG.REAL

'Having travelled to Boma, we landed there, the local health workers were waiting in front of the MAF hangar.'

(52) khai-bo-do   è   kha-lè-do   fonoa-lè   anè
sit-be.3SG.REAL-DS PAUSE walk-1PL.REAL-DS move.down-1PL.REAL ADHORT
kha-mén-é   de-té-do   khenè khaü-lalé[287] khuwol-anop
go-2PL.INTENT-EXCLM say-3PL.REAL-DS next   house-big   guest-people
lu-lu-m-ba-tél-e-kha   khaü khe-nè le-lé
enter-enter-HAB-be-3PL.REAL-TR-CONN house go-SS   enter-1PL.REAL

'They were waiting when we came and landed and they told us to go, and we went to the big house, the house where usually guests are entering, and we entered there.'

(53) le-lè-lofekho   sustèr[288] lai
enter-1PL.REAL-DS nurse   come.3SG.REAL

'We entered and the nurse arrived.'

(54) if-af-e-kholo dé-tofekho   él de-lé
this-that-TR-Q say.3SG.REAL-DS yes say-1SG.REAL

'"So this is it?" she said and I said, "Yes."'

(55) folelé-lekhu   khop rumasakit[289]   khaü kha-mén-é   dé
be.afternoon-IRR.DS there local.health.centre house go-2PL.INTENT-EXCLM say.3SG.REAL

'She said, "This afternoon you should go to the health centre over there."'

(56) dé-do   él de-nè   khai-ba-lè-do   folé-do
say.3SG.REAL-DS yes QUOTE-SS sit-be-1PL.REAL-DS be.afternoon.3SG.REAL-DS
kha-lè
go-1PL.REAL

'She said so and we said, "Yes," and waited and in the afternoon we went there.'

(57) kha-lè-lofekho mbakha-mol-me-té-dakhu   mbakha-mol-me-té-do
go-1PL.REAL-DS what-SUPP-SUPP-2PL.REAL-SS what-SUPP-SUPP-2PL.REAL-DS
ülmekhe-té-kholo de-té-tofekho   manda-è   khambom
shoot-3PL.REAL-Q say-3PL.REAL-DS   no-EXCLM village
di-khai-ba-tél-e-kha   khambom Nakhilop
open-live-be-3PL.REAL-TR-CONN village   Nakhiro.village
di-khai-ba-tél-e-kha   yanop khomi-khaüle-té-do   a   if-e-kha
open-live-be-3PL.REAL-TR-CONN people dead-INTNS-3PL.REAL-DS PAUSE this-TR-CONN

khakhua-khakhua-lo yanop lé-lé-m-ba-té   de-té-dakhu   yanop lamé
witch-witch-FOC   people eat-eat-HAB-be-3PL.REAL QUOTE-3PL.REAL-SS people tie
khamil-mo[290]
do.in.common-HAB.3SG.REAL

'We went there and they asked, "What did you do—what have you done, so that they shot you?" "No, the people who had opened up a village and lived there, the people who had opened Nakhilop village and lived there, died in mass—well, it is these witches who usually eat (their victims)—" they said, "and then they tied up all the people."'

(58) y-afé   lamé-lo   Kolufo-bolüp   fe-nè fu   Golokhofalé
his-older.brother tie-CAUS.SS Korowai-clan.territory take-SS put.3SG.REAL Golokhofalé
lamé-lo   Bafé-yano-bolüp   fe-nè fu
tie-CAUS.SS Eilanden.River-people-territory take-SS put.3SG.REAL

'"When they had tied up his older brother, they sent him to the Korowai clan territories, and having tied up Golokhofalé, they sent him to a territory of Eilanden River people."'

(59) sé   yu-fè   lebükh-ma-té-do   Yaniluma   lai-do   mesé nokhup
next he-TOP shoot-SUPP-3PL.REAL-DS Yaniruma.village come.3SG.REAL-DS next   we
laléo-alim-pekho[291]   urus-ma-té-dom-pekho[292]   mesé i-mofu
spirit-PL-COMIT   organize-SUPP-3PL.REAL-DS-and next   here-only
le-ba-lè   de-lé-dakhu[293]   sustèr dai-bo-top   de-lé
come-PERF-1PL.REAL say-1SG.REAL-SS nurse   hear-3SG.PERF.REAL-DS say-1SG.REAL

'"And as far as he is concerned, they shot him, and he came to Yaniruma village and then we together with the 'spirits' arranged (this), and then we came here," I said and the nurse listened and I told.'

(60) de-lé-lofekho   él   khombokhai[294] dé
QUOTE-1SG.REAL-DS yes all right   say.3SG.REAL

'So I told, and she said, "Yes, okay."'

(61) khombokhai dé-do   éba-té-do   ébo-do   nu
all right   say.3SG.REAL-DS sleep-3PL.REAL-DS sleep.3SG.REAL-DS I
be-ba-lé
sit-be-1SG.REAL

'She said, "All right," and then they slept, he slept and I sat down.'

(62) ébo-do   ülmekho-ülmekho-ma-té[295]
sleep.3SG.REAL-DS shoot-shoot-HAB-3PL.REAL

'He slept and they gave him several injections.'

(63) ülmekho-ülmekho-ma-té-do khomilo[296]
shoot-shoot-HAB-3PL.REAL-DS die.3SG.REAL

'They gave him several shots and he died.'

(64) khomilo-do   ü   ne lenggile-lé
die.3SG.REAL-DS Ow! I   be.frightened-1SG.REAL

'He died and "Ow!" I was frightened.'

(65) ü   khomilo   de-lé-lofekho
Ow! die.3SG.REAL say-1SG.REAL-DS.but

'"Ow, he has died!" I said.'

(66) nup-tekhé guf-è   imbo de-té-tofekho   gekhenép if-è
I-purpose you-CONN see.Q QUOTE-3PL.REAL-DS you(PL)   here-CONN
khomilo-tu   de-lé
die.3SG.REAL-EXCLM say-1SG.REAL

'They said to me, "Do you see?" but I said, "Now that you here . . . he died!"'

(67) de-lé-lofekho   lesife-té
say-1SG.REAL-DS laugh-3PL.REAL

'So I said but they laughed.'

(68) manda-é khotul-é lé   lé   melu-khail-é   de-té
no-EXCLM still-EXCLM presently presently get.up-3SG.IRR-EXCLM say-3PL.REAL

'"No, presently, by and by he will get up again," they said.'

(69) ati-wokhelimekhe-lè-dakhu a   bifukh khakhokha-lo mofu khami-mengga-lo
hold-turn-1PL.REAL-SS   PAUSE steel.knife like-FOC   only handle-with-FOC
ati-ba-té-do   ye-pan-to[297] dé
hold-be-3PL.REAL-DS it-self-FOC   cut.3SG.REAL

'We turned (to him) and, with something like a knife, they only held its handle and it cut automatically.'

(70) khami-mengga-lo ati-ba-té-do   di-bakh-i   di-bakh-i   mo nop-engga
handle-with-FOC   hold-be-3PL.REAL-DS cut-HOD-3SG cut-HOD-3SG just flesh-with
yabén-mengga keliokhmo   plasti   o   e   plasti-da
fat-with   gather.together.SS plastic.sheet EXCLM PAUSE plastic.sheet-NEG
kertase-la[298] fe-nè fu fe-nè fu-ma-té
paper-LOC   take-SS put take-SS put-HAB-3PL.REAL

'At the handle they held it, and after it had made incisions for a while, they collected the flesh and the grease and a plastic sheet, no, not plastic, they put it (repeatedly) on a piece of paper.'

(71) fo-nè fu-nè fu-ma-té   ü nup-tekhé yup if-è   ye-no-fefè
take-SS put-SS put-HAB-3PL.REAL Ow! I-BENEFIT he this-CONN his-flesh-TOP
khokhol-mekho-lu   a-nè   il-mekho   i-fè
be.white-SUPP.3SG.REAL-EXCLM that-SUPP.SS ochre-SUPP.3SG this-TOP
mbakha-mo-bo   mbakha-mo-bo[299]   de-té-tofekho   o   wa
what-SUPP-be.3SG.REAL what-SUPP-be.3SG.REAL say-3PL.REAL-DS EXCLM that
nop-da-o   wa yabén de-lé
flesh-NEG-EXCLM that fat   say-1SG.REAL

'They collected all of it, and—Oh!—then they asked me about him, "This flesh of his is white, but the ochrous stuff here, what is this?" and I said, "Oh, that is not flesh, that is grease."'

(72) wa yabén-o   yanop yabén wof-ap de-lé
that fat-EXCLM people fat   that-LOC say-1SG.REAL

'"That is grease, human grease it is," I said.'

(73) lenggile-té   lenggile-té-to   i no-fè   yabén-é if-a-fè   i-fè
amazed-3PL.REAL amazed-3PL.REAL-DS this flesh-TOP fat-EXCLM this-there-TOP this-TOP
khal-é   i-fè   yabén-é de-lé
flesh-EXCLM this-TOP fat-EXCLM say-1SG.REAL

'They were astonished, astonished they were when I said, "This here is flesh, the grease is there, this is flesh, and this is grease."'

(74) de-lé-do   lenggile-té   él   de-nè fekha³⁰⁰ bu-nè
     say-1SG.REAL-DS amazed-3PL.REAL yes say-SS one   cut-SUPP.SS
     monggol-me-té   fekha bu-nè   monggol-me-té   fekha bu-nè
     get.out-SUPP-3PL.REAL one   cut-SUPP.SS get.out-SUPP-3PL.REAL one   cut-SUPP.SS
     monggol-me-té   fekha bu-nè   monggol-me-té   mesé
     get.out-SUPP-3PL.REAL one   cut-SUPP.SS get.out-SUPP-3PL.REAL next
     wokhelimekho³⁰¹ wap ülmekho-bakha-til-e-kha mesip mesip mesip ülmekho
     return.SS   there shoot-HOD-3PL-TR-CONN again   again again   shoot
     ülmekho ülmekho ülmekho-ma-té-do   khai-ba-lè   nup-tekhé gup
     shoot   shoot   shoot-HAB-3PL.REAL-DS sit-be-1PL.REAL me-purpose you
     im-bo-m-é   de-té
     look-stay-2SG.IMP-EXCLM say-3Pl.REAL

'When I said so, they were astonished and then they cut out one, another they cut out, again another one and another one they cut out; and then just like they had given him a hypodermic syringe before, again they shot him repeatedly and while I was waiting, they said to me, "You must pay attention," they said.'

(75) gup imbo-m-é   de-té-do   nu im-ba-lé-do   sé
     you pay.attention-2SG.IMP-EXCLM say-3PL.REAL-DS I   look-stay-1SG.REAL-DS next
     a-nè   le-nè³⁰² fené-mekho   fené-mekho-do
     that-SUPP.SS come-SS breathe-SUPP.3SG.REAL breathe-SUPP.3SG.REAL-DS
     im-ba-lè-lofekho   melu bai
     look-stay-1PL.REAL-DS get.up sit.3SG.REAL

'"You must pay attention!" they said, and when I did so, he came and he breathed, I saw him breathing and then he got up and sat upright.'

(76) melu   bai-dakhu   nup laifo   nup-tekhé yup nu
     get.up.SS sit.3SG.REAL-SS I   ask.3SG.REAL me-to   he   me
     mbu-m-bakha-til-e-kholo wé   gu dé-tofekho   if-e-kha   kertase-la
     cut-SUPP-HOD-3PL-TR-Q   EXCLM you say.3SG.REAL-DS this-TR-CONN paper-LOC
     b-imo-m
     EFFORT-look-2SG.IMP

'He got up and sat upright, and he asked me, "Did they cut me loose?" he asked, and I answered, "You should look at this sheet of paper here!"'

(77) ge-nop   wap ibo   ge-yabén wap ibo   de-lé   uwa
     your-flesh there be.3SG.REAL your-fat   there be.3SG.REAL say-1SG.REAL yes
     dé-tofekho   bail-u   de-lé
     say.3SG.REAL-DS really-EXCLM say-1SG.REAL

'"Your flesh is there, and your grease is there," I said, and when he was wondering, I said, "Yes, really," I said.'

(78) gup bu-ma-tél-e-kha   gup be-lép-té-da-kholo   de-lé-lofekho   nu
     you cut-SUPP-3PL.REAL-TR-CONN you NEG-ill-3PL.REAL-NEG-Q say-1SG.REAL-DS I
     ne be-lép-té-da   dé
     me NEG-ill-3PL.REAL-NEG say.3SG.REAL

'"Now, that they have operated you surgically, do you feel hurt?" I said, but he said, "No, I don't feel pain."'

(79) nu ne lenggile-lé
     I me amazed-1SG.REAL

     'I was astonished.'

(80) nup ne lenggile-lé-lofekho è   a-fè   yo de-té-do   wof-e-kha
     I   me amazed-1SG.REAL-DS PAUSE there-TOP yes say-3PL.REAL-DS that-TR-CONN
     nop-engga yabén-mengga fo   gübo-lelo kertas fakhüp wakhum
     flesh-with fat-with   get.SS collect-be.SS paper LOC   packet
     alife-té-do   bando ai   kertas-fekho bando ai
     wrap-3PL.REAL-DS bring move.down.SS paper-CIRCUM bring move.down.SS
     alü-fe-té
     burn-put-3PL.REAL

     'I was astonished, and they said there, "Yes," and the flesh with the grease, they col-
     lected it all, and they made a packet of it and brought it outside, (wrapped) in paper
     they brought it outside and burnt it.'

(81) alü-fe-té-do   do   khofé-lelo-tofekho   diof-è   gu if-e-kha
     burn-put-3PL.REAL-DS burn.SS soot-COP.3SG.REAL-DS quickly-CONN you this-TR-CONN
     obas-é[303]   mi-m-é   de-té-do   obas   fédo-do
     medicine-EXCLM drink-2SG.IMP-EXCLM say-3PL.REAL-DS medicine give.REAL.3SG-DS
     mé-do   mesé wa khaü gilfa-lé   khaü éba-lè   lefü-lefül
     drink.3SG.REAL-DS next that house go.away-1SG.REAL house sleep-1PL.REAL day-day
     obas mi   ébo   ébo-fekho   è   lebakhop-to[304] gekhenép
     medicine drink.SS sleep.3SG.REAL sleep-3SG.REAL-until PAUSE old.lady-FOC   you.PL
     if-e-kha   lefül-è   gekhenép anè   gekhenép kha-mén-é
     this-TR-CONN day-CONN you.PL   ADHORT you.PL   go-2PL.INTENT-EXCLM
     dé
     say.3SG.REAL

     'They burnt it, so it burnt and was charred, "Quick, you should drink this medicine,"
     they said, and when he had been given medicine, he drank it, and then we went to the
     house and rested in the house, and daily he drunk medicine and rested until the old lady
     said, "As for you, today you can go home."'

(82) gekhenép anè   kha-mén-é   dé-do   él de-nè khenè
     you.PL   ADHORT go-2PL.INTENT-EXCLM say.3SG.REAL-DS yes say-SS next
     lapangga-fekho khai-ba-lè-do   pesau maun-an pesahu lai
     air.strip-CIRCUM live-be-1PL.REAL-DS aeroplane river-LOC aeroplane come.3SG.REAL

     'When she said, "You can go home," we said "Yes" and waited at the airstrip and there
     arrived a float plane.'

(83) amo-tofekho   nokhu-peninggi[305] bando-ai   fe-nè   fu-tofekho   sé
     do.3SG.REAL-DS our-evangelist   bring-descend take-SS put.3SG.REAL-DS next
     fium-ta pesahu wai-do   sé fium-ta pesahu-fekho   lelip
     land-LOC aeroplane move.down.3SG.REAL-DS next land-LOC aeroplane-CIRCUM together
     nokhu-peninggi-fekho khofu le-nè Wanggemalo   wa-lé-dakhu
     our-evangelist-COMIT   be.with.all come-SS Wanggemalo.village move.down-1PL.REAL-SS
     Wanggemalo-fosü Yaniluman wa-lè-dakhu   sé wa-mofu
     Wanggemalo-from Yaniruma   move.down-1PL.REAL-SS next there-only
     wa-me-lè-dakhu-fekho   sé i-mol-alüf-efè   sé ye keli-telo
     thus-SUPP-1PL.REAL-SS-and next this-SUPP-day-TOP next he strength-be.3SG.REAL

'So it did and it brought our evangelist down, and then a land plane came down, and by the land plane, together with our evangelist, all of us we landed in Wanggemalo village, and from Wanggemalo we landed in Yaniruma, there we did so, and nowadays he is healthy again.'

The Gom Song

Gom is the name of the sacred song sung during the final stage of the sago grub feast, when the sacred fence (*khandin damon*) is removed.[306] According to one informant, *Gom* is also sung during the dancing when a nest of parts of sago leaves is hung on the sacred central pole (*khandin du*). The same lines of the song are chanted over and over again, lines in which the boys of the clan and the sago trees are called on to grow and multiply. The verb *melu* means both 'to grow' and (when applied to humans) 'to procreate'. There are various variants of *The Gom Song*, but all have the two parallel themes of the growth and multiplication of the young males of the clan and of the sago. The song given here was sung by Delai Khawékh (Bafé-yanop), a man about 25 years old, on September 7, 1990, in the office of van Enk.

We do not know the meaning of the name of the song. There might be a link with procreation through sexual intercourse since the stem *gom* also occurs in the verb *gom-mo* 'to have sexual intercourse'. The corresponding Kombai song sung at the closing ceremony of the sacred part of the Kombai sago grub feast is called *bere* (see de Vries 1993a: 106, for a transcribed *bere* song). *Bere* denotes also the dance ('let us dance the *bere*').

Although both the *gom* and the *bere* songs extensively refer to sago subspecies and both have the prosperous growth of new sago as their theme, there are a number of differences; for example, the Kombai song refers to the *bere* man who cuts down sago trees and to the whistles between the teeth that accompany the performance of the *bere*. The Kombai song focusses on the invitation to the dance and on the sago but does not mention young men or boys.

(1)   khofél gabüm-gun[307] mbolop   gabüm-gun khofé
      boy   knee-group   older.people knee-group boy
      mano-pelu-m-é-o
      well-grow-2SG.ADHORT-EXCLM-EXCLM

      'Knee-dancing boys' group, knee-dancing older people's group, boy, you must grow well,'

(2)   khakhül   melu-m-o   lahial   melu-m-o
      khakhül.sago grow-2SG.ADHORT-EXCLM lahial.sago grow-2SG.ADHORT-EXCLM
      lé   melu-m-o   amo   melu-m-o
      kind.of.sago.tree grow-2SG.ADHORT-EXCLM   amo.sago grow-2SG.ADHORT-EXCLM

      '*Khakhül* sago tree, you should grow! *Lahial* sago tree, you should grow! Sago tree of the *Lé* kind, you must grow! Sago tree of the *Amo* kind, you must grow!'

(3)   khofé mano-pelu-m-é-o
      boy   well-grow-2SG.ADHORT-EXCLM-EXCLM
      'Boy, grow well!'

APPENDIX 1

Comparative Korowai–Kombai Basic Lexical Items

The following table is an adaptation of the 209-word list used for lexicostatistical surveys in Irian Jaya by SIL-Irian Jaya (UNCEN/SIL 1985, *Daftar Kata-Kata*). The Korowai words are written according to table 2–4. The spelling of the Kombai words follows the grapheme table of de Vries (1989) with the exception of the vowel phoneme /y/, which is written with the grapheme *ü*. When a Kombai lexical item is known to have a final consonant when followed by another morpheme (which consonant is dropped in isolation), this final consonant is written between brackets (see de Vries 1993b: 10). For example, *e* 'bird', *el-o lu* 'the voice of a bird'. Representation: *e(l)*.

We counted 44 possible cognates in 200 items, giving a cognation percentage of 22%.

Table A–1   Korowai–Kombai basic word list

English	Korowai	Kombai	Cognate
1. head	khabéan	khabiya	+
2. hair (on head)	khabéan-mukh	khabiya-lo	−
3. ear	khoto-khal	ruro	−
4. neck	khomo (fekholol)	khuma	+
5. mouth	bontebil	mogoro	−
6. tooth	lebil	iba	−
7. tongue	lép	faga	−
8. eye	lul	khoro	−
9. nose	gelip	ragu	−
10. hand	mél	i(t)	−
11. dirty	banggelèkh	khabu	−
12. hair (on body)	khal-mukh	kha-lo	−
13. elbow	bonggup	i-gabü	−
14. finger	mé-lol	i-lo	+

221

Table A–1   (*continued*)

English	Korowai	Kombai	Cognate
15. fingernail	me-singga	i-dodo	–
16. skin	khal	kha	+
17. meat/flesh	nop	khudo	–
18. fat (N)	yabén	khiya	–
19. bone	kholol	fiya	–
20. milk	am	a(m)	+
21. belly	khondul	awamu	–
22. back	banun	buma-kholo	–
23. penis	dul	rege	–
24. blood	büngga	rere	–
25. heart	debop	dümo	–
26. liver	üm	afina	–
27. foot	bél	khino	–
28. swollen	khakhé-bo	rera-khakhu	+
29. ill	lép	yabo	–
30. water	maun/akh	o(kh)	+
31. lake	difon	o-guwo	–
32. river	maél/maun/akh	wodei	–
33. to flow	khaimbo	bakhalüwa	–
34. sand	nenim/dofu	abü	–
35. sea	méan-maél	makhül-ono	–
36. fire	melil/alun	e	–
37. to heat	alü	adü	+
38. ash	anom	rinokhware	–
39. smoke	lemül	emarü	–
40. stone	ilol/khandun	riga	–
41. heavy	lüp-telo	inu-khe	–
42. slippery	fép-telo	weinagane	–
43. one	senan/lidop	raga	–
44. two	senan-afül/pol	raga-ragu	–
45. three	pinggelup	woromi	–
46. four	wayo-fül	woromi-bogo	–
47. five	wayo	abalo(f)	–
48. many	demal	biduma	–
49. little	mamap	folumo	–
50. all	kholfunè	imimo	–
51. earth/soil	mé	i(f)	–
52. dust	bulanom	bura	+
53. road	dobülop	iro	–
54. narrow	dékh-telo	muragaya/gone	–
55. wide	bau-talé	mujano/belurabo	–
56. mountain	fanip	fani	+
57. cloud	dép	le(f)	+
58. rain	maun-beol	mulü	–
59. sky	dalibün	ramokhoü	–
60. fog	dép-temül	leriyama	–
61. wind	fup	khifei	–
62. hot	mamün	mamü	+
63. cold	khagil	lokhe	–
64. thunder	khul	khumu	–(?)
65. lightning	fakhbéakh	boba	–

Table A–1   (*continued*)

English	Korowai	Kombai	Cognate
66. stick	donggop	meja	–
67. straight	godakh	bumiyo	–
68. thick	fanip-telo	fini-rabo	+
69. thin	dalap-telo	makho-rabo	–
70. sharp	fül	gabü/gerege	–
71. blunt	felil	feli	+
72. sun	mamün/lup	rei	–
73. day	lefül	rei	–
74. night	gülnanggaup	fi(m)	–
75. moon	wakhol	amanga	–
76. star	belil	mi	–
77. banana	dup	rü(l)	–
78. garden	yasim	yarimo	+
79. long grass	goglén-talé	bufo	–
80. dry	gololfobo	fu-khi	–
81. to cut	dil-mo	boroü-ma	–
82. tree/wood	du	dodo	+
83. to cleave	bamol-mo	efa-mo	–
84. branch (of tree)	letép	khabefo	–
85. leaf	mukh	lo(f)	–
86. thorn	aün	alü	+
87. fruit	du-op	dodo-lo(f)	+
88. seed	du-khabül	edofe-lo	–
89. decayed	nén-telo	bo-ge	–
90. jungle	lop	khuro	–
91. rope	nan/yebun	ri	–
92. to tie	lamé	adafe	–
93. white	khokho-lun	khu-waru	+
94. black	khofi-lun	gunü-waru	–
95. red	khafümengga	rerabo	–
96. bird	dél	e(l)	+
97. egg	lokhesukh	idi	–
98. wing	baul	yagiya	–
99. to fly	bedifo	bobukha	–
100. cassowary	küal/sanip/sandum	nuwayo	–
101. fly	lotup	luru	–
102. mosquito	letün	refiyo	–
103. dog	méan/muman	makhü	–
104. big	khonggél	mujano	–
105. small	yèn-tena	murago	–
106. this	ip	mene	–
107. that	wap	mofene	–
108. different	yani	khaifo	–
109. to bite	ü-	u-	+
110. tail	khendép	minü	–
111. fish	khelé	duwo	–
112. leech	lajo	rekhiyo	–
113. lice	meli	gu	–
114. pig	gol/wan/wangga	ai	–
115. to shoot	ül-mekho	rabiye-ne	–
116. worm	wafol	amiya	–

Table A–1   (*continued*)

English	Korowai	Kombai	Cognate
117. snake	anol	gwari	–
118. long	nggolo-lalé	rejo-rabo	–
119. short	gembenul	bogo	–
120. mouse	duo	fira	–
121. full	botèlfo	bamo-ge	–
122. house	khaim/op	a(f)	+
123. new	sol	alu	–
124. old	mülekha	muno	–
125. roofing	lél	amodo	–
126. in front of	mülgopé	rabiya/ragu	–
127. outside	khanggopé	khukhuni	–
128. inside	khaup	khalu(f)	+
129. close	khalu	deima	–
130. far	lekhingga	khiyado	–
131. people	yanop	kho(f)	–
132. good	manop	yafe-rabo	–
133. wicked	khén/letél	gabü-rabo	–
134. male	wafil	wafi(l)	+
135. female	lal	la(n)	+
136. father	até	are	+
137. mother	(ne)ni	(na)ni	+
138. child	mbam	miyo(f)	–
139. I	nup	nu(f)	+
140. you (SG)	gup	gu(f)	+
141. he/she/it	yup	khe	–
142. we	nokhup	nagu(f)	+
143. they	yèkhenép	ya	–
144. who?	yakhop	yafo(rumu)	–
145. what?	mbakha	nalufa	–
146. name	fi	fi	+
147. to come	lai	ma	–
148. to go	khai	kha	+
149. to know	khelép	khume	–
150. to listen	daé	khakhe	–
151. to search	bilai-mo	bokho-ma	–
152. to speak	u-ma	u-mo	+
153. true	mokhefup	makhano	–
154. to drink	mi	mi	+
155. to eat	lé	ande/en	–
156. to kill	ü-	u	+
157. to die	khomilo	khumolei	+
158. to scratch	gelil-mo	bokhoro-ma	–
159. to sit	ba	ba	+
160. to stand	alo	maru	–
161. not	be . . . da	fe . . . do	+
162. to bathe	dadü	akhi-mo	–
163. to fall	feli	kholüwafa	–
164. to live	khafén-telo	aluba	–
165. maternal uncle	mom	momo(f)	+
166. to spit	mekhesimpükh-mo	bendoborü	–
167. nausea	wakhali	bakhugi	–

Table A–1 (*continued*)

English	Korowai	Kombai	Cognate
168. to lay	é-bo	khalüwale	–
169. to sleep	é-lo	khunu-le	–
170. to dream	alenu-telo	u-fera	–
171. to see	i-mo	fera	–
172. to hold	ati	lefa	–
173. to give	fédo	andiya	–
174. to blow	fu-mo	fuwa-mo	+
175. to breathe	fené-mo	fina	+
176. to cough	bokokh-telo	ahüwo	–
177. to count	lamo	yukhu-mo-ne	–
178. to dig	yakhü	khüwo-ne	–
179. afraid	golo	adura	–
180. ashamed	khatakh	khara(kh)	+
181. to weep	ya-mo	bolo	–
182. to sing	èpo	gobolü	–
183. to play	kelèkh-mo	ya-ma	–
184. to push	gali-mekho	yogo-mo-ne	–
185. to wash	sukh-mo	rürü-ne	–
186. to throw	pükh-mo	fiya-mo-ne	–
187. six	gédun	igo	–
188. seven	lafol	iwamü	–
189. eight	bonggup	igabü	–
190. nine	labul	irafe	–
191. ten	main	dodoü	–
192. to rub	béal-mo	gege-me-ne	–
193. wet	fékh-telo	gu-khe	–
194. to bury	mélai-mekho	ifa-ma	–
195. sago grub	non/gékh	wo	–
196. sago	ndaü/kho	doü	+
197. husband	um	yale	–
198. wife	defol/lebakhop	khorabo	–
199. angry	khén-telo	gabü	–
200. to put	fu	fa	+

APPENDIX 2

Vocabulary

Korowai-English

In the Korowai–English vocabulary lists, the syllable receiving the main word stress in the Korowai word is underlined. Where stress is unmarked, we are uncertain about stress placement.

A

a (EXCLM)   ah!

a- (DEICT)   there; that; thus

abéakh (N)   outer layer of grilled lump of sago

abéap (N)   tortoise species

abém (N)   shrimp species

abi (VB)   to carry on the back

abokhai (VB)   to hunt; to chase

abolai (mo) (VB)   to chase; to hunt; to expel

abolo (VB)   to buy; to sell; to exchange

aboümo (VB)   to sell; to exchange

abul (NORN)   Moustached treeswift (bird)

abun (N)   fish species

abül (NKIN)   son; boy; male person; man

abüokh (N)   door; entrance

andüop (NKIN)   grandfather

Afeni (NPROP)   Afeni

afé (NKIN)   elder brother

afé (VB)   to turn

afé(n) (ADV)   always; usually

afolaü (VB)   to bring in order; to clear (*as a garden*)

afop (ADJ)   thin, skinny

Afüm (NGEOGR)   Afüm River

afü (VB)   to fight, struggle; to wrestle; to suffer

agél (N)   pipe; tube

agiop (N)   shell

anggokh (ADJ)   slow

-anggol (PKIN)   PL

-anggu (SS)   and (= -dakhu)

anggufa (Q)   why?

ai (VB)   to move down; to go out
aibum (NKIN)   child from mother's
  second marriage
aiè (EXCLM)   aiè!
aifogum (ADJ)   naked
Aim (NTRIBE)   Kombai
akéamo (VB)   to carry on the back
akh (N)   water; river
akhabop (LOC)   under
-akhu (SS)   and (= -dakhu)
-akhüp (NREL)   place
al (N)   trap (*for catching big game*)
alenul (N)   dream
-alé (N)   respected male person
alénap (ADJ)   quick-tempered, fiery,
  passionate
alèp (N)   dug-out canoe
ali (VB)   to build, construct
alifo (VB)   to wrap: to wrap in leaves
-alingga (POSTP)   without, not having
alimo (VB)   to row; to scoop
-alin (PL/PKIN)   PL
alip (DEICT)   here; this
alo (VB)   to stand; to walk
alo dimo (VB)   to defend
aloli (VB)   to stand; to set foot on
alop (NKIN)   firstborn
alun (N)   fire; fireplace
aluntalé (ADJ)   vicious
alü (VB)   to heat; to bake
alül (N)   bridge
alüm (ADV)   first; before
alümekhon (N)   moon
alümon (ADV)   next month
alüp (N)   period; day; (in former)
  time(s); the one in between
am (N)   breast (*female*)
amékhesimdop (N)   marsupial species
am gü (N)   breast milk
amin (N)   bank; edge
amo (N)   sago species
amo (VB)   to do
amodo (RELV)   thus; and; next
amonggu (EXCLM)   Ah! (*pity*)
-amol (N)   different kinds
amomengga (PART)   thus
Amosé (NPROP)   Amos
amul (ADJ)   suffering from malaria
  fevers
amül (N)   nest

amüsamün (ADJ)   wide
-an (LOC)   in; at; to
Ana (NPROP)   Ana
anè (ADH)   ADH
ano (N)   side; brink; edge
anol (N)   snake; rainbow
anolebil (N)   grinder
anom (N)   ashes
-anop (NREL)   amount
-anop (N)   people; person
antabun (N)   sharp objects; pointed
  objects
antenül (N)   nipple
ao (VB)   to put into; to plant; to cleanse
ap (N)   scabies
-ap (LOC)   there
apa (ADV)   only
apifu (VB)   to drown
até (NKIN)   father
ati (N)   bow
ati(lo) (VB)   to hold, get hold of; to
  keep; to take
atiafunakh (N)   the surrounding water
ati kilelo (VB)   to control oneself
ati-khayo (N)   bow and arrows
atun (N)   bow
aubaul (N)   joke; pleasantry
aun (N)   sago tree marrow
aup (N)   voice; sound; word; language;
  talk; story
aü (EXCLM)   ow!
aündan (ADJ)   refusing, resisting
aüfonaü (VB)   to clear; to order (*as a
  garden*)
aül (N)   rapid
aül (N)   angle; angular point
aülém (NORN)   wild pigeon (*Goura
  cristata*)
aülo (VB)   to close; to cover; to block
  (up)
aümo (VB)   to break loose
aün (N)   thorn
aüofü (VB)   to yelp
aüso (VB)   to promise (to give)
aütop (N)   place of whirlpool in the river
aw (NKIN)   elder sister
awam (N)   small seized cucumber
Awlal (NPROP)   Awlal
awü (N)   female of certain marsupials
-ayan (INTNS)   very; real

ayul (ekha) (N)   secret; taboo;
  prohibition

B

b-/be- (EFF)   try to
b-/bV- (NEG)   not
babo/beba- (VB)   to sit
babü (N)   kind of tuber
bandakh (ADJ)   hospitable; nice
bandakhol (NKIN)   wife's mother('s
  sister)
bando (VB)   to bring
bandüp (N)   sago species
Bafé (NGEOGR)   Eilanden River
banggelèkh (ADJ)   dirty
banggenénmekho (VB)   to seal up
banggil (N)   dog teeth
banggo (N)   tree stem
banggolol (N)   breastbone
banggumN   slope
bahüom (N)   sugar cane
bail (AFFIRM)   Oh, yes; possible; really
bai (N)   bow
bai/ba- (VB)   to be; to sit; to stay; to live
bai(l)mo (VB)   to hide
baimo/baimekho (VB)   to pass; to
  transgress
bajam (N)   hidden place
bajom (N)   iguana species
baka (ONOMAT)   sound of inflaming
bakhuom (N)   locust species
bakhup (N)   slope
balalmo (VB)   to roll, thunder
balebol (N)   neck
balénaup (N)   indirect talk
balép (N)   sago species
baliam (N)   sugar cane
balin (N)   rack for sago(-grub) storage
balüm (N)   mud
bamo (VB)   to call (*a pig*)
bamo(lmo) (VB)   to break
ban (N)   chest
ban (NKIN)   father-in-law; wife's parent
Banam (NTRIBE)   Citak (*people*)
bani (N)   piece of wood; sago leafstem
  panel
baniaupelu (VB)   to splutter with one's
  lips; to deny
banibol (N)   leaf stem; place for storing
  food

banté/bante- (VB)   to share; to
  distribute; to divide; to dispense
banun (NREL)   back(side)
Banyo (NPROP)   Banyo
baosamo (VB)   to pierce
bau (VB)   to stay; to be; to live
bau kilelo (VB)   to control oneself
baul (ADJ)   wide; heavy; rough
baul (N)   wing; side
baun (N)   tree species
bautalé (ADJ)   wide
baükhmo (VB)   to hit, strike
baül (N)   banian tree
baüm (N)   tree species
baüpo (VB)   to make round
bayol (N)   sago species
bayom (N)   boggy soil
bayulo (N)   mud crab species
bebal (N)   centipede species
bebén (ADJ)   strong; violent
bebéntebo (VB)   to squat
bebil (N)   bottom
bembi (ADJ)   loving, affectionate;
  compassionate
bembüo(kh) (N)   lizard species
bedi(fo) (VB)   to fly
bendé- (VB)   to hang
benggé- (VB)   to hang
bekhémo (VB)   to push forward
bekhelilé (VB)   to drown
-bekho- (INTNS)
belebél (N)   cross-beam
belén (NEG.IMP)   not; don't; do not
  need to
belil (N)   star; firefly
belüfekha (N)   domesticated pig;
  domestication
belüp (NREL)   space under the house
benén (N)   abdomen
benénmukh (N)   pubic hair
-benè (Q)   Q-marker
-benè- (HAB/ITER)
beni (NORN)   bird of paradise
bepé (VB)   to blow
besi (N)   steel wire
betél (N)   nibung palm (*Oncosperma
  filamentosum*)
betül (N)   shrimp species
béan (N)   tree (fruit) (*Ponnetia pinniata*)
bélum (N)   foot

bétom (N)   footprint
bémo (VB)   to care
béal (NORN)   honey eater species
béa(l)mo (VB)   to rub; to smear; to grease
béan (N)   tree (fruit) (*Ponnetia pinniata*)
bél (N)   foot; leg
bélol (N)   foot
béolfo (VB)   to catch
bésam (N)   necklace made of pig teeth
bésamtebil (N)   lower teeth
bétop (ADV)   after; behind
bi- (VB)   to look for
bi (ADJ)   swollen
bimbolop (ADV)   illegally; in vain; expressly
bindom (ADJ)   left; unexperienced; unacquainted with
bif (N)   (big) tortoise species
bil (N)   stone; rock
bilaimekho (VB)   to search desperately
bilaimo (VB)   to search, look for
bilamalin (ADV)   all kinds of
biléamekha (N)   length of time
binodan (ADJ)   pale blue
-bo (VB)   to be; to sit; to stay; to live
bonggol (N)   mouth
bonggup (N/NUM)   elbow; eight
bokokh (VB)   to cough
bokh (VB)   to hit, strike
bol (N)   hole; opening
bolmumu (VB)   to smile
bolüp (N)   (clan) territory; place
bolüplefupé (N)   (at) the end of the places; land of the dead
Boman (NGEOGR)   Boma village
bon (N)   end; head of tobacco pipe
bonanam (N)   festival songs
bontebil (N)   mouth
bu (ADJ)   tired
bu (ADJ)   teasing; vexing
bu (N)   vegetable (*Saccharum edule*)
bu (N)   pitfall; hole
buél (N)   varan; iguana
buél-bajom (N)   varans and iguanas
bunggul (N)   ribs of sago leaves
bulanom (N)   ash; dust
bulmekho (VB)   to be covered with
bumo (VB)   to slaughter
bumon (N)   bamboo arrow tip

buom (N)   lizard species
büakh (N)   rack
büngga (N)   blood
bülan (N)   floor; platform
bümo (VB)   to strike, hit; to beat
bün (N)   extent; stretch; stream
bün fédo (N)   to give recompensation for application of harmful magic

MB
mbakha (Q)   what?
mbakhamon (Q)   what?
mbalamo (VB)   to distribute, share, divide
mbalop (N)   place; container
mbam (NKIN)   child
mbayap (N)   penisgourd
mbelüp (N)   clearing
mbiyon (N)   coconut tree
mbonggon (N)   arrow
mbolombolop (N)   older people; parents; ancestors
mbolop (NKIN)   old man; husband's father
Mbulul (NPROP)   Mbulul

D
-da (NEG)   not; no
dabüp (N)   rattan
dambelüm (ADJ)   in vain
dada (ADJ)   like, similar; same; right as; just; according to/with
dadam (ADJ)   naughty
dadü (VB)   to swim; bathe
daél (N)   tree species
danggup (N)   locust species
dai (VB)   to hear, listen to; to obey
daibo (VB)   to know
dain (ADV)   up; on top of
Dajo (NCLAN)   Dajo clan
dakh (ADJ)   young
dakh (N)   scale of shrimp
dakhaméumo (VB)   to crawl
-dakhu (SS)   and
dal (N)   tree species
dal (ADJ)   long
dal (ADJ)   visible; appearing
dali (N)   sky
dalibün (N)   sky
dalip (DEICT)   there

dalun (ADJ)   light; clear; clever
damiabo (VB)   to expel
dami(l)mo (VB)   to open
damo (VB)   to close; to root out
damo (VB)   to inform
damol (N)   back
damon (N)   wall; panel
Damu (NPROP)   Damu
dap (N)   palm
daun (N)   ear
daup (N)   bamboo arrow tip
daüm (N)   end; finish
daya (N)   feather(s)
dayabél (ADJ)   exhausted (*after a feast*)
dayun (N)   comb
debap (N)   covering; cover; lid
debop (N)   heart
debüf (NREL)   way; by means of; by
    way of
debülop (N)   way; road
debünenul (ADV)   early in the morning
dedamol (N)   branch (*of tree*)
dedi (ADJ/ADV)   secret(ly)
dedil (N)   root
Dedilon (NPROP)   Dedilon (*female
    name*)
dediop (ONOMAT)   crack
dendü (N)   banana
defol (NKIN)   wife
dekheté(akh) (N)   sperm
delap (ADJ)   thin
demé (VB)   to tear open
demi(l) (VB)   to run
demi(l)mekho (VB)   to make
Démbol (NGEOGR)   Démbol River
dékh (ADJ)   narrow
dél (N)   bird
délamol (N)   (all kinds of) birds
délfo (VB)   to withdraw
-dém (PL/PKIN)
dén (N)   oblong slice of meat
dénufekholol (N)   pelvis bone
Dénumalé (NPROP)   Denumalé
dép (N)   cloud
dépo- (VB)   to suck; to pull
dépon (N)   tobacco
déponagél (N)   bamboo pipe for
    smoking tobacco
déptemül (N)   cloud
dèkhlèkhalé (NORN)   Fairy Wren (bird)
di (ADJ)   lacking

di (QUOTE)   to talk, speak, say; to tell
di (VB)   to pull out; to get out; to open;
    to cut off
dialun (ADJ)   clear; shining; clever
Didonalé (NPROP)   Didonalé
difo (VB)   to be almost; to arrive; to
    withdraw
difo (VB)   to be pulled out
difon (N)   lake
dil (N)   beam
dilmekho (VB)   to grip; to catch hold of
dilmo (VB)   to close; to block; to cut
dimekho (VB)   to put on; to put in
-din- (POTENT)
diof (ADJ)   quick
dip (DEIC)   there; this
ditaimekho (VB)   to begin, to start
-do(n) (DS)   and
do (VB)   to burn
dobongga (ADJ)   (well) done
dodépo (VB)   to call
dofo (VB)   to be burnt
dofu (ADJ)   stupid, dull, foolish
dofuleli (VB)   to be dark
dofusofu (ADJ)   very stupid
donggop (N)   piece of wood; spar
dokhemémo (VB)   to march in a column
    (*ants*)
dokhon (N)   small bivouac; baiting
    place
dokhul (N)   bow
doleli (VB)   to call; to invoke
dolmekho (VB)   to graze
dolokh(mengga) (ADJ)   with mischief
dolom (N)   sweet potato
domenè (NEG)   not; don't; do not need
    to
domo (VB)   to split, cleave; to burn
du (N)   wood; tree; trunk
dubaüm (N)   spars
dufol (N)   banana
dul (N)   penis
dulakh (N)   urine
dulalü (VB)   to urinate
dulekhi (wai) (VB)   to go out (*to
    urinate*)
dulekhil (N)   crowbar (*for jerking sago
    trunks open*)
duo (N)   mouse; rodent
duo (VB)   to stab; put into; stew; shoot;
    think

duobo (VB)   to pull
duop (N)   (wild) fruits
dup (N)   banana
düdümté (VB)   to make a hissing sound
  with the lips
dül (N)   crown
dül (N)   sheatfish (*Arius maculatus* v.
  sagor)
dülebil (N)   upper teeth

ND
ndafun (N)   magic power; mana
ndakhimo (VB)   to do well; to help
ndakhimon (N)   help
ndalip (DEICT)   here; this
ndaü (N)   sago
ndaülakh (N)   big piece of sago;
  chatterbox
ndemop (N)   swamp
ndewé (N)   mythical fish(es)
ndi(p) (DEICT)   here; this
ndüni (ADJ)   unhospitable; harsh

E
e (PAUSE)
-engga (POSTP)   and; with
-é (EXCLM)
é (PAUSE)
é(bo) (VB)   to sleep
-él (PKIN)   PL
él (AFFIRM)   yes
Éla (NPROP)   Ela
élo (VB)   to sleep
émol (N)   snake
énon (ADJ)   prolonged; of long duration
énonomekho (ADJ)   dumb, mute;
  speechless; stupid
énontelo (VB)   to forget
è (PAUSE)
èfop (N)   walnut-tree species (*Canarium
  commune*)
èkhmo (VB)   to weep, cry
èpalap (AFFIRM)   all right
èponaup (N)   worksong

F
fahüomo (VB)   to clear a location from
  trees and bushes
fail (N)   yellow banana
fain (N)   banana species
-faipo (VERB/INTNS)

fakh(tenè) (ADJ)   floating away
fakhbéakh (N)   lightning
fakhbéyokhofu (VB)   to jut out
fakhüo (VB)   to grunt
fala (Q)   what about?
falé (N)   break-through (*of a river
  winding*)
falé (ADJ)   crooked
falép (N)   side of upper chest
fali (VB)   to become visible; appear
falimekho (VB)   to accuse
falip (N)   lung
fanip (N)   mountains
fano (NEG)   no; not
-fap (DEICT)   that
Faül (NPROP)   name of mythical pig
Faülanop (NCLAN)   Faülanop clan;
  Faülanop people
faül (N)   swamp
faüsesaü (ADJ)   wide
fayan (N)   magic arrow carving; arrow
fayup (ADJ)   thin; supple, flexible
fefé (VB)   to turn
-fekha (INDEF)   a certain; one; some far
  away
-fekho (POSTP)   and; with; until; in, at,
  on, along; around
felép (ADJ)   lazy; not willing
feli (VB)   to fall
femé (VB)   to dress (*an arrow*)
fédo (VB)   to give
féndon (N)   cloth of thin treebark
fékh (ADJ)   wet
félelo (ADJ)   not angry anymore
Félman (NGEOGR)   Férman village
fénop (N)   pole; pillar
fép (ADJ)   slippery; smooth
fi (N)   name
fikh (N)   bamboo knife; razor blade
fil (N)   tree species
filo (VB)   to mention; to call
filolai (VB)   to mention; to recite
Filup (NGEOGR)   Firu village
fimelon (N)   intestines
finop (ADJ)   loving, affectionate;
  compassionate
fiop (N)   smoke filter in bamboo
  smoking pipe; iguana species
fium (N)   land; hill; ground
fiüm (ADJ)   much; many
fiyan (N)   kind of vegetables

fiyo (N)   long grass species
fo (VB)   to get; marry; take
fofiyu (N)   honey; well
fofo (N)   tree species
fofu (VB)   to send
Fofumon(abül) (NPROP)   Fofumonabül
fokhun (N)   male of certain marsupials
folapé (VB)   to bring
folé (VB)   to be/become afternoon
foleli (VB)   to be/become afternoon
folomonagél (N)   tobacco pipe
fonolé (VB)   to eat
fotokh (ADJ)   light
-fosü (LOC)   from; through; at
-fosübo (VB)   to be downstream
fu (VB)   to put; to set; to get; to admonish
fu (N)   big bamboo rope
fuai (VB)   to hunt
fudamo (VB)   to repay; to recompense
fundam (N)   matter; thing; management; arrangement
ful (N)   tree species
fulo (VB)   to meet
fumo (VB)   to blow
funèp (ADV)   probably; perhaps; possibly
fup (N)   wind; storm
fup lu (VB)   to blow (*as wind*)
fusa (N)   ironwood
füboli (VB)   to jump, leap
fül (ADJ)   sharp; sharpened
füolo (VB)   to cover
füomo (VB)   to clean, cleanse; to order
füon (N)   marsupial species
füp- (ONOMAT)   yell, cry; whistling sound

G
g-/gV- (POSS)   your.SG
ga (ADJ)   strong; dominating; forcing; heavy
gabün (N)   knee
gadiakhai (VB)   to help
gadilai (VB)   to abduct
gaga (ONOMAT)   voice of the Blith's hornbill
ganggail (ADJ)   much; many
ganggül (N)   baby
gailop (N)   kidney
gakholi (VB)   to hit, strike

gakhomo (VB)   to hit, strike
Galon (N)   wet season
gamo (VB)   to increase; to be strong
ganim (N)   sago species
gatakhmo (VB)   to shrug
gaul (N)   second and following layers (*of a baked lump of sago*)
gawakhomo (VB)   to hunt
gawil (N)   stairs
gayan (N)   arrow tip
ge (PERS)   you
gebelipekho (VB)   to awake with fright, start from one's sleep
gebül (N)   fibres; tissue
gembenul (ADJ)   short
gegüp (N)   head
gekhené- (POSS)   your.PL
gekhené(p) (PERS)   you.PL
gelamo (VB)   to go
gele- (VB)   to be afraid, be frightened
gelelü- (ONOMAT)   roaring of fire
gelelukh- (ONOMAT)   splashing (*sound*)
gelén (N)   vegetable
gelèkh- (VB)   to move on and on
geli (VB)   to go
geli(mo) (VB)   to press
gelibol (N)   nostril(s)
gelifekholol (N)   nose bone
gelilfo (VB)   to go away
gelip (N)   nose
gelitop (N)   nostril(s)
gelümo (VB)   to run, go fast; to travel
gelükhmo (VB)   to graze
gemélalé (ADJ)   unhospitable
genul (ADJ)   short
gédun (N/NUM)   wrist; six
gél (N)   nibung palm tree species
Gén (NPROP)   Gén
gènggèmop (N)   little water mosquito
gèkh (N)   sago grub
gikh (N)   landing stage
gil (N)   ceremonial festival place; sago grub festival
gilfo (VB)   to go away, depart; to disappear
gilmambolüp (N)   abandoned festival bivouac
Ginol (NPROP)   Ginol
giolmanop (N)   the ones who organize a sago grub festival

gipo (VB)   to erase
gisole (VB)   to be cold
gitakhul (N)   remains of abandoned festival bivouac
godakh (ADJ)   straight; right
godunalé (N)   vegetable (*Saccharum edule*)
gogelén (N)   grass
gol (N)   pig
golo (VB)   to be afraid
Golokhofalé (NPROP)   Golokhofalé
gololo (VB)   to be afraid
goloni (N)   coward
Gom (N)   Gom-song
gomo (VB)   to have sex
gu(p) (PERS)   you (SG)
gua (N)   iguana species
gufu (VB)   to claim for recompensation
gugukh (ADJ)   unclear; twofold
gul (N)   snake species
gul (N)   bottom
gum (N)   sheatfish species
gun (ADJ)   short
gun (N)   ulcer
gun (N)   family; group; clan; all of them
gunop (N)   family; clan
gü (N)   moisture; water
güboli (VB)   to come together
gübo(lmo) (VB)   to come together, meet; to collect
gülap (LOC)   upstream
gülelo (ADJ)   dark
güli (VB)   to be/become dark; to be/become night
gülnanggaup (N)   night
gülo(l) (LOC)   upstream
gümo (VB)   to play; to dance

NGG
nggaén (N)   tree (*Areca catechu*)
nggaüm (N)   end; finish
nggaümo (VB)   to collide, bump against
nggawalalun (N)   dot; burn-scars
nggawél (ADJ)   lazy; not willing
nggenggimekho (VB)   to push
nggelü (VB)   to push forward
nggé (NKIN)   friend; husband's sister
nggél (N)   old (man); aged male
nggén (N)   small palm tree species
nggonggop (N)   piece of wood

nggolo(lalé) (ADJ)   long; tall
Nggop (NPROP)   Nggop
nggul (ADJ)   discontented
Nggulumèlèp (NFAM)   Rumere

H
hey/hèé (EXCLM)   hey!
hièn(tena) (ADJ)   small; little
hüüüü (EXCLM)   huuuu

I
ibo (VB)   to be; to lay; to sleep
imban (N)   individual; member; person
indo (VB)   to heat; to bake
iè (EXCLM)   iè!
igo (N)   oar
inggenun (N)   sago leaf stem; sago washing construction
ii (EXCLM)   ii!
ilakh (ADV)   high; on top of; up
ilmekho (VB)   to be of ochre colour; to be ochrous
ilol (N)   stone; rock
imo (VB)   to look, see, watch, look at
imonè (ADV)   now
i(p) (DEICT)   here; this

K
kaél (N)   tree species
kafüol (N)   tree (*Casuarina equiaetifolia*)
kailon (N)   rib; arrow made of rib
kamèn (N)   long grass
Kawantè (NFAM)   Markus Kawangtet (*from Muyu origin*)
kembakhi (N)   aggressive ant
kembalimo (VB)   to return
Kelajafalé (NPROP)   Kelajafalé (= Kepsan Kurufe)
Kelamu (NGEOGR)   Kelamu River
kelelükhmo (VB)   to make noise
kelil (N)   strength; zest for life; mind
keliokhmo (VB)   to come together, gather together
kemél (ADJ)   used to; skilled in, expert; usual; familiar with
kélo (N)   dugout canoe
kémo (N)   tuber
kèkèkh (NORN)   white cockatoo

kilelo (VB)   to be, keep silent
kiya (ONOMAT)   crack
klèkhmo (VB)   to flirt; to defy
Kolufaup (N)   Korowai speech
Kolufo (NTRIBE)   Korowai
kombéop (N)   Jew's harp
Kou (NGEOGR)   Kouh village
Kris (NPROP)   Kris
Kuakhil (NGEOGR)   Kuakhil River
Kualégofalé (NPROP)   Kualégofalé
kuasél (N)   fishhook; pointed shell
kulekham (N)   mud crab species
küal (N)   cassowary
kükülmo (VB)   to be similar
kül (ADJ)   right; in order; according;
   like; just
külomo (VB)   to dance in the külomo
   fashion

KH
-kha (CONN)
kha (Q-WORD)   what?
khabéan (N/NUM)   head; crown;
   thirteen
khabéantokhul (N)   headache
khabél (ADJ)   tired; exhausted
khabop (N)   Vulturine parrot
khabül (N)   ulcer; ball
khambap (N)   scabies
khandin (N)   sacredness; secret
khandindamon (N)   sacred fence in
   ceremonial sago grub festival bivouac
khandul (N)   island
khandun (N)   stone; rock
khandü (VB)   to stew on hot stones
khafén (ADJ)   alive; awake; conscious
khafun (N)   blood
khafun (NKIN)   grandchild
khafüm(engga) (ADJ)   red
khafüm (N)   red soil
khagil (ADJ)   (feeling) cold
khanggop (ADJ/ADV)   high; on top of
khai (VB)   to go; to walk; to travel
khaifosaifo (ADJ)   all kinds of; each of
   them
khail (N)   rodent (*Sminthopsis
   rufigenis*)
Khailfüoalop (NPROP)   Khailfüoalop
   (name of a mythical dog)
khaim (N)   treehouse; house

khaimokh (NKIN)   brother's wife
khaimon (NKIN)   husband's brother
Khain (NPROP)   Khain
khaja (NKIN)   last born
khakheli(mo) (VB)   to split, cleave
khakhikh (N)   warning; advice;
   admonition
khakhlakh (N)   grass species
-khakho (ADV)   like
khakho (N)   small piece of wood
khakho (NREL)   inside; middle
khakholop (N)   mouth
khakhu (N)   shrimp species
khakhua (N)   (male) witch
khakhul (ADV)   yesterday
khakhuda khopé (ADV)   the day
   before yesterday
khakhü (N)   shrimp species
khakhül (N)   sago species
khal (N)   skin; flesh; meat
khala(kh) (ADJ/ADV)   high; on top of;
   up
khalan (N)   groin
khalasela (ADJ)   in vain
khalfap (N)   iguana species
khalilmekho (VB)   to be frightened; to
   wonder
khalokh (ADJ)   naughty; good for
   nothing
khalom (N)   sheatfish species
khalu (ADJ)   near; close
kham (NORN)   bird (Torrent Lark)
khami (N)   handle
khami/khai (VB)   to sit; to stay; to live
khami(l)mo (VB)   to do in common; to
   do with all
khamon (N)   hand; forepaw
khamu (VB)   to yelp
khamüsol (N)   ant species
khanap (ADJ)   happy; pleased; glad
khanél (N)   baskets for catching fish
khasam (N)   khasam dance
-khata (OBJ)   OBJECT
khatakh (ADJ)   ashamed; scandalised
-khatun (NKIN)   children of mother (. . .)
khau (N)   sweet potato
khau(p) (NREL)   inside; interior
-khaü- (INTNS)
khaü (N)   bivouac; house
khaüadop (NORN)   bird species

khaüp (LOC)   down
Khawagé (NGEOGR)   Kawagit village
Khawékh (NCLAN)   Khawékh clan;
   Khawékh people
khawil (NORN)   yearbird (Blith's
   hornbill)
khawisip (N)   penis gourd made of the
   beak of the yearbird
khayal (N)   fish species
khayal (N)   rodent species
khayan (INTNS)   very; real
khayo (ADJ)   ripe
khayo (N)   arrow
khayolamol (N)   arrows for fending off
   destruction of the universe
khayolul (N)   sclera
khe- (DEICT)   there
khebé (VB)   to totter
khebüm (N)   wasp
khedi/khedé (VB)   to kill; to terminate
khendé(mo) (VB)   to care; to watch; to
   maintain; to raise
khendép (N)   tail; dog
khendil (N)   secret magic
khejo (N)   sago leaf stem; sago washing
   construction
khejom (NORN)   bird (Brownheaded
   crow = *Corvus fuscicapillus*)
khekhin (N)   arrow tip made of
   cassowary bones
khelé (N)   fish
khelélmekho (VB)   to cut down
khelép (ADJ)   clear; clean; bright;
   plain
khelèl (VB)   to split, cleave
kheli(l)mekho (VB)   to graze; to brush
khelünakh (N)   sweat
-khelüp (DESID)
khenè (REL)   next; and; presently
khenil (N)   beginning
kheyo (N)   tree bark (nibung)
kheyop (N)   house
khél (N)   flower
khén (ADJ)   angry; fierce; aggressive
Khénalé (NPROP)   Khénalé
khésekhan (NEG)   no; not being; it is
   not
khèkh- (VB)   to make fun
Khinggo (NCLAN)   Khinggo people
   (i.e., a Kombai clan)

khil (ADJ)   strong; healthy; alive
khim (N)   mucus
khimakhmbalop (N)   sinus; nasal
   cavity
-khip (ADV)   over
khip (N)   sago beetle (*Scarabaeidae*
   spp.)
-kho(lo) (Q)   Question
kho (N)   sagotree; sago
kho- (DEICT)   there; that
khobo (VB)   come and go
khobül (N)   leg
khombokhai (AFFIRM)   please; can
khombül (N)   sago bag
khondul (N)   belly
khondulmengga (N)   pregnancy (*lit.*
   "belly.with")
Khondubidop (NPROP)   Khondubidop
khofe (VB)   to unite; mix; meet
khofé (N)   soot; charcoal
khofél (N)   youngster
khofélapa (EXCLM)   Oh boy!
khofélaup (N)   lie
khofémanop (N)   boy; male youth
khofi(lun) (ADJ)   dark; black
kho(l)fu (VB)   to unite; to mix; to be
   together; to meet
kho(l)funè (QUANT)   all (of them)
khonggekél (ADJ)   big, large; great
khonggél (ADJ)   big; large; great
khokh (ADJ)   hot; spicy
khokha (CL SIM)   like; sort of
khokholmekho (VB)   to be white
khokholun (ADJ)   white; light
khokho(l)mo (VB)   to be together
khokhu (N)   meaning
khokhukh (N)   bone; hard object
khokhukh (ADJ)   strong; hard;
   aggressive
khokhukhanop (N)   enemy
khokhül (N)   central pole (*of a
   treehouse*)
khokhün (ADJ)   abandoned; discarded
khokhüneni (N)   garden products
khol (N)   tree bark fibres
khol-mekho/-mo (VB)   to take a walk
kholmo (VB)   to meet
kholofudamo (VB)   to replace; to
   recompense
kholokholop (NREL)   each other

kholol (N)   bone; hard object; stem
khololanop (N)   enemy
kholomon (N)   breakthrough at river
winding
kholop (NREL)   each
kholopamo (VB)   to reciprocate
kholü(kh)- (VB)   to treat with magic;
neutralise bad magic
kholükhmo (VB)   to break down
-kholüp (DESID)
Khomei (NCLAN)   Khomei people, clan
khomi (VB)   to be unconscious; to
transform; to change way of existence
khomilo (ADJ)   unconscious; dead
khomofekholol (N/NUM)   neck; eleven
khomolamol (ADJ)   all kinds of
khomul (N)   necklace; string
khomulo (N)   mudcrab species
khomülepé (ADV)   the day before
yesterday
khonai (VB)   to go
khonum (N)   fish species
khop (DEICT)   there; that
khopésambo (VB)   to be invited
Khosomalé (NPROP)   Khosomalé
khosübo(l) (ADV)   downstream there
khosükhop (DEICT)   (down) there; that
khosül (N)   sago
khotogèlmo (VB)   to be fed up with
khotokhal (N/NUM)   ear; auricle; twelve
khotop (N)   ear
khotu(l) (ADV)   still
khoyo (N)   scale (*shrimp*)
Khufom (NPROP)   Khufom
khugol (N)   frog
khul (N)   shell string (kauri)
khul (N)   intestines
khul (N)   stone axe
khul (N)   sky
khulbün (N)   sky
khum (N)   sago species
khup (ADJ)   right; good; clever; skilled
khup (N)   time
khuwolanop (N)   guest
khuwolmo (VB)   to visit
khüfolun (N)   shadow
-khül (PKIN)   PL
khül (N)   shell money; shell string
khül (N)   column (*of ants*)
khül (N)   bees wax

khülekhelimo (VB)   to march in a row
(*of ants*)
khülo(l) (ADV)   upstream
khülul (N)   pupil and iris (*eye*)
khün (N)   sweat
-khüp (DESID)

L

-la (LOC)   at; on; in
labodi (VB)   to join; to follow; to add
labul (N/NUM)   upperarm; nine
labul (N)   cockroach
labulop (N)   wild apple; wild apple tree
labun (N)   arrow tip
labunop (N)   upper arm muscles
lambiakh (N)   verandah
lambil (N)   family; group of close
relatives
lambil (N)   (nibung) tree
lambimatimo (VB)   to sneeze
laf (N)   nibung tree
lafi(l) (VB)   to cut
lafimekho (VB)   to knock over
lafiyol (N)   lizard species
lafol (N/NUM)   forearm; seven
langgamo (VB)   to eat; consume food
langgéntop (N)   ulcer
lahial (N)   sago species
lai (VB)   to come; build; hatch; to break;
to be broken
lai (INTNS)
lai(l)mo (VB)   to break
laibo(l) (VB)   to be born
laibolekha (N)   descent
laifo (VB)   to break
laifo (VB)   to ask; to question; to
interrogate
laifu (VB)   to produce; to bring forth
lailo (ADV)   returning
lailo (VB)   to cause
laimanggü (VB)   to fold
laimekho (VB)   to hide thoroughly; to
bury
laimofo (VB)   to break loose
lakh (N)   poisonous snake
lakha (N/NUM)   elbow; eight
lakhato(l)mo (VB)   to shoot
lakhatop (NREL)   the underneath
lakhebé (VB)   to make
lakhefi (VB)   to open

lakheli- (VB)   to pour
lakhi(l)mo (VB)   to stew with leaves
lakhul (ADJ)   former; discarded
lakhup (N)   stone
lakhup duo (VB)   stew with hot stones in big leaf-packages
lal (NKIN)   daughter; girl; female
lal (N)   floor-beam; bottom-beam
-lalé (ADJ)   big, great, large
-lalé (INTS)   very
laléo (N)   spirit; bad spirit; demon
laléo-aup (N)   Indonesian language
laléo-ndaü (N)   bread
laléo-khal (N)   clothing
laléo-menil (N)   matches
lalobop (N)   mouth
Lalop (NGEOGR)   Lalop River
lalum (NKIN)   daughter's husband
lam (N)   tree species
lamé (VB)   to tie; to play; to dance
lamélo (VB)   to tie; to bind
lamo (VB)   to wrap in leaves
lamo (VB)   to count
lamoda- (VB)   to touch with something
lamol (N)   world, universe; place; clan territory
lamolaup (N)   myth; world history
lamon (N)   bunch; packet
lamotelokhai (VB)   the world will be destroyed
lamunalé (N)   hair decoration
lamü (VB)   to pound (*sago*)
lamükh (VB)   to hew out
lamül (N)   green cucumber
lanéam (N)   wet season
lanol (N)   tree species
-lanukh (ADV)   only
lanumo (VB)   to command
laopo (VB)   to move up and down
laul (N)   rodent species
laün (NKIN)   foster-
laün (N)   Pandanus fruit
laünbün (= laünkhul) (N)   freshwater fish species
laünkhul (= laünbün) (N)   freshwater fish species
lawa (N)   rock; stone; food wrapped in leaves
layo (N)   leech
layop (N)   cassava

lebakhop (N)   old lady
lebé (VB)   to pick; to gather
lebidi (VB)   to quarrel; to abuse (*each other*)
lebil (N)   tooth
lebilekhul (N)   gum
lebükh (VB)   to shoot
lembémo (VB)   to flirt
lembul (ADJ)   bad; wrong; ugly; dirty; inefficient
lefaf (ADV)   finished
lefé (N)   banana species
Lefilkhei (NCLAN)   Lefilkhei clan
lefu (N)   end, finish
lefu (INDEF)   some . . . other(s)
lefu (N)   ulcer
lefugop (ADV)   all kinds of
lefukokop (ADV)   all kinds of
lefulmekho (VB)   to finish, terminate
lefül (N)   day; time
lefül (N)   fish species
lefüta (ADV)   at noon
lenggili (VB)   to be frightened
lenggotena (N)   small piece of
lekhal (ADJ)   tall; big
lekhalekha (N)   winding (*as a river*)
lekheli (VB)   to unfasten; to carry out; to finish
-lekhé(n) (NREL)   because; for; in order to
lekhingga (ADJ)   far; faraway
lekhül (N)   trunk
lekhüpwaila (N)   all kinds of
lelé- (VB)   to come
leléal (ADJ)   happy; contented; glad; pleased
leléalmo (VB)   to accept
lelèmbelè (ADJ)   shrieking
leléf/lelép (N)   higher grounds
lelida (ADJ)   pretty; attractive; handsome
lelip (ADV)   together
lelua (N)   dirt; feces
lelup (N)   sprig; planting
lelül (N)   infected wound; infection
Lemakha (NFAM)   Lemakha people
lemakhal (N)   lie, falsehood
Lemé (NGEOGR)   Lemé River
lemilé (VB)   to die down (*fire*); to decrease
lemu (N)   cough

lemül (N)   smoke; cloud
-lena (DIMIN)   small, little
lenan (N)   armpit
lenan (N)   lizard species
lenup (ADJ)   sleepy
lenutép (ADJ)   sleepy
lepé (VB)   to meet
lepélo (VB)   to shut; to get hold of
lepun (N)   container made of folded
   sago leaf stem
lesifu (VB)   to laugh
lesukh (ADJ)   brave
letél (ADJ)   angry; strong; aggressive
letép (N)   root
letün (N)   mosquito
lé (ndé/nté) (VB)   to eat
lé (N)   sago species
-lè (DISJ)   or
léam (N)   side (*of a building*)
léf (N)   tongue
lékh (N)   nose decoration of pig tusk
lé khomo (VB)   to associate with; to mix
   with
lél (N)   roof
lél (N)   centipede species
lénté (VB)   to itch
lép (ADJ)   ill, sick; longing for; suffer;
   feel hurt
lidop (NUM)   one
lil (N)   vagina
lilol (N)   lie, falsehood
lilomo (VB)   to tell lies
lilop (N)   arrow tip
-lo(n) (FOC)
-lo(n) (INSTR)   with; by
-lo(p) (DS)   and; but
lofekha (N)   wild pig
-lofekho (DS)   and; but
lokhesukh (N)   egg
lokhesukhop (N)   scrotum; testicles
lokhetikh (N)   small bat species
lokhmekho (VB)   to parallel
lokhté (VB)   to go away, depart; to
   disappear
lokhul (N)   forehead; head; brains
lokhulkholol (N)   frontal bone
lokhutokhul (N)   headache
lokhül (N)   body; corpse
lol (N)   big lizard species
lolol (N)   goods; luggage; things

lonoptabül (N)   rattan shingles
lop (N)   place; circumstance; jungle;
   forest
lotup (N)   fly
-lu (FOC)
lu (VB)   to rub; to smear; to grease
lu (VB)   to move up; to ascend; to enter;
   to cross
lubul (ADJ)   busy
lungga (N)   food; game
lul (N)   leaves
lul (N)   eye
lulgelip (N)   face (*human*)
lulkhal (N)   eyelid
lulkholol (N)   brow
lulop (N)   eye; black decorative dots at
   the margin of a shield
lup (N)   banana sprig
lup (N)   small fish species
lup (N)   sun
lüfekhemi (VB)   to take rest
lül (N)   barrier; blocking; fallen down
   trees
lülmo (VB)   to moisten; to rub
lüma (N)   sheat fish species
lüp (ADJ)   heavy

M
m (PAUSE)
-ma (REL)   also
-ma (LOC)   at; to
Mabül (NGEOGR)   Mabül village;
   Mabül River
mabün (PL of abül) (N)   sons
mambisi (N)   uterus
mambüm (NKIN)   children
manda (NEG)   no; not; it is not
mandil (N)   arrow
mandum (N)   fish species
maél (N)   water; river
maf (N)   picture; shadow; image
mafém (N)   nothing; no
mafakh (N)   mirror; reflected image
Mafém (NPROP)   Mafém (*female name*)
mafial (N)   small piece of wood
mafom (N)   mafom snake
mafüm (N)   lizard; salamander
mangga (N)   dry sago leaves
manggaka (CIRCUM)   at; in; along;
   around

Manggél (NGEOGR) Manggél village
manggumbalop (N) lower jaw
manggum (N) cheek
manggumkholol (N) cheek bone
mahüankho(sol) (N) (fresh) Pandanus
  fruit
mahüokh (N) shrimp species
mahüon (N) word; story; language;
  voice; advice
main (NUM) shoulder; ten
makh (NKIN) grandmother
makhaya(l) (N) bat species
makhil (N) aereal roots
makhol (N) mouth of river; deep water
Makhyuni (NPROP) Makhyuni
mal (N) spear
malan (N) snake species
Maliaufalé (NPROP) Maliaufalé
malin (N) shell money; shell string
  (*kauri*)
maman (N) out of order
mamap (ADV) a little; a bit; slightly
mamün (N) sun; hotness
mamüngga (N) blood
manian (N) stick for picking breadfruits
Manianggatun
  (NCLAN) Manianggatun clan;
  Manianggatun people
manol (ADJ) white; light; bright
manop (ADJ) good; in order; right;
  beautiful; attractive; clean
manop (N) chest
manopo (VB) to heal; to order
manütul (N) navel
Map (N) MAF (Mission Aviation
  Fellowship)
masekha (N) secret; taboo; prohibition
maselop (N) tree species
maun (N) water; river; rain
maun fu (VB) to rain
maunggél (N) bamboo pipe for
  drinking-water storage
maun langga (N) fish (*lit.* river-food)
maünan (N) rattan
mayokh (EXCLM) help!; oh, dear!
mayokh (N) friends
mayum (N) sago species
mefekha (NKIN) last born
-mengga (POSTP) with; and
mekhesim (N) spittle

-mekho (SUPP)
mekho (VB) to fill; to load; to put
  into
melé (VB) to move; to be in motion;
  to loosen; to finish
melibol (N) fireplace
meli (N) louse
melil (N) fire; firewood
melitemül (N) smoke
meli yabo (VB) to pick lice
melo (ADJ) stiff (of penis erectus)
melu (VB) to get up; to move up; to
  awake; to grow; to resurrect
melun (N) gall bladder
memil (N) vein
menakholol (N) rib
menél (N) young girl; maiden
menè(l) (ADV) quickly
menil (N) fire; firewood
mesendip (ADV) repeatedly; again
mesendipo (VB) to prepare and serve
mesé (ADV) again; and then; next
mé- (VB) to move, be in motion
mé (N) earth
méan (N) dog
méanmaél (N) the great water surrounding the world (*lit.* dog water)
mébol (N) grave
mél (N) hand; forepaw
mélaimekho (VB) to bury
mél endü (VB) to point to; to indicate
mélol (N) hand; fingers
mén (NREL) side; bank
mèkhmo (VB) to squeak
mi (VB) to drink
Milofakh (N) Milop River
milon (N) sago species; fire guard (at
  sago grub festival)
minamo (VB) to shine; to flash
Minu (NPROP) Minu (*female*)
Mip (N) Mip River
misafi (N) luggage; goods; things
-mo (SUPP)
mo (VB) to do; to make
modol (NKIN) younger sister
mofekha (NKIN) younger brother
mofekhup (ADJ) true; reliable
mofu (ADV) only
monggo(fo) (VB) to get out; to unload
mokukh (VB) to suck (*sweets*)

mokhemükh (N)   ant species
molun (N)   tree species
molüp (N)   fly species
mom (NKIN)   mother's brother
mo<u>mul</u> (ADJ)   longing; desiring; covetous
munggofo (VB)   to set (*sun*)
mukh (N)   hair; leaf
<u>M</u>ukhalé (NPROP)   Mukhalé
mul (NKIN)   father's sister
<u>mu</u>man (N)   dog
<u>mu</u>mengga (N)   dog
mup (N)   last piece of baked lump of sago
mup (ADJ)   very good
<u>mü</u>ndiop (ADV)   at once; suddenly; quickly
<u>mü</u>fekholol (N)   backbone
mül (N)   handle
mül(ekha) (NREL)   former; before; front
<u>mü</u>lalüp (ADV)   in the past; in former times
<u>mü</u>lanop (N)   people of former times
<u>mü</u>lgop (NREL)   front(side)

N
n-/nV- (POSS)   my
na- (POSS)   my
Nabé<u>kha</u> (NTRIBE)   Nombéakha
nabul (NKIN)   wife's sibling
nai (VB)   to move down; to go out
Nai<u>lop</u> (NGEOGR)   Becking River (Ndeiram Kabur)
Nakhi<u>lop</u> (NGEOGR)   Nakhiro village
nakhup (DESID)   it is good
nan (N)   rope (of rattan); wire
nanafo (VB)   to do nothing
na<u>ném</u> (ADJ/ADV)   secret/ly; silent/ly; illegal/ly; being in rest; illicit/ly
nanü (NKIN)   son's wife
Naomi (NPROP)   Naomi
<u>nau</u>matélekha (N)   sago
ne (PERS)   I; me
ne<u>ni(l)</u>fo (VB)   to be much; to be many
ne<u>nim</u> (N)   sand
néakhméokh- (VB)   to speak inside (oneself); to think
nén (ADJ)   rotten; tainted
nèkhmo (VB)   to ask for; to claim
Nènèp (NPROP)   Nènèp
ni (NKIN)   mother; lady; woman

ni-até (NKIN)   parents (*lit.* mother-father)
ninggün (N)   dirt
ni<u>okh</u> (N)   mother
nokho (NKIN)   friend; husband's sister
no<u>khu-</u> (POSS)   our
no<u>khu(p)</u> (PERS)   we; us
no<u>lé</u> (VB)   to eat
non (N)   sago grub
nop (N)   flesh; meat
nu(p) (PERS)   I; me

O
-o (VOC)
-o (EXCLM)   -o!
-o (COORD)   and
O (EXCLM)   oh!
ol(ekhi) (N)   feces
olaibo (VB)   to clear a path while dancing
oldintai (VB)   to clear a path while dancing
op (N)   fruit

P
-pa(n) (REL)   also; self
pa (ONOMAT)   crack
palu- (VB)   dancing fashion
palua (N)   fish (*Plotosus canius* v. angguilaris)
-pé(n) (LOC)   at; in; on
peli (ADJ)   blunt
pingg(ul)up (N/NUM)   middle finger; three
pi<u>pe</u>(mo) (ONOMAT)   sound of khejom bird
pofule<u>li</u> (VB)   to be silent
pol (NUM)   two; a couple of
pükh (N)   arrow
pükh (ONOMAT)   crack
<u>pü</u>khmo (VB)   to throw away

S
sa<u>bül</u> (NKIN)   nephew; cross male child
Sabül (NGEOGR)   Sabül River
sa<u>ndum</u> (N)   cassowary
sahü<u>o</u> (N)   small bat species
<u>sa</u>khu (N)   banana
salal (NKIN)   niece; cross female child
Sali (NGEOGR)   Sali River

sa**nip** (N)   cassowary
saukh (N)   tobacco
Saul (NPROP)   Saul
saündal (N)   little sticks; calendar
seng**gili** (VB)   to be frightened; to be amazed
se**mail** (N)   crocodile
senan (N/NUM)   little finger; one
senanafül (N/NUM)   ring finger; two
sé (ADV)   next; again
sékh (N)   skirt; sago palm fiber material for making skirts
sél (N)   crispy sago marrow
Sèmbelèfalé (NPROP)   Sèmbelèfalé (*male name*)
Sèifabül (NPROP)   Sèifabül
sèip (N)   shudder; magic trance
sèipengga lal (N)   woman who maintains contacts with the spirits
si(si) (N)   legs; feet
sim (N)   smoking rack
simbelu (N)   tuber (*Colocasia*)
singga (N)   fingernail
sikh (ADJ)   delicious; fine
Silam (NPROP)   mouse-like animal; Silam
silup (N)   forehead decoration
sim (ADJ)   pushing against
siop (N)   lower end
sip (N)   root end; beak
sol (ADJ)   new; fresh
solditai- (VB)   begin
sop (NKIN)   father's sister's husband
sumo (VB)   to smell
sü (N)   tobacco
-sü (LOC)   from; through; at
sübap (ADV)   downstream
sübo(l) (VB)   to be downstream
süfap (ADV)   downstream
süom (N)   oily layer covering swampy water

T

-ta (LOC)   at; on; in
tambiakh (N)   veranda
Takhanè (NPROP)   Takhanè
takhebé (VB)   to make
takhefi (VB)   to open
takhul (ADJ)   former; discarded
-talé (ADJ)   big, great, large

-talé (INTNS)   very
tamon (N)   bunch; packet
tamükh (VB)   to hew out
-tanukh (ADV)   only
tebé (VB)   to pick; to gather
-tekhé(n) (NREL)   because; for; in order to
telida (ADJ)   pretty; attractive; handsome; nice
temül (N)   smoke
-tena (DIMIN)   small, little
-tè (DISJ)   or
-to(n) (FOC)
-to(n) (POSTP)   with; by
-to(p) (DS)   and
-tofekho (DS)   and; but
tonggo (ADJ)   many; much
tom (N)   mark
top (N)   place; circumstance
-tu (FOC)

U

u (EXCLM)   wow!
u(mo) (VB)   to talk; to tell; to speak
umbontafekho (N)   clearing (*jungle*)
udediop (N)   situation; circumstances
ukh (N)   small cucumber
ul (N)   season; time; period
um (NKIN)   husband
Uni (NGEOGR)   Uni village
utebo (VB)   being the growing season of . . .
-uwo (EXCLM)   uwo

Ü

ü (EXCLM)   oh!
ü(l) (VB)   to kill; to beat, hit; to cut down
Ügo (NGEOGR)   Ugo village
ülekhal (N)   floor platform
ülelo (VB)   to yell, shout; to cry
ülfo (VB)   to vanish, disappear; to come to an end; to burn down quickly
ülfo (VB)   to kill
ülmekho (VB)   to shoot; to hit
ülmo (VB)   to kill; to hit; to cut
ülo (VB)   to drown
-ülop (ADV)   like
üm (N)   liver
ün (NREL)   side; roof-ridge

üop (N)   goods; things; message
ütelo (ADJ)   over; gone

W

wa(p) (DEICT)   there; that; thus
wambon (N)   tree (fruit) (*Ponnetia pinniata*)
wafil (N/NKIN)   male adult; husband
Wanggemalo (NGEOGR)   Wanggemalo village
wai (VB)   to move down; to go out
wailo (ADJ)   going down
wakhai (ADJ)   discontented
wakhalimo (VB)   to vomit
wakhan (ADV)   left
wakhatum (N)   folktale(s)
wakhél (N)   handle; arrow stem
wakhol (N)   moon
wakhum (N)   package; wrapping
wakhum (NORN)   wild chicken
wakhumekho (VB)   to chase; to hunt
wali (VB)   to be, become light/day
walelélekhu (ADV)   tomorrow
waleli (VB)   to be, become light/day
waliop (N)   swamp
walukh (ADJ)   ill, sick
walüp(i) (ADV)   halfway
walü(p) (N)   oar
wan(gga) (N)   pig
wanum (N)   tree (*with thorny branches and lianas*)
wayafül (N/NUM)   index finger; four
wayo (N)   tortoise species
wayo (N/NUM)   thumb; five
wé (EXCLM)   Wow!
wé (ADJ)   continuous
wél (N)   torch
wémekho (VB)   to turn turtle
wof- (DEICT)   there; that; thus
wokaka (ADV)   all kinds of
wokhelimekho (VB)   to turn; to return; to do again
Wokhemél (NPROP)   Wokhemél
wol(iol) (N)   symbol; drawing; picture
wola (N)   world, universe
wolalelokhai (VB)   the world will be destroyed
wolamaman (N)   destruction of the universe

wolop (N)   menstruation
Wolop (NGEOGR)   Wolop River
wolumon (N)   shield
wotop (N)   sacred place
wotuwo (N)   tree species
wü (EXCLM)   wü!

Y

y-/yV- (POSS)   his; her; its
ya (EXCLM)   yes
yabén (N)   fat; grease
yabibo (VB)   to cover (cf. süom)
yabo (VB)   to pick (*lice*)
Yambim (NPROP)   Yambim
yambim (N)   tree species
yafé (VB)   to roll
yafikh (N)   sago pounding stick
yafil (N)   snake
yafin (N)   stairs of a treehouse
yafo (VB)   to block; to close
Yafufla (NGEOGR)   Yafufla village
yafun (N)   roll
yagua (N)   nose decoration of pig tusk
yakhasél (N)   wound
yakhatimekho (VB)   to abandon; to renounce; to resist
yakhofekha (Q)   who?; who
yakhonggolol (N)   coccyx
yakhomo (VB)   to harm someone
yakhop (Q)   who?; who
yakhuol (N)   tree species
yakhü (VB)   to dig
yal (N)   cassowary legbone; dagger
yalé (N)   respected person
yalén (N/NKIN)   old man; respected man; husband
yaléyalén (N)   older people; ancestors
yaliaémo (VB)   to show
yalikhomo (VB)   to show
yalomo (VB)   to hit with nettles
Yalul (NPROP)   Yalul
yalün (N)   nettle
yame- (VB)   to tie up
yamo (VB)   to weep, cry, wail
yamolomo (VB)   to stew in leaves
yani (ADJ)   other; different
Yaniluman (NGEOGR)   Yaniruma village; Yaniruma River
yanogun (N)   patriclan; group; family
yanop (N)   people; person

yanopkhayan (N)   soul (*lit.* the very person)

yasim (N)   garden

yaüap/yaüp (ADV)   downstream; down there

yawol (N)   breadfruit (*Artocarpus*)

ye (PERS)   he; she; it

ye- (DEICT)   here

ye- (VB)   to sleep

yealé (NKIN)   husband

yebom (NKIN)   great-grandchild; great-grandparent

yebun (N)   rope; rattan rope

yefo(lo) (VB)   to close; to block up

yekhené- (POSS)   their

yekhené(p) (PERS)   they; them

yelüp (N)   arrow

yemül (N)   flying fox

yenalfayan (N)   magic arrow

yè (ADV)   again

yo (EXCLM)   yes

Yohanem (NPROP)   Johannes Veldhuizen

yokholmo (VB)   to vomit

yolmo (VB)   to whistle

yumfayan (N)   magic arrow

Yuni (NPROP)   Yuni

yu(p) (PERS)   he; she; it

English–Korowai

See the preceeding listing for the word categories and stress placement of the Korowai words.

A

a certain (INDEF) -fekha
a couple of; a few (NUM) pol
a little (ADV) mamap
to abandon (VB) yakhatimekho
abandoned (ADJ) khokhün
abandoned feast bivouac
  (N) gilmambolüp
abdomen (N) benén
to abduct (VB) gadilai
to abuse (VB) lebidi
to accept (VB) leléalmo
to accuse (VB) falimekho, falimo
to add (VB) labodi
to admonish (VB) fu
admonition (N) khakhikh
advice (N) khakhikh, mahüon
aerial roots (N) makhil
to be affectionate (VB) bembi, finop
after; behind (ADV) bétop
again (ADV) mesendip, mesé, mesi(p),
  sé, yè
aged male (N) nggél
aggressive (ADJ) khén, khokhukh,
  letél
alive (ADJ) khil, khafén
all kinds of (ADJ/ADV) bilamalin,
  khomolamol, lekhüpwaila, lefukokop,
  khaifosaifo, lefugop, wokaka
all right (AFFIRM) èpalap
all of them (QUANT) kho(l)funè
along (CIRCUM) -fekho
also (REL) -ma, -pa(n)
always (ADV) afé(n), aféngga
amount (N) -anop
ancestors (N) mbolombolop, yaléyalén
angle; angular point (N) aül
angry (ADJ) khén, letél
ant (*species*) (N) kembakhi, khamüsol,
  mokhemükh
appear(ing) (ADJ) fali; dal
Areca catechu (N) nggaén
armpit (N) lenan
around (CIRCUM) -fekho
arrangement (N) fundam

to arrive (VB) difo
arrow (N) hayo, pükh
arrow stem (N) wakhél
arrow tip (N) labun
arrow (made of leaf rib) (N) kailon
arrow (*types*) (N) bumon, daup, fayan,
  gayan, khekhin, lilop, mandil,
  mbonggon, yelüp
to ascend (VB) lu
ashamed (ADJ) khatakh
ashes (N) anom, bulanom
to ask for (VB) nèkhmo
to ask (a question) (VB) laifo
at noon (ADV) lefüta
at once (ADV) mündiop
attractive (ADJ) lelida, manop,
  telida
auricle (N) khotokhal
awake (ADJ) khafén, melu
to awake with fright (VB) gebelipekho

B

baby (N) ganggül
back(side) (NREL) banun, damol
backbone (N) müfekholol
bad (ADJ) lembul
bad spirit (N) laléo
baiting place (N) dokhon
to bake (VB) alü, indo
ball (N) khabül
bamboo knife (N) fikh
bamboo pipe for storage of water
  (N) maunggél
banana (N) dendü, dufol, dup, sakhu;
  (*species*) fain, lefé
banana sprig (N) lup, lelup
banian tree (N) baül
bank (of river) (N) amin, mén
barrier (N) lül
bat (*species*) (N) lokhetikh, makhaya(l),
  sahüo
to bathe (VB) dadü
to be (VB) bo, bai/ba-, bau, ibo
to be born (VB) laibo(l)
to be the season of (VB) utebo

to be/come afraid (VB)   gele-, golo,
  gololo
to be/come afternoon (VB)   foleli, folé
to be/come almost (VB)   difo
to be/come amazed (VB)   senggili
to be/come broken (VB)   lai
to be burnt (VB)   dofo
to be/come cold (VB)   gisole
to be/come covered with
  (VB)   bulmekho
to be/come dark (VB)   dofuleli, güli
to be/come day (VB)   waleli, wali
to be downstream (VB)   -fosübo, sübo(l)
to be/come fed up with
  (VB)   khotogèlmo
to be/come frightened (VB)   gele-,
  khalilmekho, lenggili, senggili
to be a guest (VB)   khuwolmo
to be invited (VB)   khopésambo
to be in motion (VB)   melé, mé-
to be(come) light (VB)   wali, waleli
to be many (VB)   neni(l)fo
to be much (VB)   neni(l)fo
to be night (VB)   güli
to be ochrous (VB)   ilmekho
to be pulled out (VB)   difo
to be/come silent (VB)   pofuleli, kilelo
to be similar (VB)   kükülmo
to be strong (VB)   gamo
to be together (VB)   kho(l)fu,
  khokho(l)mo
to be/come unconscious (VB)   khomi
to be/come visible (VB)   fali
to be white (VB)   khokholmekho
beak (N)   sip
beam (N)   dil
to beat (VB)   bümo, ü(l)
beautiful (ADJ)   manop
because (NREL)   -lekhé(n), -tekhé(n)
beeswax (N)   khül
before (NREL)   alüm, mül(ekha)
to begin (VB)   ditaimekho, solamo,
  solditai
beginning (N)   khenil, khenikhenil
behind (ADV)   bétop
being in rest (ADJ)   naném
belly (N)   khondul
big (N)   -talé, khonggekél, khonggél,
  lekhal
big bamboo rope (N)   fu

big lump of sago (N)   ndaülakh
to bind (VB)   lamélo
bird (N)   dél
birds (coll. N)   délamol
bird of paradise (N)   beni
bivouac (N)   khaü
bivouac, small (N)   dokhon
black (ADJ)   khofi(lun)
Blith's hornbill (N)   khawil
to block (up) (VB)   aülo, yefo(lo),
  dilmo, yafo
blood (N)   büngga, khafun, mamüngga
to blow (wind) (VB)   fup lu; (trans.
  VB)   bepé, fumo
blunt (ADJ)   peli
body (N)   lokhül
boggy soil (N)   bayom
bone (N)   khokhukh, kholol
bottom (body part) (N)   bebil
bottom (of an object) (N)   gul
bottom beam (N)   lal
bow (N)   ati, atun, bai, dokhul
bow and arrows (N)   ati-khayo
boy (son) (N)   abül; (youngster)
  (N)   khofémanop
brains (N)   lokhul
branch (tree) (N)   dedamol
brave (ADJ)   lesukh
bread (N)   laléo-ndaü
breadfruit (Artocarpus) (N)   yawol
to break (VB)   bamo(lmo), lai, lai(l)mo,
  laifo
to break down (VB)   kholükhmo
to break loose (VB)   aümo, laimofo
breast (female) (N)   am
breastbone (N)   banggolol
breast milk (N)   am gü
bridge (N)   alül
bright (ADJ)   khelép, manol
to bring (VB)   bando, folapé
to bring forth (VB)   laifu
brink (N)   ano
brother's wife (N)   khaimokh
brow (N)   lulkholol
brownheaded crow (N)   khejom
to brush (VB)   kheli(l)mekho
to build (VB)   ali, lai
to bump against (VB)   nggaümo
bunch (N)   lamon, tamon
to burn (VB)   do, domo

to burn down (VB)   ülfo
burn scars (*body decoration*)
  (N)   nggawalalun
to bury (VB)   laimekho, mélaimekho
busy (ADJ)   lubul
to buy (VB)   abolo
by means of (NREL)   debüf
by way of (NREL)   debüf

C
calendar (N)   saündal
to call (VB)   dodépo, doleli
to call (*a pig*) (VB)   bamo; (*mention*)
  (VB)   filo
to care (VB)   bémo, khendé(mo)
to carry on the back (VB)   abi, akéamo
to carry out (VB)   lekheli
cassava (N)   layop
cassowary (N)   küal, sandum, sanip
cassowary legbone (N)   yal
Casuarina equiaetifolia (N)   kafüol
to catch; get hold of (VB)   dilmekho,
  béolfo
cause (VB)   lailo
centipede (*species*) (N)   bebal, lél
central pole (N)   khokhül
charcoal (N)   khofé
to chase (VB)   abokhai, abolai(mo),
  wakhumekho
cheek (N)   manggum
cheekbone (N)   manggumkholol
chest (N)   ban, manop
child (N)   mbam, (PL: mambün)
Citak (*tribe, people*) (N)   Banam
to claim recompensation (VB)   gufu,
  nèkhmo
clan territory (N)   bolüp, lamol
clan (N)   gun, gunop
to clean (VB)   manop
to clean; cleanse (VB)   füomo, manopo
clear (ADJ)   dalun, dialun, khelép
to clear (*as a garden*) (VB)   aüfo,
  naüfahüomo, afolaü
to clear a path by dancing
  (VB)   olaibo, oldintai
clearing (N)   umbon(tafekho), mbelüp
to cleave (VB)   domo, khakheli(mo),
  khelèl
clever (ADJ)   dalun, dialun, khup
close (ADV)   khalu

to close (VB)   aülo, damo, dilmo, yafo,
  yefo-(lo)
clothing (*Western style*) (N)   laléo-khal
cloud (N)   dép, déptemül, lemül
coccyx (N)   yakhonggolol
cockatoo, white (N)   kèkèkh
cockroach (N)   labul
coconut (N)   mbiyon
coconut tree (N)   mbiyon
cold (ADJ)   khagil
to collect (VB)   gübo(lmo)
to collide (VB)   nggaümo
Colocasia (N)   simbelu
column (*of ants*) (N)   khül
comb (N)   dayun
to come (VB)   lai, lelé-
to come and go (VB)   khobo
to come together (VB)   gübo(lmo),
  güboli, keliokhmo
to come to its end (VB)   ülfo
to command (VB)   lanumo
compassionate (ADJ)   bembi, finop
conscious (ADJ)   khafén
to construct (VB)   ali
to consume food (VB)   langgamo
container (N)   mbalop
contented (ADJ)   leléal
continuous (ADJ)   wé
to control oneself (VB)   atikilelo,
  baukilelo
corpse (N)   lokhül
cough (N)   bokokh
to cough (VB)   lemu
to count (VB)   lamo
cover (N)   debap
to cover (VB)   yabibo, aülo, füolo
covetous (ADJ)   momul
coward (N)   goloni
to crack (N/ONOMAT)   dediop, kiya,
  pa, pükh
to crawl (VB)   dakhaméumo
crispy sago marrow (N)   sél
crocodile (N)   semail
crooked (ADJ)   falé
to cross (VB)   lu, tu
cross beam (N)   belebél
cross female child (N)   salal
cross male child (N)   sabül
crowbar (*for jerking sago trunks open*)
  (N)   dulekhil

crown (*of head*) (N) khabéan; (*of tree*)
(N) dül
to cry (VB) èkhmo, füp-, ülelo, yamo
cucumber (*species*) (N) awam, lamül, ukh
to cut (VB) di, dilmo, lafi(l), ülmo
to cut down (VB) khelélmekho, ü(l)
to cut off (VB) di

D

dagger (*made of cassowary legbone*)
(N) yal
to dance (*different fashions*)
(VB) gümo, külomo, khasam, lamé,
palu-
dark (ADJ) gülelo, khofi(lun)
daughter (N) lal
daughter's husband (N) lalum
day (N) alüp, leful
day before yesterday (N) khomülepé,
khakhuda khopé
dead (ADJ) khomilo
to decrease (VB) lemilé
deep (*place in river*) (N) makhol
to defend (VB) alo, dimo
to defy (VB) klèkhmo
delicious (ADJ) sikh
demon (N) laléo
to deny (VB) baniaupelu
to depart (VB) gilfo; (go away)
(VB) lokhté
descent (N) laibolekha
desiring (ADJ) momul
destruction of the universe
(N) wolamaman
to die down (fire) (VB) lemilé
different (ADJ) yani, yanisani
to dig (VB) yakhü
dirt (N) lelua, ninggün
dirty (ADJ) banggelèkh, lembul
to disappear (VB) gilfo, ülfo
discarded (ADJ) khokhün, lakhup,
takhul
discontented (ADJ) nggul, wakhai
to dispense (VB) banté/bante-,
mbalamo
to distribute (VB) banté/bante-, mbalamo
to divide (VB) banté/bante-, mbalamo
to do (VB) mo, amo
to do again (VB) wokhelimekho
to do in common (VB) khamilmo

to do nothing (VB) nanafo
to do well (VB) ndakhimo
to do with all (VB) khamilmo
dog (N) khendép, méan, muman,
mumengga
dog teeth (N) banggil
domesticated pig (N) belüfekha
dominating (ADJ) ga
don't! (NEG.IMP) belén, domenè
door (N) abüokh
dot (N) nggawalalun
dots at shield margins (N) lulop
down (there) (ADV) khaüp, yaüp, yaüap
downstream (there) (ADV) khosübo(l),
sübap, süfap, yaüap, yaüp
drawing (N) wol(iol)
dream (N) alenul
to drink (VB) mi
to drown (VB) apifu, bekhelilé, ülo
dry sago leaves (N) mangga
dugout canoe (N) alèp, kélo
dull (ADJ) dofu, dofusofu
dumb (ADJ) énonomekho
dust (N) bulanom

E

each (NREL) kholop
each of them (ADJ) khaifosaifo
each other (NREL) kholokholop
ear (N) daun, khotokhal, khotop
early in the morning (ADV) debünenul
earth (N) mé
to eat (VB) lé(ndé/nté), fonolé,
langgamo, nolé
edge (N) amin, ano
egg (N) lokhesukh
eight (NUM) bonggup, lakha
elbow (N) lakha, bonggup
elder brother (N) afé
elder sister (N) aw
eleven (NUM) khomofekholol
end (N) bon, daüm, lefu, nggaüm
enemy (N) khokhukhanop, khololanop
to enter (VB) lu, tu
entrance (N) abüokh
envy (N) kelil
to erase (VB) gipo
to exchange (VB) abolo, aboümo
exhausted (*after a feast*)
(ADJ) dayabél, khabél

to expel (VB)   abolai(mo), damiabo
expressly (ADV)   bimbolop
extent (N)   bün
eye (N)   lul, lulop
eyelid (N)   lulkhal

F
face (N)   lulgelip
fairy wren (N)   dèkhlèkhalé
to fall (VB)   feli
falsehood (N)   lemakhal, lilol
familiar with (ADJ)   kemél
family (N)   gun, gunop, lambil, yanogun
far; far away (ADV)   lekhingga
fat (N)   yabén
father (N)   até
father-in-law (N)   ban
father's sister (N)   mul
father's sister's husband (N)   sop
feather(s) (N)   daya
feces (N)   lelua, ol(ekhi)
feel hurt (ADJ)   lép
female (N)   lal
festival place (N)   gil
festival song (N)   bonanam
fibres (N)   gebül; (sago palm) for
   making skirts (N)   sékh
fierce (ADJ)   khén
fiery (ADJ)   alénap
to fight (VB)   afü
to fill (VB)   mekho
filter in smoking pipe (N)   fiop
fine (ADJ)   sikh
finger(s) (N)   mélol
fingernail (N)   singga
to finish(ed) (VB)   lefulmekho, lekheli,
   melé, daüm, nggaüm, lefu, lefaf
fire (N)   alun, melil, menil
firefly (N)   belil
fire guard (at sago grub festival)
   (N)   milon
fireplace (N)   alun, melibol
firewood (N)   melil
first (ADV)   alüm
firstborn (N)   alop
fish (N)   khelé
fishhook (N)   kuasél
fishing basket (N)   khanél
fish (species) (N)   abun, khonum,
   khayal, lefül, lup, mandum

five (NUM)   wayo
to flash (VB)   minamo
flesh (N)   khal, nop
flexible (ADJ)   fayup
to flirt (VB)   klèkhmo, lembémo
floating away (ADJ)   fakh(tenè)
floor (N)   bülan
floor-beam (N)   lal
floor platform (N)   ülekhal
flower (N)   khél
fly (N)   lotup
to fly (VB)   bedi(fo)
fly (species) (N)   molüp
flying fox (N)   yemül
to fold (VB)   laimanggü
folktale(s) (N)   wakhatum
to follow (VB)   labodi
food (N)   lungga
food wrapped in leaves (N)   lawa
foolish (ADJ)   dofu
foot (N)   bél, bélol, bélum, si(si)
footprint (N)   bétom
for (NREL)   -lekhé- (n), -tekhé- (n)
forearm (N)   lafol
forehead (N)   lokhul
forehead decoration (N)   silup
forepaw (N)   khamon, mél
forest (N)   lop
to forget (VB)   énontelo
former (ADJ)   lakhul, mül(ekha), takhul
four (NUM)   wayafül
fresh (ADJ)   sol
friend (N)   nggé, nokho
friends (N)   mayokh
frog (N)   khugol
from (LOC)   -fosü, -sü
front(side) (NREL)   mülgop, mül(ekha)
frontal bone (N)   lokhulkholol
fruit (N)   op
fruits (N)   duop

G
gall-bladder (N)   melun
game (food) (N)   lungga
garden (N)   yasim
garden products (N)   khokhüneni
to gather together (VB)   keliokhmo,
   lebé, tebé
to get (VB)   fo, fu
to get hold of (VB)   ati(lo), lepélo

to get out (VB)   di, monggo(fo)
to get up (VB)   melu
girl (N)   menél
to give (VB)   fédo
glad (ADJ)   khanap, leléal
to go (VB)   gelamo, geli, khai, khonai
to go away (VB)   gelilfo, gilfo, lokhté
to go down (VB)   ai, nai, wai, wailo
to go fast (VB)   gelümo
gone (ADJ)   ütelo
good (ADJ)   khup, manop
good for nothing (ADJ)   khalokh
goods (N)   lolol, misafi, üop
to go out (VB)   ai, nai, wai
Goura cristata (N)   aülém
grandchild (N)   khafun
grandfather (N)   andüop
great-grandchild (N)   yebom
great-grandparent (N)   yebom
grandmother (N)   makh
grass (N)   gogelén
grass (*species*) (N)   khakhlakh
grave (N)   mébol
to graze (VB)   dolmekho, gelükhmo,
   kheli(l)mekho
grease (N)   yabén
great (ADJ)   -talé, lalé, khonggekél,
   khonggél
great water surrounding the world
   (N)   méanmaél
grinder (N)   anolebil
to grip (VB)   dilmekho
groin (N)   khalan
ground (N)   fium
group (*relatives*) (N)   gun, yanogun;
   (*close relatives*) (N)   lambil
to grow (VB)   melu
to grunt (VB)   fakhüo
guest (N)   khuwolanop

H
hair (N)   mukh
hair decoration (N)   lamunalé
halfway (ADV)   walüp(i)
hand (N)   khamon, mél, mélol
handle (N)   khami, mül, wakhél
handsome (ADJ)   lelida, telida
to hang (VB)   bendé-, benggé-
happy (ADJ)   khanap, leléal
hard (ADJ)   khokhukh

hard object (N)   kholol, khokhukh
to harm someone (VB)   yakhomo
harsh (ADJ)   ndüni
to hatch (VB)   lai
to have sex (VB)   gomo
he (PERS)   ye, yu(p)
head (N)   gegüp, khabéan, lokhul
headache (N)   khabéantokhul,
   lokhutokhul
head of tobacco pipe (N)   bon
to heal (VB)   manopo
healthy (ADJ)   khil
to hear (VB)   dai
heart (N)   debop
heat (N)   mamün
to heat (VB)   alü, indo
heavy (ADJ)   baul, ga, lüp
help (N)   ndakhimon
to help (VB)   gadiakhai, ndakhimo
her (PERS)   y-/yV-
here (ADV)   alip, dip, i(p), ndalip,
   ndi(p), ye-
to hew out (VB)   lamükh, tamükh
hidden place (N)   bajam
to hide (VB)   bai(l)mo, laimekho
higher grounds (N)   leléf/lelép
hill (N)   fium
his (POSS)   y-/yV-
to hit (VB)   ülmekho, ülmo, baükhmo,
   bokh, bümo, gakholi, gakhomo, ü(l)
to hit with nettles (*magic cure*)
   (VB)   yalomo
to hold (VB)   ati(lo)
hole (N)   bol, bu
honey (N)   fofiyu
honey eater (*species*) (N) béal
hospitable (ADJ)   bandakh
hot (ADJ)   khokh
house (N)   khaim, khaü, kheyop
to hunt (VB)   abokhai, abolai(mo), fuai,
   gawakhomo, wakhumekho
husband (N)   um, wafil, yalén, yealé
husband's brother (N)   khaimon
husband's father (N)   mbolop

I
I (PERS)   ne, nu(p)
iguana (N)   buél; (*species*) (N)   fiop,
   bajom, gua, khalfap
ill (ADJ)   lép, walukh

illegal/ly (ADJ)   bimbolop, naném
illicit/ly (ADJ)   naném
image (N)   maf
in (CIRCUM/LOC)   -an, -la, -pé- (n), -ta, -fekho
increase (ADV)   gamo
index finger (N)   wayafül
to indicate (VB)   mél endü
indirect talk (N)   balénaup
individual (N)   imban
Indonesian language (N)   laléo-aup
inefficient (ADJ)   lembul
inexperienced (ADJ)   bindom
infected wound (N)   lelül
infection (N)   lelül
to inform (VB)   damo
in former times, in the past
   (ADV)   mülalüp, mülekhufefè
inhospitable (ADJ)   gemélalé, ndüni
in order (ADV)   kül, manop
in order to (NREL)   -lekhé(n), -tekhé(n)
inside, interior (N)   khakho, khau(p)
to interrogate (VB)   laifo
intestines (N)   fimelon, khul
in vain (ADV)   bimbolop, dambelüm,
   khalasela
to invoke (VB)   doleli
ironwood (N)   fusa
island (N)   khandul
it (IMPERS)   ye, yu(p)
it is not (NEG)   khésekhan, manda
itching (ADJ)   lénté
its (POSS)   y-/yV-
it's a pity! (EXCLM)   amonggu

J
Jew's harp (N)   kombéop
to join (VB)   labodi
joke (N)   aubaul
to jump (VB)   füboli
jungle (N)   lop
jut out (VB)   fakhbéyokhofu

K
to keep (VB)   ati(lo)
kidney (N)   gailop
to kill (VB)   khedi/khedé, ü(l), ülfo,
   ülmo
knee (N)   gabün

to knock over (VB)   lafimekho
to know (VB)   daibo
Kombai (people, tribe) (N)   Aim
Korowai (people, tribe) (N)   Kolufo
Korowai language (N)   Kolufaup,
   Kolufomahüon

L
lacking (ADJ)   di
lake (N)   difon
land of the dead (N)   bolüplefupé
landing stage (N)   gikh
language (N)   aup, mahüon
large (ADJ)   -talé, lalé, khonggekél,
   khonggél
last born (N)   khaja, mefekha
last piece of baked lump of sago
   (N)   mup
to laugh (VB)   lesifu
to lay (VB)   ibo
lazy (ADJ)   felép, nggawél
leaf (N)   mukh
leaf stem (N)   banibol, khejo
leaf stem container (N)   lepun
to leap (VB)   füboli
leaves (N)   lul
leech (N)   layo
left (ADJ)   bindom, wakhan
leg (N)   bél, khobül, si(si)
lid (N)   debap
lie (N)   khofélaup, lemakhal, lilol
light (ADJ)   dalun, khokholun, manol,
   walun
light (ADJ)   fotokh
lightning (N)   fakhbéakh
like (ADJ)   dada, kül
to listen to (VB)   dai
little (ADJ)   hièn-, -tena
little finger (N)   senan
to live (VB)   bo, bai/ba-, bau, khai
liver (N)   üm
lizard (species) (N)   buom, bembüo(kh),
   lafiyol, lol, lenan, mafüm
to load (VB)   mekho
locust (species) (N)   danggup, bakhuom
long (ADJ)   dal, nggolo(lalé)
longing (ADJ)   momul
longing for (ADJ)   lép
long grass (N)   kamèn; (species)
   (N)   fiyo

to look (at) (VB)   imo
to look for (VB)   bilaimo, bi-
to loosen (VB)   melé
louse (N)   meli
loving (ADJ)   bembi, finop
lower end (N)   siop
lower jaw (N)   manggumbalop
lower teeth (N)   bésamtebil
luggage (N)   lolol, misafi
lung (N)   falip

M
MAF (Mission Aviation Fellowship)
   (N)   Map
mafom snake (N)   mafom
magic arrow (N)   yumfayan,
   yenalfayan
magic arrow carving (N)   fayan
magic defense arrows (N)   khayolamol
magic power (N)   ndafun, khendil
magic trance (N)   sèip
maiden (N)   menél
to make (VB)   demi(l)mekho, mo,
   lakhebé, takhebé
to make fun (VB)   khèkh-
to make hissing sound with the lips
   (VB)   düdümté
to make noise (VB)   kelelükhmo
to make round (VB)   baüpo
male adult (N)   wafil
male youth (N)   khofémanop
man (N)   abül
mana (N)   ndafun
management (N)   fundam
many (ADJ)   fiüm, ganggail, tonggo
to march in a row, column (*ants*)
   (VB)   dokhemémo, khülekhelimo
to marry (VB)   defol fo
marsupial (*species*)
   (N)   amékhesimdop, füon
matches (N)   laléo-menil
meaning (N)   khokhu
meat (N)   khal, nop
to meet (VB)   fulo, gübo(lmo), kho(l)fu,
   khofe, kholmo, lepé
member (N)   imban
menstruation (N)   wolop
to mention (VB)   filo, filolai
message (N)   üop
middle (NREL)   khakho

middle finger (N)   pingg(ul)up
mirror (N)   mafakh
to mix (with) (VB)   lé khomo, kho(l)fu,
   khofe
to moisten (VB)   lülmo
moisture (N)   gü
moon (N)   alümekhon, wakhol
mosquito (N)   letün
mother (N)   ni, niokh
mother's brother (N)   mom
mountains (N)   fanip
mouse (N)   duo
moustached tree swift (N)   abul
mouth (N)   bonggol, bontebil,
   khakholop, lalobop
mouth of river (N)   makhol
to move (VB)   mé-, melé
to move down (VB)   ai, wai, nai
to move on and on (VB)   gelèkh-,
   laopo
to move up (VB)   melu, lu, tu
much (ADJ)   fiüm, ganggail, tonggo
mucus (N)   khim
mud (N)   balüm
mud crab (*species*) (N)   bayulo,
   kulekham, khomulo
mute (ADJ)   énonomekho
my (POSS)   n-/nV-
myth (N)   lamolaup, wolaup
mythical fish(es) (N)   ndewé

N
naked (ADJ)   aifogum
name (N)   fi
narrow (ADJ)   dékh
nasal cavity (N)   khimakhmbalop
naughty (ADJ)   dadam, khalokh
navel (N)   manütul
near (ADV)   khalu
neck (N)   balebol, khomofekholol
necklace (N)   khomul
necklace made of pig tusk (N)   bésam
nephew (N)   sabül
nest (N)   amül
nettle (N)   yalün
to neutralise bad magic
   (VB)   kholü(kh)-
new (ADJ)   sol
next (ADV)   mesé, mesi(p), sé, amodo,
   khenè

next month (ADV)   alümon
nibung tree (*species*) (N)   lambil, laf,
  gél
nice (ADJ)   lelida, telida
niece (N)   salal
night (N)   gülnanggaup
nine (NUM)   labul
nipple (N)   antenül
no; not (NEG)   -da, b-/bV-, fano,
  khésekhan, mafém, manda
nose (N)   gelip
nose bone (N)   gelifekholol
nose decoration of pig tusk (N)   yagua,
  lékh
nostril(s) (N)   gelibol, gelitop
not angry anymore (ADJ)   félelo
not willing (ADJ)   felép, nggawél
nothing (ADJ)   mafém
now (ADV)   imonè

O

oar (N)   igo, walü(p)
to obey (VB)   dai
oblong slice of meat (N)   dén
oh, boy! (EXCLM)   khofélapa
oh, dear! (EXCLM)   mayokh
oh, yes (AFFIRM)   bail
oily layer that covers swampy water
  (N)   süom
old (man) (N)   nggél
older brother (N)   afé
older people (N)   mbolombolop,
  yaléyalén
older sister (N)   aw
old lady (N)   lebakhop
old man (N)   mbolop, yalén
on (CIRCUM   -fekho, -la, -pé(n), ta
on top of (NREL)   dain
Oncosperma filamentosum (N)   betél
one (NUM)   lidop, senan
one; a (INDEF)   -fekha
only (ADV)   -lanukh, -tanukh, apa,
  mofu
to open (VB)   dami(l)mo, di, lakhefi,
  takhefi
opening (N)   ol
or (DISJ)   -tè,—lè
organizer(s) of a sago grub festival
  (N)   giolmanop
other (ADJ)   yani, yanisani

our (POSS)   nokhu-
out of order (ADJ)   maman
outer layer of grilled lump of sago
  (N)   abéakh
over (LOC)   khip; (*gone*) (ADJ)   ütelo

P

package; packet (N)   lamon, tamon,
  wakhum
pale blue (ADJ)   binodan
palm (N)   dap
Pandanus fruit (N)   laün, mahüankho
panel (N)   damon
parallel (ADJ)   lokhmekho
parents (N)   ni-até, mbolombolop
to pass (VB)   baimekho, baimo
passionate (ADJ)   alénap
patriclan (N)   yanogun
pelvis bone (N)   dénufekholol
penis (N)   dul
penis gourd (N)   mbayap
penis gourd made of the beak of the
  Blith's Hornbill (N)   khawisip
people (N)   -anop, yanop
people of former times (N)   mülanop
perhaps (ADV)   funèp
period (N)   alüp, ul
person (N)   -anop, imban, yanop
to pick (VB)   lebé, tebé; (*lice*)
  (VB)   (meli) yabo
picture (N)   maf, wol(iol)
piece of wood (N)   donggop, bani,
  nggonggop
to pierce (VB)   baosamo
pig (N)   gol, wan(gga)
pillar (N)   fénop
pipe (N)   agél
pitfall (N)   bu
place (N)   bolüp, lamol, lop, mbalop,
  top
place for storing food (N)   banibol
plain (ADJ)   khelép
to plant (VB)   ao
platform (N)   bülan
to play (VB)   gümo, lamé
pleasantry (N)   aubaul
pleased (ADJ)   khanap, leléal
Plotosus canius (N)   palua
pointed objects (N)   antabun
pointed shell (N)   kuasél

to point to (VB)   mél endü
poisonous snake (N)   lakh
pole (N)   fénop
Ponnetia pinniata (**matoa**) (N)   béan
possible (ADJ)   bail
possibly (ADV)   funèp
to pound (*sago*) (VB)   lamü
to pour (VB)   lakheli-
pregnant (ADJ)   khondulmengga
to prepare and serve (VB)   mesendipo
to press; knead (VB)   geli(mo)
pretty (ADJ)   lelida, telida
probably (ADV)   funèp
to produce (VB)   laifu
prohibition (N)   ayul(ekha), masekha
prolonged (ADJ)   énon
to promise (*give something*) (VB)   aüso
pubic hair (N)   benénmukh
to pull (VB)   dépo-, duobo
to pull out (VB)   di
pupil and iris (*eye*) (N)   khülul
to push (VB)   nggenggimekho
to push forward (VB)   bekhémo,
   nggelü
pushing against (ADJ)   sim
to put (VB)   fu
to put into (VB)   duo, ao, mekho,
   dimekho
to put on (VB)   dimekho

Q
to quarrel (VB)   lebidi
to question (VB)   laifo
quick/ly (ADV)   diof, menè(l), mündiop
quicktempered (ADJ)   alénap

R
rack (N)   büakh
rack for sago(-grub) storage (N)   balin
rain (N)   maun
rainbow (N)   anol
to raise (*pigs, dogs*) (VB)   khendé(mo)
rapid (N)   aül
rattan rope (N)   yebun
rattan shingles (N)   lonoptabül
razor blade (N)   fikh
really (AFFIRM)   bail
really; very (INTNS)   -ayan, khayan
realm of the dead (N)   bolüplefupé
to reciprocate (VB)   kholopamo

to recite (VB)   filolai
**recompensation for application of
   harmful magic** (N)   bün
to recompense (VB)   fudamo,
   kholofudamo
red (ADJ)   khafümengga
red soil (N)   khafüm
reflected image (N)   mafakh
refusing (ADJ)   aündan
reliable (ADJ)   mofekhup
remains of abandoned festival bivouac
   (N)   gitakhul
to renounce (VB)   yakhatimekho
to repay (VB)   fudamo
repeatedly (ADV)   mesendip
to replace (VB)   kholofudamo
to resist (VB)   yakhatimekho
respected male person (N)   -alé, yalén
to resurrect (VB)   melu
to return (VB)   kembalimo,
   wokhelimekho
rib (*leaf*) (N)   kailon; (*body*)
   (N)   menakholol
ribs of sago leaves (N)   bunggul
right (*good*) (ADJ)   godakh, khup, kül,
   manop
right (*direction*) (ADJ)   khup
ring finger (N)   senanafül
ripe (ADJ)   khayo
river (N)   akh, maél, maun
river-food (*fish*) (N)   maun langga/
   tangga
road (N)   debülop, debüf
to roar (*fire*) (VB)   gelelümo
rock (N)   bil, ilol, khandun, lawa
rodent (N)   duo
rodent (*species*) (N)   khayal, laul
roll (N)   yafé, yafun
roof (N)   lél
roof ridge (N)   ün
root (N)   dedil, letép
root end (N)   sip
to root out (VB)   damo
rope (*rattan*) (N)   nan, yebun
rotten (ADJ)   nén
rough (ADJ)   baul
to row (VB)   alimo
to rub; smear (VB)   béa(l)mo, lülmo
to rumble (*thunder*) (VB)   balalmo
to run (VB)   demi(l-), gelümo

S

Saccharum edule (N)   bu, godunalé
sacred fence in ceremonial sago grub festival (N)   khandindamon
sacredness (N)   khandin
sacred place (N)   wotop
sago (*species*) (N)   khakhül, khum, lé, milon, mayum, bayol, amo, balép, bandüp, ganim, lahial
sago bag (N)   khombül
sago beetle (*Scarabaeidae* spp.) (N)   khip
sago grub (N)   gèkh, non
sago grub festival (N)   gil
sago leafstem (*panel*) (N)   bani, inggenun, khejo
sago pounding stick (N)   yafikh
sago, sago tree (N)   kho, khosül, naumatélekha, ndaü
sago tree marrow (N)   aun
sago washing construction (N)   khejo, inggenun
salamander (N)   mafüm
same (ADJ)   dada, kükül
sand (N)   nenim
to say (VB)   di
scabies (N)   ap, khambap
scale (*shrimp*) (N)   dakh, khoyo
scandalised (ADJ)   khatakh
sclera (N)   khayolul
to scoop (VB)   alimo
scrotum (N)   lokhesukhop
to seal up (VB)   banggenénmekho
to search (VB)   bilaimekho, bilaimo
season (N)   ul
second and following layer of a baked lump of sago (N)   gaul
secret (N)   ayul(ekha), masekha
secretly (ADJ)   naném
to see (VB)   imo
self (REL)   -pa(n)
to sell (VB)   aboümo
to send (VB)   fofu
to set (VB)   fu; (*sun*) (VB)   munggofo
to set foot on (VB)   aloli
seven (NUM)   lafol
shade; shadow (N)   maf
shadow (N)   khüfolun
to share (VB)   banté/bante-, mbalamo
sharp; sharpened (ADJ)   fül

sharp objects (N)   antabun
she (PERS)   ye, yu(p)
sheatfish (*species*) (N)   dül, gum, khalom, lüma
shell (N)   agiop
shell money (*string*) (N)   malin, khul, khül
shield (N)   wolumon
to shine (VB)   minamo
shining (ADJ)   dialun
to shoot (VB)   duo, lakhato(l)mo, lebükh, ülmekho
short (ADJ)   gembenul, genul, gun
shoulder (N)   main
to shout (VB)   ülelo
to show (VB)   yaliaémo, yalikhomo
shrieking (ADJ)   lelèmbelè
shrimp (*species*) (N)   betül, abém, khakhü, khakhu, mahüokh
to shrug (VB)   gatakhmo
shuddering (ADJ)   sèip
to shut (VB)   lepélo
sick (ADJ)   lép, walukh
side (N)   ano, baul, mén, ün; (*building*) (N)   léam; (*upper chest*) (N)   falép
silent/ly (ADV)   naném
silhouette (N)   maf
similar (ADJ)   dada, kükül
to splutter with one's lips (VB)   baniaupelu
sinus (N)   khimakhmbalop
to sit (VB)   bo, babo/beba-, bai/ba-, khami
situation (N)   udediop
six (NUM)   gédun
skilled in (ADJ)   kemél, khup
skin (N)   khal
skinny (ADJ)   afop
skirt (N)   sékh
sky (N)   dali, dalibün, khul, khulbün
to slaughter (VB)   bumo
to sleep (VB)   é(bo), élo, ibo, ye
-sleepy (ADJ)   lenup, lenutép
slightly (ADV)   mamap
slippery (ADJ)   fép
slope (N)   bakhup, banggum
slow (ADJ)   anggokh
small (ADJ)   hièn, -lena
small piece of wood (N)   mafial, khakho, lenggotena

small palm tree (N)   nggén
to smear (VB)   béa(l)mo, lülmo
to smell (VB)   sumo
to smile (VB)   bolmumu
Sminthopsis rufigenis (N)   khail
smoke (N)   lemül, melitemül, temül
smoking rack (N)   sim
smooth (ADJ)   fép
snake (N)   anol, émol, yafil; *(species)*
  gul, malan
to sneeze (VB)   lambimatimo
some . . . other(s) (INDEF)   lefu . . . lefu
son (N)   abül (PL mambün)
son's wife (N)   nanü
soot (N)   khofé
sort of (NREL)   khokha
soul (N)   yanopkhayan (*lit.* 'the very
  person')
sound (N)   aup
sound of inflaming (ONOM)   baka
sound of khejom bird
  (ONOM)   pipe(mo)
space under the house (N)   belüp
spar (N)   donggop, dubaüm
to speak (VB)   di, u(mo)
to speak inside (*oneself*)
  (VB)   néakhméokh
-spear (N)   mal
speechless (ADJ)   énonomekho
sperm (N)   dekheté(akh)
spicy (ADJ)   khokh
spirit (N)   laléo
spittle (N)   mekhesim
splashing (*sound*) (ONOM)   gelelukh-
to split (VB)   domo, khakheli(mo),
  khelèl
to squat (VB)   bebéntebo
to squeak (VB)   èkhmo
to stab (VB)   duo
stairs (N)   yafin, gawil
to stand (VB)   alo, aloli
star (N)   belil
to start (VB)   ditaimekho, solamo,
  solditai-
to start from sleep (VB)   gebelipekho
to stay (VB)   bo, bai/ba-, bau, khai,
  khami
steel wire (N)   besi
stem (N)   kholol
stepbrother (N)   aibum

to stew (*with leaves*) (VB)   lakhi(l)mo,
  khandü, yamolomo, duo; with hot
  stones in leaf packages (VB)   lakhup
  duo
stick for picking breadfruits
  (N)   manian
stiff (of penis erectus) (ADJ)   melo
still (ADV)   khotu(l)
stone (N)   bil, ilol, khandun, lakhup,
  lawa
stone axe (N)   khul
storm (N)   fup
story (N)   aup, mahüon
straight (ADJ)   godakh
stream (N)   bün
strength (N)   kelil
stretch (N)   bün
to strike (VB)   baükhmo, bokh, bümo,
  gakholi, gakhomo
string (N)   khomul
strong (ADJ)   bebén, ga, khil,
  khokhukh, letél
to struggle (VB)   afü
stupid (ADJ)   dofu, énonomekho
to suck (VB)   dépo-; (sweets)
  (VB)   mokukh
suddenly (ADV)   mündiop
to suffer (VB)   afü, lép
suffering from malaria fevers
  (ADJ)   amul
sugarcane (N)   bahüom, baliam
sun (N)   lup, mamün
supple (ADJ)   fayup
swamp (N)   faül, ndemop, waliop
sweat (N)   khelünakh, khün
sweet potato (N)   dolom, khau
to swim (VB)   dadü
swollen (ADJ)   bi
symbol (N)   wol(iol)

T
taboo (N)   ayul(ekha), masekha
tail (N)   khendép
tainted (ADJ)   nén
to take (VB)   ati(lo), fo
to take rest (VB)   lüfekhemi
to take a walk (VB)   kholmo,
  kholmbekho
talk (N)   aup
to talk (VB)   di, u(mo)

tall (ADJ)   lekhal, nggolo(lalé)
to tear open (VB)   demé
teasing (ADJ)   bu
to tell (VB)   di, u(mo)
to tell lies (VB)   lilomo
ten (NUM)   main
to terminate (VB)   khedi/khedé,
    lefulmekho
testicles (N)   lokhesukhop
that (DEICT)   -fap, a-, kho-, khop,
    khosükhop, wa(p), wof-
the one in between (NREL)   alüp
their (POSS)   yekhené-
them (PERS)   yekhené-
there (LOC)   khosükhop; kho(p); -a(p),
    dali(p), khe-, wa(p)
they (PERS)   yekhené- (PL)
thin (ADJ)   afop, delap, fayup
thing (N)   fundam, lolol, misafi, üop
to think (VB)   khul duo, fimelon duo,
    néakhméokh-
thirteen (NUM)   khabéan
this (DEICT)   alip, dip, i(p), ndalip, ndi(p)
thorn (N)   aün
thorny tree branches and lianas
    (N)   wanum
thoroughly (ADV)   laimekho
three (NUM)   pinggup, pinggulup
through (CIRCUM)   -fosü, -sü
throw away (VB)   pükhmo
thumb (N)   wayo
thus (DEICT)   a-, wa(p), wof-,
    amomengga
to tie up (VB)   yame-, lamé, lamélo
time (N)   khup, alüp, lefül, ul
tired (ADJ)   bu, khabél
tissue (N)   gebül
to (CIRCUM)   -an, ma
tobacco (N)   dépon, saukh, sü
tobacco pipe (N)   déponagél,
    folomonagél, süagél
together (ADV)   kho(l)fu, lelip,
    walelélekhu
tongue (N)   léf
tooth (N)   lebil
torch (N)   wél
Torrent lark (N)   kham
tortoise (species) (N)   abéap, bif, wayo
to totter (VB)   khebé
to touch with something (VB)   lamoda-

to transform (VB)   khomi
to transgress (VB)   baimekho, baimo
trap (for catching big game) (N)   al
to travel (VB)   gelümo, khai
to treat with magic (VB)   kholü(kh)-
tree (N)   du; (species) lam, yakhuol,
    maselop, wanum, molun, wotuwo,
    yambim; daél, baüm, fil, baun, fofo,
    dal, ful, kaél, lanol
tree bark fibers (N)   khol
treebark-cloth (N)   féndon
treehouse (N)   khaim
tree stem (N)   banggo
true (ADJ)   mofekhup
trunk (N)   du, lekhül
to try to (VB)   - b-/be-
tube (N)   agél
to turn (VB)   afé, fefé,
    wokhelimekho
to turn turtle (VB)   wémekho
twelve (NUM)   khotokhal
two (NUM)   pol, senanafül
twofold (ADJ)   gugukh

U
ugly (ADJ)   lembul
ulcer (N)   gun, khabül, langgéntop, lefu
unclear (ADJ)   gugukh
unconscious (ADJ)   khomilo
under (NREL)   akhabop
underneath (ADJ)   lakhatop
to unfasten (VB)   lekheli
to unite (VB)   kho(l)fu, khofe
universe (N)   lamol, wola
to unload (VB)   monggo(fo)
until (CIRCUM)   -fekho
upper arm muscles (N)   labunop
upperarm (N)   labul
upper teeth (N)   dülebil
upriver, upstream (ADV)   gülap,
    gülo(l), khülo(l)
to urinate (VB)   dulalü
urine (N)   dulakh
us (PERS)   nokhu(p)
usual; usually (ADV)   kemél, afé(n)
uterus (N)   mambisi

V
vagina (N)   lil
to vanish (VB)   ülfo

varan (N)   buél
varans and iguanas (N)   buél-bajom
vein (N)   memil
veranda (N)   tambiakh, lambiakh
very (ADV)   -ayan, -khayan, -lalé, -talé,
very good (ADJ)   mup
very stupid (ADJ)   dofusofu
vexing (ADJ)   bu
vicious (ADJ)   aluntalé
violent (ADJ)   bebén
visible (ADJ)   dal, dalun
to visit (VB)   khuwolmo
voice (N)   aup, mahüon
voice of Blith's hornbill (N)   gaga
to vomit (VB)   wakhalimo, yokholmo
vulturine parrot (N)   khabop

W

to wail (VB)   yamo
to walk (VB)   alo, khai
wall (N)   damon
walnut tree (*Canarium commune*)
   (N)   èfop
warning (N)   khakhikh
wasp (N)   khebüm
to watch (VB)   imo, khendé(mo)
water (N)   akh, maél, maun
water mosquito (N)   gènggèmop
way (N)   debüf, debülop
we (PERS)   nokhu(p)
to weep (VB)   èkhmo, yamo
well (N)   fofiyu
well done (ADV)   dobongga
wet (ADJ)   fékh
wet season (N)   Galon, lanéam
what (Q)   mbakha, mbakhamon-
whirlpool in the river (N)   aütop
to whistle (VB)   yolmo
whistling sound (N)   füp-
white (ADJ)   khokholun, manol
who (Q)   yakhofekha, yakhop
why (Q)   anggufa
wide (ADJ)   amüsamün, baul, bautalé,
   faüsesaü
wife (ADJ)   defol
wife's mother('s sister) (ADJ)
   bandakhol

wife's parent (ADJ)   ban
wife's sibling (ADJ)   nabul
wild apple; wild appletree
   (ADJ)   labulop
wild pig (ADJ)   lofekha
wind (ADJ)   fup
winding (*as a river*) (ADJ)   lekhalekha
wing (ADJ)   baul
wire (ADJ)   nan
witch (male) (ADJ)   khakhua
to withdraw (VB)   délfo, difo
without (POSTP)   -alingga
**woman who maintains contacts with
   spirits, medium** (N)   sèipengga
   lal
to wonder (VB)   khalilmekho
wood (N)   du
word (N)   aup, mahüon
worksong (N)   èponaup
world (N)   lamol, wola
wound (N)   yakhasél
to wrap (VB)   alifo
to wrap in leaves (VB)   alifo,
   lamo
wrapping (N)   wakhum
wrestle (VB)   afü
wrist (N)   gédun
wrong (ADJ)   lembul

Y

yell (VB)   füp-, ülelo
yellow banana (N)   fail
yelp (VB)   aüofü, khamu
yes (AFFIRM)   ya, yo, él
yesterday (ADV)   khakhul
you (PL) (PERS)   gekhené(p)
you (SG) (PERS)   gu(p), ge
young (ADJ)   dakh
young girl (N)   menél
younger brother (N)   mofekha
younger sister (N)   modol
youngster (N)   khofél
your (PL) (POSS)   gekhené-
your (SG) (POSS)   g-/gV-

Z

zest for life (N)   kelil

Indonesian Loanwords in Korowai

Indonesian source words are glossed only when semantic changes have occurred.

andu (N)   towel (< Ind. handuk)
anggaman (N)   church service (< Ind. agama 'religion')
atulan (N)   rules; regulations (< Ind. aturan)

bapa (N)   mister; father (< Ind. bapak)
bayarmo (VB)   to pay (< Ind. membayar)
bayu (N)   shirt (< Ind. baju)
bendélekhal (N)   flag; colours (< Ind. bendera)
belanggan (N)   pan (< Ind. belangan)
berdoa (VB)   to pray (< Ind. berdoa)
bési (N)   steel axe; steel wire (<besi 'iron')
betégé (N)   can (< Ind. belek)
bifukh (N)   pisau (< Ind. pisau)
botolo (N)   bottle (< Ind. botol)
bugu/buku (N)   book (< Ind. buku)

mbagu (N)   nail (< Ind. paku)
mbisi (N)   steel axe (< Ind. besi 'steel')

derom, ndelom, ndolom (N)   barrel (< Ind. derum)

èletè (N)   (head of) administrative section of village (< Ind. RT = 'rukun tetangga')

fensin (N)   mononatrium glutaminate (for flavoring food) (< Ind. vetsin)

fènmekho (VB)   participate in general elections (< Ind. mengisi pening; this compound is formed of *fèn* 'badge' + *mekho* 'to put in'; these badges play a role in the registration procedures for the general elections in Indonesia)

gelégagi (N)   saw (< Ind. gergaji)

nggalam (N)   salt (< Ind. garam)
nggulun (N)   teacher; evangelist (< Ind. guru)

ili (N)   helicopter (< Ind. helikopter)
isilamo (VB)   to take a rest (< Ind. istirahat)

kafula (N)   chief; head; leader (< Ind. kepala)
kafulansi (N)   head of government-appointed citizen guards (< Ind. kepala hansip)
kain (N) cloth; rag of cloth (< Ind. kain)
kapolsek (N)   head of police subdistrict (< Ind. abbrev. KaPolSek = Kepala Kepolisian Sektor)
kasè(n) (N)   tape recorder (< Ind. kaset)
kasiamata (N)   glasses (< Ind. kaca mata)
kasiamolo (N)   diving glasses (< Ind. kaca molo)
kasikelajamo (VB)   to set under penal servitude (< Ind. kasih kerja = memberi kerja)
kawamül (N)   wire (< Ind. kawat + Korowai *mül* 'front')
kawas (N)   wire (< Ind. kawat)
kelaja (N)   work; settlement (< Ind. kerja 'work')
kelesas, kertase (N)   sheet of paper (< Ind. kertas)
kolé(menil) (N)   matches (< Ind. korek (api), forms a compound with *menil* 'fire')
kopi, kopimaun (N)   coffee (< Ind. kopi)
kuali (N)   frying pan (< Ind. kuali)
kurusi (N)   chair (< Ind. kursi)
khamba (N)   steel axe (< Ind. kampak)
khambom (N)   village; settlement (< Ind. kampung)

ladiop (N)   radio receiver (< Ind. radio)
lapanggan, lapangga (N)   airstrip (< Ind. lapangan 'field')
lembaya (N)   Christian worship; Christian religious activities (< Ind. sembayang)
lembayakhaü (N)   church building (< Ind. sembayang 'to worship', forms a compound with *khaü* 'bivouac')
limalatu (NUM)   five hundred (< Ind. lima ratus)
loko (N)   cigarettes (< Ind. rokok)
loti (N)   bread (< Ind. roti)

mandelé, mandeli (N)   local health care worker (< Ind. mantri kesehatan)
manggon (N)   cup (< Ind. mangkok)
map (N)   M.A.F. (= Mission Aviation Fellowship)
matiolu (N)   hammer (< Ind. martelo)
minggü (N)   week (< Ind. minggu)
mina, minya (N)   oil; fuel (< Ind. minyak)
minyalampu (N)   generator (< Ind. minyak 'fuel' + lampu 'lamp')

molo, kasiamolo (N)   diving glasses (< Ind. kaca molo; molo 'to dive' not occurring in Standard Indonesian)
müsi (N)   making music with nonindigenous instruments (< Ind. musik 'music')

nelon (N)   nylon wire (< Ind. tali nelon)

obasé, obas (N)   medicin (< Ind. obat)

pal (N)   machete (< Ind. parang)
pelasi, plasti (N)   plastic; plastic bag; plastic sheet (< Ind. plastik)
pelüsi (N)   police (< Ind. polisi)
pen(d)éta (N)   missionary; reverend (< Ind. pendeta 'pastor')
penétu (N)   lid (< Ind. penutup)
peninggi (N)   evangelist (< Ind. guru penginjil)
pepèl (N)   agricultural development worker (< Ind. abbreviation PPL)
pesahu (N)   aeroplane (< Ind. pesawat terbang)
pilin (N)   dish (< Ind. piring)
pilosé (N)   pilot (< Ind. pilot)

rumasakit (N)   local health centre (< Ind. rumah sakit)

sabu, sabun, safu (N)   soap (< Ind. sabun)
samasama (ADV)   together (< Ind. bersama-sama)
sendél (N)   center (< Ind. senter)
sèndokh (N)   spoon (< Ind. sendok)
sekhula (N)   school (< Ind. sekolah)
selatu (NUM)   one hundred Indonesian Rupiah (< Ind. seratus 'one hundred')
selèn(a) (N)   shorts; trousers (< Ind. celana)
selènbayu (N)   clothing (< Ind. celana 'trousers' + baju 'shirt')
selibulimalatu (NUM)   one thousand five hundred Indonesian Rupiah (< Ind. seribu limaratus 'one thousand five hundred')
semén (N)   cement (< Ind. semen)
sentala (N)   military (< Ind. tentara)
sesial (ADJ)   of the social development project (< Ind. sosial 'social')
sénsol (N)   chain saw (< Ind. sensor)
sèn (N)   zinc (< Ind. seng 'zinc roofing')
siama (N)   head of administrative subdistrict (< Ind. camat)
siapamo (VB)   to hold ready (< Ind. siapkan)
sombaku (N)   tobacco (< Ind. tembakau)
soko, tokop (N)   store; shop (< Ind. toko)
sokop (N)   shovel (< Ind. sekop)
sundi (N)   hypodermic syringe (< Ind. suntik)
sulasé (N)   letter (< Ind surat)
susèl, suster, soster (N)   nurse (< Ind. suster)

tyarimo (VB)   to look for (< Ind. mencari)

uan (N)   money (< Ind. uang)
urusmo (VB)   to organize; to arrange (< Ind. mengurus)

wakélé (N)   deputy (< Ind. wakil)
wotan (N)   forest; wood (< Ind. hutan)

yalin (N)   fishing net (< Ind. jaring)
yandala (N)   window (< Ind. jendela)
yelasé (N)   snare; trap (< Ind. jerat)
yondon (N)   Johnson outboard engine (< Ind. Johnson)
yosu (N)   Johnson outboard engine (< Ind. Johnson)

APPENDIX 4

Korowai Inhabitants

Inhabitants of desa Yaniruma and desa Manggél, according to the census 1991/1992.

Personal name	Clan name[b]	Gender	Family Members/Relationship
A. Desa Yaniruma RT I: Yaniruma, January/February 1992[a]			
1. Luomo	Khombonggai*		4
2. Rembaüo	Khombonggai*		7
3. Tetenaré	Milofakhanop		4
4. Khauaré	Milofakhanop		4
5. Sapuru	Sendékh		5
6. Ainalop	Bilambanén		3
7. Bulalé	Sendékh		2
8. Yalul	Sendékh		2
9. Ela	Molonggai		2
10. Kubenalé	Nambul		2
11. Ayanalé	Sendékh		6
12. Fianalé	Molonggai		3
13. Khaüfalé	Dajo		4
14. Meséfalé	Khawékh		5
15. Raifalé	Khawékh		4
16. Kefalé	Sendékh		3
17. Fenelun	Molonggai		3

a. The Indonesian acronym RT refers to administrative village sections (see chapter 1, Korowai villages).
b. Clan names marked with an asterisk refer to Kombai-speaking groups.

Personal name	Clan name[b]	Gender	Family Members/Relationship
	B. Desa Yaniruma RT V: Mabül, February, 4, 1992		
1. Wanggép	Ngguali	♂	H of 2
2. Gembil	Awop	♀	W of 1
3. Bémalé	Lefilkhei	♂	eB of 4
4. Yawalalé	Lefilkhei	♂	yB of 3
5. Lumalé	Lemakha	♂	H of 6
6. Amondu	Lemakha	♀	W of 5
7. Sapu	Lefilkhei	♂	H of 8
8. Mim	Lemakha	♀	W of 7
9. Non	Khalikhatun	♀	D of 7
10. Bonggolo	Lemakha	♂	H of 11
11. Mopun	Lemakha	♀	W of 10
12. Lamufon	Lemakha	♀	W of 10
13. Khaléap	Lemakha	♀	D of 10
14. Lapil	Lemakha	♂	S of 10
15. Luter	Bafiga	♂	eB of 16
16. Lomunalé	Bafiga	♂	yB of 15
17. Bowas	Awop	♂	eB of 18
18. Dunom	Awop	♂	yB of 17
19. Filalé	Bafiga	♂	H of 20
20. Gison	Bafiga	♀	W of 19
21. Laléo	Bafiga	♀	D of 19
22. Olakh	Bafiga	♂	S of 19
23. Baé	Bafiga	♀	
24. Bandé	Bafiga	♂	
25. Khemuno	Bafiga	♂	
26. Sirifanus	Bisom	♂	
27. Sifalé	Naüp	♂	H of 28; eB of 29
28. Tai	Maüp	♀	W of 27
29. Baüom	Maüp	♂	yB of 27
30. Baülalé	Lemakha	♂	H of 31
31. Baüop	Lemakha	♀	W of 30
32. Feyagé	Lemakha	♂	yB of 30
33. Atunalé	Lemakha	♂	yB of 30
34. Dokél	Lemakha	♂	yB of 30
35. Yakobus	Lemakha	♂	yB of 30
36. Kholualé	Lefilkhei	♂	H of 37
37. Lalambé	Lefilkhei	♀	W of 36
38. Dagi	Alemél	♂	H of 39
39. Mbaüwo	Alemél	♀	W of 40
40. Lukas	Alemél	♂	S of 38
41. Wambiyo	Alemél	♀	M of 42
42. Lalalé	Alemél	♂	S of 41
43. Fianalé	Bisom	♂	H of 44
44. Yakhalé	Bisom	♀	W of 43
45. Alsapu	Bisom	♀	D of 43
46. Papaum	Bisom	♂	yB of 43
47. Maléafu	Bisom	♂	yB of 43
48. Delai	Khawékh	♂	H of 49
49. Lodün	Khawékh	♀	W of 48
50. Yotelina	Khawékh	♀	D of 48
51. Lefum	Khawékh	♂	

(*continued*)

Personal name	Clan name[b]	Gender	Family Members/Relationship
52. Yefu	Khawékh	♂	
53. Mbasi	Ngguali	♂	H of 54
54. Maleol	Ngguali	♀	W of 53
55. Biato	Ngguali	♂	H of 56
56. Lanumon	Ngguali	♀	W of 55
57. Yemén	Ngguali	♂	

C. Desa Yaniruma RT VI: Férman, February 10, 1992

1. Dofualé	Khomei	♂	H of 2
2. Silép	Molonggatun	♀	W of 1
3. Khaüfalé	Lefilkhei	♂	
4. Kaüol	Molonggatun	♂	eB of 5
5. Tolo	Molonggatun	♂	yB of 4
6. Fofo	Lefilkhei	♂	eB of 7
7. Lalambe	Lefilkhei	♂	yB of 6
8. Kheléalé	Nanokhatun	♂	H of 9
9. Khofol	Nanokhatun	♀	W of 8
10. Bilaündop	Dajo	♂	H of 11
11. Sayap	Khomei	♀	W of 10
12. Mbèkh	Nggokhoni	♂	
13. Khaufalé	Dajo	♂	H of 14 and 15; F of 16
14. Nanggon	Walofekhatun	♀	W of 13
15. Khuon	Khomei	♀	W of 13
16. Baüon	Dajo	♂	S of 13
17. Gasiyon	Walofekhatun	♂	
18. Müfalé	Khomei	♂	H of 19
19. Lamofu	Faülanop	♀	W of 18
20. Banggilalé	Khomei	♂	H of 21
21. Maelalum	Khomei	♀	W of 20
22. Afünaüp	Khomei	♀	D of 20
23. Lulalé	Khomei	♂	F of 24
24. Malualé	Khomei	♂	S of 23
25. Didonalé	Lemakha	♂	H of 26
26. Dinggokh	Khalikhatun	♀	W of 25
27. Bilai	Lemakha	♂	yB of 25
28. Fufua	Khomei	♂	F of 29
29. Khaükhalé	Khomei	♂	S of 28
30. Lefelalé	Khomei	♂	H of 31
31. Duop	Khomei	♀	W of 30
32. Khaüalé	Dajo	♂	

D. Desa Manggél RT I: Manggémakhol, January/February 1992

1. Fünéya	Aimbon*	2
2. Hakha	Khomei	5
3. Damunalé	Khomei	6
4. Khakhlakh	Khomei	6
5. Khofimalé	Dajo	4
6. Yakop	Dajo	3
7. Waliaré	Molonggatun	2
8. Yasüalé	Molonggatun	2
9. Ayaré	Khenei	2
10. Majai	Khenei	3

Personal name	Clan name[b]	Gender	Family Members/Relationship
11. Samaré	Mifanop		2
12. Büakhabül	Dajo		4
13. Khaélalé	Khenei		2
14. Tamanuaré	Mifanop		3
15. Abukh	Boluop		2
16. Büalé	Khomei		2
17. Bailum	Dajo		4
18. Mailu	Mifanop		3
19. Yenggénalé	Boluop		3
20. Déalé	Khenei		4
21. Nggalakhalé	Mifanop		2
22. Yamalé	Khomei		2
23. Feyoko	Nandup		2

E. Desa Manggél RT II: Yafufla, January/February 1992

1. Balayo	Khomei*		3
2. Rekhudayo	Khomei*		2
3. Bofo	Khomei*		4
4. Laté	Mariap		4
5. Nggailu	Wafüop		6
6. Lopio	Mariap		3
7. Semani	Bainggatun		4
8. Imou	Mifanop		3
9. Wakejaw	Marüo		5
10. Ngganapi	Malinggatun		4
11. Ayanaré	Apü		4
12. Yabé	Bainggatun		6
13. Balimanaré	Lénggatun		2
14. Kobong	Bainggatun		2
15. Epularé	Makhé		3
16. Paulalé	Makhé		3
17. Popohüo	Kubalopohu*		3

References to the Korowai in the Missionary Magazine *TOT ANN DE EINDEN DER AARDE* (*TADEDA*)[a]

Abbreviations used in this appendix:

AvH	A. van Houdt	JBKdV	J. B. K. de Vries
Acc	based on the written account/	JJPK	J. J. P. Klopstra
	report of	JK	Jac. Kruidhof
Aut	author of the article	JV	Joh. Veldhuizen
CJH	C. J. Haak	LJdV	L. J. de Vries
CS	C. Stam	MEvEB	M. E. van Enk-Bos
DJZ	D. J. Zandbergen	MKD	M. K. Drost
GJvE	G. J. van Enk	OJD	O. J. Douma
HRM	H. R. Munneke	RH	R. Houwen
HV	H. Venema	SB	S. Bakker

TADEDA, vol. 1 (1976/77):
  1 (April 1976) 8–9   Aut: OJD   Acc: JBKdV
     Kouh en de Koroway (1) (Strategies to contact the Korowai)
  2 (May 1976) 30–31   Aut: CS   Acc: JBKdV
     Het bijgeloof van de Koroways (Kombai views on Korowai religion—Rebabu complex)

a. *Tot aan de einden der aarde:* information about the missionary work of the Reformed churches in the Netherlands and about the activities of De Verre Naasten, c.o. J. van der Graaf, Volksparksingel 59, 7513 CS Enschede, Netherlands.

11 (March 1977) 248–249   Aut: MKD   Acc: JK
   Nieuw Gebied etc. (The borders of Korowai tribal area)

TADEDA, vol. 2 (1977/78):
 2 (May 1977) 30–31   Aut: MKD   Acc: CJH
   Ds. Haak weer in de Kombay (Fear of Korowai toward police)
 4 (Juli/August 1977) 80–81   Aut: RH   Acc: DJZ
   Goed nieuws uit Firiwage—Van Firiwage naar Biwage—De Tsawkwambo's (Relationships between Korowai and Tsawkwambo)
 7 (November 1977) 151   Aut: CS   Acc: JV
   Eerste rapport br. Veldhuizen (First encounter with Korowai from border area
   Korowai-Tsawkwambo—June/July 1977)
 9 (January 1978) 204–205   Aut: CS   Acc: JV
   Een weg zoeken (Efforts to contact Korowai via Waliburu—October 1977)
10 (February 1978) 232   Aut: CS   Acc: JV
   Contacten zoeken (Plans to switch to the Western access road, via Citak area; first
   encounter with Korowai in downstream Becking River area)

TADEDA, vol. 3 (1978/79):
 1 (April 1978) 16–17   Aut: CS   Acc: JV
   Het werk van br.Veldhuizen (Evaluation of efforts to contact via Citak area)
 3 (June 1978) 56–57   Aut: CS   Acc: JV
   De Korowai (Strategy to contact the Korowai within the framework of the general
   missionary approach of the Reformed Missions in Southern Irian Jaya; meeting H.
   Griffioen and John Veldhuizen with Korowai at Tsawkwambo sago grub festival)
 7 (November 1978) 164–165   Aut: CS   Acc: ?
   Koroway (Investigations with respect to strategy and language learning; troubles with
   establishing contact via Tsawkwambo people; notes on location of Korowai area)
 7 (November 1978) 186–187   Aut: ?   Acc: ?
   Werkzaamheden in Waliburu (Geographical investigations concerning the Korowai
   area)
 8 (December 1978) 200–203   Aut: CS   Acc: —
   Een nieuw gebied (Venema partially available for work in Korowai)
10 (February 1979) 267–268   Aut: CS   Acc: JV
   De eerste kontakten met de Korowai (Expedition Veldhuizen up the Becking River,
   October 1978)
11 (March 1979) 284–286   Aut: CS   Acc: JV
   Nog eens: naar de Korowai [Expedition Veldhuizen up the Becking River, October
   1978 (cont.)]

TADEDA, vol. 4 (1979/80):
 2 (May 1979) 35   Aut: JK   Acc: JK
   Kerkelijke stand van Honya en Tiau (Contacts Citak people from Sagis and Ziobok
   with Korowai)
 3 (June 1979) 52–53   Aut: OJD   Acc: JV
   Kontakten met de Korowai [Korowai from Afiüm River area to Tiau (Citak)]
 7 (November 1979) 168–169   Aut: OJD   Acc: JV
   Contacten met de Korowai [Expedition March/April 1979 upstream Becking River
   (incl. map)]

8 (December 1979) 190–191   Aut: OJD   Acc: JV
Op zoek naar de Korowai (Surveys upstream Becking and Eilanden rivers by helicopter)
9 (January 1980) 210–211   Aut: OJD   Acc: JV
De weg naar de Korowai (Expeditions along Eilanden River/Becking River; relationships Kombai–Korowai and Citak–Korowai)
11 (March 1980) 257   Aut: OJD   Acc: HV
De Korowai is open (Yaniruma as a strategic location; Rebabu concept)

TADEDA, vol. 5 (1980/81):

3 (June 1980) 70–71   Aut: OJD   Acc: JV
Yaniruma (First development of Yaniruma as a village)
4 (July/August 1980) 92–95   Aut: OJD   Acc: JV
Pinksteren en Korowai [Kombai view on Korowai; acceptance of contact goods; further contacting strategies; kinship relationships between Ugo (Kombai) and Korowai clans at the Becking riverbanks; tentative division of Korowai area into three regions]
7 (November 1980) 180–181   Aut: OJD   Acc: JV
De Korowai—Brief uit Yaniruma (Village absenteeism)
9 (January 1981) 228f.   Aut: OJD   Acc: JV
Terug onder de Korowai [Opening of former Firu village; relationships Nombéakha (Kombai)–Korowai]
11 (March 1981) 77   Aut: OJD   Acc: JV
Om het hart van de Korowai (Northern border: quick comparison of Korowai with Ulakhin language; similar counting system)

TADEDA, vol. 6 (1981/82):

1 (April 1981) 15   Aut: OJD   Acc: JV
Met z'n drieën in Irian—Korowai (Veldhuizen available full-time for work in Korowai area)
5 (September 1981) 102–103   Aut: OJD   Acc: JV
Naar de Korowai (Relationships Korowai–Tsawkwambo)
6 (October 1981) 130–131   Aut: LJdV   Acc: LJd
Achtergronden van taalkundig werk op het zendingsveld (Acculturation problems)
7 (November 1981) 156   Aut: RH   Acc: PRB
De Tsawkwambo (Relationships between Tsawkwambo and Korowai; investigations of Baas)
8 (December 1981) 176–177   Aut: OJD   Acc: HV, JV
Het leven onder de Korowai (Village development in Yaniruma; helicopter surveys over Korowai area)

TADEDA, vol. 7 (1982/83):

1 (April 1982) 13   Aut: OJD   Acc: JV
Ook voor de Korowai komt er een strip: rustig aan en met veel vakantie (Village development in Yaniruma)
4 (July/August 1982) 88–89   Aut: OJD   Acc: JV
Het evangelie onder Korowai (Contacts with Korowai clans at Eilanden riverbanks via Citak from Bidnew)
8 (December 1982) 190–191   Aut: OJD   Acc: HV
Onder de Korowaiers (Great sago grub festival near Yaniruma; religious features; rebabu concept; use of stone axe)

11 (March 1983) 268–269 Aut: OJD Acc: JV
De eerste Korowai-kampong? (No Afiüm Korowai in Mbasman)

TADEDA, vol. 8 (1983/84):
3 (June 1983) 62–63 Aut: OJD Acc: ?
Een zendeling voor de Korowai (Venema available for work in Korowai)
6 (October 1983) 138–139 Aut: OJD Acc: HV
Yaniruma (Korowai reactions at a solar eclipse; protection magic; lamol concept)
9 (January 1984) 208–209 Aut: HRM Acc:—
Waar haalt Groningen de moed vandaan? (General strategy; missionary manpower for the Korowai project)
10 (February 1984) 234–235 Aut: OJD Acc: JV HV LJdV
Yaniruma (Expedition to Manianggatun territory)

TADEDA, vol. 9 (1984/85):
2 (May 1984) 46–47 Aut: OJD Acc: HV
Onder de Korowai . . . (Eating of human flesh; sago grub festival)
3 (June 1984) 56–57 Aut: OJD Acc: HV
Ds. H. Venema en zijn werk (Fear of Citak raid)
5 (September 1984) 104–105 Aut: OJD Acc: HV LJdV
Om het hart van de Korowai (Village absenteeism; Korowai language learning; contacts with Korowai in Mbasman)
7 (November 1984) 150–151 Aut: HV Acc:?
De versperring moet weg [Mukhalé Manianggatun opens a village (Fumbaum) in his territory]
8 (December 1984) 170–171 Aut: OJD Acc: JV
De Korowai (Local census in Yaniruma)
9 (January 1985) 196–197 Aut: OJD Acc: LJdV, JV
Taalstudie (Relation between Korowai and Wambon language; Korowai kinship terminology)
10 (February 1985) 222–223 Aut: HV Acc: HV
Dagtocht op de Neilop (Stay in Manianggatun at breadfruit season)

TADEDA, vol. 10 (1985/86):
1 (April 1985) 12–13 Aut: OJD Acc: LJDV
Hoe wordt het hart van de Korowai bereikt? (Sorcery and accusations of sorcery; symbolic character of sorcery among Kombai and Korowai; avenge methods)
2 (May 1985) 38–39 Aut: OJD Acc: ?
Het leven in Yaniruma (Korowai woman abducted; authority crisis among Korowai group in Yaniruma)
3 (June 1985) 58–59 Aut: OJD Acc: LJd
Postwerk en taalwerk (Two expeditions upstream, Becking River—Manianggatun territory)
4 (July/August 1985) 88–89 Aut: OJD Acc: JV
Veel geduld met de Korowai! (December 1984 great sago grub festival near Yaniruma; reasons for village absenteeism; influence/authority of Gambünalé Molonggai; sorcery along the Eilanden riverbanks)
5 (September 1985) 120–121 Aut: OJD Acc: HV
In het Korowai-gebied [April 1985 sago grub festival near Yaniruma (Malegop as organiser); expedition to Fumbaun; skulls and bones along the road]

6 (October 1985) 140–141   Aut: LJdV   Acc: HV
Berichten uit Yaniruma [First entrance of local government officials (subdistrict level)
in Korowai area—Fumbaum]

TADEDA, vol. 11 (1986/87):
 1 (April 1986) 3–5   Aut: OJD   Acc: HV
Yaniruma (Korowai people from Eilanden River territories in Yaniruma)
 4 (July/August 1986) 86–88   Aut: OJD   Acc: HV
Opening van het Korowai-gebied (February 1986 expedition to Yafufla, passing
Manianggatun, Khomei, Boluop, and Mifanop territories; stay overnight at
Manggélmakhol; meeting with Galikhatun people)
 7 (November 1986) 155–156   Aut: OJD   Acc: HV
Afscheid van Yaniruma [Korowai people from Nakhilop (Fumbaum) attend National
Celebrations in Bomakia, August 1986]
10 (February 1987) 218–219   Aut: OJD   Acc: LJdV
Het boeiende taalwerk (Sociolinguistic aspects; pidginisation)

TADEDA, vol. 12 (1987/88):
 1 (April 1987) 8–9   Aut: OJD   Acc: JV
Prediking onder de Korowai (New village at Manggémakhol, halfway between
Yaniruma and Yafufla end, 1986; initiated by Khomei people)
 3 (June 1987) 60–61   Aut: OJD   Acc: GJvE HV JV
Entrée in Yaniruma (Van Enk starts to work in Yaniruma)
 7 (November 1987) 152–153   Aut: OJD   Acc: GJvE
Ds. G. J. van Enk onder de Korowai (Language learning; pregnancy and delivery in
the Korowai population of Yaniruma)
 8 (December 1987) 176–177   Aut: JV   Acc: JV
Yaniruma, Yafufla en Bofo I [Short ethnohistorical sketch of Yafufla area and its
people: first contacts with Bofo Khomei (Kombai from Yafufla area) in 1980; contacts
April 1982; missionary expeditions February 1986 and September 1986; contact gifts
refused; efforts of Kepsan Kurufe to contact Bofo; revenge of sorcery at Yafufla]
 9 (January 1988) 200–201   Aut: JV   Acc: JV
Yaniruma, Yafufla en Bapak Bofo II [Ethnohistorical sketch of Yafufla area and its
people (cont.); Bofo Khomei visits Yaniruma May 31, 1987; first signs of initiatives
for opening a village at Yafufla]
10 (February 1988) 232–233   Aut: SB   Acc: JV
Een nieuwe start (Plans for further development at new village at Yafufla; Kombai
majority in Yaniruma)
11 (March 1988) 252–253   Aut: AvH   Acc: JPDG
Dat ellendige absenteïsme! (Village in Kombai–Korowai border area: Khaipelambürü)
11 (March 1988) 254–255   Aut: SB   Acc: GJvE
Evangelisten (Village absenteeism at Nakhilop)

TADEDA, vol. 13 (1988/89):
 4 (July/August 1988) 20–21   Aut: SB   Acc: LJdV
Met de linguïst op tournee (Trips to Khawékh territories and to Manggél via Nakhilop
village; the way to find a sorcerer; Nakhilop village closed)
 6 (October 1988) 18–19   Aut: SB   Acc: GJvE
Sociale spanningen in een jonge gemeente (Korowai custom to kill one of newborn
twins)

7 (November 1988) 18–19   Aut: SB   Acc: GJvE
Yafufla (History of opening a village at Yafufla, August/September 1987)
8 (December 1988) 18–19   Aut: SB   Acc: GJvE
Yafufla II (History of opening a village at Yafufla, August/September 1987. Removal of arrowtips from body of wounded Korowai man in Boma by Jannie Velvis)

TADEDA, vol. 14 (1989/90):

5 (September 1989) 18–19   Aut: SB   Acc: GJvE
Taalwerk in Mangge (Korowai language learning; description of road Yaniruma–Manggél; September/October 1988 expedition to Yafufla)
6 (October 1989) 18–19   Aut: SB   Acc: GJvE
Heksenterreur (Trip to Molonggai territory; sorcery and black magic)
8 (December 1989) 18–19   Aut: SB   Acc: GJvE
Als geest op een feest (Risks during expedition to sago grub festival in Khomei Walofekhatun territory; lamol complex; contacts with older Khomei Khayakhatun people)
10 (February 1990) 18–19   Aut: SB   Acc: MEvEB
De vrouwen van Mangge (Informal health education for Korowai in Manggél)
11 (March 1990) 18–19   Aut: SB   Acc: JV
Cursus voor de bevolking van Yaniruma (Informal education of Korowai and Kombai people of Yaniruma; about Korowai worldview and thinking on life and death)

TADEDA, vol. 15 (1990/91):

1 (April 1990) 18–19   Aut: SB   Acc: LJdV
Taalperikelen rond "hart" en "buik" (Kombai view on residence of thinking and feeling; Korowai language study)
2 (May 1990) 20–21   Aut: SB   Acc: GJvE JV
Hoe Korowai en Kombai-mensen over de dood denken (Differences in worldview and view on humankind of Korowai and Kombai; rebabu complex in Kombai; consciousness and unconsciousness, life and death)
5 (September 1990) 3–5   Aut: SB   Acc: GJvE
Bij het interview met Wandeyop Weremba: Vreemdelingschap in Mangge (Kombai Christian view on sorcery; Kombai living among Korowai; village absenteeism in Manggél)
6 (October 1990) 15–17   Aut: LJdV   Acc: LJdV
De veldlinguïst vertelt (Notes on Korowai kinship system)
8 (December 1990) 18–19   Aut: SB   Acc:—
Familie Veldhuizen, adieu! (Historical overview of efforts to contact Korowai since 1973; overview of Veldhuizen's stay in Korowai area)
9 (January 1991) 16–17   Aut: SB   Acc:—
Tuan Korowai I (Overview of Veldhuizen's stay in Korowai area)
10 (February 1991) 18–19   Aut: SB   Acc:—
Tuan Korowai II (Overview of Veldhuizen's stay in Korowai area)
11 (March 1991) 24   Aut: GJvE   Acc:—
Hoe moet het verder? (Questions about the future of the missionary work among the Korowai)

TADEDA, vol. 16 (1991/92):

2 (May 1991) 28–29   Aut: SB   Acc: LJdV
Een onrustige periode (Notes on Korowai language, kinship issues; tourists in Korowai area)

3 (June 1991) 20–21   Aut: SB   Acc: LJdV
Post- en bijbelvertaalwerk [Various contacts between Korowai and outside world (tourists; Japanese TV productions; gold and oil companies)]

4 (July/August 1991) 18–19   Aut: SB   Acc: GJvE
Op zijn post (Notes on accounts in Indonesion news magazine *Tempo*, February 1991; Indonesian Department of Social Welfare pays attention to 'recently discovered' tribe, named Korowai)

5 (September 1991) 18–19   Aut: SB   Acc: LJdV
De linguïst in Yaniruma en Boma (Expedition to Manggél village)

9 (January 1992) 15–17   Aut: SB   Acc: GJvE
Verontruste Korowai-mannen—Een interview met ds. Van Enk (Genres in Korowai oral tradition; criteria of discretion concerning the genres)

TADEDA, vol. 17 (1992/93):

2 (May 1992) 3   Aut: AvH   Acc:—
Boekbespreking: Rijke de Wolf, Sapuru, Uitgeverij van Wijnen, Franeker 1992 (Book review of *Sapuru*, a novel by Rijke de Wolf)

3 (June 1992) 15–17   Aut: SB   Acc: GJvE
Diep het Korowai-gebied in [February 1992 expedition to Bainggun area; contacts with Kheney, Bumkhey, and Sendékh (Baféyanop) people]

5 (September 1992) 18–19   Aut: SB   Acc:—
Afscheid van dr. L. J. de Vries (De Vries's contributions to studies in Korowai language and culture)

6 (October 1992) 15–17   Aut: SB   Acc:—
Ds. Henk Venema gerepatrieerd (Historical overview of Venema's stay among the Korowai)

7 (November 1992) 19   Aut: SB   Acc:—
Visum afgewezen (Problems about missionary manpower for work in Korowai area)

9 (January 1993) 7   Aut: HV   Acc:—
Van Hemmen: SAP-docent (Van Hemmen as successor of van Enk)

11 (February 1993) 44–49   Aut: HV   Acc:—
Groningen/Irian Jaya (Historical overview of the efforts of Groningen to bring the gospel to, among others, the Korowai)

TADEDA, vol. 18 (1993/94):

1 (April 1993) 3–5   Aut: SB   Acc:—
Afscheid van de familie Van Enk (Historical overview of van Enk's stay among the Korowai)

6 (October 1993) 3–5   Aut: HV Acc: JJPK
Moord of executie? (Sorcery and murder in Yaniruma)

Notes

Chapter 1

1. It is quite possible that there were incidental contacts between the Korowai people and outsiders before the missionary period, which started in 1978. In 1959–1960, a French expedition headed by Gaisseau seems to have crossed Korowai territory on its way to the Mek region (cf. Godschalk 1993: 22). The Reverend J. Klamer, the ZGK missionary from 1959 to 1973 in the Kawagit area, reported incidental contacts with some Korowai clans who lived west of the Tsawkwambo village Waliburu and the Kombai-Wanggom village Firiwagé (reports in Missionary Archives of Reformed Church of Spakenburg-Zuid). Kawagit was a mission station on the Digul River (see map 2, Korowai area).

2. A summary of the history of the Korowai project from a missionary perspective was presented by Venema (1993: 44–47). The relevant missionary accounts of Veldhuizen are deposited with the secretary of the Irian Commissie van de Gereformeerde Kerk van Groningen-Noord. For a global account of Veldhuizen's first contacts with the Korowai, see Veldhuizen 1982. Van Enk (1993) presents a detailed history of the first period of contacts between the Korowai and the mission (1978–1991), using both written missionary reports and a tape-recorded indigenous oral account as his sources. The transcription of that oral account was included in this book as the *Khenil-khenil* text (in chapter 6).

3. In the accounts of Veldhuizen (e.g., 1978: 4–6), this man is called Guop. Nggop was the son of a Kombai father and a Korowai mother, kidnapped by the Citak from Tiau on one of their numerous raids. This background made him an ideal go-between for establishing relations with the Korowai in the Kombai-Korowai border area, especially the fact that the Korowai men in that area were his mother's brothers. See below, Cultural relationships, for the Korowai avunculate (MB-Ss dyad).

4. Korowai clans in the vicinity of Yaniruma are Bilambanén, Khawékh, Molonggai, Sendékh, and Wahüop (see map 4). Kombai clans from the Ndeiram Hitam area are Aimbakharun, Ambüakharun, Alera, Eluaru, Kambuaru, Khombonggai, and Milofakhanop.

5. The Nombéakha (Korowai: Nabékha) is a small Kombai subtribe.

6. In chapter 6, there is a real-life narrative (text *Mukhalé*) in which the young Mukhalé plays a central role.

7. The population of Nakhilop comprised people of the following clans: Bolüop, Dajo, Faülanop, Nggokhoni, Khomei Khajakhatun, Khenei, Manianggatun, and Molonggatun.

8. Manggémakhol < *Manggél* 'Manggél River' + *makhol* 'mouth'.

9. Cf. van Enk 1993: 24, n. 61. Because of trips into Korowai territory by Wandeyop Weremba, many contacts were established with various Khomei subclans who have territories along the banks of the Fukh River. Some of these Khomei people moved to Manggél. Other Korowai clans contacted by Weremba were Dajo (upstream), Khelékhatun, Mifanop, and Nandup.

10. There are traditional ties between the Korowai-speaking clans and the Kombai-speaking clans in the border area with the same clan names, for example, the Korowai Khomei (sub)clans and the Kombai Khomei (sub)clans. Such ties are also reflected in the text *Origin of the Khomei Clan*, line (13), in chapter 6, a totem story of the *laibolekha mahüon* genre. Van Enk (1987: 18–23) reports on the opening of Yafufla, which involved the two Korowai clans Mariap and Malüo.

11. Mabül is located at the coordinates 139,35° and 5,40°; compare the coordinates of Yaniruma: 139,41° and 5,40° (Klopstra 1992: 82). According to the data of the census of the Desa Yaniruma of 1992, the following Korowai clans were involved in the formation of Mabül: Alemél, Awop, Bafiga, Bisom, Guali, Khalikhatun, Lefilkhei, Lemakha, and Maüp.

12. The Kombai raided the Korowai clans Salékh en Sèifanop (van Enk 1990a: 16–17).

13. Since we have tried to mention in this book all publications on Korowai that have appeared thus far, we add here that de Wolf is also the author of an article that appeared in the Dutch newspaper, *Nederlands Dagblad*, December 22, 1990, pp. 14–15, entitled '*Een volk dat in duisternis ronddwaalt*'. The topic of that article is the events taking place in the first part of the text Mukhalé, the real-life narrative, in chapter 6.

14. From Yafufla the following route was taken on February 26, 1992, during a ten hours' walk: via the Mariap territory, across the Mip R(iver), via Malüo T(erritory), Gémom R., Molonggatun T., Khayokha R., Khénakh R., Yenikhatun T., Walofa R., Makhé T., Afiüm R., Fefiü R., Dajo T. (upstream), Dakhé R., Yokhtél R., Lemakha T., Bumkhei T., Khomun R., Khelikhatun T., Mabül R., Naüp R., Khamun R., Imon R., Bakhtokh R., Bemim R., Aun R., Alukh R., Khenei T., to reach the Bafé R. (= Eilanden River).

15. The contrast between high and low grounds is expressed by the adjectives *khalakh* 'high' and *khaüp* 'low'. Two other relevant Korowai terms are *leléf-anop* (from *lelép* 'higher ground' and *yanop* 'person'), referring to the people living on the higher ranges of hills found in the low country between the Bafé and the Nailop rivers; and *bayom-anop* (from *bayom* 'low peat' and *yanop* 'person'), referring to people who inhabit low, boggy soils.

16. It is not clear why the upriver Korowai are called Stone Korowai. Maybe the vast stone banks in the shallow upriver parts of the Becking, used by the Korowai as roads, is the explanation.

17. In the story of origin of the Khomei clan (see chapter 6), the Lemé River (Indonesian: Kali Semin) is mentioned in close connection with the Kuakhil River, which we have not yet been able to identify.

18. The contour of the Jayawijaya Range, called *fanip* by the Korowai, is visible and is thought of as part of the sky.

19. Two Korowai names for unidentified rivers in the trans-Eilanden area are the Sali

and the Wolop; there is a reference to the Wolop River in the *Ginol Silamtena* text, line (10), in chapter 6. The Wolop is possibly in the Brazza River area.

20. The absence of a clearly marked monsoon (dry and wet periods/seasons) is reflected in the fact that the concept of '(monsoon) season' does not seem to have been lexicalised. There are, however, periphrastic expressions to denote dry and wet periods/seasons (*Galon élo* 'Galon is asleep' = dry season and *Galon béboda* 'Galon does not sleep' = wet season; also *lanéam* 'wet period/season'). There are a number of 'seasonal' expressions with the verb form *utebo* for periods when certain trees bear fruit or when certain game is hunted, as in *béan utebo* '(it is) the season of the Ponnetia pinniata fruit' (in local Indonesian: '*musim matoa*'); *yawol utebo* '(it is) breadfruit (*Artocarpus*) season'; *bu utebo* '(it is) the season of Saccharum edule'; *bif utebo* '(it is) tortoise season'.

21. The Awyu-Ndumut family is placed by Voorhoeve (1975: 27) in the Trans-New Guinea Phylum (TNGP) of Papuan languages, a hypothetic genetic grouping comprising about 500 of the 750 Papuan languages (McElhanon and Voorhoeve 1970; McElhanon, Voorhoeve, and Wurm 1975; Wurm 1972, 1982). See Pawley (1995) for a recent discussion of the TNGP hypothesis.

22. We base this statement on information given by Sapuru Sendékh in February 1992.

23. The Reverend P. R. Baas (1988), who studied Citak culture for more than ten years, recorded and transcribed a major part of the Citak oral tradition, both songs and narratives.

24. The Korowai term *èponaup* (< *èp-mo-n-aup* 'worksong-SUPP-INF-voice') is probably based on Citak *üèp* 'worksong'.

25. Boelaars (1970: 220) suggests that the 'two-roads' idea might have its origin in missionary preaching on heaven and hell.

26. Our informants from the Digul area were Kristian Wandenggei (Kawagit area, Wanggom) and Kefas Hetowanggom-Maukay (Wambon, Manggelum area). This magic is called *tiruan* 'imitation' in local Indonesian.

27. The Korowai characterise such persons with the expression *ye-fi   khalakh   melé-lu-mbo*' his-name   high   moving-move.up-PROGR.3SG.REAL'. Another term that denotes the main characteristic of the big man is *bebén* 'strong, violent'.

28. The informant Fénélun Molonggai said that there were no such *wotop* places on his territories but that this was exceptional.

29. This subdivision is reflected in the *Origin of the Khomei Clan* text in chapter 6, the story of the descent of the Khomei, lines (11) and (12).

30. The element *-khatun* follows proper names of females and means 'children/offspring of mother X', for example, *Nggainggatun* (< Nggain-*khatun* 'children of mother Nggain').

31. First, the creator-spirit smears the backbone of the mythical pig Faül with dog fat [line (18)] and with fat of the *bebal* centipede [line (21)]. This backbone is used to form the sky. Second, the older brother (of the older brother-younger brother dyad, which forms the original couple) applies animal fat before he has sexual intercourse with his younger brother-turned-sister [line (35)].

32. Compare the expression *dil akhabopta babo* 'he sits under the house', lit. 'cross-beam underside.at he.sits'.

33. The bark is carefully knocked loose with stone axes and peeled off the tree in its entirety. Sudarman (1987) has recorded this technique in her film.

34. The noun *damon* is a nominal infinitive of the verb *damo* 'to close'.

35. The Korowai term *èleté*, a loan based on the Indonesian acronym *RT*, indicates both the village section and the headman of the section (Indonesian: *ketua RT*). The headmen of the *rukun tetangga* are locally recruited, just like the *kepala hansip* (Korowai: *kafulansip*) 'head of civil guard'; the *èleté* and the *kafulansip* have institutional authority in the village section in a way unknown to the Korowai, who are used to informal 'big man' forms of leadership in egalitarian contexts.

276 NOTES TO PAGES 24-31

36. *Khaü* means 'bivouac', that is, a temporary dwelling on the ground in distinction to the permanent treehouses (*khaim*).

37. According to the instructions for the census, every individual had to be registered under a family head or head of a household (Indonesian: *k.k.* = *kepala keluarga*). The division into households was done rather loosely. The actual number of inhabitants is bigger since people from other areas, employed by the mission or the government and living in Yaniruma, are not included in the count. See appendix 4 for lists of inhabitants recorded during the 1991/1992 census.

38. The village Nakhilop, opened by Mukhalé Manianggatun (the central participant in the *Mukhalé* text in chapter 6), fell apart in the course of 1987 when a number of deaths were ascribed to *khakhua* witchcraft, which triggered bloody revenge. Some of the population withdrew to their clan territories in the jungle and some moved to Manggél.

39. Compare Yaniruma coordinates 139,41° 5,40° (Klopstra 1992: 82). Petocz (1987: 260) notes for Yaniruma the coordinates 139,46° 5,25°, based on data from the Associated Mission Aviation (AMA), the Mission Aviation Fellowship (MAF), and Regions Wings (RG) (241).

40. The inhabitants moved to Yaniruma and Manggél, not long after the local census of 1992.

41. This negative attitude of older people toward the village is often accompanied by warnings that the world will soon come to an end if the young people live in villages [see *lamol/wola* and *mbolombolop*; see also chapter 6, below, Some central ideological notions, under text of *Khenil-khenil*, lines (65)–(75)].

42. In opposition to wild pigs (*lofekha*). General names for pigs are *gol, wan*, and *wonggan*.

43. *Khendép* means 'tail'. The term is also used to denote dogs. The verb used for raising pigs (*khendémo*) is a verbalisation of the noun *khendép* 'tail'.

44. The general term for hunting is *gawakhomo*. There is a special verb denoting the hunting of big game: *golsanipo < gol* 'pig' + *sanip* 'cassowary' + *-mo* 'SUPP'.

45. *Mafüm   ye-gun   kholfunè* literally means '*mafüm* its-group all.of'.

46. We mention the *kailon* arrows since the same type of arrow plays a role in the myth of origin *Ginol Silamtena* [see line (20) in chapter 6] when the sky is formed, and in the ritual of the shooting of *kailon* arrows into the roof of the festival bivouac by little boys (see Sago, below, and figure 1–9).

47. *Maun-makhol   yefole-té* 'river-mouth   dam.up-3PL.REAL'. Cf. van Baal 1982: 7f. and Schoorl 1957 for a description of a similar technique. The term for the opening of the dam that causes the water to flow away through the baskets and the fish to get trapped is *maétakhe-fimekho*. This term is also used in the origin myth *Ginol Silamtena* [cf. line (14)] to refer to the stream, which is 'opened' to clean out the remnants of the first creation, destroyed by fire.

48. Similar developments concerning crocodiles as game animals have been reported for other Papuan societies, for example, Yimas (Foley 1991: 12).

49. The expression in Korowai is *semail-kholol-fekho   mahüankho-sol-fekho   maun fe-nè mekhe-té* 'crocodile-bone-and pandanus.fruit-young-and   river   put-SS   put.in-REAL.3PL.

50. For the *ayulekha* concept, see below, Some central ideological notions; for the genre *laibolekha mahüon* 'stories of descent' , see Oral tradition.

51. Other Korowai nouns for sago are *khosül, ndaü*, and *naumatélekha*.

52. With thorny stem (Indonesian: *sagu duri*): *balép, bayol, khum*, and *lé*; without thorns (Indonesian: *sagu licin*): *amo, bandüp, lahial*, and *milon*; we do not know whether the *ganim* and the *mayum* have a thorny subspecies or not.

53. For example, the old Awolalop, a leading figure in the Bolüop clan (see map 4), was generally known for this virtue.

54. Two points in particular need further study: first, the relation between the sago grub festival, which focusses on life and procreation, and the *khakhua* complex, which focusses on death and destruction; second, the question of to what extent and in which ways sexual fertility is symbolised in the feast, for example, in possible symbolic links between semen and *milon* sago grub grease (see below). Consider also the fact that the noun *dul* 'penis' occurs in *dul-e-khil*, lit. 'penis health' or 'penis vitality' (perhaps 'penis life force'), the name of the special crowbar used in the feast for opening the rotting sago trunks, which contain the mature sago grubs that are ready to be harvested.

55. The term *gil* primarily refers to the sacral feast bivouac (cf. *gil alibaté* 'they have built a festival bivouac') but also indicates the feast itself.

56. A striking difference with the Kombai festival concerns the time at which the sacred fence is broken down. The Kombai break down the fence in the presence of close relatives just before the guests arrive (Venema 1989: 49, 50), whereas the Korowai perform this ritual only after the guests from outside have departed.

57. Cf. above, Territories and treehouses of Korowai clans; see below, Some central ideological notions, for the distinction between spirits (*laléo*) and ancestral spirits (*mbolombolop*).

58. The term *belil* 'star' is also used to denote fireflies.

59. Especially in the planning and timetable for the sago grub festival this function of the moon comes to the fore (see table 1–5). The time-indicating function of the moon is also evident in the other word for moon, *alümekhon* (< *alüp* 'time' + *mekho* 'SUPP' + *-n* 'NOM').

60. With *-telo* 'to be', *mamün* forms the adjective *mamüntelo* 'hot, warm'. Persons suffering from malaria fevers (*amul*) often sit in the sun (*mamünta bau*) to neutralise the heat of the fever and remove the pain in the muscles.

61. In the *Ginol Silamtena* text [see line (17)], the backbone is shot into its high position by a volley of small *kailon* arrows of the creator-spirit to form the sky. Given our limited knowledge of the Korowai culture, such mythological material is extremely difficult to interpret. For example, we do not know whether the custom to shoot volleys of *kailon* arrows (shot by small boys) into the roof of the festival bivouac (see figure 1–9) at the end of the sago grub festival is linked to the *kailon* shooting of *Ginol Silamtena*. Much more research is needed to establish links between Korowai myths (like *Ginol Silamtena*) and Korowai rituals (like the rituals of the sago grub feast). The same holds for the relationship between the slaughter of the mythical pig Faül and the subsequent use of his meat and bones in the construction of heaven and earth in the Ginol myth and the ritual of the pig sacrifice.

62. The term *nokhu-yanop* 'our people' often occurs in stories of descent. In names of clans, *yanop*, or *-anop* frequently occurs, for example, *Mifanop* 'people of the Mip River', *Khandunanop* 'stone people', and *Milofakhanop* 'people of the Milop River' (*Milof-akh* 'Milop River').

63. For example, *Yaniluma(n-anof-)imban* 'someone of Yaniruma' or *Lefilkhei-imbam-pekha* 'a certain individual of the Lefilkhei people'.

64. *Lül   aüle-té* 'barrier.of.branches.and.leaves   close-REAL.3PL'.

65. *Khomu-ngga   mahüon* 'be.dead-INF.CONN   word'.

66. Such links between dying and losing consciousness are widespread in New Guinea, for example, in the neigbouring mountain culture of the Una (Louwerse 1987: 96). For an example of *Seelenwanderung* in the texts, see *The Resurrection Story*, lines (23)–(25), in chapter 6. The man who comes out of his grave in that text tells the people who buried him, 'I died [*khomile-lé*] and I went there but halfway there was a barrier and I returned . . .' *Khomilo* in its two senses, 'to die' and 'to be unconscious', contrasts with *khafén-telo* 'to live; to be conscious'.

67. For example, *The Resurrection Story* and the *wakhatum* story of the Fofumonalin brothers (see chapter 6).

68. For example, lines (8) and (11) in *Ginol Silamtena* (chapter 6).

69. The term *khabéan* '(crown of the) head' is the most frequent. The term *lokhul* 'head' occurs in the idiom *lokhutokhul* 'headache', a reduplication of *lokhul*, and in *lokhulmukh* 'hair of the head', a synonym of *khabéanmukh*. A third word for 'head' is *gegüp*.

70. The short form *lul* 'eye' is most frequently used in compounds like *lul-khal* 'eye-skin = eyelid', *lul-kholol* 'eye-bone = brow', *khayo-lul* 'sclera', and *khü-lul* 'pupil and iris'. The term *lulop* is used metaphorically for the black decorative dots at the margin of festive shields (*wolumon*). Compounds with *gelip* are *geli-top* 'nose-place' and *geli-bol* 'nose-hole' for indicating the nostrils.

71. Sometimes *khoto-khal* 'ear-skin = auricle' and rarely *daun* (< *dau-n* 'to.hear-NOM').

72. The words *mamüngga* 'warmth' and *khafun* 'redness' are also used to denote blood.

73. Hair plays a role in divination aimed at finding out whether someone with a serious illness will become healthy again or not. Nails are used to detect *khakhua* witches (see below, Some central ideological notions).

74. Informants who have some command of Indonesian always translate *ayul* with *larangan* 'prohibition'.

75. Food taboos can be linked to specific ages, periods, sexes, and conditions like menstruation and pregnancy. Sometimes the taboo concerns forbidden combinations of food items or specific ways to prepare a given food. Food taboos can be linked to specific locations, totem animals, specific (magical) hunting techniques, and specific functions such as the taboos that should be kept by the *milon* 'guard of the sacred fire' during the sago grub festival.

76. The extinction of the entire *Faülanop* clan referred to in the *Mukhalé* text (chapter 6), is ascribed to the use of 'forbidden arrow tips'.

77. The word *mbolombolop* is a reduplication of *mbolop*. The term is restricted to male ancestors, just like the synonymous term *yaléyalén* 'ancestors' [a reduplication of *yalén* 'respected (old) man'].

78. See, for example, *The Resurrection Story* (chapter 6). In that tale, the ancestors are called *mül-anop* 'people of former times'. *Mül* can be used for both time and space ('in front of; ahead; former; before'), for example, *Nokhu bétop yekhené mül* 'we (walked) behind, they (went) ahead'; *mül-alüp* '(in) former days; in the past'; *mülekha mahüon* 'stories of the past'.

79. The technical term for casting spells is *ndafun filolai* 'to name *ndafun*', often in combination with ritual actions that are beneficial, as in the case of healing magic (*manopo, kholükhmo*), or destructive, as in 'bespeaking' sago (*khola ndafun fu*) that will be eaten by an enemy.

80. The Korowai describe this curing as follows: *Bon mekhesim lül-mo menil alü mamün-me-nè khabéanta lamoda-té-do khabéantekhul manda-lelo* 'they spit on a tobacco pipe's head and heat it in the fire, and they touch the head and then the headache is gone'.

81. The verb *lé/fonolé* is not a technical term for 'magically eating' or for 'eating of human flesh' but the general verb for eating, which is also applied to 'normal' eating. Notice that for the Korowai, just as for the Marind-Anim (van Baal 1981: 196), there is no distinction between 'magically' eating human flesh and 'really' eating human flesh; or to be more precise, in their verbal reports the distinction is not discernible, says van Baal, 'when the Marind-anim talk about it [i.e., magic cannibalism], no one would guess that they were talking about symbolic action'. This fact makes it often extremely hard for students of these cultures, if they have not witnessed the reported actions with their own eyes, to find out whether a report by an informant refers to symbolic/magic actions or to 'real' actions. Van Baal himself was misled by very realistic reports on cannibalism that turned out to be reports on magic cannibalism.

82. According to Wandeyop Weremba, who worked almost ten years as an evangelist in the Korowai area, the actions of the *khakhua* follow from his evil disposition (cf. Bakker 1990: 3–5). The *khakhua* cannot change himself since he is controled by his destructive urges. Van Baal (in a personal letter to L. de Vries of December 30, 1989) wrote that he had found the notion of the internal, uncontrolable urge to perform black magic, contrasting with voluntary harmful magic, in the Bird's Head area of Irian Jaya (see Bergh 1961) but never in south coast cultures. In a recent publication by Groen (1991) on Kombai *kakuarumu*, the existence of the involuntary 'dispositional' form of black magic (in the Kombai area often thought of as hereditary) in Awyu cultures is confirmed.

83. The return of the *khakhua* is linked to his ascribed intention to eat more of the dead body of his victim. For necrophagy in the context of sorcery in some highland Papuan cultures of Papua New Guinea, see Sterly (1987: 25).

84. If the *khakhua* is someone who lives in a *kampong*, he is sometimes punished 'modernly', by prolonged forced hard labour and by various forms of ill treatment. From the Indonesian verbs *kasih* 'to give' and *kerja* 'to work', the Korowai verb *kasikelajamo* 'to set under penal servitude' is derived and is used to denote the *kampong*-style punishment of *khakhua*. These are the forms of punishment that we saw during our stay in the area. The accused may also be brought to unpacified areas for the traditional punishment. We have never witnessed the traditional punishment accorded to *khakhua* in unpacified areas (the killing and eating of the *khakhua*).

85. Similar killing and unceremonial cannibalisation of sorcerers or witches after formal public accusation and trial occurs or occurred in other Awyu groups like the Kombai and the Wambon. It has also been reported for Stickland-Bosavi groups (Knauft 1993: 212). A detailed study of Gebusi sorcery and cannibalism is presented in Knauft (1985).

86. *Lembul* 'bad; out of order; ugly; dirty; inefficient' and *manop* 'good; in order; beautiful; attractive; clean' are two opposite adjectives with a very general meaning. Of course, in specific contexts, they can be replaced by more marked words. In ethical contexts, *lembul* can be replaced by words like *dadamtelo/dadamtalé* 'naughty', *aluntalé* 'vicious', *dolokhmengga* 'with mischief', *khalokhtelo* 'good for nothing', *khén* 'aggressive', and *gemélalé/ndüni* 'inhospitable'. Physically and/or mentally handicapped people are also called *lembul* 'not in order'. In the sense of mentally handicapped, *lembul* can be replaced by the more specific term *énonomekho* 'unable to say or do anything that makes sense'. In a hygienic sense, a more specific word is *bangglèkh* 'dirty'. In an aesthetic sense, *lelida* 'handsome; pretty' can replace *manop*.

87. We have not found any links between Sèifabül and the tremors (shiver/shudder) of earthquakes. The neighbouring Citak also have a shiver-spirit, called Ayai-ipit 'shiver-man'. According to Baas (in personal communication), the Citak shiver-man is linked to earthquakes, and he thinks that the Citak got their shiver-man from the Kombai Refafu tradition (also Rebabu/Tefafu; see Kamma 1975: 23, 118, n. 2). Refafu is a Kombai sleeping spirit who causes earthquakes when he turns in his sleep. According to the Kombai, Refafu lives (and sleeps) on Korowai territory, and the dangers associated with waking up this sleeping spirit formed one of the arguments the Kombai used to prevent missionaries from entering Korowai territories. (Notice the sound similarities between Sèif-abül and Ref-afu).

88. The *ndewé* fish are described as very big *lüma* and *gum* fish, that is, sheatfish species.

89. De Vries (1993a) discusses possible links between orality and patterns of clause combining in Awyu languages.

90. The totem story included in *The Origin of the Khomei clan* (chapter 6) deviates from this pattern because the former is complemented by other mythological material.

Chapter 3

1. The data are written in phonemes represented by the graphemes in table 2–4. Stress is not written except in examples (10)–(16), where the accent indicates stress. In the glossary (appendix 2), stress is marked by underlining.

2. For morphophonemic changes in these and following examples, see chapter 2. Only when a morphophonemic change has not been covered there do we pay attention to that change in this chapter.

3. There is variation of /i/ and /é/ in the last syllable of *khonggél* 'big'.

4. For the change from /t/ to /l/ see chapter 2, Morphophonemic changes.

5. The verb *isilama* 'to pause, have a rest' is a loan word from Indonesian *beristirahat* 'to pause', phonologically adapted and integrated in the Korowai lexicon with the support verb *mo* (see Verbs, below).

6. The /o/ and /a/ vary in *wofekha*, /o/ being predominant.

7. Usually these are points on the hand, arm, shoulder, and head. An interesting exception is Alamblak of Papua New Guinea, which had both a men's and a women's tally system. The latter used two low points, the breasts, to the exclusion of points on the face (Bruce 1984: 320).

8. By *relational noun*, we mean a noun that is used to express specific grammatical relations.

9. The use of attributive suffixes with body-part/number words when they are used as numerical modifiers in noun phrases has also been reported for Wambon (de Vries and Wiersma 1992: 45), Kombai (de Vries 1993b: 40), and Telefol (Healy 1965: 28). Telefol belongs to the Ok family, the eastern neighbour of the Awyu family, to which Korowai, Kombai, and Wambon belong. Note the differences in sources for the attributive suffixes: the Telefol attributive suffix *-kal* is derived from the locative postposition *-kal* 'at', for example, 'five' ('at left thumb'), the Korowai attributive suffix from a noun meaning 'amount' and the Kombai and Wambon attributive suffixes from a word meaning 'also, added'. For a detailed discussion of counting systems in Awyu languages, see de Vries (1995a).

10. See chapter 2 for the morphophonemic changes affecting *lefül* 'day' in the examples in table 3–3.

11. The /f/ of *-fekha* changes into /p/ after nasals.

12. See Dik (1989: 280) for focality as a cross-linguistic characteristic of question words.

13. Bernard Comrie (in personal communication) pointed out that the use of verbal expressions for (some) question-words is not rare cross-linguistically, citing examples from Haruai (*pöd r-ön* 'how' lit. 'how do-SS') and Japanese (*doo site* 'how/why' lit. 'in-what-way do-ing').

14. The support verb *mo-* has a longer allomorph, *mol-*, which occurs in this example. The form without the /l/ is by far the most frequent.

15. The word *manderi* is a loan word from Indonesian (*mantri*) that refers to local primary health-care workers.

16. The DS suffix on the verb is caused by the experiential construction, in which the experiencer is never the subject (first argument). More literally, this example could be rendered as 'It is malaria to me and I sit in the sun.' See below, The verb *telo* 'to be', for experiential constructions.

17. We do not have many data on *-ma*. Thus far we have found it only with human noun phrases.

18. *Mbam-mengga* > *mbamengga*.

19. *Pilin* 'plate' and *sabun* 'soap' are Indonesian loan words (see appendix 3).

20. The /f/ of *-fekho* changes into /p/ after nasals.

21. There are similar sets of dimensional relational nouns in other Awyu languages; see Drabbe (1957: 41) for Aghu (Jair), de Vries (1986) for Wambon, and de Vries (1989: 184) for Kombai.

22. See below, The verb *-telo* 'to be', for agreement phenomena in experiential constructions.

23. *Manop-mo-* > *manopo-* [regressive (total) assimilation; cf. chapter 2, Assimilation].

24. The Kombai cognate support verb *-ma* and the Wambon *-mo* have this same function; in these Awyu languages many Indonesian verb loans were already integrated with the support verbs in the lexicon (see de Vries 1989: 14, 139).

25. The final /l/ of *di* 'cutting' is dropped only in the stem form.

26. Sometimes *woliolao*, from *woliol* 'decorative carving; symbol' and *ao* 'to plant'.

27. This possibility was suggested to us by William Foley.

28. *Ate-un-kha* > *atungga;* see chapter 2, Assimilation, for the fusion of /n/ + /kh/ > /ngg/.

29. Onomatopoeia, that is, sound of sudden inflammation.

Chapter 4

1. *Pilin* 'plate' and *sabun* 'soap' are Indonesian loan words (see appendix 3).

2. *Subject* is used in this book in the semantic sense of the first argument of the verb. Thus with action predications, the actor or agent is the subject; in stative predications, the entity predicated to be in a certain state is the subject.

3. The verb appears in the 3SG form because of the experiential construction of the clause ['It is ill (to) me and . . .'].

4. In this chapter, we focus on the main function of the connective *-kha* in clauses. The connective also occurs with other elements—first, occasionally with independent pronouns, as in (a); secondly, with the adverb *afén* 'usually' as in (b); and third, with possessive prefixes to form words for 'mine', yours', and so on:

(a) yakhof-e-kha-lo   wof-e-kha   de-mémo?
    who-TR-CONN-FOC that-TR-CONN say-3SG.IMM.REAL
    'Who just said that?'

(b) afé-ngga   wa-mol-mo
    usually-CONN thus-do-do.3SG.REAL
    'He usually does like that.'

(c) waf-è   na-kha
    that-CONN my-CONN
    'That is mine.'

(d) if-è   ne-ni   ya-kha
    this-CONN my-mother her-CONN
    'This is my mother's.'

5. The infinitive marker *-n* and the connective *-kha* have fused to become *-ngga* in this example.

6. Topic markers have been found in many Papuan languages to express the setting or theme of initial adverbial clauses, for example, Hua (Haiman 1978, 1980), Usan (Reesink 1987), and Wambon and Kombai (de Vries 1989).

7. The morphophonemics behind this form is

fédo-un-kha-efè > *fédonggafè*
give-INF-CONN-TOP

8. Bromley (1981) reports that recapitulatory verbs are used also in Dani conversations as a regular linking device between utterances of different speakers; the second speaker starts his or her turn with the recapitulation of the last verb of the first speaker.

9. Experiential constructions (see chapter 3, The verb *-telo* 'to be') are an important exception to the rule that the referent of the subject is the topic of the clause. In such constructions, the experiential verb does not agree with the experiencer who is the topic of the clause, for example, *nokhu kelil ütelo* 'we are depressed' lit. '(to) us the zest for life is gone'. The verb *ütelo* is a 3SG form that agrees with the subject *kelil* 'zest for life' and not with the human experiencer, which is the topic of the clause 'about' which something is asserted. See note 2 for the notion subject.

10. This section is based on de Vries (1995b).

Chapter 5

1. This chapter is a revised version of van Enk and de Vries (1993).

2. As far as we know, in Korowai the following terms are used for expressing adoptive relationships: *Laün-até* or *mahüan-até* 'foster father'; *laün-abül* or *mahüan-abül* 'foster son'; *laüne-lal* or *maüane-lal* 'foster daughter'. The nouns *laün* and *mahüan* are also used to denote the *Pandanus* tree. We do not know what the connection is between the *Pandanus* meaning and the adoptive relationship meaning, if there is a connection at all.

We have the impression that the terms *laün-até, mahüan-até,* and so on denote the kind of relation called in Indonesian *anak piara*, a common term in eastern Indonesia for an adoptive parent-child relationship in which the adopted child is a nonrelative who has a different status in the household than the other children, often approaching domestic helper. In gratitude for being adopted and also in exchange for food and other things like education, the *anak piara* is expected to do domestic chores.

3. Not frequently used is *-mefekha* 'last born'.

Chapter 6

1. To indicate that the present story has its origin in the oral tradition, the narrator uses a fixed formula that points to unspecified ancestors as the source for the story. See chapter 1, Some central ideological notions, for the concept of the *mbolombolop* 'ancestors'.

2. Events that occurred more than two generations ago are situated in *mülalüp* 'in former times'.

3. Corpses have to be buried the same day or the next day before it becomes really hot. The Korowai prefer the next day in order to mourn, to give relatives from other places the possibility to see the corpse before it is buried, and to facilitate detection of possible black magic. (See chapter 1, Some central ideological notions, under *khakhua*).

4. Korowai burials usually take place under or at least near the treehouse of the one who died. In this story the grave is situated somewhere on the clan territory, not far from the treehouse mentioned in the text.

5. The word *khaim* means (one of) the treehouse(s) on the clan territory of the person who died.

6. The relatives of the buried person usually stay a couple of days in the vicinity of the grave to deliberate about issues related to deaths, such as recompensation arrangements (see chapter 1, Some central ideological notions, under *kholofudamo*), and often also measures concerned with the detection of and revenge on *khakhua* witches seen as responsible for the death (see chapter 1, under *khakhua*).

7. This is a 'false' DS marking, possibly triggered by the quotation clause. See chapter 4, Chaining linkage.

8. The apparently dead person comes back to consciousness at the time it had become dark, so he has been in the grave for at least 12 hours, namely, from *debünenul* 'daybreak' to *güledo* 'it became dark'. See table 1–6.

9. Usually Korowai graves are shallow, so the buried man could survive this adventure easily. He only had to get through the thin layer of earth that covered him and to push up the panel of sago leaf ribs, which forms the covering of the grave.

10. The man was not able to run fast because his body was covered with dried-up clay.

11. Notice the repetition of the hodiernum form *khebakhi* 'he walked', expressing the relatively long distance the man had to go to reach the treehouse. This indicates that the grave was not under the treehouse in which his relatives intended to spend the night.

12. Going upstairs, the leading character of the story still was hindered by the muddy layer covering his body.

13. The repetition of the verb *lu* 'to go upstairs' also causes some kind of tension in the story, in anticipation of the shock of the relatives who in an instant will meet the resurrected dead man.

14. See chapter 1, Territories and treehouses of Korowai clans, for stairs and for construction.

15. Note the increased tension because of the repeated use of the verb *khebémo* 'to move to and fro'.

16. As an intermezzo in the report about the man going upstairs, continued in (18), the story changes its point of view to the house's interior, where the relatives have their own obvious thoughts while observing the moving stairs. In this way the Korowai listeners to the story are forced to revel in the surprising event that is going to occur.

17. First the people see the mud-covered head appearing in the light that shines from within the treehouse. The basic meaning of the verb *dalmekho* 'to appear' is 'to shine'.

18. See chapter 1, Some central ideological notions, for the *laléo* 'demon' concept.

19. For the *khomilo* concept, see chapter 1, Mankind, under *yanopkhayan* 'soul'.

20. This refers to the journey of the soul (in Korowai: *yanopkhayan* 'the very man') to his own clan territory in the land of the deceased (see chapter 1, Universe and Mankind).

21. See chapter 1, Universe, for this 'big road' that links the realms of the living and of the dead.

22. Note that the quotation started in (4) is maintained consistently and closed in a proper way with the quotation marker *dédakhufekho* 'he said and . . .'.

23. See introduction to *The Resurrection* text.

24. *Wofè* 'there' refers to the clan territory.

25. See chapter 3 for the derivation of habitual verbs (HAB) with the support verb *-ma-/-mo*. This type of habitual form is used consistently in this procedural text.

26. The *ol* 'feces' in this context includes the *ol*-containing parts, that is, the intestines.

27. The women of the clan are responsible for cleansing the dirty intestines in the river; the verb *ao-* basically means 'to plant/to put into' or 'to poke' (i.e., a little twig into the intestines for removing the feces).

28. In this DS transition, the subject reference switches from the women to the men. Now that the preliminary cleansing task of the women is finished, the sacred part of the ceremony starts, in which the women are excluded (see chapter 4 for switch reference).

29. Before the men start to carry out the ceremonial allocation of the pig-meat,the women are summoned to stay together in the treehouse, that is, at a certain distance from the ceremonies.

30. That is, when the women have gathered together in the treehouse.

31. See chapter 1, Territories and treehouses of Korowai clans and Some central ideological notions, under *mbolombolop* for *wotop* 'sacred place associated with dead ancestors'.
A *wotop* can be marked by a bend in the river, a particular tree, or a hill.

32. The verb *dolelimaté* 'they call / they invoke' refers to a compulsory way of addressing or invoking the ancestral spirits.

33. The quote marker has been omitted. See also (13), (15), and (22).

34. Namely, another *wotop* in the clan territory.

35. During this pause, the spirits of the ancestors are supposed to consume the parts of
the pig meat.

36. Notice the omission of plural suffixes on this and the following kinship nouns. For
the kinship terms, see chapter 5 (on *mom* 'maternal uncle', *sabül* 'nephew', *afé* 'older brother',
aw 'older sister', *modol* 'younger sister', *mofekha* 'younger brother', and *ni* 'mother').

37. The avunculate (cf. chapter 1, Cultural relationships, under social and political
organisation; kinship) is relevant here: the mother's brothers (*mom*) and sister's sons (*sabül*)
are the only people from outside the performing clan who are allowed to attend the ceremony.
Usually a couple of days before performing the sacrifice, the members of the clan send a
message to related clans with the request not to visit their territory during the ceremonies.

38. That is, the women of that particular clan; cf. (4).

39. See chapter 4 for the topic marker *-(f)efé*. The topical participant 'the one who created the universe' is identified in (4) as Ginol Silamtena.

40. This 'false' SS form is discussed in chapter 4, Chaining linkage. We have rendered
the verb *fu* 'to put' in the free translation with 'to create'. Obviously, by using terms like
'creation' and 'soul', we just give an imperfect and very rough indication of the meaning of
such terms, which should be analysed in the context of Korowai culture (see chapter 1, Korowai
views of universe and man).

41. This story is part of a series of stories about the origin of the universe. The demonstrative *a* is used to mark definiteness here. The mythical female participant, in (6) identified
as Wokhemél Yambim, is supposed to be known to the listeners.

42. This refers to the construction used for sago production: to wash the sago flour out
of the sago tree's fibres, the women use a construction of two sago leaf stems (*khejo* or
inggenun). See chapter 1, Sago.

43. For the procedure followed in the production of sago flour, see chapter 1, Sago.

44. Synonymous with *khejo* 'sago leaf stem'; hence (*pars pro toto*) 'sago flour-wash-
ing construction'.

45. Tobacco is considered to be a carrier of *ndafun* 'power' (see chapter 1, Some central ideological notions, under *ndafun*). The informant suggested that the woman performed
the ritual of putting tobacco leaves at the top of the *inggenun* construction to provoke the
destructive activities of Ginol.

46. Ginol is the 'one who created the universe' and as such is the leading character of
this story.

47. A mythical animal with the appearance of a mouse. Used as a apposition to the proper
name Ginol it may be considered an epithet: Ginol the Little Mouselike.

48. Usually there are many dry sago leaves at the sago-pounding location.

49. Usually there is a small fire where people produce sago for roasting pieces of fresh
sago marrow as a titbit. In this story, apparently the fire was dead.

50. See chapter 4 for the expletive use of 'dearness' relationship terms.

51. Lexicalized serial root construction; see chapter 3, Dependent verb forms. The meaning of the verb stem *di-* is not clear.

52. With the names Wokhemél Yambim the mythical female being, introduced in (2),
is identified. *Yambim* is also a kind of hardwood.

53. This is an onomatopeic verb, using a quotative construction (see chapter 3, Quote marking).

54. For -*fo* in the form *ülfo*, see chapter 3, Derivation of verbs. Note the 'false' SS marker -*dakhu*.

55. The verb *afü/afu(l)/afe* basically means 'to quarrel; to fight; to wrestle'; hence 'to wrestle in thoughts > to wonder'.

56. Or *Hemiprocne mystacea*; see Beehler, Pratt, and Zimmerman (1986: 136, plate 128).

57. See chapter 1, Mankind, under *yanop-khayan* for this transformation.

58. The demonstrative marks definiteness here. The Wolop River is presupposed to be known to the listeners.

59. The Wolop River is one of the wide streams northwest of the Eilanden River, located in or close to the Brazza region of southern Irian Jaya (see map 2).

60. *Laünbün* or *laünkhul* is a small fish with a red-brown belly; its appearance is like that of the *Ophiocephalus* (Indonesian: *Ikan gabus*).

61. Serial root construction. Note that *demé*- 'to tear' in this context means 'to be torn open so that you could look inside the chest'. The gaping wound was caused by the fire.

62. The words *khomolamol*, *lekhüpwaila*, and *bilamalin* have the same meaning according to the Korowai informant, namely, 'all/various kinds of'. The piling up of these words indicates that Ginol is shoving aside literally everything.

63. The intensifier -*lalé* refers to the totality of the scorched remains of an earlier universe.

64. In the spoken text, the focus marker -*to* is emphasized strongly.

65. Cf. previous footnote.

66. *Maél lakhafimekho*, lit. 'to open the water(s)', points to the action of giving way to the water of a blocked-up river. See chapter 4, Means of subsistence, for fishing techniques. Especially during longer spells of dry weather, the Korowai block up streams to catch fish. For a description of a fishing technique like this, see van Baal (1982: 7) and Schoorl (1957: 65).

67. With these words the first episode is summarised.

68. According to the informant, *fonggalingga lunè* has the same meaning as *fo anolmekho* [see (12)].

69. Faül is described by informants as a piglike animal.

70. The use of -*fefè* indicates that the preceding clauses of (17) present the given framework for the information to follow in (17): 'Given that Faül came swimming downward and that (Ginol) killed and slaughtered him. . .' (see chapter 4 for -*(f)efè*).

71. The *méan* 'dog' is introduced without further identification. There might be a link with the *méan* of the mythical sea *méan-maél*, lit. 'dog-water' (see chapter 1, Universe).

72. Cf. chapter 3, Derivation of verbs; the form *bulfo* has the same meaning as *bul-mekho*.

73. See chapter 1, Territories and treehouses of Korowai clans, for contexts in which smearing with the fat (*yabén*) of animals occurs.

74. The difference in grammatical meaning between *béalfo* and *béa(l)mo* is explained in chapter 3, Derivation of verbs.

75. The verb root *lamé*- usually refers to 'the quick (dancing) entrance of the guests at a sago grub festival place'. The *lamé* dancing act is translated in Indonesian with *main* 'to play'. The stem *abo*- basically means 'to hunt/chase'; together with *lu*- 'to move up', this serial root construction points to the action of 'chasing upward in a hurry' (cf. in Dutch: '*snel omhoogjagen*').

76. *Yelüp*, *fayan*, *mandil*, and *mbonggon* are arrows that differ from one another with respect to the carved decoration at the top of the shaft. Arrows with these decorations are used as magical protection devices, so-called 'arrows of the universe'. See chapter 1, Some central ideological notions, under *lamol* for references to pictures of these carved decorations.

77. The *tamon* 'bunch' contains the four kinds of arrows mentioned.

78. The various kinds of *kailon* ('little arrows made of leaf ribs') also play a role in the Korowai sago grub festival (see chapter 1 table 1–7) and when young boys shoot volleys of *kailon* arrows into the roof of the festival bivouac to further the prosperous growth of new sago.

79. The *lé* sago tree has a long trunk and is not so large as the *mayum*, quite a big species of sago.

80. According to the informant, one has to imagine the shooting as a continuous hail of arrows, which is the way of transporting Faül's *müfekholol* to its proper position so that it can form the firmament.

81. The DS marker *-do* reflects the switch from the backbone of Faül, which is the subject of *lu khalakhmekhodompekho* to Ginol, the subject of *dibéalfo*.

82. *Lamol fu* 'he created the world' h.l. as a concluding statement after the description of Ginol activities in (17) to (21). This conclusion is resumed by means of a tail-head linkage in the next line.

83. First the seed capsule, indicated by the diminutive *-tena*, of the *dabüp* rattan bursts open, after which the plant is growing (25).

84. This is an onomatopeic verb, using a quotative construction (see chapter 3, Quote marking).

85. Note that the narrator corrects himself by changing the SS marker (25) into a DS marker.

86. The information stated in the present clause is resumed and amplified in the following ones.

87. Serial root construction with *monggo* 'to move out/unload' and *feli/felé* 'to fall (down)'.

88. The noun *gun* 'group/family/clan' is normally used for groupings of animate entities (humans and animals), for example, *yano-gun*, (lit. 'people-group') 'family' or 'clan'; *duo-gun* 'rodents' (lit. 'mouse-group'). Here the collectivity of heavenly bodies is meant.

89. *Feletél-anop*, lit. 'they fell down-people', that is, 'people who fell down'. Normally, the connective *-kha* links prenominal modifiers to their head nouns (see chapter 4); thus:

feletél-e-kha   *yanop*
they.fell.down-TR-CONN   people

90. *Wolakholol*, lit. 'universe-bone', that is, 'world, earth'. See chapter 1, Man, under *lokhül* for uses of *kholol* 'bone'.

91. From *khendémo* (< *khendép* 'tail' + *mo* 'SUPP'), meaning 'to heed; to watch for', 'to raise (pigs)'; h.l. 'to care for'.

92. Ingressive use of *-mba* is discussed in chapter 3, Inflection.

93. There are at least two different Lefilkhei groups that occupy different, nonadjacent territories (see chapter 1 for this distant type of interclan relationship, marked by the optional addition of geographical terms to the names of the clans). The Lefilkhei man of this text was identified by informants as a member of the Walüpta Lefilkhei clan living at the banks of the Nélaf River (see map 4). There is a certain relationship between the narrator's own clan (Khomei-Khayakhatun) and the Lefilkhei-Nélafanop clan with respect to bride giving. The narrator, for instance, is married to Silép Lefilkhei-Nélafanop.

94. *Khufom* is a water spirit with unpredictable behaviour. Ginol here denies the self-identification of the man as a member of the Lefilkhei people. Note that the name Khufom is used frequently by Korowai people as a swearword, like Ginol's name (see chapter 4 under expletive nouns).

95. The connection between this antagonistic dialogue of Ginol and the Lefilkhei man and the creation of mankind is not clear to us. Maybe *fekhalalé* 'the big one', who is introduced below, can be identified with the Lefilkhei man.

96. Cf. the comment on *aful* in (8).

97. For the kinship nouns *alop* 'firstborn' and *mefekha* 'last born', see chapter 4, Subordinate linkage with *-kha*. The compound *dabüpefekha*, consisting of *dabüp* 'kind of rattan' and *mefekha* 'last born', shows regressive assimilation (cf. chapter 2).

98. Freshwater fish with the appearance of the *Clarius* (*melanoderma*).

99. *Lu* is the 3SG REAL form of *lülmo* 'to moisten'.

100. *Malan:* a nonpoisonous, brightly green snake.

101. The sago grubs (*non*), which had been bred in the very lower end (*sip*) of the *milon* sago treetrunk, are usually very fat. The Korowai smear the fat of the *sip non* at a new trap to ensure successful hunting. Notice that the theme of the *milon* sago, which occurs in this context of sex and reproduction, returns in the sago grub festival, in the name of the guard of the sacred fire (*milon* 'guard of the sacred fire'; see chapter 1, Sago). We do not know which body parts the older brother smeared with grub fat (his penis?).

102. See chapter 2, Chaining linkage, for false DS markings that precede quotes.

103. The name Faül, first introduced as a participant in (17), is here used as a swearword. See chapter 4 for the use of *nggé* and *Faül* as expletive nouns.

104. See chapter 1, Some central ideological notions, under *ayulekha*. Given the context, probably the incest taboo is meant here.

105. Cf. the comment on *batélfekho* in (32).

106. The verb *dimekho* 'to put in' refers here to the sexual act.

107. The ample presentation of a time frame actually takes up the whole range of clauses within (39).

108. Lit.: 'struggling with her belly'.

109. The brown-headed crow, or *Corvus fuscicapillus*. See Beehler, Pratt, and Zimmerman (1986: 233, plate 55). This bird as a rule starts to sing very early in the morning, and therefore is called in Indonesian *burung siang* 'morning bird'.

110. Nominal infinitive *lungga* (< *lu-* 'to eat' + *-n-* 'INF' + *-kha* 'CONN') 'food'.

111. See map 4.

112. The *buom* 'small white lizard' represents a small kind of lizard that lives in people's houses. The *bembüo* 'small brown wood lizard', which lives in the trees, is called the *nggé*, lit. 'friend' of the *buom*. This expression is generally used to indicate some kind of kinship, affinity, similarity, or community of attributes, qualities, or properties, even in the case of inanimate referents.

113. The informant added the explanation *yelokhesukh laidakhu* 'its egg broke (hatched) and. . .'. Since the little brown wood lizard is the subject of *laidakhu* and of the next clause, this is an SS transition.

114. The language helper at this point added the information that the *bembüo* in the meantime had procreated lots of people.

115. *Wola-khip*, lit. 'earth-over', usually indicates the sky; here it is used for pointing to 'higher place(s/d) place'.

116. The sentence *Wofè nokhup laibokhafefè* is the answer to the question 'Please could you tell me something about the origin of your kindred [the Khomei people)?'.

117. *Khinggo* is the name of a Kombai clan. This clan's territory is situated a few hundred metres upstream from Manggél village along the south bank of the Becking River.

118. It is not clear why this unexpected SS marking occurs here.

119. The informant stated that the Khomei man's dog was of a small size; the Khinggo man's dog was a big one.

120. Khailfüoalop, actually means 'little earth-rat's firstborn', h.l. the name of the Khomei man's dog. The *khail* rat was identified by the informants as the *Sminthopsis rufigenis* (Menzies & Dennis 1979: plate 1a).

121. In line (5) there are several unexpected DS markings for which we do not have an explanation.

122. That is, the man who, as the owner of the big dog, was supposed to be responsible for the death of the little dog.

123. The verb *kholükhmo* 'break (down)' h.l. intransitive. The breaking down of the tree was caused by the wind.

124. The DS marking here is a 'false' one for which we do not have an explanation.

125. *Khanggofekho* = *khalakhofekho* (< *khalakh* 'high' + *khop* 'DEICT' + *-fekho* 'CIRCUM').

126. The noun *daüm* = *nggaüm* 'border; end'. There are a few other words that show phonemic variation between /d/ and /ngg/ (e.g. *donggop/nggonggop* 'piece of wood').

127. The switch-reference neutral form *bau*, according to the informant, may be replaced with the DS form *babodo* 'sit.3SG.REAL.DS'.

128. *Aful amodo* here paraphrased by the informant as *ye khul duol amodo* 'he thought and . . .'.

129. The DS marking here is a 'false' one since the subject stays the same.

130. In (11) and (12), the narrator refers to the division of the Khomei into subclans, namely, the Khayakhatun, Walofekhatun, and Walüfekhatun (cf. map 4; see also chapter 1 for subclan divisions of this type).

131. What is meant is the lower grounds along the banks of the Fukh River, where the Khomei-Khayakhatun subclan has its territory.

132. The Citak, an Asmat tribe, it is claimed here, originated from the same ancestor as the Khomei clan.

133. The Kuakhil River and Lemé River (Korowai for Ndeiram Hitam) run through the area of the Kombai tribe. *Kuakhil* is a Kombai word. The informant was not able to indicate the location of the Kuakhil exactly, but he was sure about a location somewhere in the area close to the head of the Ndeiram Hitam River (see map 3).

134. *Ifekho* 'here', that is, the banks of the Fukh River and the Afiüm River.

135. Notice that the partitioning of a set of participants into subsets leads here to a DS marking.

136. 'At the other side' (i.e., of the Fukh River); *ména* < *mén-ma* 'side-LOC'.

137. That is, at the south bank of the Becking River (location of the present village Yaniruma).

138. The person addressed in the last lines of the discourse is the man who is present at the recording session in the missionary's office.

139. Mbulul and Yalul are members of the Sendékh clan, living near the banks of the (Nailop) Becking River, southwest from the Khomei territoria (see map 4).

140. See chapter 1 for the Korowai sago grub festival.

141. The serial verb construction *lé-khami-* 'eat-sit' is generally used to denote being together in fellowship and harmony.

142. *Khondubidop* < *khondul* 'belly' + *bidop* 'swelled'.

143. By taking this measure, the oldest brother and the other ones behind urge the youngest to open a garden for himself and to plant his sprigs in his own place.

144. In the mother's brother–sister's son dyad, the mother's brother has to support his sister's son. The territory of the mother's brother is the place to go to in case of troubles, as Khondubidop does in this story. See chapter 1, Cultural relationships, under social and political organization; kinship.

145. What is meant here is 'You should let me know when the bananas of the just-planted tree can be harvested.'

146. The bat reports that the banana tree that Khondubidop had planted in his new planting area bears fruit.

147. That is, the first of the Lanialin 'Lani sisters'. In Korowai folktales, the Lani sister(s) often form the female counterpart of (the) Fofumon brother(s).

148. The sister has changed herself into a *makhaya* bat by applying well-known forms of magic by which people can change themselves into animals (especially birds) and back (see chapter 1, Man, under *yanopkhayan* for *khomilo* 'to transform'). Here the sister has changed into a bat to facilitate the eating (stealing?) of the bananas. The Korowai and the Kombai usually claim that they do not perform these kinds of magic, which they ascribe to the tribes living along the banks of the Digul River. In both Kombai and Korowai myths and folktales, however, this type of magic plays an important role, for example, the *Ginol Silamtena* text [see (11)ff.].

149. It is understood here that she changed back into a human being.

150. It is understood here (and in the following lines) that they had sexual intercourse after the woman came down from the tree.

151. The form *mo* probably means 'he saw that', parallel to *imotofekho* in (16).

152. While Khondubidop was walking from his uncles' place to the place in his own territory where he had planted the banana tree, the Lani sisters had eaten the bananas in the upper parts of the tree. At this point in the story Khondulbidop appears on the scene and sees the youngest Lani sister eating the last bananas low in his tree.

153. The form *amobodo* seems to function here as a relational verb, meaning 'and/next (I tell you)', comparable to *amodo* (see chapter 4, Discourse linkage verbs).

154. According to the informant, *Khondubidop* was angry for two reasons, first, because of all the work he had done in vain and, second, because he felt his rights to marry the other Lani-sisters had been violated by his brothers.

155. The intestines of slaughtered animals are a normal part of the Korowai diet. The cleansing of intestines is done by women.

156. In the following section of the tale, the preparations for the sago grub (ceremonial) feast are sketched in a very compact manner. See table 1–7.

157. See table 1–7, A: 3.

158. See table 1–7, A: 4.

159. *Naumatélekha* is an idiomatic expression for sago.

160. See table 1–7, C: 13.

161. See table 1–7, C: 14.

162. See table 1–7, C: 15.

163. The *banibol* are food storage places, made of sago leaf stems and tied along the bivouac side walls.

164. See table 1–7, C: 16.

165. See table 1–7, C: 18.

166. Lines (68)–(70) correspond to the activities mentioned in table 1–7, D: 19–21.

167. That is, the guests invited to partake in the ceremonies of the sago grub festival Cf. table 1–7, G: 30.

168. For a description of the *khasam* dance, see chapter 1, Sago.

169. Lines (73)–(76) correspond to the activities mentioned in table 1–7, G: 33–34.

170. For the events described in lines (77)–(81), cf. table 1–7, H: 35–36.

171. The *bandüp* is described by the informant as a kind of small, thorny sago tree.

172. The Korowai women use the fibres from the top of the sago palm for making skirts, in contrast to mountain tribes of New Guinea who use grass species.

173. According to the narrator and the informant this quotation (question) is addressed to the skirt material.

174. The verb *gümo* means 'to dance' or 'to play'. The ways in which she danced/played was like the courtship dance of the *beni* 'bird of paradise.'

175. That is, the treehouse of the Lani sisters.

176. Together they slept in the treehouse, although Khondubidop was not aware of it.

177. The *ukh* and the *lamül* cucumbers may not be eaten in combination with pig meat (food taboo).

178. According to informants, she gave the cucumbers after she had transformed herself back into a human being.

179. The expression 'sit and eat' refers to being harmoniously together. Throughout this tale the ups and downs of the human relationships are phrased in terms of sharing, offering, and refusing food. Offering food to someone of the opposite sex who is not a legal marriage partner has very strong sexual meanings in the Korowai society, as well as in the Kombai and other societies in the area.

180. The narrator is a member of the Sendékh clan whose territory is on the northern bank of the Becking River. See map 4.

181. Namely, before 1978, when the missionary Johannes Veldhuizen entered the Korowai territories via the Becking River (see chapter 1).

182. See chapter 1, Some central ideological notions, for the *laléo* 'demon/bad spirit' concept, which is applied in this text to Johannes Veldhuizen and his Papuan assistants. The term is often used for potentially dangerous intruders with whom no relationship of any sort has been established. At the time of this narration, the narrator had a confidential relation with Veldhuizen. Since the initial contact is the theme of this text, the perspective on Veldhuizen and his assistants is rather consistently the perspective of the people who first met Veldhuizen. However, the narrator's present perspective on Veldhuizen, and also the shifting attitude of other Korowai people in later stages of the contact, is expressed in phrases that denote Veldhuizen, such as *nokhu-laléo* 'our demon' in (29) and *yalé(n)* 'respected man' in (42), (58), (61), (70), and (71).

183. Lit. 'the time without the coming of the bad spirit'.

184. *Khaibalè* = *khamibalè* 'we stayed'.

185. *Yemén* 'this side', that is, the southern bank of the Becking River; the perspective of the narrator is from Yaniruma village.

186. *Abémekho* 'to carry on the back' < *abé* 'to carry' + *mekho* 'to put in (a net bag)'; the net bag is usually carried on the back.

187. Onomatopeic form, often in quotative construction, here constructed with support verb.

188. Informants paraphrased the idiom *khebümtada kembakhilada* as follows:

khebüm-pekho kembakhi-fekho
wasp-COORD   aggressive.ant.species-COORD

khul-melun duo-mon-alingga
intestines-gall put.into-INF-without

'without thinking of *khebüm* or *kembakhi*'

189. *Baja-mekho* 'to hide' = *bai-mekho* 'to hide' = *balin-mekho* lit. 'to put into a hidden place'.

190. The idiomatic expression *wola-lelo-khai*, lit. 'earth will be', always functions as a warning: 'the earth will get to its end'. The expression is synonymous with *lamo-telo-khai* (*lamol* 'earth'). See chapter 1, Some central ideological notions, for the *lamol/wola* concept.

The idiom has the form of an experiential construction with -*telo* (see chapter 3), in which the verb is a 3SG form, never agreeing with the experiencer (like *nokhu* in this line); thus, '(to) us the world will end'.

191. The speaker quoted here is the missionary Johannes Veldhuizen.

192. The subject of *ima-té-tofekho* 'they saw' is *mbolombolop* 'the older people'.

193. *Bimo* 'investigate;inspect' < *b-* 'try to' + *imo* 'see'.

194. Perhaps *nè = fenè* 'taking'.

195. For *yanop* '(human) person' and *laléo* 'demon/bad spirit', see chapter 1, Mankind and Some central ideological notions.

196. This form can be paraphrased as 'the things he used to unload'.

197. *Baup-da*, 'NEG-word-NEG' = 'there should be no word', explained by the informant as 'Do not resist anymore!'.

198. I *yanop* 'this people' that is, the Milofakhanop-clans, living on both banks of the Becking River in the area of the Sokom River mouth, in the Yaniruma area.

199. The narrator points to a spot some 2 miles downstream from the present Yaniruma village.

200. *Yano-fekho* 'with the people', that is, the people who join the missionary's patrol.

201. *Ili-bümonaup* 'the beating sound of the helicopter('s machine)'.

202. For *kelaja* 'village' and Korowai villages, see chapter 1.

203. The first expeditions of Johannes Veldhuizen started from the mission station Tiau in the area of the Citak tribe; cf. map 3 and chapter 1, Recent history of contact.

204. See chapter 1, Recent history of contact, for background information on the man Nggop. We have not been able to identify Kualégofalé.

205. That is, at the place where the little Yaniruma river flows into the Sokom River. This location still provides a natural landing place for the dugouts of the Yaniruma village people.

206. The word *lapangga* 'airstrip' derives from the Indonesian expression *lapangan terbang* 'airfield'.

207. See chapter 1 for Korowai villages. The word *khambon* is a loan from Indonesian *kampong* 'village'.

208. That is, not far from the landing place at the banks of the Sokom River.

209. The missionary pointed to the higher sandy grounds at the banks of the Yaniruma River.

210. The word *nggulun* 'evangelist' is a loan from Indonesian *guru* 'teacher'.

211. Kristian Wandenggei, an early convert from the Kawagit area (Wanggom tribe), from 1979 to 1992 was involved in the building up of the Yaniruma mission station and the opening of the Korowai clan territories.

212. Epithet-shaped proper name for Kepsan Kurufe, an early Christian convert who originates from the Kawagit area. However, Kurufe's (perhaps Kombai pronunciation of *Kolufo* 'Korowai') roots lay in one of the Korowai territories in the Becking River's downstream area. Kurufe, like Kristian Wandenggei, was in the service of Yaniruma's mission station during the years 1979 to 1992 (see chapter 1).

213. The noun *wotan* is a loan from Indonesian *hutan*. The whole phrase translates the expression *orang hutan*, a phrase often used in local Indonesian for people who still live permanently in their clan territories and not in the *kampung*, or village.

214. The expression 'spirit's language' refers to Indonesian. See chapter 1, Some central ideological notions, under *laléo*.

215. Alveolar click sounds are used when people emphatically indicate that they do not want or like something.

216. *Kelaja* 'work' from Indonesian *bekerja* 'to work'; in this context the expression

refers to work at the mission station (building and maintenance of the airstrip, roads, etc.). The word *selén* 'shorts' derives from Indonesian *celana* 'trousers' and *bayu* from Indonesian *baju* 'shirt'. The compound *selén-bayu* denotes nonindigenous clothing in general. For razor blades (local Indonesian: *silet*) and mirrors (Indonesian: *kaca muka*), Korowai words are used. *Fikh* 'bamboo splinter; knife', often very sharp, is used for the razor blade; *maf-akh*, a compound of *maf* 'shadow/image' and *akh* 'water', is used for mirror.

217. In this 'shopping list' there occur several loans from (the local variety of) Indonesian: *sabu* from *sabun* 'soap', *nggalam* from *garam* 'salt', and *molo* from the local Indonesian expression *kaca molo* 'diving glasses'. See appendix 3 for loan words from Indonesian.

218. The narrator suggests that the people who insist on staying far from the village had secret aims concerning contact with the white people. The verb *khu-laimekho*, lit. 'to bury in the intestines', means 'to hide the real aim'. See chapter 1, Mankind, under *lokhül* 'body' for *khul/fimelon* 'intestines'.

219. See chapter 1, Some central ideological notions, for *ayul* 'taboo; prohibition'.

220. The word *aturan* is a loan from Indonesian *aturan* 'rules.'

221. The noun *udediop* points to situations of peace and safety, in general to positive situations.

222. That is, the work that had to be done to get an airstrip in Yaniruma. Hundreds of Kombai and Korowai people had been involved in this project, starting in 1983 and finishing in 1985.

223. The narrator uses first the Korowai word for 'together' (*lelip*) and then the Indonesian word *sama-sama*.

224. A settlement in Manggél was opened by the end of 1986. See chapter 1, Recent history of contact.

225. See chapter 1, Recent history of contact, for the opening of Yafufla in September 1987, Mabül village in 1989, and Férman in the course of the year 1990.

226. The Nabékha people are considered a subtribe of the large Kombai tribe.

227. The word *siama* is a loan from Indonesian *camat* 'head of government subdistrict'.

228. Nabékha people moved into Yaniruma village in 1985. See chapter 1, Recent history of contact.

229. The term *aibum* points to the younger stepbrother of ego, that is, a child from ego's mother's second marriage. The first *aibum* mentioned in this story was identified by the informant as Unalé, a member of the Khomei Walofkhatun clan (see map 4).

230. The verb *non u-* 'to cut sago grubs' refers to the felling of the sago trees in which the sago beetle will deposit its eggs and in which the grubs will mature, but the verb is also used to refer to the sago grub festival as a whole. See chapter 1, Sago, for the background of this text.

231. The Sékh and Tabul are clans that live together on a clan territory along a branch of the Mabül River.

232. Someone from the feast-giving clan had come to invite them.

233. A *dokhon* is a small bivouac, used as a halting place during the journey to a feast.

234. See chapter 1, Sago, for the *külomo* way of dancing.

235. See chapter 1, Sago, for the *khasam* dance.

236. See chapter 1, Some central ideological notions for *ayul*.

237. *Khasam lamé-* 'to tie the *khasam*' is the idiom for dancing the *khasam*.

238. The verbs *oldintai-* and *olaibo-* denote the act of clearing a path to the festival place by dancing on young trees and small bushes.

239. The Indonesian loan *kelaja* 'work' (< Indonesian *bekerja* 'to work') is here used to refer to a *kampong*-like settlement. See chapter 1, Recent history of contact and Korowai villages: settlement and housing patterns.

240. The exclamation *üü* marks the end of the *khasam* entrance dance.

241. They took the sago grub parcels down from the high racks (*balin*) in the festival bivouac. See table 1–7, D: 20 and D:21.

242. After the celebrations the narrator and his stepbrothers stayed overnight in the half-way shelter.

243. *Minya* is from Indonesian *minyak tanah* 'petrol'; the fuel was bought at the mission station Yaniruma.

244. Minu is the name of a young man of the Dambol clan (Silom's son).

245. That is, at the next festival place, in the Khomei Walofekhatun area, near the banks of the Afiüm River.

246. The verb *gil alü-dilme-* means 'to finish celebrating'.

247. See chapter 1, Mankind, for the the notion *fimelon* 'intestines' as the seat of emotions and thoughts.

248. See chapter 1, Territories and treehouses of Korowai clans, for the construction of the treehouse and for treehouse stairs. For security reasons, normally the stair pole is fastened only with its upper end while its lower end is left hanging freely. The woman descended to fasten the stair pole below also, to help the movements of the upper end from attracting the attention of the victim of the planned murder.

249. Here, and in many other places in this text, demonstratives are used as markers of definiteness, with proper names and other definite noun phrases.

250. This scene is strongly reminiscent of that in *The Resurrection Story* (19), where, also at the climax of the story, the mud-covered face of the dead man appears in the treehouse entrance lit by the fire inside. The dramatic entrance of Mukhalé in the treehouse to kill his brother is also told from the perspective of the inside of the treehouse, from the fireplace, the light of which shines on the face of the person entering.

251. They took fire from the house that they had burned down and brought it with them to Mukhalé's house. Although in itself there is nothing unusual in transporting fire (a burning piece of wood) from one house to another, here they take the fire from the house of the killed man to the house of the killer, his own brother. We do not know whether this act has a special meaning in this context. *Melil* may mean both fire and firewood, but it seems unlikely that they took firewood with them.

252. Bafén is the name of the woman, the wife of the murdered man.

253. Nénép is the name of the victim of the fratricide.

254. The interjection *ü* is used to express pity, and the killer interprets the reaction of pity as disapproval of his act.

255. See chapter 1, Some central ideological notions, under *kholopamo* for recompensation claims in Korowai society. The recompensation claims of the close relatives of the murdered man were usual and legitimate, and the reaction of Mukhalé to these claims was considered very bad by the informants.

256. The term *laünabül* 'foster son' (see chapter 5, n. 2) probably refers to the son of the murdered older brother.

257. This child was born to Mukhalé and his second wife.

258. Dedilon (possibly of the Lemakha clan) was the fourth wife of Mukhalé, the Khawékh woman was the third, and the Dajo woman was the second.

259. Mafém is a woman of the Faülanop. It is not clear why her name is mentioned here.

260. The death of Mafém's father is attributed to the *khakhua* type of witchcraft, which involves eating the vital organs of the victim in a magical fashion (see chapter 1, Some central ideological notions, under *khakhua*).

261. The witch's hands are tied together.

262. *Fenè fu-* is idiom for 'to send'.

263. For the custom to send *khakhua* witches to other clans to be executed, see chapter 1, Some central ideological notions.

264. The expression *ülnè alü nontédo* refers here to eating human flesh. See chapter 1, Some central ideological notions.

265. *Mbolop* refers to the father of Mafém, whose death had triggered witchcraft accusations and who was referred to in line (28).

266. That is, Golokhofalé, who was sent to the Lemakha people.

267. According to the informant, a brother of Mukhalé had put a spell on the Faülanop people by secretly burning an *ayulekha daup* in one of their treehouses (see chapter 1, Some central ideological notions, under *ayulekha*).

268. The actors of this verb are the members of the Manianggatun clan (of Mukhalé), who are murdering people everywhere. The Faülanop people really have been slaughtered within the course of one year (1986–1987). The killings mentioned here took place in August–October 1987. These events also form the background of the fact that Nakhilop village was abandoned (see also chapter 1, Recent history of contact).

269. Here the narrator refers to himself and to his own activities at the time Didonalé arrived in Yaniruma.

270. *Naném* 'secretly'; *naném fo-* 'to take secretly (theft; adultery)'; *naném-anop* 'thief' (compound of *naném* and *yanop* 'person').

271. These verbs together denote the actions of getting out of the house, standing on the house balcony, and shouting out your grief all over.

272. Amosé, that is, Amos Yaléhatu (Yalénggatun), a Tsawkwambo man, employed as a carpenter at the mission station of Yaniruma.

273. This refers to Didonalé, who entered Yaniruma on October 12, 1987 (van Enk 1987: 24).

274. Literally 'yes, no' but perhaps better translated as 'well . . .' since the function of these words in dialogues seems to be to announce a major or lengthy contribution to the conversation (here in response to the question about why he had been shot).

275. Literally, *pükh* means 'thing which is thrown'.

276. From Indonesian *manteri kesehatan* 'health worker', local primary health-care worker.

277. *Bumo-* 'to slaughter flesh' is here glossed as 'to incise'.

278. In the village Boma on the Mappi River (see map 3), where the mission had a regional health center with (very) basic surgery facilities.

279. The subjects of *deté* are the local workers employed at the mission station.

280. Loan from Indonesian *uang* 'money'. The Mission Aviation Fellowship (MAF) flight was needed because the distance between Boma and Yaniruma is 50 kilometres. The pilot had to be paid in Indonesian currency, that is, in *rupiahs*.

281. Loan from Indonesian *cari* 'to look for, to search'.

282. Derived from Indonesian *siap* 'ready, prepared'.

283. From Indonesian *pesawat terbang* 'aircraft'. In this section suddenly the 'modern' world enters the text, and this is reflected in the sudden appearance of many Indonesian loan words.

284. From Indonesian *bayar* 'to pay'.

285. Notice the 'false' SS form of the verb, possibly a speech error.

286. *Map* from MAF. Boma is an MAF base, which includes a float plane facility. The shape of the hangar of the float plane in Boma made the narrator choose the term *khaü* 'bivouac'.

287. The term *khaü-lalé* 'big bivouac' refers to the accomodation for guests at the missionary compound in Boma, not far from the local health center.

288. *Sustèr* 'nurse' is a loan from Indonesian *suster* (< Dutch *zuster*). The nurse referred to here was Jannie Velvis, working for the Dutch mission-related development organization De Verre Naasten in Bomakia from 1976–1988. We mention her here because her account of this same story was summarized in the mission periodical *TADEDA*, vol. 13, no. 8 (December 1988), 13.

289. From Indonesian *rumah sakit* 'hospital'.

290. The narrator gave the following local Indonesian paraphrase of *yanop lamé khamilmo*: *semua orang ikat* ('all people in ties').

291. The expression *laléo-alin* refers here to the missionaries and native mission personnel (see chapter 1, Some central ideological notions, for the *laléo* concept).

292. The verb form is based on the loan *urus* from Indonesian *mengurus* 'to arrange, organise, manage something'.

293. Notice the 'false' SS marking that precedes the clause with the nurse as subject; this is probably a speech error.

294. Idiom that means something like 'all right'.

295. The verb *ülmekho-* means 'to shoot (with arrows)' and is used here to refer to injections with needles.

296. For the *khomilo* concept see under *yanop khayan* in chapter 1, Mankind.

297. With these words, the narrator describes the semiautomatic surgical knife that the nurse used.

298. Both *plasti* 'plastic' and *kertase* 'paper' are loans from Indonesian *plastik* and *kertas*.

299. Jokingly, the local health workers tried to check the narrator's anatomical knowledge. The Korowai are viewed as cannibals in Boma.

300. The correlative clitics *fekha . . . fekha* ('one. . .another') refers to the broken arrowtips, which they removed from the back.

301. *Wokhelimekho* 'return.SS' or 'again and again'.

302. *Anè lenè* = 'he came', denoting the return of the wandering soul (*yanopkhayan*) from the road (*debüloptalé*) to the land of the dead ones (cf. chapter 1, Universe and mankind).

303. From Indonesian *obat* 'medicine'.

304. *Lebakhop* 'respected old woman' is a polite way of referring to the nurse, Jannie Velvis. She told the authors that Didonalé had to swallow a lot of antibiotics because one of his lungs was hit by an arrowtip. After Didonalé's return to the Korowai area, where people have still tried to kill and eat him, he warned them that he was so full of medicine now that they had better not eat him.

305. *Nokhu-peninggi* 'our evangelist' (from Indonesian *penginjil* 'evangelist') refers to Markus Kawangtet, a Muyu evangelist working in Yaniruma, who was on his way from the Digul area (Kouh) to Yaniruma; he was flown in by float plane to Boma, changed to a regular plane there, and together with the narrator and the patient flew via the Kombai village Wanggemalo to Yaniruma.

306. See table 1–7, H: 38.

307. *Gabüm gun*: the people who come and dance in the preparation of the sago grub feast when the sago trees are felled in which the grubs will be bred. The term *gabüm* denotes how that dance is performed.

References

van Baal, Jan. 1966. *Dema. Description and analysis of Marind-anim culture.* The Hague: Nijhoff.

van Baal, Jan. 1981. *Man's quest for partnership.* Assen: Van Gorcum.

van Baal, Jan. 1982. *Jan Verschueren's description of Yéi-Nan culture. Extracted from the posthumous papers.* The Hague: Martinus Nijhoff.

van Baal, Jan, K. W. Galis, and R. M. Koentjaraningrat. 1984. *West Irian, a Bibliography.* Dordrecht: Foris.

Baas, Peter R. 1988. Mondelinge overleveringen, liederenschat van de Citak clan Vaw. Unpublished MS, Mission of the Reformed Churches.

Baas, Peter R. 1990. Agama dan Kebudayaan Orang Citak, Bagian suku yang hidup di Amazu dan daerah sekitarnya, Khususnya di Desa Ndeiram Atas dan Desa Ndeiram Kabur. Unpublished MS, Mission of the Reformed Churches.

Bakker, Sybe. 1990. Bij het interview met Wandeyop Weremba: Vreemdelingschap in Mangge. *Tot aan de einden der aarde*, vol. 15, no. 5, 3–5.

Bakx, Fons. 1992. *De gedachtenverdrijver. De historie van de mondharp.* Antwerpen: Hadewijch.

Bean, Susan. 1981. Referential and indexical meanings of 'amma' in Kannada: mother, woman, goddess, pox and help! In *Language, culture and cognition*, ed. Ronald W. Casson, 188–202. New York: Macmillan.

Beehler, Bruce M., Thane K. Pratt, and Dale A. Zimmerman. 1986. *Birds of New Guinea.* Princeton, N.J.: Princeton University Press.

Bergh, R. 1961. Soeangi in de Vogelkop. MA thesis, Department of Cultural Anthropology, Leiden University.

Beversluis, A. J. 1954. Bossen. Nieuw Guinea, De ontwikkeling op economisch, sociaal en cultureel gebied. In *Nederlands en Australisch Nieuw Guinea*, vol. 2, ed. W. C. Klein, 276–356. 's-Gravenhage: Staatsdrukkerij.

Boelaars, Jan H. M. C. 1970. *Mandobo's tussen de Digoel en de Kao, bijdragen tot een etnografie*. Assen: Van Gorcum.

Boelaars, Jan H. M. C. 1981. *Head-hunters about themselves, an ethnographic report from Irian Jaya, Indonesia*. The Hague: Nijhoff.

Braak, C. 1954. Klimaat. Nieuw Guinea, De ontwikkeling op economisch, sociaal en cultureel gebied. In *Nederlands en Australisch Nieuw Guinea*, vol. 2, ed. W. C.Klein, 42– 66. 's-Gravenhage: Staatsdrukkerij.

Bromley, H. Myron. 1981. *A grammar of Lower Grand Valley Dani*. Pacific Linguistics Series, C-63. Canberra: Australian National University Press.

Bruce, Les. 1984. *The Alamblak language of Papua New Guinea (East Sepik)*. Pacific Linguistics Series, C-81. Canberra: Australian National University Press.

Bruce, Les. 1986. Serialisation: The interface of syntax and lexicon, 21–37. Pacific Linguistics Series, A-70. Canberra: Australian National University.

Casson, Ronald W., ed.. 1981a. *Language, culture and cognition*. New York: Macmillan.

Casson, Ronald W. 1981b. The semantics of kin term usage: Transferred and indirect metaphorical meanings. In *Language, culture and cognition*, ed. Ronald W. Casson, 230–243. New York: Macmillan.

Chafe, Wallace. 1987. Cognitive constraints on information flow. In *Coherence and grounding in discourse*, ed. Russell Tomlin, 20–51. Amsterdam: John Benjamins.

Comrie, Bernard. 1985. *Tense*. Cambridge: Cambridge University Press.

Dik, Simon C. 1989. *The theory of Functional Grammar. Part 1: The Structure of the Clause*. Dordrecht: Foris.

Dixon, Robert M. W. 1989. The Dyirbal kinship system. *Oceania*, vol. 59, no. 4: 245–268.

Douma, Okke J. 1983. Yaniruma. *Tot aan de einden der aarde*, vol. 8, no. 6, 138–139.

Drabbe, Peter 1950. Twee dialecten van de Awyu-taal. In *Bijdragen tot de Taal-, Land- en Volkenkunde*, vol. 105, 93–147.

Drabbe, Peter 1955. *Spraakkunst van het Marind. Zuidkust Nederlands Nieuw-Guinea*. Wien-Moedling: Drukkerij Missiehuis St. Gabriël.

Drabbe, Peter 1957. *Spraakkunst van het Aghu-dialect van de Awjutaal*. Den Haag: Nijhoff.

Drabbe, Peter 1959. *Kaeti en Wambon. Twee Awju-dialecten*. Den Haag: Nijhoff.

van Eechoud, Jan P. K. 1962. *Etnografie van de Kaowerawédj (Centraal Nieuw-Guinea)*. 's Gravenhage: Nijhoff

van Enk, Gerrit J. 1987. Rapport 1.02 juli tot en met december 1987. Unpublished report to the Reformed Church of Groningen-Noord.

van Enk, Gerrit J. 1990a. Rapport 1.11 januari tot en met februari 1990. Unpublished report to the Reformed Church of Groningen-Noord.

van Enk, Gerrit J. 1990b. Rapport 1.12 over de periode maart tot en met april 1990. Unpublished report to the Reformed Church of Groningen-Noord.

van Enk, Gerrit J. 1993. Khenilkhenil, In the Beginning, History of the Korowai Mission Project (1978–1991) described by an indigenous participant. *Reflection. International Reformed Review of Missiology*, vol. 3, no. 34, 16–43.

van Enk, Gerrit J., and Lourens J. de Vries. 1993. Korowai Kinship Terminology. *Irian, Bulletin of Irian Jaya*, vol. 21, 91–103.

Foley, William A. 1986. *The Papuan languages of New Guinea*. Cambridge: Cambridge University Press.

Foley, William A. 1991. *The Yimas language of New Guinea*. Stanford, Cal.: Stanford University Press.

Godschalk, Jan A. 1993. Sela valley. An ethnography of a Mek society in the Eastern Highlands, Irian Jaya, Indonesia. Ph.D. thesis, Free University of Amsterdam.

Gressitt, J. Linsley, and R. W. Hornabrook. 1985. *Handbook of Common New Guinea Beetles*.

Wau Ecology Institute Handbook No. 2. Port Moresby: National Library Papua New Guinea.

Griffioen, D. 1983. De Irianees, zijn land en geschiedenis. In *Een open plek in het oerwoud*, ed. Tjerk S. de Vries, 11–21. Groningen: De Vuurbaak.

Griffioen, H., and J. Veldhuizen. 1978. Verslag van een sagorupsenfeest in de Tsawkwambo. Unpublished MS, Mission of the Reformed Churches.

Groen, J. P. D. 1991. *Kakuarumu. Missiologische aspecten van een centraal gegeven in de Kombai cultuur.* Kampen, Neth.: Kok.

Gundel, Jeanette K. 1988. Universals of topic-comment structure. In *Studies in Syntactic Typology*, ed. Michael Hammond et al., 209–239. Amsterdam: Benjamins.

Haiman, J. 1978. Conditionals are topics. *Language*, vol. 54, 564–589.

Haiman, J. 1980. *Hua: A Papuan language of the Eastern Highlands of New Guinea.* Amsterdam: Benjamins.

Hannay, Michael. 1985. Inferrability, discourse-boundness and sub-topics. In *Syntax and pragmatics in functional grammar*, ed. A. M. Bolkestein, C. de Groot, and J. L. Mackenzie, 49–63. Dordrecht: Foris.

Healy, Phyllis M. 1964. *Teleéfoól quotative clauses.* Pacific Linguistics Series A-3. Canberra: Australian National University.

Healy, Phyllis M. 1965. *Telefol noun phrases.* Pacific Linguistics Series B-4. Canberra: Australian National University.

Healy, Phyllis M. 1966. *Levels and chaining in Telefol sentences.* Pacific Linguistics Series B-5. Canberra: Australian National University.

Kamma, Freerk C. 1975. *Religious texts of the oral tradition from western New-Guinea (Irian Jaya). Part A: The origin and sources of life. Religious texts translation series Nisaba*, vol. 3. Leiden: E. J. Brill.

Kamma, Freerk C. 1978. *Religious texts of the oral tradition from western New-Guinea (Irian Jaya). Part B. The threat to life and its defence against "natural" and "supernatural" phenomena. Religious texts translation series Nisaba*, vol. 8. Leiden: E. J. Brill.

Klopstra, Jacob J. P. 1992. Rapport 4—December 1992. Unpublished report, De Gereformeerde Kerk van Groningen-Noord.

Knauft, Bruce M. 1985. *Good company and violence: Sorcery and social action in a Lowland New Guinea society.* Berkeley: University of California Press.

Knauft, Bruce M. 1993. *South coast New Guinea cultures: History, comparison, dialectic.* Cambridge: Cambridge University Press.

Kroneman, Dick, and Lloyd Peckham. 1988. Kopka and Momina survey report. Unpublished report, Abepura (Irian Jaya), Summer Institute of Linguistics.

Kruidhof, Jouk. (n.a.). *Pelajaran Citak.* Internal publication, Mission of the Reformed Churches.

Kunst, Jaap. 1967. *Music in New Guinea.* The Hague: Nijhoff.

Lakoff, George, and M. Johnson. 1980. *Metaphors we live by.* Chicago: University of Chicago Press.

Lambrecht, Knud. 1988. Presentational cleft constructions in spoken French. In *Clause combining in grammar and discourse*, ed. John Haiman and Sandra Thompson, 136–179. Amsterdam: John Benjamins.

Laycock, Donald C. 1975. *Observations on number systems and semantics. New Guinea area languages and language study, vol. 1: Papuan languages and the New Guinea linguistic scene*, ed. Stephen A. Wurm, 219–233. Pacific Linguistics Series C-38. Canberra: Australian National University.

Leroux, C. C. F. M. 1950. *De bergpapoea's van Nieuw-Guinea en hun woongebied*, vol. 3. Leiden: E. J. Brill.

Longacre, Robert E. 1972. *Hierarchy and universality of discourse constituents in New Guinea languages, vol. 1: Discussion.* Washington, D.C.: Georgetown University Press.

Lounsbury, Floyd G. 1964. A formal account of the Crow- and Omaha-type kinship terminologies. In *Explorations in cultural anthropology*, ed. Ward H. Goodenough, 351–391. New York: McGraw-Hill.

Louwerse, Jan. 1987. Una (West-New Guinea) worldview and a Reformed model for contextualizing cross-cultural communication of the Gospel. Ph.D. thesis, School of World Mission, Fuller Theological Seminary, University of Michigan, Ann Arbor.

McElhanon, Kenneth A., and C. L. Voorhoeve. 1970. *The trans-New Guinea phylum: Explorations in deep-level genetic relationships.* Pacific Linguistics Series B-16. Canberra: Australian National University.

McElhanon, Kenneth A., C. L. Voorhoeve, and S. A. Wurm. 1975. *The trans-New Guinea phylum in general. New Guinea area languages and language study, vol. 1: Papuan languages and the New Guinea linguistic scene*, ed. S. A. Wurm, 299– 322. Pacific Linguistics Series C-38. Canberra: Australian National University.

Menzies, J. I., and Elisabeth Dennis. 1979. *Handbook of New Guinea rodents.* Wau Ecology Institute, Handbook no. 6. Port Moresby: National Library Papua New Guinea.

Merrifield, W. R. 1983a. Comments on kinship notation. In *Gods, heroes, kinsmen. Ethnographic Studies from Irian Jaya, Indonesia*, ed. W. R. Merrifield, M. Gregerson, and D. C. Ajamiseba, 177–188. Dallas/Jayapura: International Museum of Cultures/Cenderawasih University.

Merrifield, William R. 1983b. Some typological comments. *Gods, heroes, kinsmen. Ethnographic Studies from Irian Jaya, Indonesia*, ed. W. R. Merrifield, M. Gregerson, and D. C. Ajamiseba, 291–296. Dallas/Jayapura: International Museum of Cultures/Cenderawasih University.

Merrifield, William R., M. Gregerson, and D. C. Ajamiseba, eds. 1983. In *Gods, heroes, kinsmen. Ethnographic Studies from Irian Jaya, Indonesia.* Dallas/Jayapura: International Museum of Cultures/Cenderawasih University.

Ong, Walter J. 1982. *Orality and literacy.* London: Routledge.

Pawley, Andrew. 1995. C. L. Voorhoeve and the trans–New Guinea phylum hypothesis. Tales of a concave world. In *Liber Amicorum Bert Voorhoeve*, ed. C. Baak, M. Bakker, and D. van der Mey, 83–123. Leiden: Department of Languages and Cultures of South-East Asia and Oceania of Leiden University.

Petocz, Ronald G. 1987. *Konservasi alam dan pembangunan di Irian Jaya, strategi pemanfaatan sumber daya alam secara rasional.* Jakarta: Pustaka Grafiti.

Pétrequin, Pierre, and Anne-Marie Pétrequin. 1993. *Écologie d'un outil: la hache de pierre en Irian Jaya (Indonésie).* Monographie du CRA 12. Paris: CNRS Éditions.

Pinkster, Harm, and Inge Genee, eds. 1990. *Unity in diversity. Papers presented to Simon C. Dik on his 50th birthday.* Dordrecht: Foris.

Prince, Ellen. 1981. Towards a taxonomy of given/new information. In *Radical pragmatics*, ed. P. Cole, 223–256. New York: Academic Press.

Reesink, Ger P. 1983. Switch-reference and topicality hierarchies. *Studies in Language*, vol. 7, 215–246.

Reesink, Ger P. 1987. *Structures and their functions in Usan, a Papuan language of Papua New Guinea.* Amsterdam: Benjamins.

Scheffler, Harold. 1978. *Australian kin classification.* Cambridge: Cambridge University Press.

Schneider, David M. 1984. *A critique of the study of kinship.* Michigan: University of Michigan Press.

Schoorl, Johan W. 1957. *Kultuur en Kultuurveranderingen in het Moejoe-gebied.* Den Haag: J. N. Voorhoeve.

Silzer, Peter J., and Heljä Heikkinen Clouse. 1991. *Index of Irian Jaya languages*. Special publication of Irian, Bulletin of Irian Jaya. Jayapura: Cenderawasih University and Summer Institute of Linguistics.

Smoltczyk, Alexander, and George Steinmetz. 1996. Wo die Welt noch keine Kugel ist. *Geo Magazine*, no. 1 (January), 10–37.

Stam, C. Koroway. 1978. *Tot aan de einden der aarde*, vol. 3, no.7, 164–165.

van Steenis, C. G. G. J. 1954. Vegetatie en flora. Nieuw Guinea, De ontwikkeling op economisch, sociaal en cultureel gebied. In *Nederlands en Australisch Nieuw Guinea*, vol. 2, ed. W. C. Klein, 218–275. 's-Gravenhage: Staatsdrukkerij.

Steinmetz, George. 1996. Irian Jaya's people of the trees. *National Geographic*, vol. 189, no. 2, 34–43.

Sterly, Joachim. 1987. *Kumo. Hexer und Hexen in Neu-Guinea*. München: Kindler Verlag.

Sudarman, Dea. 1987. *Korowai*. Documentary film. Social Sciences Foundation of Indonesia.

Taylor, Michael, and Judy Hallet. 1994. *Lords of the Garden*. Documentary Film. Smithsonian Institution/Hearst Entertainment.

Thurman, R. C. 1975. Chuave medial verbs. *Anthropological Linguistics*, vol. 17, no. 7, 342–352.

Trompf, Garry W. 1991. *Melanesion religion*. Cambridge: Cambridge University Press.

Turner, Mark. 1987. *Death is the mother of beauty*. Chicago: University of Chicago Press.

van der Velden, Jacobus A., ed. 1982. *Een weg in de wildernis. Gedenkboek ter gelegenheid van 25 jaar zending op Irian Jaya door de Groninger kerken (1956–1981)*. Groningen: Boon.

Veldhuizen, Johannes. 1978. Rapport 4–22/78. Unpublished report to the Church of Groningen-Noord.

Veldhuizen, Johannes. 1982. De Korowai. In *Een weg in de wildernis. Gedenkboek ter gelegenheid van 25 jaar zending op Irian Jaya door de Groninger kerken (1956–1981)*, ed. Jac. van der Velden, 29–38. Groningen: Boon.

Venema, Henk. 1989. Sago grub festival. *Irian, Bulletin of Irian Jaya*, vol. 17, 38–63.

Venema, Henk. 1993 GGRI Irian Jaya en Groningen. *Tot aan de einden der aarde*, vol. 17, no. 11, 44–48.

Venema, Henk. In press. *Jemaat Yesus Kristus dan Pesta Ulat Sagu, Seri Gereja & Kebudayaan*, no. 1. Jakarta: Yayasan Komunikasi Bina Kasih.

Versteeg, Henry. 1983. Zijn stam en taal. In *Een open plek in het oerwoud*, ed. Tjerk S. de Vries, 21–25. Groningen: De Vuurbaak.

Voorhoeve, Cornelis L. 1965. *The Flamingo Bay dialect of the Asmat language*. Den Haag: De Nederlandsche Boekdrukkerij.

Voorhoeve, Cornelis L. 1975. *Languages of Irian Jaya: Checklist, preliminary classification, language maps, wordlists*. Pacific Linguistics, Series B-31. Canberra: Australian National University.

Voorhoeve, Cornelis L. 1980. *The Asmat languages of Irian Jaya*. Pacific Linguistics Series B-108. Canberra: Australian National University.

de Vries, Lourens. 1985. Topic and focus in Wambon discourse. In *Syntax and pragmatics in functional grammar*, ed. A. M. Bolkestein, C. de Groot, and J. L.Mackenzie, 155–180. Dordrecht: Foris.

de Vries, Lourens. 1986. *The Wambon relator system*. Working Papers in Functional Grammar 17. Amsterdam: Institute for General Linguistics of the University of Amsterdam.

de Vries, Lourens. 1987. Kombai kinship terminology. *Irian, Irian Bulletin of Irian Jaya*, vol. 15, 105–118.

de Vries, Lourens. 1989. Studies in Wambon and Kombai. Aspects of two Papuan languages of Irian Jaya. Unpublished Ph.D. thesis, University of Amsterdam.

de Vries, Lourens. 1990. Some remarks on direct quotation in Kombai. In *Unity in diversity*, ed. H. Pinkster and I. Genee, 291–308. Dordrecht: Foris.

de Vries, Lourens. 1993a. Clause combining in oral trans-New Guinea languages. *Text, An Interdisciplinary Journal for the Study of Discourse*, vol. 13, no. 3., 481–502.

de Vries, Lourens. 1993b. *Forms and functions in Kombai, an Awyu language of Irian Jaya*. Pacific Linguistics Series B-108. Canberra: Australian National University Press.

de Vries, Lourens. 1995a. Number systems of the Awyu languages of Irian Jaya. *Journal of the Royal Institute of Linguistics and Anthropology at Leiden*, vol. 150, no. 3, 539–576.

de Vries, Lourens. 1995b. Spirits and friends: Expletive nouns in Korowai of Irian Jaya. Tales of a concave world. *Liber Amicorum Bert Voorhoeve*, ed. C. Baak, M. Bakker, and D. van der Mey, 178–188. Leiden: Department of Languages and Cultures of South-East Asia and Oceania of the Leiden University.

de Vries, Lourens, and Robinia Wiersma. 1992. *The morphology of Wambon of the Irian Jaya Upper-Digul area*. Royal Institute of Linguistics and Anthropology. Leiden: KITLV Press.

Wierzbicka, Anna. 1992. *Semantics, culture and cognition: Universal human concepts in culture-specific configurations*. New York: Oxford University Press.

Wilson, John. 1989. The Yali and their environment. *Irian, Irian Bulletin of Irian Jaya*, vol. 17, 19–37.

Wimbish, John S. 1990. *Shoebox, a data management program for the field linguist*. Ambon: Summer Institute of Linguistics and Pattimura University.

de Wolf, Rijke. 1990, December 22. Een volk dat in duisternis ronddwaalt. *Nederlands Dagblad*, 14–15.

de Wolf, Rijke. 1992. *Sapuru. Een novelle*. Franeker: Uitgeverij Van Wijnen.

Wurm, Stephen A. 1972. The classification of Papuan languages and its problems. *Linguistic Communications*, vol. 6, 118–178.

Wurm, Stephen A., ed. 1975. *New Guinea area languages and language study, vol. 1: Papuan languages and the New Guinea linguistic scene*. Pacific Linguistics Series C-38. Canberra: Australian National University.

Wurm, Stephen A. 1982. *Papuan Languages of Oceania*. Tübingen: Gunter Narr.

INDEX

abdomen. *See* body(-parts)

absenteeism, 6, 26, 291 n.213

abül (son, male), 142, 158, 163, 171, 208, 210–211, 282 n.2

abusive words, 44

acculturation, 4, 10, 46. *See also* cultural integration

address forms, 127, 129, 135, 137, 140, 141, 149

administrative system. *See* Indonesia, Republic of

adornments, 28, 44, 49, 50, 51. *See also* decoration/decorative motifs

adverbial clause, 115, 116, 118

afé (elder brother), 39, 144, 162, 168, 173–175, 207, 208, 209, 210, 211, 213, 216, 284 n.36, 293 n.250, 293 n.256

Afiüm River, 6, 18, 274 n.14, 288 n.134, 293 n.245

after-life. *See khomilo*-concept

afü/afu- (to quarrel, to wrestle, to struggle), 162, 164, 171, 172, 285 n.55, 287 n.108, 288 n.128

age. *See* time(-concept)

Aghu language, 9, 17, 281 n.21

aggressiveness, 15, 49

aibum (stepbrother), 203–204, 292 n.229

Aibum text, 155, 203–205

Aim. *See* Kombai

Aimbon, Füneya, 6

aircraft. *See* travelling

airstrip. *See* travelling

Alamblak (Papua New Guinea), 280 n.7

Allied International, mineral company, 7

allophones, 9

Alukh River, 274 n.14

aluntalé (vicious), 279 n.86

alveolar click sound, 198, 291 n.215

AMA (Associated Mission Aviation), 276 n.39

Amboruma. *See* Yaniruma

Ambüakharun, Yanggio, 5

Amutai, Dominikus, 6

anatomy, knowledge of, 42, 295 n.299

ancestors. *See mbolombolop*; time(-concept)

andüop (grandfather), 143

anemia. *See* diseases

animal fat, 21, 28, 166, 168, 169, 275 n.31, 277 n.54, 285 n.73. *See also* rituals

animals, 11, 15, 21, 23, 27, 37, 40, 41, 42, 47, 52, 53, 155, 276 n.48, 278 n.75, 284 n.47, 285 n.69, 286 n.88, 289 n.148, 289 n.155

animate entities, 286 n.88

Arius maculatus v. sagor, 28

Artocarpus. See trees

arrows, 11, 27, 28, 36, 47, 51, 52, 213, 285–86 nn.76–77

arrowtips, 28, 156, 205, 295 n.300, 295 n.304

ayulekha daup/bumon (forbidden arrowtips), 44, 45, 278 n.76, 294 n.267

with carved decorations, 11, 12, 285 n.76

magic application, 44

303

patriclan, 15
pause, 115, 120, 122, 123, 124
Pawley, Andrew, 275 n.21
Peckham L., 9–10
penal servitude, 279 n.84
penis gourd, 28, 44, 171–172
perception clause, 109, 114, 115, 118
perfect, 92
person, concept of, 40–42
    emotional states and processes, 42–43
    evil disposition, 47, 279 n.82
    feeling, 43
    gun/gunop/yanogun (group), 17, 41, 171,
        173, 220, 286 n.88, 295 n.307
    human relationships, 290 n.179
    imban (individual), 41, 156, 167, 170, 194,
        214, 277 n.63
    kelil/kelitelo (zest for life), 42, 219
    khal (body/meat/skin), 42
    khén/khéntelo (anger/angry, aggressive), 43,
        178, 179, 183, 279 n.86
    khil/khitelo (healthy), 42, 161, 162, 169, 277
        n.54
    lokhül (body), 40, 42–44
    maf (shadow), 40, 41–42, 48
    nggul/nggutelo (discontented), 176
    yanop (person/people), 3, 18, 19, 26, 40–41,
        50, 160, 161, 168, 173, 182, 189–190,
        192, 193, 195, 196, 199, 202, 209, 212,
        213, 214, 215, 217, 291 n.198, 277 n.62,
        291 n.195, 291 n.200, 294 n. 270, 295
        n.290
    See also body(parts); diseases; vital organs;
        yanopkhayan(-concept)
Petocz, Ronald G., 8, 29, 276 n.39
Pétrequin, Anne-Marie, 11
Pétrequin, Pierre, 11
petrol, 205
phonemes, 54–64
physical geography, 7–8
pigs (*gol*), 11, 24, 159–162, 185, 187–188
    back(-bone), 161, 165, 286 n.28
    blood, 28
    chest(-bone), 161, 165
    contrast between domesticated and wild, 27,
        276 n.42
    exchange, 27, 48
    feces, 160, 283 n.26
    festival, 14, 26
    forepaw, 162
    head, 161, 162
    hunting, 27
    intestines, 160, 283 nn.26–27, 289 n.155
    kidney, 160
    leg, 160
    mouth, 162
    in myth, 275 n.31, 277 n.61
    pork, 162, 188, 290 n.177

raising, 11, 27, 49
sacrifice, 14, 18, 27, 45, 49, 159–162, 277
    n.61
shooting of wild pigs, 27, 187–188
tail, 286 n.91
teeth, 27, 50, 76
trapping of wild pigs, 21, 27
pig sacrifice (text/procedure), 106, 126, 127,
    135, 136, 137, 138, 155, 159–162
    attendance restrictions, 283 nn.28–29, 284
        n.37
    cleansing intestines, 137, 160, 283 nn.26–27
    consumption by the spirits, 284 n.35
    performing clan, 284 n.37
    sacred part of the ceremony, 283 n.28, 284
        n.37
Pisa language, 9
plural, 65
police. *See* Indonesia, Republic of
politeness, 148, 149, 150
Ponnettia pinniata. See trees
potatoes, sweet, 27, 35, 38
pork. *See* pigs (*gol*)
power, 15. *See also* aggressiveness, strong man
    concept
power-words (*ndafun-mahüon*), 52. *See also*
    magic
Pratt, T. K., 285 n.56, 287 n.109
precontact period, 4, 29, 273 n.1, 290
    n.181
pregnancy, 43, 44, 47, 278 n.75
Prince, Ellen, 135, 137
procedural discourse, 135
procreation, 34, 37, 44, 220, 277 n.54, 287
    n.114
progressive, 92–93
prohibitions. *See ayul*(-*ekha*-concept)
prosperity, 37, 52, 220, 286 n.78
protection. *See khayolamol* (arrows of the
    universe); magic; treehouse
protein, 28

quotative complement. *See* verbs of thought
quotation (in discourse structure), 283 n.22
quotative construction, 285 n.53, 286 n.84,
    290 n.187
quote marking, 104–105

raids, organised, 7, 15, 273 n.3, 274 n.12
rain(fall), 8, 29, 52. *See also* climatological
    conditions; magic
rainbow, 40
rainforest, tropical, 7
rattan, 22, 28, 166, 167, 286 n.83, 287 n.97
razor blades (*fikh*), 189, 190, 192, 199, 201,
    291–292 n.216
realis, 90
reality and magic, 278 n.81